40 QUESTIONS ABOUT Mormonism

Kyle Beshears

Benjamin L. Merkle, Series Editor

40 Questions About Mormonism

Published by Kregel Academic, an imprint of Kregel Publications, 2450 Oak Industrial Dr. NE, Grand Rapids, MI 49505-6020.

This book is a title in the 40 Questions Series edited by Benjamin L. Merkle.

Italics in Scripture quotations indicate author's added emphasis.

All Scripture quotations, unless otherwise indicated, are from the King James Version.

Library of Congress Cataloging-in-Publication Data
Names: Beshears, Kyle author
Title: 40 questions about Mormonism / Kyle Beshears.
Other titles: Forty questions about Mormonism
Description: First edition. | Grand Rapids, MI : Kregel Academic, [2026] | Series: 40 questions | Includes bibliographical references and index.
Identifiers: LCCN 2025038935 (print) | LCCN 2025038936 (ebook)
Subjects: LCSH: Church of Jesus Christ of Latter-day Saints—Doctrines—Miscellanea | Latter Day Saint churches—Doctrines—Miscellanea
Classification: LCC BX8635.3 .B47 2026 (print) | LCC BX8635.3 (ebook)
LC record available at https://lccn.loc.gov/2025038935
LC ebook record available at https://lccn.loc.gov/2025038936

ISBN 978-0-8254-4749-5
ISBN 978-0-8254-7866-6 (epub)
ISBN 978-0-8254-5471-4 (Kindle)

Printed in the United States of America

26 27 28 29 30 31 32 33 34 / 5 4 3 2 1

"*40 Questions About Mormonism* makes a strong bid to become the go-to Christian resource on Mormonism. As a long-time pastor in Utah, I appreciate the thoroughness and accuracy of the information it presents as well as its engaging tone. Drawing on the author's admirable grasp of Christian history, and biblical theology, as well as his solid research into Latter-day Saint doctrine, history and culture, the book analyzes all the important issues that divide Mormonism from traditional Christianity. It does so, not only with depth and insight, but also with the graciousness and fairness that invites Mormons to listen."

—Ross Anderson
Author of *Understanding Your Mormon Neighbor*

"It is always difficult for someone outside a particular religious movement to understand enough of the ins and outs of that movement to write about it completely accurately, especially when others want to know what is *the* position, when in fact there is a range of perspectives. It is doubly difficult when that religious movement is not completely other but emerges from various common origins and has become a major rival for converts. Kyle Beshears has nevertheless made an admirable effort in this volume and presented as helpful a set of answers to his forty questions as any traditional Christian has compiled to explain the Church of Jesus Christ of Latter-day Saints as it exists today. Warmly recommended."

—Craig L. Blomberg
Distinguished Professor Emeritus of New Testament, Denver Seminary

"The product of many years of study and dialogue, *40 Questions About Mormonism* is eminently smart, accessible, fair, and generous. I wish I had this book as a Mormon missionary talking to evangelical Christians, so I would better understand their sincere faith and they would better understand mine. As a lifelong member of the LDS Church, I can say it feels good to be seen. As a scholar of Mormonism, I admire Beshears's careful attention to detail and nuance. This marks a new standard for evangelical Christians' study of and pastoral approach to Latter-day Saints."

—Patrick Q. Mason
Arrington Chair of Mormon History and Culture, Utah State University

"When I first began working as one of Kyle Beshears's editors, he told me he wanted to give Latter-day Saints a fair hearing while also not watering down his own theological commitments as an evangelical Protestant. I think he has succeeded brilliantly. He explains Mormon beliefs, practices, and history with enough respect that LDS readers will not only recognize themselves in these pages but even learn new things about their faith. His fellow evangelicals, too, will come away with a greater appreciation of the key religious differences between themselves and Latter-day Saints, while also finding common ground they never previously suspected."

—Jana Riess
Author of *The Next Mormons* and senior columnist for Religion News Service

"*40 Questions About Mormonism* is an invaluable resource for Christians, religious scholars, and anyone interested in understanding the Church of Jesus Christ of Latter-day Saints. Its blend of historical analysis, theological comparison, and practical advice makes it a standout work in its field."

—Sandra Tanner
Co-founder of Utah Lighthouse Ministry

"Beshears is to be congratulated on producing a most helpful volume that is based on first-rate scholarship, mutual respect, and a keen understanding of both the LDS tradition and his own Christian tradition. Incorporating an irenic approach, Beshears makes a good faith effort to describe his LDS dialogue partners and their beliefs in a way that they would not only recognize but perhaps also be hard pressed to improve. At the same time, the author makes clear the numerous ways in which the traditions differ from one another, clearing the ground for respectful and productive conversations. Both those new to the study of Mormonism and those who have studied the topic for years will benefit from this excellent, sincere engagement. Beshears has done a great service for readers of all sorts, and this primer is destined to have a long shelf-life indeed."

—John Christopher Thomas
Senior Professor of Biblical Studies, Pentecostal Theological Seminary
Director of the Centre for Pentecostal and Charismatic Studies, Bangor University

"Kyle Beshears challenges Christians to engage in charitable, winsome, and informed dialogue with Latter-day Saints. His *40 Questions About Mormonism* is a lucid primer on Mormon theology and practice. Highly recommended."

—John G. Turner
Author of *Joseph Smith: The Rise and Fall of an American Prophet*

To the students of Mars Hill Church (Mobile, Alabama)
who have traveled to Utah since 2014,
building bridges through charitable dialogue
and a faithful witness of the Lord Jesus Christ.

Contents

Part 4: The Beliefs of Mormonism

Part 5: Approaching Mormonism

Abbreviations

Abr.	The book of Abraham
ACD	Thomas C. Oden, ed. *Ancient Christian Doctrine*, 5 vols. (Downers Grove, IL: IVP Academic, 2009–2010)
ANF	Alexander Roberts and James Donaldson, eds., *Ante-Nicene Fathers: The Writings of the Fathers Down to A.D. 325*, 10 vols. (Peabody, MA: Hendrickson, 1994)
BY	Brigham Young
BYU	Brigham Young University, Provo, UT
CCC	*Catechism of the Catholic Church*
CDBY	Richard S. Van Wagoner, *The Complete Discourses of Brigham Young*, 5 vols. (Salt Lake City: Signature Books, 2009)
Conf.	St. Augustine, *Confessions*, trans. Thomas Williams (Indianapolis: Hackett, 2019)
CSB	Christian Standard Bible
D&C	Doctrine and Covenants
Dialogue	*Dialogue: A Journal of Mormon Thought*
EJ	*Elders' Journal of the Church of (Jesus Christ of) Latter Day Saints* (Kirtland, OH), 1837–1838
EMD	Dan Vogel, ed., *Early Mormon Documents*, 5 vols. (Salt Lake City: Signature Books, 1996–2003)
emend.	*emendata* (Lat.), meaning "corrected," to indicate grammatical changes for readability
EMS	*The Evening and the Morning Star* (Independence, MO and Kirtland OH), 1832–1834
ESV	English Standard Version
Gk.	Greek language
Heb.	Hebrew language
JD	*Journal of Discourses*, 26 vols., reported by George D. Watt et al. (London: Latter-day Saints' Book Depot, 1851–1886)
Inst.	John Calvin, *Institutes of the Christian Religion*, trans. Henry Beveridge (Peabody, MA: Hendrickson, 2008)
Interpreter	*Interpreter: A Journal of Latter-day Saint Faith and Scholarship*, 2012–present
JBMS	*Journal of Book of Mormon Studies*

JS	Joseph Smith
JSJ	Joseph Smith, journal entry
JSP	Matthew C. Godfrey, R. Eric Smith, and Ronald K. Esplin, eds. *The Joseph Smith Papers*, 28 vols. (Salt Lake City: Church Historian's Press, 2008–23). Volumes are referred to by their series: Documents (D), Revelations and Translations (R), Histories (H), Journals (J), Council of Fifty Minutes (C), and Manuscript Revelation Books (MRB). Taken from online collection at www.josephsmithpapers.org if no series indicated.
JST	Joseph Smith Translation
KJV	King James Version, Authorized Version of the Bible
Lat.	Latin language
LW	Jaroslav Pelikan and Helmut T. Lehmann, eds., *Luther's Works*, 55 vols. (St. Louis: Concordia Publishing House, 1955–1986)
M&A	*Latter Day Saints' Messenger & Advocate* (Kirtland, OH), 1834–1837
MS	*The Latter-Day Saints' Millennial Star* (Liverpool), 1840–1970
MSG	The Message
NIV	New International Version
NT	New Testament, Christian scriptures
OT	Old Testament, Hebrew scriptures
RSC	Religious Studies Center, Brigham Young University, Provo, Utah
T&S	*Times & Seasons* (Nauvoo, IL), 1839–46
WWJ	Dan Vogel, ed., *The Wilford Woodruff Journals*, 6 vols. (Salt Lake City: Signature Books, 2020)

Introduction

My journey into understanding Mormonism began not with curiosity but with caution. As a traditional Christian, I had been raised with a clear message: Mormons were trapped in a cult, a counterfeit of Christianity that was best left alone. The directive was clear—if you must engage, study up to pull them out. This mindset shaped my early approach. Armed with evangelical countercult literature, I felt prepared to confront and correct. But my first real encounter with a Mormon missionary left me more confused than confident.

"But your church teaches that you'll become the god of your own planet one day," I insisted, my finger jabbing the air between us.

The missionary's eyebrows raised. He paused, carefully considering his next words. "You know," he began, his voice calm and measured, "it's not exactly like that. We believe we can become *like* God, yes. But it's more about experiencing the fullness of what Heavenly Father wants for his children." He tilted his head, looking at me curiously. "Don't you believe God wants us to become more like him?"

I opened my mouth to argue, then closed it again. The words stuck in my throat as I realized that yes, I did believe something like that. It frustrated me how easily the missionary swatted away everything I thought was true about his beliefs. Was he lying, or was I lied to? Was the truth somewhere in the middle? This interaction shook my certainty and sparked a realization: Perhaps my understanding of Mormonism was built on the sands of "heresy hearsay," the peculiar mix of secondhand information and accusations of doctrinal deviation that often characterizes an outsider's perspective of a group not their own.

What began as a mission to save Mormons from their beliefs transformed into a genuine quest for understanding. I had to find out the truth, and doing so has led to a lifelong journey of trying to understand Mormonism—not just its doctrines but its people, culture, and the ways its adherents live out their faith. Along the way, I've encountered surprises that challenged my preconceptions. I've found areas of common ground I never expected, and I've gained a deeper appreciation for Latter-day Saint culture. At the same time, I've come to recognize our real differences more clearly, free from the fog of misunderstanding and caricature—differences that are serious and, in some instances, utterly irreconcilable.

In many ways, this book is a report of that journey and an invitation for other Christians to join me on the way. It's a journey of discovery, one that passes through convictions we share with Mormonism while also recognizing our differences. It's a primer to understand not only a religion but also its people, the Latter-day Saints, whom God loves as deeply and sincerely as he does anyone in the world (see John 3:16–17).

For readers approaching this book with skepticism or preconceptions like my initial ones, I invite you to set them aside for a moment. You may find, as I did, that firsthand learning and genuine dialogue can lead to surprising insights and a more Christlike approach to understanding Mormonism.

As we embark on this exploration together, you'll encounter some of the most intriguing aspects of Mormon belief and practice. From the bold claims of Joseph Smith's "First Vision" to the complex theology of eternal progression, from the communal strength of Latter-day Saint family networks to the sacred rituals of their temples, we'll examine Mormonism with both scholarly rigor and empathetic understanding to shape our approach to the religion and its people.

By way of introduction, it's important first to define a few terms: "Latter-day Saint," "Mormonism," and "traditional Christianity."[1] Latter-day Saints are people whose religious and cultural convictions and practices are formed and informed by Mormonism. This term describes the nineteenth-century religious tradition started by Joseph Smith, whose remarkable claims and experiences led his followers to believe in a restoration of the Christian faith and to establish the Church of Jesus Christ of Latter-day Saints in 1830. Mormonism is as much a culture as it is a religion, one that is deeply influenced by the collective history, beliefs, and experiences of a unique people. Mormons, as they are commonly called, self-identify as Christian because of the centrality of Jesus Christ's atoning death and resurrection in their doctrine of salvation. But Latter-day Saints, as they are formally called, distinguish themselves from traditional Christians in four categories: history, authority, doctrine, and practices.

Four Basic Distinctives of Mormonism

First, the story of Mormonism. In a vision, Smith claimed to encounter God, who appeared to him as two separate and distinct beings, the Father and the Son. During this "First Vision," as it is known, Smith was instructed to refrain from aligning with any Christian denomination in anticipation of the faith's complete restoration. Years later, an angel revealed the location of buried plates to Smith, which he excavated. The plates were golden in appearance and inscribed with a record containing an account of the ancient Americas. Once miraculously translated, Smith published this record as the Book of Mormon,

1. For the definition of "traditional Christianity," see page 15.

a scriptural companion to the Bible, thus its subtitle "another testament of Jesus Christ." The Book of Mormon is the keystone text of LDS scripture.

Second, the authorities of Mormonism. Along with the Bible and Book of Mormon, Latter-day Saints accept two additional texts they consider to be scripture: Doctrine and Covenants and Pearl of Great Price. These four standard works represent the scriptural authority of the LDS Church, which may be added to by new revelation in the future. Openness to more revelation stems from the doctrine of continuing revelation, especially through modern prophets. Only prophets may speak authoritatively and finally for God to the church, although God also speaks directly to individual members and influences nonmembers. Revelation flows from God through prophets to the world through the medium of the priesthood and the mediation of church leadership—or "General Authorities"—by official revelations, semi-revelatory statements, or "proclamations," which are speeches delivered at bi-annual meetings called "General Conference," and various other works and writings. Relatedly, Latter-day Saints affirm the restoration of priesthood authority, which they believe traditional Christianity forfeited through apostasy. God later restored his authority to speak and act on his behalf through Joseph Smith, who ordained others to the priesthood in a lineage that extends to this day. Latter-day Saints also look to family, individual conscience, and the promptings of God's Spirit to guide them.

Third, the doctrine of Mormonism. Latter-day Saints understand God differently than classical Christian theism, which describes him as the simple, immutable, immaterial, ungenerated, and eternal first cause of all things. In Mormonism, God is the complex, mutable, quasi-material, partially generated, and the eternal first cause of the universe, though not of all things. God is married to a Heavenly Mother, who together are the eternal parents of all human spirits. Humanity lived together in premortality until being sent to earth for mortal probation. All God's children are promised glorious exaltation in the afterlife through faith and obedience to him, meaning salvation is inclusive of all people because everyone will resurrect after death into one of three eternal kingdoms. The degree of glory to be enjoyed in the afterlife depends on one's faith and obedience in this life.

Fourth, the practices of Mormonism. Latter-day Saints place heavy emphasis on the binding power of priesthood ordinances, especially as they are related to the eternality of families. Each family has the potential to last forever by being sealed together in ordinances for time and eternity. Sealings occur by rituals performed in temples, which are sacred spaces for other ordinances like baptism for the dead and the endowment, a ceremony of religious instruction and covenant making. Latter-day Saints also participate in public rituals, like congregational worship and the sacrament, or the Lord's Supper, as complements to their personal spiritual devotion. Mormonism is also a conversionary religion; every member must place faith in Jesus Christ, repent from sin, become baptized by immersion under a proper authority, and receive the gift of the Holy Ghost by the laying on of hands. For this reason, Latter-day Saints evangelize to people with no faith and proselytize people from other faiths.

This book is organized around these four basic distinctives—story, authority, doctrine, and practices.

What's in a Name?

It wasn't long after the founding of the Church of Jesus Christ of Latter-day Saints before its members were first called "Mormons" and their religion "Mormonism." These labels were used by early skeptics and critics of the church, drawing on the most unique part of the new religion, the Book of Mormon. Derogatively naming a religious minority is nothing new. Most Christian denominations were nicknamed for a person or practice, like the Calvinists and Quakers. But the Mormons were not called Smithites, like the Lutherans who followed Martin Luther, nor were they identified by a particular practice, like Baptists. They were named for their unique scripture, the Book of Mormon, which is perhaps why Latter-day Saints eventually donned the title with pride.

But not everyone likes the term. Some prefer to be called by the title given in their scripture, "Latter-day Saints," which is especially true of members of the Church of Jesus Christ of Latter-day Saints headquartered in Salt Lake City.[2] Still, not everyone who identifies with Smith's tradition are members of the church. There are many divisions of Mormonism, each with its own way of self-identification, like Community of Christ, Church of Jesus Christ ("Bickertonite"), Church of Jesus Christ of Latter-Day Saints ("Strangite"), Remnant Fellowships ("Snufferite"), and Apostolic United Brethren. What unites these diverse groups is their belief in Joseph Smith as a prophet and the scripture he brought forth, the Book of Mormon. *40 Questions About Mormonism*, however, will focus mainly on the church based in Salt Lake City, which prefers not to be called "Mormon." In charitable respect, I will describe the Church of Jesus Christ of Latter-day Saints by its full name at its first reference in each question, abbreviating it to "LDS Church" or simply "church" afterward, and I will restrict my use of "Mormon" and "Mormonism." But I will not completely abandon those terms, partly due to the need for contrasting the Latter-day Saint (or LDS) tradition from traditional Christianity, and

2. When Joseph Smith founded his church in 1830, it was initially called the Church of Christ. Four years later, church leaders modified the name to the Church of the Latter Day Saints, possibly to distinguish it from other Church of Christ churches. In 1838, Smith reported receiving a revelation that established the church's official title as the Church of Jesus Christ of Latter Day Saints. This name was later canonized into the church's scripture, Doctrine and Covenants (115:4).

neither will I adopt the church's preferred terminology of "restored gospel" or "Restoration" due to personal convictions.

By "traditional Christianity," I mean the faith that holds to four things:

1. the Holy Bible alone as inspired scripture (i.e., not the Book of Mormon, Doctrine and Covenants, nor Pearl of Great Price);
2. the ecumenical creeds (e.g., Apostles' Creed, Nicene Creed, Athanasian Creed);
3. the classical Trinitarian person and work of God;[3] and
4. the practicing of ethical teachings and spiritual imperatives from God.

The first point rallies around common authority, the Word of God inspired by him. Nearly all Christianity believes in the Bible's inspiration, to one degree or another, including Mormonism, although it adds other texts to its list of inspired writings on par with the Bible. Confessing the ecumenical creeds further differentiates the two traditions. Traditional Christianity affirms these doctrinal statements, even those Protestants wary of the role creeds play as an authority. Mormonism, however, struggles to see some of its doctrinal distinctives in them, like its conception of the Godhead. Traditional Christianity confesses the Holy Trinity—God is one being in three persons: Father, Son, and Holy Spirit—which contrasts to the Mormon Godhead as three distinct beings and three different persons. Finally, a traditional Christian is one who practices their faith, confessing to "be ye doers of the word, and not hearers only" (Jas 1:22). Christianity cannot be reduced to merely a collection of theological propositions and ethical instructions. It is a living and active faith that ought to produce holiness, human flourishing, and thankful praise to God.

I hope *40 Questions About Mormonism* is an informative, trustworthy, and helpful guide on your journey of approaching the religion. But more importantly, I pray that this book will honor and glorify the Lord Jesus Christ.

3. I define classical Trinitarianism as the belief in one God who exists eternally in three persons—Father, Son, and Holy Spirit—who are ungenerated, co-equal, and co-eternal, sharing one divine essence.

PART 1

Studying Mormonism

QUESTION 1

Why Should Traditional Christians Learn About Mormonism?

"Do not waste time bothering whether you 'love' your neighbour; act as if you did. . . . When you are behaving as if you loved someone, you will presently come to love him."[1]

~ C. S. Lewis

"You have heard of MORMONISM—who has not?"[2] New York journalist James Bennett asked this question in 1831, just sixteen months after Joseph Smith sparked the Mormon movement. News about the unfamiliar religion traveled fast as reporters struggled to satisfy public curiosity. Eager to add his voice to a growing chorus of journalists, Bennett cranked out his article, which ended up being a mixture of fact and fiction. Readers learned how Smith established the Church of Christ (as it was then known) after claiming to have discovered gold plates, the source material for the Book of Mormon. All that is true. Yet Bennett also reported how Smith thought of himself as a second messiah and how his wife, Emma, caused half the plates to vanish magically after sneaking a forbidden peek at them. None of that is true.

Bennett's article is a fitting parable for non-Mormons. We may have heard of Mormonism, but how well do we truly understand it? Like Bennett, some things we know are true, but other things are probably false, and our alloyed beliefs affect the way we view Latter-day Saints. But let's not get ahead of

1. C. S. Lewis, *Mere Christianity* (New York: Macmillan, 1980), 116.
2. James Gordon Bennett, "Mormonism—Religious Fanaticism—Church and State Party," *Morning Courier & Enquirer* (New York City), August 31, 1831. Reproduced in Leonard J. Arrington, "James Gordon Bennett's 1831 Report on 'The Mormonites,'" *BYU Studies* 10, no. 3 (1970): 357.

ourselves. Having begun to ask forty questions about Mormonism, we should explore our motivations for answering those questions. So, why should traditional Christians learn about Mormonism?

Common Reasons

Traditional Christians have implicitly pondered this question for as long as the Church of Jesus Christ of Latter-day Saints has existed. Typically, answers fall into one of four categories: exposing Mormonism, comparing it with Christianity, equipping Christians for evangelism to Latter-day Saints, or engaging Mormonism's cultural influence.

Early Mormon missionaries shocked Christians by their success. How could anyone believe Smith, they wondered? Christians believed Mormon missionaries deceived potential converts by withholding damaging information, prompting an aggressive mission of "exposing" Mormonism to prevent conversion. They produced a host of anti-Mormon exposés in newspaper articles, tracts, and books that frustrated Mormon missionary efforts. One of the earliest and most popular of these works, *Mormonism Unvailed* (1834), set the tone for countless exposés that followed. Among the most influential of these in recent generations is Walter Martin's *The Maze of Mormonism* (1962),[3] Jerald and Sandra Tanner's *Mormonism: Shadow or Reality?* (1963),[4] and Ed Decker's film *The God Makers* (1982),[5] which made a particularly strong impression on the evangelical imagination about Mormonism.[6] *The God Makers* was shown to countless churches across the United States. For many traditional Christians, it was their first exposure to Mormon doctrine, one that framed Mormonism as a sinister counterfeit of Christianity.[7]

Latter-day Saints are generally not shy about their doctrine, though, especially concerning God and scripture. Some beliefs and practices they hold privately, like temple rituals. But enough is taught about them publicly to convince traditional Christians that Smith's movement has irreversibly

3. Walter R. Martin, *The Maze of Mormonism* (Grand Rapids: Zondervan, 1962).
4. Jerald and Sandra Tanner, *Mormonism: A Study of Mormon History and Doctrine* (Salt Lake City: Utah Lighthouse Ministry, 1963). This book was subsequently published as *Mormonism: Shadow or Reality?*
5. According to Decker, on December 31, 1982, the film debuted at Grace Community Church, then led by evangelical preacher John MacArthur, who thought it was "dynamite" and encouraged evangelicals: "Get your Mormon friends to view it!" Ed Decker and Dave Hunt, *The God Makers: A Shocking Exposé of What the Mormon Church Really Believes* (Eugene, OR: Harvest House, 1984), 16.
6. I define *evangelical* to mean any orthodox Protestant person in the network of global communities marked by adherence to *sola scriptura* and strongly influenced by Christocentrism, conversionism, sanctification, and evangelism.
7. See J. B. Haws, *The Mormon Image in the American Mind: Fifty Years of Public Perception* (New York: Oxford University Press, 2013), 112–25.

departed from the historic faith, so exposing Mormonism seems less necessary. These traditional Christians prioritize comparing LDS and Christian beliefs. In this vein, Mormonism is typically classified as an irregular extension of Christianity or rejected altogether as a sect "outside the historic Christian faith," explained one Roman Catholic writer.[8] Conservative Protestants commonly view Mormonism as a counterfeit of orthodoxy, so Christians are encouraged to study the real thing to spot the fake. For example, Walter Martin's popular *Kingdom of the Cults* devotes a large section to comparing Mormon beliefs with those of evangelicalism.[9] Martin invited his readers to reexamine orthodox beliefs carefully to gain the ability "to detect those counterfeit elements so apparent in the cult systems, which set them apart from Biblical Christianity."[10] Martin's general posture is defensive, warning Christians not to be persuaded by Mormonism.[11]

For others, though, comparing beliefs is insufficient. Driven by evangelistic impulse, the primary reason Christians should study Mormonism is to engage it, not avoid it. Presently, this is the most popular reason given among evangelical authors who write on Mormonism.[12] Still, others add a final concern: the growing population and influence of the LDS Church. According to official tallies, the global membership of the church surpassed that of the Southern Baptist Convention, the largest Protestant denomination in the United States. In 2019, investigative reporters discovered the church was wealthier than many Fortune 500 companies.[13] Latter-day

---

8. Isaiah Bennett, *Inside Mormonism: What Mormons Really Believe* (San Diego: Catholic Answers, 1999), 14.
9. Walter R. Martin, *The Kingdom of the Cults: An Analysis of the Major Cult Systems in the Present Christian Era* (Grand Rapids: Zondervan, 1965).
10. Martin, *The Kingdom of the Cults*, 16.
11. Some traditional Christians opt to avoid Mormonism altogether, interpreting the biblical warning to shun anyone who deviates from orthodoxy as applying to Latter-day Saints (see 2 John 10). The warning, however, is not one of personal engagement but congregational association. The writer is not "forbidding private hospitality, but rather an official welcome into the conversation, with the widespread opportunities which would then be available for the heretics to promote their cause." Stephen S. Smalley, *1, 2, 3 John*, Word Biblical Commentary 51 (Dallas: Word, 1984), 333.
12. For example, see Bill McKeever and Eric Johnson, *Answering Mormons' Questions: Ready Responses for Inquiring Latter-day Saints* (Grand Rapids: Kregel, 2012); Eric Johnson and Sean McDowell, eds., *Sharing the Good News with Mormons: Practical Strategies for Getting the Conversation Started* (Eugene, OR: Harvest House, 2018); Eric Johnson, *Introducing Christianity to Mormons: A Practical and Comparative Guide to What the Bible Teaches* (Eugene, OR: Harvest House, 2022); and Corey Miller and Ross Anderson, *Responding to the Mormon Missionary Message: Confident Conversations with Mormon Missionaries (and Other Latter-day Saints)* (Abbotsford, WI: Aneko Press, 2023).
13. Jon Swaine, Douglas MacMillan, and Michelle Boorstein, "Mormon Church Has Misled Members on $100 Billion Tax-Exempt Investment Fund, Whistleblower Alleges," *The Washington Post*, December 17, 2019.

Saints currently enjoy leadership and influential roles in business, politics, media, and culture. That's a lot of power, and Christians ought to be aware of Mormon influence.

There is a growing sense, however, that a fifth reason is appropriate for the secular age in which we live. At a very basic level, traditional Christians and Latter-day Saints share the belief that religion is important and should be promoted and protected in public spaces. True, we hold serious theological differences that pit our traditions against each other, and those should not be ignored or trivialized. In large measure, this book is devoted to exploring those differences. But perhaps Christians ought to consider studying Mormonism to aid us in developing a closer social alliance. We are, after all, experiencing the same challenges caused by increasing secularism, whether expressed as indifference to faith or enmity toward it.

In 2013, R. Albert Mohler addressed a large crowd at Brigham Young University. The president of The Southern Baptist Theological Seminary may have seemed like a strange guest speaker before a mostly Latter-day Saint audience, but his message certainly resonated with many in the audience. He contended for a closer relationship between Christians and Latter-day Saints in an increasingly secular culture built on common convictions yet without jettisoning their differences. Mohler pithily concluded, "I do not believe that we are going to heaven together, but I do believe we may go to jail together."[14] If Mohler's prediction seems dramatic, the impulse behind it is not. As traditional theology and conservative morality are challenged, traditional Christians and Latter-day Saints will inevitably share common ground. Willingness to get to know our new neighbors may surprise us with fruitful partnerships, like mutual support on social issues. Studying Mormonism, then, gives traditional Christians the vocabulary and knowledge to coordinate and promote areas in which we share genuine agreement.[15]

The Greatest Reason? The Greatest Commandment

But culture is fluid and merely temporary in the grand scheme of redemption, and we belong to an eternal kingdom with irrevocable decrees on how its people should live. There must be an ultimate reason why traditional Christians ought to study Mormonism, one on which all others depend, making it more important than all the rest.

---

14. "A Clear and Present Danger: Religious Liberty, Marriage, and the Family in the Late Modern Age," presented by R. Albert Mohler, Brigham Young University, Provo, UT, October 21, 2013.
15. For an insightful essay on the like-mindedness between traditional Christians and Latter-day Saints, see J. B. Haws, "Mormons and Evangelicals in the Public Square," in *Talking Doctrine: Mormons and Evangelicals in Conversation*, ed. Richard J. Mouw and Robert L. Millet (Downers Grove: IVP Academic, 2015), 90–99.

Let's return for a moment to the question at hand: Why should traditional Christians learn about Mormonism? The standard answer (especially among the missionally minded) is the Great Commission, but the correct answer is the Greatest Commandment because it's impossible to fulfill the former without the latter. After all, before Jesus mandated his Great Commission (see Matt 28:18–20), he issued the Greatest Commandment, to love God holistically and to love one's neighbor as oneself (see Matt 22:37–40). This is not to pit one against the other. Love that lacks a gospel witness has no home in the kingdom of God, but a gospel witness that lacks love is equally foreign. You cannot bear witness to the Lord Jesus while harboring apathy or fear or hate against those for whom he died and rose again. So when it comes to studying Mormonism, first things first. If Christians are called to love their Latter-day Saint neighbors as themselves, how can we possibly do so without knowing anything about them, their beliefs, or their lives? We'll be just like James Bennett, the journalist who had heard of Mormonism but apparently didn't know any Latter-day Saints, let alone love them.

With love of Latter-day Saints as our chief motivation, our study of Mormonism takes on a virtuous form. We break away from the tired pattern of mistrust that has marred our relationship for generations. We'll have no appetite for digesting poor resources, the kinds that introduce us to mere caricatures, Latter-day Saints who exist only in a hostile or naive imagination. We'll fact-check what we hear and read, like Bennett's false claims about second messiahs and disappearing plates. But we'll also latch on to genuine and significant differences, seeking truth beneath the authority of Christ through scripture. Part of what it means to love a person is to know them as truly as possible, even the bits we disagree on.

So again, why should traditional Christians study Mormonism? Because we are commanded to love our neighbors as ourselves, and it's hard to love someone without taking the time to get to know them. Only then may we move forward together.

Summary

Since the founding of the Church of Jesus Christ of Latter-day Saints, traditional Christians have learned about Mormonism to expose it, to compare it to traditional Christianity, to equip Christians for missionary work among Latter-day Saints, and to engage its social and political influence. Yet for Christians hoping to communicate their faith clearly to Latter-day Saints, a sincere love of neighbor must precede all other reasons for learning about Mormonism. The Lord Jesus commanded his followers to love their neighbor as themselves, and it is impossible to love someone fully without knowing them truly. Therefore, obedience to the Greatest Commandment ought to be the core motivation for traditional Christians to learn about Mormonism because all subsequent reasons for study are inevitably shaped by love (or its absence).

REFLECTION QUESTIONS

1. Reporter James Bennett knew about Mormonism but didn't really know Mormonism. How is Bennett an analogy for traditional Christians today?
2. Which of the four common questions traditional Christians ask of Mormonism are you most drawn to, and why?
3. How did you first learn about Mormonism, and how has that experience shaped your perception of Latter-day Saints?
4. Do you agree that traditional Christians and Latter-day Saints ought to form a closer social relationship? Why or why not?
5. What is the relationship between the Greatest Commandment and the Great Commission, and how does this inform your approach to Mormonism?

QUESTION 2

How Have Christians Approached Mormonism Throughout History? (Part 1)

"The greatest fraud of our time in the field of religion is most certainly one Joseph Smith."[1]
~ Diedrich Willers, Protestant Minister, 1830

From its inception, the Church of Jesus Christ of Latter-day Saints has contrasted itself against the Christianity from which it emerged. Joseph Smith lamented the faith in his day as irredeemably fractured. He believed that "there was no society or denomination that built upon the gospel of Jesus Christ," later clarifying this criticism came directly from God in a vision.[2] Since the apostolic era, a complete loss of authority and authenticity had thrust Christianity into the throes of apostasy. Its redemption could only come by a great restoration led by Smith, who donned a prophet's mantle, brought forth new scripture, and gathered a Zionist community.

Smith's message was shocking to those who viewed Mormonism as a heretical wildfire needing to be extinguished. From the 1820s–1890s, traditional Christians generally approached Mormonism as foolishness to avoid, a fraudulent religion to expose, and a foreign culture to oppose.[3]

1. Diedrich Willers to "Reverend Brethren," June 18, 1830, translated by Neal Chandler, *EMD* 5:271.
2. JS, ca. 1832 history, H1:11.
3. For these three phases, I draw from J. Spencer Fluhman's insightful observation that Christians "first found Mormonism to be a fake religion, then an alien or foreign religion, and finally a merely false one." J. Spencer Fluhman, *"A Peculiar People": Anti-Mormonism*

Mormonism as Foolishness to Avoid

Skeptics rolled their eyes when word spread in Smith's hometown that he had discovered ancient artifacts. "Jo[seph] Smith told the story," recalled Lorenzo Saunders, "but he told so many stories, it was a hard thing to get the fact in any way or shape."[4] Smith had garnered a reputation for scrying, the act of using enchanted objects to see beyond the physical realm. Neighbors employed his services on expeditions to retrieve lost possessions or locate buried treasure. So when Smith claimed he had unearthed precious relics, he was often brushed aside. But not everyone thought his tale was hard to believe. In mid-nineteenth-century rural New York, many people embraced an enchanted worldview. One man remembered Smith relaying his story to mixed reactions. Some folks "did not believe a word they heard," casting it aside as foolishness, but Smith captured the imagination of others who "[rubbed] their eyes in wonder."[5]

His story became especially intriguing when considering its religious elements, such as encounters with angels, newly discovered scripture, and the restoration of Christianity. As Smith's movement gained momentum, skeptics cautioned potential converts to steer clear of what they thought was foolishness. They may have been bothered by his stories, but his religious claims deeply concerned them. At first, Christians "only laughed at the ridiculousness of the thing"[6] when Smith published the Book of Mormon in 1830, dismissing it as a "silly fabrication of falsehood" to dupe the gullible for worldly gain.[7] But they were soon pleading with potential converts to stay away from Smith's book and the church he founded that same year. When that didn't work, they employed less sophisticated techniques like banging together kettles and tin pans to drive off LDS missionaries at public speaking engagements.

Still, Smith continued to win converts. Convinced Smith was a charlatan, his opponents took to subverting and suppressing his fledgling movement. Mormonism evolved from foolishness to avoid to a fake religion to expose.

Mormonism as a Fake Religion to Expose

"Every age of the world has produced impostors and delusions," wrote Alexander Campbell of Mormonism in 1831.[8] Campbell, a founder of the Disciples of Christ movement, was joined by others who viewed Joseph Smith

---

and the Making of Religion in Nineteenth-Century America (Chapel Hill: University of North Carolina Press, 2012), 9.

4. Lorenzo Saunders Interview, November 12, 1884, *EMD* 2:159.
5. "Origin of Mormonism," *San Francisco Chronicle*, May 14, 1893.
6. John A. Clark, "Gleanings by the Way. No. VII," *The Episcopal Recorder*, September 12, 1840.
7. Larry E. Morris, ed., *A Documentary History of the Book of Mormon* (New York: Oxford University Press, 2019), 83.
8. Alexander Campbell, "Delusions," *The Millennial Harbinger* 2, no. 2 (February 2, 1831).

as simply one more example of the many charlatans throughout history. He was nothing more than a con man, and the Book of Mormon was his con. To them, the "Golden Bible" was a knockoff, a hodgepodge of material imported from sermons, scripture, and Shakespeare.

At first, critics attributed Smith's success to the gullibility of the naive. But when the church began to swell with rational and educated people, they changed their tune. Charles H. Spurgeon, the famous London preacher, captured how traditional Christians felt about the power behind Mormonism's rise. "What has been its strength?" he wondered. "Simply this—the assertion of power from heaven." He didn't believe in Smith's claims, of course: "There never could be a delusion more transparent, or a counterfeit less skilful [*sic*] and more lying upon the very surface," Spurgeon clarified.[9] But by appealing to heaven, Smith tapped into the latent desire within people who yearned for immediate encounters with God. So early converts were drawn to Smith's dynamic leadership, his new-yet-ancient Christianity, and the unique identity that came with belonging to a budding Zionist community. As a result, traditional Christian churches lost followers.

Losing followers became a personal matter for Alexander Campbell when Sidney Rigdon, an eloquent and influential preacher in Campbell's movement, converted to Mormonism and took hundreds with him. These people were being deceived, critics reasoned, so the antidote to conversion was exposing Smith as the con man he was. Few worked harder to expose Mormonism than newspaperman Eber Dudley Howe. When the church relocated its headquarters to Howe's hometown in northern Ohio, he took advantage of his proximity to warn potential converts away in a series of articles. Howe encouraged his readers to do as the Ephesians did: test false apostles and reject them by their failures (see Rev 2:1–2).[10] But his focus turned to exposing Mormonism after his wife, Sophia, expressed interest in joining the church. By 1834, Sophia converted, prompting her husband to publish *Mormonism Unvailed* the same year, the first exposé of Mormonism and arguably the most influential to date.

The book featured affidavits calling into question the history and character of Smith. It also promoted a theory that suggested the Book of Mormon was largely plagiarized from an unpublished romance novel. Countless works after *Mormonism Unvailed* drew inspiration from it whether in name or content, including *Exposure of Mormonism* (1838), *Mormonism Unmasked, Showed to Be an Impious Imposture* (1840), *Abominations of Mormonism Exposed* (1852), *Mormonism Unveiled* (1877), and *Mormonism Exposed* (1908).

These works all follow familiar patterns of painting Joseph Smith as an imposter, the Book of Mormon as a fraudulent artifact, and the church as

---

9. Charles H. Spurgeon, *The New Park Street Pulpit: Containing Sermons Preached and Revised by the Rev C. H. Spurgeon*, vol. 2 (Pasadena, TX: Pilgrim Publications, 2006), 182.
10. Eber D. Howe, "The Book of Mormon," *Painesville Telegraph* (New York), reprinted in *Poughkeepsie Journal* (New York), January 5, 1831.

a cartel of dubious financial dealings, secret rituals, heresies, and polygamy. The mission of anti-Mormon sleuths was simple: to bring to light all these strange, esoteric, and immoral elements of Mormonism for the public. Smith's following would dwindle into obscurity if people could only know the truth.

Yet no matter how hard they tried, the magnetic pull of Mormonism continued to lure people toward it. When exposing Mormonism failed to hamper its growth, Christians resorted to social oppression and violent persecution.

Mormonism as a Foreign Culture to Oppose

As Mormonism grew, so did Smith's power and influence. Americans from all backgrounds became anxious over the communal nature of Mormon gathering places in Kirtland (Ohio), Independence (Missouri), and Nauvoo (Illinois). Smith's consolidated power over his religious community—and his growing political influence—culminated in an 1844 candidacy for US president. Christians across denominational boundaries willingly set aside their differences to oppose a mutual enemy. "[T]his was common among all the sects," said Smith, "all united to persecute me."[11]

He was right. While Latter-day Saints and traditional Christians shared varying levels of responsibility for the conflict between their communities, in 1844 some men became consumed by hate and murdered Joseph Smith. Members of the ecumenical mob included self-professed Christians like Thomas C. Sharp, son of a Methodist preacher, and Levi Williams, a Baptist minister. "Smith was killed, as he should have been," wrote Methodist minister William Brownlow, as he giddily congratulated the murderers: "Three cheers to the brave company who shot him to pieces!"[12] Not all Christians joined the cheering. "Nothing can be more impolitic, or unjust, or farther removed from the spirit of the gospel, than to oppress and persecute any set of men on account of their religious tenets," wrote an Episcopalian minister.[13]

By the mid-1850s, most Latter-day Saints fled to the Great Basin under Brigham Young's leadership. They sought isolation, wishing to be left alone. But Americans feared a future Mormon state would create an imbalance of power between Salt Lake City and Washington. Worse yet, in 1857 a Mormon militia disguised as Native Americans ruthlessly attacked and killed a wagon train of emigrants passing through Mountain Meadows (southern Utah), partly in revenge for the oppression they faced in Missouri and Illinois.[14] As a result, Mormonism became less of a fake religion to expose than a foreign culture to oppose.

---

11. JS, H1:216 [Joseph Smith–History 22].
12. William G. Brownlow, "Death of Joe Smith," *The Jonesborough Whig and Independent Journal* (Tennessee), July 24, 1844.
13. John A. Clark, "Gleanings by the Way. No. VI," *The Episcopal Recorder*, September 5, 1840.
14. See Ronald W. Walker, Richard E. Turley Jr., and Glen M. Leonard, *Massacre at Mountain Meadows* (New York: Oxford University Press, 2011); Richard E. Turley Jr. and Barbara

In the 1860s, Samuel Clemens—more commonly known as Mark Twain—met Brigham Young while traveling through the American West. Clemens expected to encounter an "ignorant savage" who would confirm all his anti-Mormon prejudices, but instead he found himself enjoying the company of a kind, "dignified, self-possessed old gentleman."[15] Still, Clemens's opinion of the prophet-president was mainly negative. For him, Young was the undisputed head of religious fanaticism, seated in Salt Lake City, "the capital of the only absolute monarch in America" and home to the prophet's polygamous "harem."[16]

Many non-Mormons shared Clemens's cynical esteem for Young in the second half of the nineteenth century. On the one hand, federal powers recognized the Mormons' vital role in its colonization of the West. Manifest destiny—with its upending and displacement of countless Native tribes—would have been far more challenging without the use of Mormon-built infrastructure. On the other hand, however, Americans feared a Mormon-majority West. They suspected Latter-day Saints of wanting to build a community isolated from broader society, one that might even break away from the nation altogether.

Their concern was not unfounded. In 1844, shortly before his death, Joseph Smith organized a secret council that plotted the formation of a theocratic republic somewhere in the West. Latter-day Saints lost confidence in the government to protect them from persecution, especially after their forced expulsion from Missouri in 1838. If the United States and its Constitution could not guarantee their safety and religious freedom, then Latter-day Saints would form their own nation and laws. But the separatist plans perished with Smith, and after Brigham Young submitted a proposal to create the US State of Deseret in 1849, Congress rejected it as too ambitious, let alone suspicious.

Over the years, political tension and conflict between Latter-day Saints and others only exacerbated the "Mormon question," or what was to be done about growing Mormon influence and power. Traditional Christians latched on to two concerns. The first was hierarchy. They argued Brigham Young was a despot who ruled unchallenged over his desert fiefdom. The church hierarchy was wholly un-American. Republicanism and democracy, not despotism and theocracy, ought to reign unchallenged from San Francisco to Washington. They pressed for any legal action possible to curb the influence of the LDS hierarchy.

Polygamy was the second issue. In 1852, LDS leadership officially acknowledged the practice, although polygamy was practiced much earlier. By the mid-1850s, Brigham Young had married approximately four dozen women. Activists

---

Jones Brown, *Vengeance Is Mine: The Mountain Meadows Massacre and Its Aftermath* (New York: Oxford University Press, 2023).

15. Mark Twain, *Roughing It* (Hartford, CT: American Publishing Company, 1872), 112.
16. Twain, *Roughing It*, 120.

worked tirelessly to keep polygamy at the forefront of the public's perception of Mormonism. Their efforts influenced a series of legal maneuvers from Washington that prevented Utah's admission into the Union until 1896, six years after the church officially forbade plural marriage. Still, the public was wary of Mormonism, fearing Mormons were more loyal to their church than to their nation. At the time, Latter-day Saints swore a ritual oath to avenge the blood of Joseph Smith.[17] So when LDS apostle Reed Smoot was elected to the US Senate in 1903, thousands petitioned a campaign to unseat him, which ultimately failed.[18]

Eventually, in the decades following Utah's statehood, a period of "accommodation gradually brought [Mormonism] and the American public to terms," explained historian Jan Shipps.[19] But not everyone accepted those terms, especially Christians, "who continued to charge that Mormonism is a Christian heresy."[20] For them, Mormonism was no longer a foreign culture to oppress, but instead it became viewed as a false religion to evangelize, a posture that will be explored in the next question.

REFLECTION QUESTIONS

1. What do you believe attracted people to Joseph Smith's message in the early days of Mormonism? What repelled others from him?

2. At first, traditional Christians simply dismissed Mormonism as foolishness. What do you think about this approach?

3. An early approach to Mormonism by traditional Christians was to test Joseph Smith as a prophet according to biblical standards. What do you imagine were the results?

4. The emigration of Latter-day Saints to the Great Basin created a significant physical and cultural distance from other Americans. How might this have affected the way traditional Christians approach Mormonism?

5. How does understanding the first six decades of LDS-Christian relationship shape how you approach Latter-day Saints today?

---

17. Devery S. Anderson, ed., *The Development of LDS Temple Worship: 1846–2000* (Salt Lake City: Signature Books, 2011), 163.
18. See Michael Harold Paulos and Konden Smith Hansen, eds., *The Reed Smoot Hearings: The Investigation of a Mormon Senator and the Transformation of an American Religion* (Logan, UT: Utah State University Press, 2021).
19. Jan Shipps, *Sojourner in the Promised Land: Forty Years Among the Mormons* (Urbana, IL: University of Illinois Press, 2000), 53.
20. Shipps, *Sojourner in the Promised Land*, 53.

QUESTION 3

How Have Christians Approached Mormonism Throughout History? (Part 2)

"It is somewhat surprising that such a field for missionary labor was neglected so completely and so long. For at least fifteen years the voice of a Christian minister was never heard in Salt Lake City."[1]
~ John Hanson Beadle, Protestant Minister, 1870

The previous question chronicled how, from the earliest days of the Church of Jesus Christ of Latter-day Saints to the dawn of the twentieth century, traditional Christians initially approached Mormonism as foolishness to avoid, then a fraud to expose, and later a foreign culture to oppose. But from the beginning of the twentieth century onward, resistance to Mormonism waned as Americans gradually accepted the Latter-day Saints. Still, for many traditional Christians—especially evangelicals—Mormonism retained lingering threats to society and promulgated heretical ideas about salvation. For them, Mormonism was no longer primarily a foreign culture to oppose but a false religion to evangelize.[2]

So what change led to such acceptance, and how did the relationship between Latter-day Saints and traditional Christians evolve during the change?

1. John Hanson Beadle, *Life in Utah . . . to the Present Time* (Philadelphia: National Publishing Company, 1870), 527.
2. For these phases, I continue from the previous question to draw from J. Spencer Fluhman's observation that Christians "first found Mormonism to be a fake religion, then an alien or foreign religion, and finally a merely false one." J. Spencer Fluhman, *"A Peculiar People": Anti-Mormonism and the Making of Religion in Nineteenth-Century America* (Chapel Hill: University of North Carolina Press, 2012), 9.

The Earliest Calls for Missions Among the Mormons

After the US Civil War, Americans looked westward for the future of their reunified nation. Generous land grants and the discovery of precious metals made the allure of western migration nearly impossible for pioneering emigrants to resist. Christians leveraged this growth for missionary activity. Eastern churches commissioned and supported missionaries to preach to unchurched mining communities, Native American tribes, and Hispanic Catholics.

But Latter-day Saints were not considered proper objects of evangelism, at least not initially. The church dominated Utah Territory; Mormons were everywhere, and their influence was felt in nearly every crevice of politics. The separation of church and state was almost nonexistent. Challenging a *de facto* religious state was a tall order for a supposedly domestic mission field. Besides, the Great Basin was too remote and inhospitable for missionaries. Few believed the Mormons could survive the desert conditions long term. The famous Baptist preacher Charles H. Spurgeon offered his prediction that "the whole settlement of the Mormonites must entirely be broken up" after reading news about their struggles to tame the wild West.[3] And after the Mountain Meadows Massacre of 1857, public media vilified LDS leaders as bloodthirsty theocrats who led a flock of barbarous serfs, so the mission was considered too dangerous.

It took two decades after Latter-day Saints began colonizing the West for missionaries to receive calls to Mormon lands. Interestingly, these calls were not predominantly issued from Christian settlers looking for pastors, nor from missionaries who felt compelled to evangelize the Mormons. Instead, the calls mainly came from US federal officials stationed in the Salt Lake valley, like Colonel Patrick Connor, the commanding officer of Camp Douglas (adjacent to Salt Lake City). In 1864, he complained to eastern Protestants that "while the Several denominations of the church Send their missionaries to the 'uttermost parts of the earth,' it has never been Seriously thought that here [Salt Lake City] is to be found the grandest field for Missionary labor."[4]

His call was answered. The same year, Congregationalist minister Norman McLeod was appointed as chaplain to Connor's camp. McLeod's efforts led to many firsts for Protestants in Utah: the first non-LDS church service in the first non-LDS church building with the first Protestant Sunday school.[5] Within a decade, nearly every major denomination in the United States was represented

3. Charles Haddon Spurgeon, "What Are the Clouds?," in *The New Park Street Pulpit Sermons*, vol. 1 (London: Passmore & Alabaster, 1855), 279.
4. "A Mission to Utah," *The Home Missionary* (New York), May 1865.
5. In 1862, Presbyterian chaplain John Anderson likely held the first non-LDS Christian service in the Utah Territory. The congregation gathered in a small meeting tent at Camp Douglas. Still, McLeod is considered the Protestant pioneer of Utah for his long-lasting contributions.

in Utah: Roman Catholics (1866), Episcopalians (1867), Presbyterians (1869), Methodists (1871), and Baptists (1871), all of whom reported to their national network of churches on the need for evangelization in Utah.[6]

Mormonism as a False Religion to Evangelize

By the 1870s, Protestants became convinced of a missional need among the Mormons. They looked at LDS leaders as immoral tyrants and Mormons as hostages of a devilish power. After touring Utah, Jonathan Blanchard, the first president of Wheaton College, declared it an evangelical duty to liberate the Great Basin from the "modern Saracens of Salt Lake," likening Mormons to Turkish Muslims.[7] Utah was compared to the "heathen" nations abroad, devoid of Christian conscience, overrun by wickedness, and in desperate need of the gospel.

It was not Mormonism's doctrinal deviations from orthodoxy that first spurred traditional Christian evangelism; rather, it was the religion's peculiar practices, especially plural marriage. Polygamy, not polytheism, was the greater threat. True, Christians felt compelled to preach doctrine unadulterated by Mormon dogma. But they were equally burdened for the plural wives, whom they considered hostages in spurious and abusive marriages.

A twofold strategy developed among missionaries: to sermonize and serve the Mormons. Male clergy employed tried-and-true practices, like traveling preaching circuits, to supply empty pulpits among the few scattered congregations while also attempting to stir revivals and preach to Latter-day Saints in public spaces. Women took a quieter approach. They established schools and mercy ministries with the hope of converting children and the former wives of polygamous men. Wealthy churches in the eastern United States supported the missionaries, spurred on to give money by reports of oppression from polygamous wives who wanted out of their plural marriages but felt too embarrassed and trapped to leave.[8]

Both male and female missionaries found their work extremely difficult. Most Latter-day Saints were once traditional Christians themselves, especially former Protestants, so convincing them to return to their old religion was a monumental task. Moreover, Latter-day Saints harbored resentment toward Protestantism, which they viewed as irredeemably fractured, spiritually powerless, and one of the mechanisms that expelled them from their eastern settlements. Mormons were a peculiar people, and Protestants played a significant role in making them so. When missionaries spoke, Latter-day Saints

6. Based on the research of Thomas Edgar Lyon, "Evangelical Protestant Missionary Activities in Mormon Dominated Areas: 1865–1900" (PhD diss., University of Utah, 1962).
7. "Missionary Intelligence: Montana," *The Home Missionary* (New York), January 1865.
8. Fanny Stenhouse, *"Tell It All": The Story of a Life's Experience in Mormonism* (Hartford, CT: A. D. Worthington, 1874), 421–22.

listened politely but largely remained loyal to their religious community. As one Mormon remarked about a Baptist missionary, "He is neither mistreated nor openly ostracized—he just does not belong."[9]

Moreover, the old methods of evangelism, which worked so well in the eastern United States, failed in the Mormon West. In 1871, Methodists held a revival in Salt Lake City. Thousands of Latter-day Saints attended for a few days; yet in the end, only a single convert joined the tiny Wesleyan community. And Protestant women were shocked to encounter Mormon women who not only preferred polygamy but viewed it as a sacred duty that was, in a salvific sense, morally superior to monogamy—not all polygamous women wanted out. And not all Mormon parents were comfortable enrolling their children in Protestant schools, despite their high quality and low cost. "Mormon group solidarity proved an enormous obstacle to the missionary work of Protestants at the turn of the twentieth century," observes one historian.[10]

Missionaries continued receiving support and persisting in their work. Besides evangelism, churches expected them to promote grassroots opposition to the LDS Church, which Protestants viewed as a threat to American democracy and Christianity. So when missionaries were not busy preaching and teaching, they called for political resistance against Mormon bids for Utah's statehood unless the church abandoned plural marriage. Their efforts paid off. In 1890, LDS officials stayed the practice of polygamy, and Christians celebrated their influential role in the change.

But this victory was costly for missionaries in Utah. The end of polygamy was also the end of evangelical interest in its anti-polygamy crusade, and as interest waned, so did missionary funding. Two years later, the economic crisis of the Panic of 1893 further restricted missionary support in Utah. Then, in 1896, Utah gained statehood and built state schools that eventually edged out private Protestant schools. Worse yet, after decades of effort, the Protestant population was minuscule, rising from 0.7 percent to 2.2 percent from 1870 to 1906, and "only in the same proportion as the [non-Mormon] immigration to Utah."[11] Only a handful of Protestant churches in Utah were self-supporting in the early twentieth century.[12] Put bluntly, it was too expensive to convert Mormons. With little to show for their efforts, Protestants were faced with the decision to abandon or reinforce their mission among the Mormons.

---

9. Quoted in R. Maude Ditmars, "A History of Baptist Missions in Utah, 1871–1931" (master's thesis, University of Colorado, 1931), 28.
10. Charles Randall Paul, *Converting the Saints: A Study of Religious Rivalry in America* (Draper, UT: Greg Kofford Books, 2018), 224.
11. Ferenc Morton Szasz, *The Protestant Clergy in the Great Plains and Mountain West, 1865–1915* (Albuquerque: University of New Mexico Press, 1988), 171.
12. Szasz, *The Protestant Clergy in the Great Plains and Mountain West*, 171.

From Menace to Moral Other: 1920s–Present

For some Protestants, the answer seemed obvious: leave the Mormons alone. In the early twentieth century, liberal theology reshaped missionary concerns within American Protestantism. Social issues, like poverty and alcoholism, led some to question why resources were being allocated to convert industrious, teetotaling Mormons. Besides, millions more souls in foreign lands were bereft of the gospel. Weren't denominational resources better spent overseas? With the Mormons' abandonment of polygamy came an abandonment of the mission to Mormons.

But with the rise of fundamentalism and neo-orthodoxy, evangelicals retained a sense of missional duty to Latter-day Saints, even as missionary support diminished. In 1922, one Baptist periodical bemoaned how Utah was a "land of neglected evangelization," echoing the same sentiment expressed by Colonel Connor more than fifty years earlier.[13] Other evangelicals felt the same way and renewed their vision of Utah as a foreign mission field in the nation's backyard.

Yet, unlike previous generations, evangelicals were now more concerned about Mormon heterodoxy than with its controversial practices. Perhaps this is because in the face of secularization both groups increasingly recognized their shared moral convictions, such as traditional family values, individualism, and American exceptionalism. Despite these rallying points, evangelicals continued to view Mormonism as a threat to orthodoxy. An obvious question, therefore, needed an answer: How could Latter-day Saints be such morally upstanding people while holding such heretical doctrines? And how might evangelicals justify evangelizing a people who, on the surface, looked so familiar to themselves?

The answer soon percolated: Mormonism was a counterfeit of Christianity. Enough of the true faith was present to compel Latter-day Saints toward Christian morality; however, Mormonism was bankrupt when it came to salvific power, like all monetary counterfeits. It looked like salvation but lacked the power to save. This counterfeit theme ran consistently throughout influential evangelical literature from the essay on Mormonism in *The Fundamentals* (1910) to Walter Martin's *Kingdom of the Cults* (1965), echoes of which are heard to this day.

Thus, throughout the twentieth century, the traditional Christian approach to Mormonism took on a new and complicated form. Liberal Protestants grew more affirming of Mormonism, which Latter-day Saints welcomed; however, their relationship was stifled by their church's conservative stance on social and political issues. And while evangelicals found themselves increasingly aligned with Latter-day Saint social conservativism,

13. Henry Jacobs, "Utah: The Land of Neglected Evangelization," *The Baptist* (Chicago), September 30, 1922.

they remained adamant that Mormonism was an unorthodox expression of Christianity. Evangelicalism tends to be the loudest on this point—especially seen in its cottage industry of countercult and evangelism books—but they are certainly not alone. Regardless of their theological interpretive frameworks, traditional Christians generally hesitate to classify Mormonism as being near themselves because of Joseph Smith's incredible claims of authority and his religion's radical theological departure from creedal Christianity, both of which will be explored in subsequent questions.

Summary

As Latter-day Saints began colonizing the Great Basin, traditional Christians hesitated to view them as a people warranting missionary attention. It wasn't until parallels were drawn between the Mormon West and the "heathen" nations that Protestant denominations were spurred to support missionary efforts among the Latter-day Saints. Protestant missionaries struggled to convert Mormons, many of whom had left Protestantism for the Church of Jesus Christ of Latter-day Saints. Still, missionaries enjoyed marginal success in providing private education to Latter-day Saint children to evangelize them. But interest waned for supporting missions after the church prohibited plural marriage and liberal Protestants refocused their missionary efforts toward social campaigns. Evangelicals, however, have largely retained a missional sense of duty toward Latter-day Saints to this day.

REFLECTION QUESTIONS

1. Were you surprised to learn Protestants generally did not consider Mormonism a mission in the mid-nineteenth century? Why or why not?

2. What obstacles did Protestant missionaries face in Utah? What challenges might they face today?

3. It is often said theology drives missions. How did liberal and neo-orthodox theology influence Protestant missions toward Latter-day Saints?

4. Evangelical literature on Mormonism tends to frame the religion as a counterfeit of Christianity. Do you agree with that assessment? Why or why not?

5. What are some ways Latter-day Saints and traditional Christians might ally themselves in political and social spheres today?

PART 2

The Story of Mormonism

QUESTION 4

Who Was Joseph Smith?

"Joseph [Smith] is a man of God, a prophet of
the Lord set apart to lead the people—
If we observe his words it will be well with us;
if we live righteously on earth,
it will be well with us in Eternity."[1]
~ Lucy Mack Smith, Mother of Joseph Smith

Perhaps no question is more central to Mormonism than the one concerning its founder. Who was Joseph Smith? The answer anticipates decisions about his claims to divine revelation with all the attendant mysteries and difficulties. Was he truly a prophet of God, as he said? If so, then how do his believers reconcile the unpolished character of his mission and message? Smith himself expected this dilemma: "I never told you I was perfect," he confessed, "but there is no error in the revelations which I have taught."[2] Those who don't believe him are faced with deciding whether he was a fallen prophet, misguided visionary, pious fraud, con man, or something else altogether. And then there are the myriad influences on Smith's life. How did his relationships, experiences, and environments shape his beliefs and actions? The celebrated scholar of Mormonism Jan Shipps rightly argued the "mystery of Mormonism cannot be solved until we solve the mystery of Joseph Smith," the main piece of the religion's "prophet puzzle."[3]

Many people have attempted to solve the prophet puzzle, which has proven to be a herculean task. First, there's the fact that it's a *prophet* puzzle,

1. Nauvoo Relief Society Minute Book, p. 24, *JSP*.
2. JS, H, 1838–1856, vol. F-1, *JSP*, 21.
3. Jan Shipps, "The Prophet Puzzle: Suggestions Leading Toward a More Comprehensive Interpretation of Joseph Smith," *Journal of Mormon History* 1 (1974): 19.

fitting together the pieces of a man's life who claimed to speak for God. Was he a true prophet or a false one, and how could we tell? Was he even a prophet at all if, "in these last days" (Heb 1:2) God has spoken finally by his only begotten Son, the Word of God (see John 1:1), and not a mere man? Regardless of how one answers these initial questions, biographers must bend Smith's jagged corners to fit the smooth contours of his life, and vice versa. At times he displayed inflexibility, a short temper, and image consciousness; yet he also showed brilliance, compassion, and peacemaking. Neither polemic nor hagiographic versions of Smith's life satisfy. Perhaps, as some suggest, he should be measured by his sincerity.[4] Was there ever a "mismatch of interior disposition and external actions" between Smith's heart and his hands?[5]

Regardless of the answer, new questions arise, especially for traditional Christians. If his motives were insincere, then could he still have expressed truth? After all, said Paul, "Some indeed preach Christ even of envy and strife" (Phil 1:15), but it bothered him little because Christ is nevertheless preached (see Phil 1:18). The matter then becomes one of distilling sweet water from a bitter fountain, if possible (see Jas 3:10–12).

But if Smith was sincerely wrong, does that excuse his errors? Smith could have deceived himself and unintentionally led people astray. What "blind leaders of the blind" happily lead their followers "into the ditch" (Matt 15:14)? Perhaps, then, discerning Smith's sincerity is a moot point. After all, in his oft-quoted statement, Smith said: "No man knows my history; I cannot tell it. I shall never undertake it."[6] How is it possible to solve the prophet puzzle when the pieces are practically unknowable even to the prophet himself?

But his life's story, integrated as it is into Mormonism, invites all to try anyhow. Over the next two questions, we'll explore Joseph Smith's persona and position in the Church of Jesus Christ of Latter-day Saints so that readers may fit the pieces of his life together in their own minds.

The Early Life of Joseph Smith

Joseph Smith Jr. was born in Sharon, Vermont, on December 23, 1805, to Joseph Smith Sr. and Lucy Mack Smith, the fourth of nine children. The Smiths were farmers whose several financial setbacks and relocations afflicted the family with challenges during Joseph's adolescent years, leaving him, he explained, "deprived of the bennifit of an education suffice it to say I was mearly instructtid in reading [and] writing."[7] Those around him described

4. See Laurie F. Maffly-Kipp, "Tracking the Sincere Believer: 'Authentic' Religion and the Enduring Legacy of Joseph Smith Jr.," in *Joseph Smith Jr.: Reappraisals After Two Centuries*, ed. Reid L. Neilson and Terryl L. Givens (New York: Oxford University Press, 2009), 175–88.
5. Maffly-Kipp, "Tracking the Sincere Believer," 178.
6. JS, discourse, *T&S*, August 15, 1855, 5:617.
7. JS, ca. 1832 history, H1:11.

Joseph as "quite illiterate"[8] and "generally ignorant in common learning."[9] Joseph was quick to admit his scholarly shortcomings—his "weakness to a learned world"[10]—especially his poor grammar and "inability in conveying [his] ideas in writing."[11]

Still, "he always seemed to reflect more deeply than common persons his age," recalled his mother, especially "upon everything of a religious nature."[12] Her son was bright, inquisitive, and filled with charisma, all characteristics that would later influence the development of his religious beliefs. Neighbors remembered him as "a real clever, jovial boy,"[13] even if, at times, he came across as "pompous [and] pretentious."[14]

The Smiths moved to Palmyra, New York, in 1816, near the site of the future Erie Canal. They worked in a store and as hired hands until they could lease a one-hundred-acre lot just south of town. There, the Smiths constructed a modest cabin and cleared land to establish a farm. The family's reputation among their neighbors was mixed. On the one hand, the Smiths labored exhaustively to make their farm productive and to secure financial peace. They felled thousands of trees to clear enough land to plant crops and a large orchard. Eventually, they produced sugar and started a small cooperage. But on the other hand, they struggled economically, which led some neighbors to complain about the Smiths. More than anything, it was the treasure digging that raised their neighbors' eyebrows. The family was rumored to divert their time and energy away from farming toward excavating treasure with magical seer stones, which cast a shadow over their reputation. "In short, not one of the family had the least claims to respectability," said one acquaintance bluntly.[15] "They were poor as well as worthless,"[16] claimed another neighbor, a point amplified by fifty-one others who asserted the family was "destitute of that moral character, which ought to entitle them to the confidence of any community."[17] Others didn't mind the Smiths, describing them as "big hearty fellows"[18] and a "good family"[19] who made "good neighbors."[20] Either way, the Smiths were marginalized,

8. *EMD* 2:122.
9. *EMD* 3:7.
10. JS to Noah C. Saxton, January 4, 1833, D2:351.
11. JS to Emma Smith, June 6, 1832, D2:256 (emend.).
12. Lavina Fielding Anderson, *Lucy's Book: A Critical Edition of Lucy Mack Smith's Family Memoir* (Salt Lake City: Signature Books, 2001), 335.
13. *EMD* 2:121.
14. *EMD* 2:209.
15. *EMD* 2:22.
16. *EMD* 3:15.
17. *EMD* 2:48.
18. EMD 2:137
19. *EMD* 2:139.
20. *EMD* 2:156.

"a low family and of no account in the community," whether by their own doing, prejudice, or both.[21] Discerning the Smiths' character is difficult. Were they an innocent and industrious family misunderstood by outsiders, or was the family business a blend of agriculture and duplicity? One thing about them, however, was clear: the Smiths valued religion.

Years earlier, after a lifetime of resisting the gospel, Joseph's grandfather, Solomon Mack, was converted after heeding Christ's invitation to "come unto me, all ye that labour and are heavy laden, and I will give you rest" (Matt 11:28). Having repudiated his Universalist convictions, Mack was pressed by the weight of his sin until, after a series of nightly visions—seeing lights and hearing his name called—he prayed for mercy and finally "found Christ's promises verified that what things soever ye ask in prayer, believing, ye shall receive."[22] It was in the gospel promise of rest where Mack found redemption.

His grandson Joseph later found himself in a similar condition, weighed down by the guilt of sin. Although he was raised by "goodly Parents who spared no pains to instructing me in the christian religion,"[23] he said, and even though he believed the Bible "contained the word of God,"[24] he was unsure of his salvation. "I felt to mourn for my own sins," he wrote, and worse, "for the sins of the world."[25] He sensed a sort of universal apostasy "from the true and living faith" among those who claimed Christ's name, evidenced by their "contentions and divisions." (see question 6).[26]

Joseph's own home was not spared. His father, Joseph Sr., once a founding member of a Universalist society, later rejected organized religion in favor of individualist spiritualism, a position Joseph Jr. seemed to share. "I can take my Bible, and go into the woods, and learn more in two hours, than you can learn at [church] in two years," he reportedly told his mother, Lucy.[27] But she felt differently, preferring instead to align herself with Presbyterianism, a more structured form of faith. The fiery revivalism of the Second Great Awakening only added to Joseph Jr.'s confusion. At camp meetings, preachers stirred up crowds to repent and receive the Holy Spirit. Joseph said he wanted "to feel & shout like the Rest but could feel nothing."[28] At an early age, he sought a quiet, personal revival in a grove near his family's cabin. There, Joseph claimed to commune directly with God, a pivotal moment that marked the beginning of Mormonism (see question 7). The vision was followed by angelic encounters,

---

21. *EMD* 2:188.
22. Solomon Mack, *A Narraitve* [sic] *of the Life of Solomon Mack . . . Was Converted to the Christian Faith* (Windsor, VT: 1811), 23.
23. JS, ca. 1832 history, H1:11.
24. JS, ca. 1832 history, H1:11.
25. JS, ca. 1832 history, H1:12.
26. JS, ca. 1832 history, H1:11 (emend.).
27. *EMD* 1:307.
28. Alexander Neibaur, journal entry, May 24, 1844, *JSP*.

the discovery of ancient gold plates, the publication of the Book of Mormon, and the humble beginning of a tiny church that grew from a handful to millions.

A Prophet Under Pressure

The growth of the church came at a tremendous cost to Smith. At first, he weathered rhetorical criticism from skeptics. The public fixated on Mormon heterodoxy, like the Book of Mormon and the church's charismatic practices. Skeptics pitied the Mormons as "a deluded set of men"[29] mesmerized by the "fanatic illusions"[30] of a false prophet who "pretends to cast out devils, to give the Holy Ghost by laying on of hands, to heal the sick, &c."[31] "Jo Smith" took the brunt of public criticism as clergy railed against him in the pulpit and pamphleteers did so in print. But in 1832, rhetorical opposition swelled into violent intimidation. Smith was abducted, beaten, and tarred and feathered.[32] The mob hoped to silence the would-be prophet, but in the long run, their actions had the opposite effect. Smith wore the scars of persecution proudly. In the years to come, many of his followers would share in his suffering. In fall of 1838, for example, at Hawn's Mill in Missouri, an anti-Mormon militia massacred seventeen men, women, and children.[33] Smith constantly faced challenges protecting his followers and dealing with church opposition.

Legal challenges also plagued the prophet. Smith was arrested and faced trials on numerous occasions. He was charged with fraud, adultery, and treason, among other allegations. Smith often pled his innocence despite being vilified. "These are falsehoods," he once said, decrying how his own "mormon dissenters are running through the world and spreading various foul and libelous reports."[34] Antagonism and persecution from external opposition permeated Smith's anxiety, but he found relief by interpreting his enemies' resentment as a sign of God's favor. In stirring up the people against Mormons, Smith said his critics hoped "to gain the friendship of the world because they know that we are not of the world and the world hates us" (see John 15:19).[35] Let anti-Mormons befriend the world; the Saints were friends of Zion.

But all was not well in Zion. While external enemies battered the church, internal dissent threatened Smith's leadership. Some Mormons challenged him, especially his decisions around financial stewardship and doctrinal developments,

29. *Illinois Patriot* (Jacksonville), September 16, 1831, reprinted in *The United States Gazette* (Philadelphia), October 14, 1831.
30. *Phenix Gazette* (Alexandria, VA), March 18, 1831.
31. "The Mormon Delusion," *Hampshire Gazette* (Northampton, MA), April 27, 1831.
32. Richard Lyman Bushman, *Joseph Smith: Rough Stone Rolling* (New York: Knopf, 2005), 178–80.
33. Bushman, *Joseph Smith: Rough Stone Rolling*, 365–66.
34. JS to the Church in Caldwell County, December 16, 1838, D6:304–05.
35. JS to the Church in Caldwell County, 305.

which led to factions. In 1837, a small but powerful schism led by Warren Parrish claimed ownership of the Mormons' first temple in Kirtland, Ohio. Parrish, who served Smith as a clerk, broke from his prophet after the two exchanged accusations of financial mismanagement. And later, in 1844, William Law, formerly Smith's counselor, organized a breakaway congregation in Nauvoo, Illinois, then the headquarters of the church. Law's group opposed polygamy and polytheism, which they accused Smith of having introduced after becoming a fallen prophet.

Under constant pressure from enemies without and dissenters within, Smith emerged not as a weathered leader but as a prophet increasingly defined by bolder claims, expanding authority, and escalating demands for loyalty.

A Prophet of Paradox

Smith was a pastoral and compassionate leader. He celebrated with newlyweds at weddings, attended the sick, and wept with mourners at funerals. He advocated for victims of domestic abuse,[36] prayed over a crisis pregnancy,[37] and consoled a woman whose baby died on Christmas Eve.[38] Smith was hospitable, having received many people into his home, so much so that at times he described being "hindered by a multitude of visitors" but received them as gifts: "May God grant to continue his mercies unto my house," he prayerfully journaled.[39]

Smith's compassionate hospitality stemmed from genuine concern about his community's welfare. He desired to alleviate poverty among his people and encouraged his followers to "cultivate sympathy for the afflicted among us."[40] During church trials, Smith sometimes "acted on the part of the defence for the accused to plead for mercy."[41] He was patient with those he found to be sincerely humble and quick to reject those who were not.[42]

But Smith was also short-tempered. For example, when the governor of Illinois, Thomas Ford, issued a warrant for Smith's arrest in June 1843, he fiercely prophesied "in the name of the Lord God" that Ford was damned and his "carcass will stink on the face of the earth."[43] A little more than a week later, a calmer Smith yielded to Christ's command to love one's enemies (see Matt 5:43–44), rightly recognizing that "if we would s[e]cure & cultivate the love of others we must love others, even our enemies."[44] In the face of adversity, Smith rightly

36. JSJ, October 29, 1835, J1:76.
37. JSJ, October 29, 1835, J1:75–76.
38. JSJ, December 24, 1842, J2:193.
39. JSJ, September 22, 1835, J1:62.
40. JSJ, April 16, 1843, J2:358.
41. JSJ, September 29, 1835, J1:67.
42. See, for example, JS's warm treatment of Baptist inquirer John Hollister [JSJ, December 4, 1835, J1:115–16] compared to Robert Matthews, or "Joshua the Jewish minister," who JS suspected as being a fraud [JSJ, November 9–11, 1835, J1:87–95].
43. JSJ, June 30, 1843, J3:48 (emend.).
44. JSJ, July 9, 1843, J3:55.

advised his people to "be cool, be deliberate [and] be wise."[45] Had he consistently practiced his own advice, perhaps he would have lived longer. His short temper prompted his rash decision to order Nauvoo's militia, which he controlled, to destroy a printing press after it published unflattering information about him. This event was the catalyst that led to his death in 1844 (see question 9).

Still, Smith strove to respect all people. "I feel myself bound to be a friend to all the sons of Adam," he wrote, "whether they are just or unjust, they have a degree of my compassion & sympathy."[46] These words take on more significance knowing Smith wrote them about John C. Bennett, a con man who quickly rose through church ranks only to be outed for moral hypocrisy, a vice that Smith despised.[47] "I love that man better who swears a stream as long as my arm, and administering to the poor and dividing his substance, than the long smoothed faced hypocrites,"[48] he said, because he believed "it is the delight of my soul to be honest."[49] Yet despite his disdain for duplicity, Smith was occasionally guilty of it. In May 1844, after enduring years of accusations of adultery for practicing "Spiritual wifeism,"[50] he very publicly denied his involvement with polygamy, which would have been a shock to the women with whom he had privately entered into celestial marriage.[51] True, Joseph dearly loved his first (and only legal) wife, Emma, whom he called "the choice of my heart,"[52] yet he caused her deep, emotional pain. She "wept considerable"[53] after being presented with a supposedly "Holy Law,"[54] the "new and an everlasting covenant"[55] of marriage in which her husband was commanded by God to take additional wives (see D&C 132:1–2, 34–39, 51–52).

Perhaps this kind of conflicted incongruity is to be expected from a man who said he was simply "but a man" and that his followers "must not expect him to be perfect."[56] "I don't want you to think I am very righteous," he said, "for I am not very righteous."[57] Still, as admittedly flawed as he was, Smith

45. JSJ, June 30, 1843, J3:43.
46. JS to James Arlington Bennet, JSJ September 8, 1842, in J2:138–39.
47. See Andrew F. Smith, *The Saintly Scoundrel: The Life and Times of Dr. John Cook Bennett* (Urbana, IL: University of Illinois Press, 1997).
48. JS, discourse, May 12, 1843, D12:321 (emend.).
49. JSJ, September 22, 1835, J1:62.
50. JS, discourse, May 26, 1844, D15:51.
51. Todd Compton, *In Sacred Loneliness: The Plural Wives of Joseph Smith* (Salt Lake City: Signature Books, 1997), 4–6. See also George D. Smith, *Nauvoo Polygamy: ". . . But We Called It Celestial Marriage"* (Salt Lake City: Signature Books, 2011), 223–24.
52. JSJ, August 16, 1842, J2:94.
53. According to JS's scribe William Clayton, in *An Intimate Chronicle: The Journals of William Clayton,* ed. George D. Smith (Salt Lake City: Signature Books, 1995), 110.
54. Clayton, *An Intimate Chronicle*, 110.
55. JS, revelation, July 12, 1843, D12:467 [D&C 132].
56. JSJ, October 29, 1842, J2:164.
57. JSJ, May 21, 1843, J3:20 (emend.).

claimed to be God's prophet. Whether or not one accepts his claim inevitably frames their understanding of his character, life, and legacy.

Summary

The story of Joseph Smith is woven into a complex tapestry of his iconoclastic religious activity, controversial leadership, and enigmatic personal character. From modest beginnings, he emerged as the founder of one of America's most unique and influential religious movements. The story of the Church of Jesus Christ of Latter-day Saints is impossible to tell without Smith, whose incredible claims to spiritual authority invite us to piece together the puzzle of his life. What image emerges, of course, depends on how one fits together the pieces of Smith's character and story with the incredible spiritual claim that "there is no error in the revelations which I have taught."[58] Why Smith felt this was the case will be explored in the next question.

REFLECTION QUESTIONS

1. Do you agree that with the prophet puzzle, that the "mystery of Mormonism cannot be solved until we solve the mystery of Joseph Smith"?[59]
2. What did you know about Joseph Smith before reading this question? What did you learn from this question?
3. What was life like for Joseph Smith as a boy, and how might his early experiences have shaped his later life?
4. What are some significant events in Joseph Smith's life?
5. Do you believe Joseph Smith was a prophet? Why or why not?

58. JS, H, 1838–1856, vol. F-1, *JSP*, 21.
59. Shipps, "Prophet Puzzle," 19.

QUESTION 5

Why Was Joseph Smith Considered a Prophet, Seer, Revelator, and Translator?

"Praise to the man who commun'd with Jehovah,
Jesus anointed 'that Prophet and Seer'"[1]
~ William W. Phelps, Latter-day Saint Hymnist

When he penned his autobiography in 1832, Joseph Smith intertwined the "marvelous experience" of his personal story with "an account of the rise of the church" he founded, and with good reason.[2] He knew how indispensable his story was to understand the Church of Jesus Christ of Latter-day Saints, and vice versa. Without him, the church would not exist, and if not for its remarkable rise Smith's name would have faded into obscurity.

But his story does not begin with the church. Like so many of his peers during the Second Great Awakening, the sinful state of his soul haunted Smith before a holy God. The evangelical revival that swept through rural New York blanketed his hometown with calls to repent and join a church. Baptists, Methodists, and Presbyterians "were active in getting up and promoting this extraordinary scene of religious feeling in order to have every body converted," he recalled.[3] Smith listened to their calls and yearned deeply for forgiveness, having "felt to mourn for my own sins," but he also felt lost in the cacophony of religious competition and the anxieties that attended them.[4]

1. William W. Phelps, "Joseph Smith," *T&S*, August 1, 1844, 5:607.
2. JS, ca. 1832 history, H1:10.
3. JS, H1:208 [Joseph Smith–History 6].
4. JS, ca. 1832 history, H1:12.

Even his own home was divided on religious matters. His father, a spiritual seeker, rejected all churches as hopelessly wayward, while his mother joined with the Presbyterians. Smith felt compelled to answer the question of which church was true before he could find salvation.

Around this time, in the 1820s, Smith claimed he had experienced a series of visions that led him to "true" religion (see question 7), which eventually culminated in the establishment of the Church of Jesus Christ of Latter-day Saints in Fayette, New York, on April 6, 1830. Smith claimed to receive a revelation naming himself "a seer, a translator, a prophet, an apostle" chosen by God to lead the new congregation.[5] Near the end of his life, Smith reflected on his time leading the church, highlighting his accomplishments in four ways: "by the voice of truth; by the accomplishments of virtue; by the blessings of pure religion; and by the holy revelations of God."[6] For Smith, these modes (i.e., seer, translator, prophet, and apostle) and means (i.e., truth, virtue, religion, and revelations) enabled him to reestablish God's true church on earth. To understand Smith, it's important to grasp what he meant by these modes and means.

Joseph Smith as Latter-day Seer and Translator

At first glance, traditional Christians might find the title "seer" to be foreign or even fabricated, but the concept has biblical origins. The Hebrews began to view the term *seer* as an antiquated description for prophets by the time of their divided kingdom (see 1 Sam 9:9). In OT histories, seers functioned much in the same way as prophets (see 1 Sam 9:19; 2 Kgs 17:13; 1 Chr 21:9–10). They spoke on behalf of God to reveal the mysteries of his will. But seers were susceptible to corruption and could abuse their position to manipulate people for selfish gain (see Mic 3:5–7), so only the virtuous seers enjoyed true authority from God (see Mic 3:8). Centuries later, early church father Jerome discerned another unique quality to OT seership, believing that Christ, who was prefigured in the Law and Prophets, was "seen" by them. "That is why the prophets were called seers," he explained. "They saw him whom others did not see."[7]

The Book of Mormon expands seership to incorporate the function of a "revelator," which included the ability to recover hidden truth (see Mosiah 8:16–17). The term *revelator* is unique in LDS scripture; it appears only once in the Book of Mormon and is absent from the Bible. In Smith's day, the term was often associated with the book of Revelation (see D&C 77:2; 128:6). On the island of Patmos, John the Revelator received an incredible vision of God's

5. JS, H1:368 [D&C 21:1].
6. JS to James Bennet, March 17–18, 1843, D12:70.
7. Alister E. McGrath, ed., *The Christian Theology Reader*, 5th ed. (Oxford: Wiley Blackwell, 2017), 81.

kingdom unfolding with an angel as his guide. He was instructed by Christ to record his vision for the benefit of the church (see Rev 1:11). This role is possibly what Smith sought to emulate having donned the title of revelator (see D&C 100:11; 107:92; 124:94, 125). Smith claimed to have experienced heavenly visions, and his angel guide, Moroni, led him to discover sacred knowledge—all to offer the church "certainty of all things pertaining to the things of [Christ's] kingdom on the earth."[8] As a revelator, Smith believed he possessed new and clarifying truth.

Smith also believed that he was gifted with a seer's power to recover lost truth from the past by retrieving forgotten or discarded doctrine through revelation or translation of rediscovered scripture (see Mosiah 8:13). This practice was "unquestionably rare, if not unique" among religious visionaries contemporary to Smith, setting him apart from potential competitors and setting him up for leadership of the church.[9] Instead of championing his interpretation of the Bible among alternatives, from the summer of 1830 to July 1833 he revised the Bible itself (Joseph Smith Translation, or the Inspired Version) to align with his vision of its ancient purity. And rather than appealing to known extrabiblical works, Smith translated new scripture from ancient plates and papyri, which led to the publication of the Book of Mormon and the book of Abraham. As a seer, Smith believed he could perceive hidden spiritual truth.

Smith's role as seer and translator enabled him to create religious products that attracted converts to early Mormonism. People unsatisfied by the limitations of the canonical record of the Bible were captivated by the prospect of modern revelation and new scripture, both produced by a man who testified of sharing similar experiences to their faith's most respected figures and promised to retrieve the pure religion they preached and practiced. Naturally, Smith viewed himself as occupying the same roles as the Bible's main authors: prophets and apostles.

Joseph Smith as Latter-day Prophet and Apostle

"Thus saith the Lord." With these prefatory words, prophets in the OT prepared the ears of people, their nation, and even foreigners in faraway lands to hear from the voice of God. The calling of a prophet by God and the closeness of their relationship set them apart from their community as divine messengers. The Holy Spirit inspired their words and empowered their holiness (see 2 Sam 23:2; Isa 61:1; Ezek 36:27). For God, the purity of his message must come through a worthy messenger, so the claim to prophethood was also a claim to holiness. Ideally, righteous prophets who faithfully modeled God's

---

8. MRB, 561 [D&C 100:11], *JSP*.
9. Michael Hubbard MacKay, Mark Ashurst-McGee, and Brian M. Hauglid, "Introduction," in *Producing Ancient Scripture: Joseph Smith's Translation Projects in the Development of Mormon Christianity* (Salt Lake City: University of Utah Press, 2020), 7.

purposes delivered his word, and a single sour note in the harmony of his prophetic choir warranted the rejection of a fallen or false prophet (see Deut 18:22). For Christians, the chorus of OT prophetic voices sung beautifully about a future Messiah, Jesus Christ, whose life, death, and resurrection secured all the promises of God foretold by the prophets (see Luke 24:27; 2 Cor 1:20; Heb 1:1).

Like the prophets, NT apostles received a divine commission by Christ to carry forward his word, being inspired by the Holy Spirit in their communication and character. The Greek word *apostolos* highlights the missional and authoritative nature of "one who is sent" to represent their sender. Jesus called apostles during his earthly ministry, and others—like Matthias (see Acts 1:26) and Paul (see Acts 9:15; Gal 1:1)—were called after Christ's ascension. The apostles embarked on a lifelong commitment as messengers of Christ, even at the cost of their freedom and lives. Their messages were both backward- and forward-facing, reminding believers of Christ's work begun and hoping for his future work completed. The apostles also engaged in evangelism and discipleship, especially in Paul's missionary journeys and his pastoral mentorship.

Joseph Smith clearly envisioned himself as a latter-day prophet-apostle, having modeled his office after Moses and the twelve apostles. The First Vision is filled with elements from the biblical accounts of prophets and apostles encountering God (see question 7). Early LDS revelations described how Smith received divine words "even as Moses"[10] and reiterated Smith's appointment "to preside over the whole church & to be like unto Moses,"[11] i.e., the prophetic head of God's community. Smith was, however, quick to point out his fallibility. "A Prophet is not always a Prophet," he clarified, because prophets are only so "when he is acting as such."[12] But when he functioned as God's prophet, his voice carried divine authority. Smith's revelations frequently emulated OT prophecy by calling the hearer to "hearken" or "behold," and then offered direct instruction or guidance in tandem with revealing God's character and will. And many of Smith's letters to his congregations are rich with NT apostolic allusions, adaptations, and quotes. Smith addressed the "saints scattered abroad" when writing from jail in 1838 (see Jas 1:1; 1 Pet 1:1). "We glory in our tribulation" (see Rom 5:3), he explained, because God would save the saints, and promised his people that the "God of peace shall be with you" (see Rom 15:33; Phil 4:9).[13]

Mormonism understands Smith's privilege to speak on God's behalf as beginning with his First Vision, expanding at his recovery of an ancient scriptural record, and culminating when John the Baptist, Peter, James, and

---

10. MRB, 51 [D&C 28:2].
11. JS, revelation, November 11, 1831, D2:135 [D&C 107:91 (partial)].
12. JSJ, February 8, 1843, J2:256.
13. JS to the Church in Caldwell County, December 16, 1838, D6:298–310.

John descended from heaven to ordain him (see question 19). As a prophet-apostle, Smith believed he—and only he—could proclaim new, divine truth authoritatively and definitively on behalf of God in the latter days.

Joseph Smith, Authority, and Traditional Christianity

It was this unprecedented combination of authority—seer, translator, prophet, and apostle—that set Smith apart from competing spiritual revolutionaries of his day. He founded the LDS Church when some traditional Christians hungered for a fresh movement of God, more than what established denominations offered. Their anxious souls yearned for forgiveness, theological clarity, and assurance of faith. Various preachers and visionaries heralded the renewal of the Spirit who empowered both tranquil revival and charismatic phenomena. They looked back to prophets and apostles who reminded the Christians of what they already knew to be true: the sufficient message of the Bible called them to delight in and serve God.

Smith was different. His fourfold office did not simply revive old truth; rather, it laid new foundations. Unlike traditional Christians who saw the Bible as a sufficient and fixed canon, Smith regarded it as inspired but incomplete (see question 12). So he revised its words, restored what he believed had been lost, and stretched its length. But this was only the beginning. Through ongoing revelation, Smith redefined the nature of God, expanded the possibilities of progressive salvation, and reconstructed temples as the stage for sacred ordinances and eternal covenants. All the distinctive marks of Mormonism trace back to him. He offered not simply restoration, but expansion. Indeed, more is what Smith claimed Mormonism—from the root "more good"—offered the world.[14] Therefore, how a person understood Smith's authority was inseparable from how they heard his invitation: to receive more, to become more, or to walk away.

Within traditional Christianity, Smith's claim to stand among—or even beyond—the biblical prophets and apostles exceeds the boundaries of legitimate spiritual authority. Christians believe that God has spoken fully and finally in his Son, the very Word of God incarnate (John 1:1, 14), who has fulfilled all divine purposes and plans for redemption as communicated by his gospel and the teachings of his apostles in the Bible (see John 1:1, 14; Heb 1:1–3). From this view, Smith's additional revelations are not merely unnecessary; rather, they are incompatible. It is not prophecy itself that Christians reject, but the content and claims of Smith's prophethood, which they find misaligned with the gospel once for all delivered to the saints (see Jude 3; 1 Thess 5:20–21).

---

14. So Smith: "The word MORMON; which means, literally, *more good*" (JS to the Editor *T&S*, ca. May 20, 1843, in D12:319, emphases original). JS elsewhere defined "the word Mormon" as "More—Good" (JSJ, May 20, 1843, J3:19).

Traditional Christianity rejects Smith's invitation for more by framing him in terms like the rival apostles of the NT period. Paul wrote to the Corinthian church concerned after learning about the church's encounter with disciples of "another Jesus," the bearers of "another spirit" and the harbingers of "another gospel" (2 Cor 11:4). These "apostles" apparently accused Paul of withholding aspects of the gospel from the Corinthians, which he vehemently denied. He cautioned against superlative apostles, those who viewed themselves as having achieved the highest attainable level of apostleship. Paul said these super-apostles promised more than was necessary or warranted.

Although it is natural to empathize with the spiritual anxiety and confusion Smith experienced in his childhood, traditional Christians find themselves at odds with the man he became. Near the end of his life, Smith believed his role as latter-day prophet-apostle had become so important to the redemption of humanity that he publicly boasted about his accomplishments and triumphs against enemies, going so far as to accept the threefold honorific title of "Prophet, Priest & King" traditionally reserved by Christians for Christ alone. Latter-day Saints interpreted the gesture within a symbolic, temple-centered framework and saw it as a preview of exalted status promised to the faithful. Even so, from a traditional Christian perspective, the act gestures toward a self-understanding that elevates Smith's role far beyond that of a merely human teacher or spiritual guide.[15]

Even after his death, church leaders insisted that Smith retained his authority postmortem in heaven as "a king and priest unto the most high God."[16] To be clear, Smith *was never* and *is not* worshiped in the LDS Church; no orthodox Latter-day Saint would even consider it. But Smith is elevated so high that he has become the subject of praise as the man who "commun'd with Jehovah," as the LDS hymn declares.[17] "If ever you enter into the Kingdom of God," claimed Brigham Young, "it is because Joseph Smith let you go there."[18] Perhaps this high veneration, more than anything, prevents traditional Christians from approaching his claims in the first place. In the end, it is not so much the *why* of Smith's mission but the *how* that distances him from the traditional Christian community.

---

15. C:96. Relatedly, in a sermon delivered the month before his death, Smith reportedly declared: "I have more to boast of than ever any man had. I am the only man that ever has been able to keep a whole church together since the days of Adam—a large majority of the whole have stood by me:—neither Paul, John, Peter nor Jesus ever did it. I boast that no man ever did such a work as me—the followers of Jesus ran away from him, the Latter Day Saints never ran away from me yet" (JS, discourse, May 26, 1844, D15:47).
16. BY, "An Epistle of the Twelve," *T&S*, August 15, 1844, 5:618.
17. William W. Phelps, "Joseph Smith," *T&S*, August 1, 1844, 5:607.
18. *CDBY* 2:853.

Summary

The story of Mormonism is intertwined with Joseph Smith, who adopted a fourfold office of seer, translator, apostle, and prophet to form the Church of Jesus Christ of Latter-day Saints. As seer, Smith believed he possessed the ability to retrieve forgotten knowledge to progress his restoration of the Christian faith. As revelator and translator, he produced revelatory "translations" that extended the scriptural canon. As prophet and apostle, he set himself atop an ecclesiastical hierarchy to lead the first Latter-day Saints and guide the development of early Mormonism. For these reasons, traditional Christians hold Joseph Smith at arm's length.

REFLECTION QUESTIONS

1. Do you agree that the story of the LDS Church is intertwined with that of Joseph Smith? If so, how does this shape and inform your study of Mormonism?

2. What is a "seer" according to Mormonism, and what is the significance for Joseph Smith adopting that role in the early LDS Church?

3. What does it mean that Joseph Smith was the translator for the LDS Church? How does this role fuse his legacy to the standard words of LDS scripture?

4. Joseph Smith believed the offices of prophet and apostle were to be restored in the end times. Do you agree or disagree, and how might you communicate your view to a Latter-day Saint?

5. What does it mean to you that Joseph Smith accepted the titles of prophet, priest, and king?

QUESTION 6

What Is the Great Apostasy?

"For a season the powers of evil triumphed,
and the spirit of apostasy ruled [the church]."[1]
~ James E. Talmage, Latter-day Saint Apostle, 1911–1933

It must have been an uncomfortable excursion for the disciples when Christ led them to the district of Caesarea Philippi, an area far from their Jewish homeland and rife with Gentile paganism. But it was worth the discomfort. There, in the most unlikely place, Jesus promised the disciples that he would build his church through them and that "the gates of hell shall not prevail against it" (Matt 16:18). It was a victorious declaration over a war already won. The church would batter down the gates of hell, invading the enemy's spiritual kingdom. Heaven's conquest over hell is inevitable. "Go ye therefore" (Matt 28:19), the resurrected Christ later commissioned his disciples, commanding them to spread his message bolstered by a promise: "I am with you always, to the end of the age" (Matt 28:20 CSB).

Throughout the centuries, Christians have interpreted Christ's words to mean the church would never fail while also acknowledging the challenges it faces. Externally, the church has weathered opposition, oppression, and persecution. Internally, episodes of heresy and seasons of compromise and apathy have all threatened the church's life. Rebellion, whether against God's people or by them, has called into question the church's survivability.

The apostle Paul warned the church of such apostasy. In fact, the day of the Lord would not come "unless the apostasy comes first" (2 Thess 2:3 CSB). Apostasy (Gk. *apostasia*) is the manifestation of rebellion, a faithless and destructive pride that leads to betraying and falling away from God and his will (see Josh 22:16, 22; Jer 2:17, 19; Acts 21:21). But when exactly

1. James E. Talmage, *The Great Apostasy* (Salt Lake City: Deseret, 1909), 23.

would that apostasy come, how pervasive would it be, and what signs would accompany it?

Apostasy in Protestant Thought

By the sixteenth century, Protestant Reformers criticized the Roman Catholic Church for being too focused on power and wealth, failing to see its own corruption. Martin Luther likened Rome to a spiritual Babylon, abusing and oppressing captive souls. And John Calvin felt that the popes were prideful men who donned Christ's name as a pretext to consolidate their own power. The papacy paved the way for the antichrist to sit atop the institutional church. Reformers sought to rehabilitate Christianity by reforming the church and returning *ad fontes* (Lat. "to the sources") to retrieve the gospel from the Bible.

Although the heirs of the Reformation agreed with Luther and Calvin that Roman Catholicism was corrupt, some expressed concerns about the Protestant movement they produced. Chief among them were issues of authenticity and disunity, both rooted in authority. How could Protestant churches preach a pure gospel while retaining Roman residue in their practices, like human-made creeds, ecclesiastical hierarchies, and liturgies and ceremonies? And why had the tradition fractured if evidence of true faith is unity (see John 17:22)? It only took fifty years from when Luther published his *Ninety-Five Theses* for Western Christianity to partition into Catholicism, Lutheranism, Anabaptism, Anglicanism, Swiss Reformed churches, and Presbyterianism, with more denominations on the horizon.

Critics thought the problem lay in the pedigree of Protestant clergy who traced their origin of authority through Rome. As English Separatist Henry Barrow argued, "If the Church of Rome be no true church, then the ministers made therein are no true ministers," but because Protestant ministers were either "made in" or "fetched from" Rome, the clergy were wholly "Romish, antichristian and false."[2] By receiving their ministerial heritage from Rome, Protestants had unwittingly opened the "scars of the old and first apostasy from the gospel," becoming as unrecognizable from the apostolic church as Roman Catholicism itself.[3]

Still, Barrowe held out hope. In all the "defection, corruption, [and] apostasy" of the universal church, he believed that "God still reserved a seed, a little poor remnant."[4] Channeling Martin Luther, he compared Catholic and Protestant churches to a spiritual Babylon, an evil power that had taken the true church into captivity and hidden it from the world. For this reason, Separatists, as their name implies, separated from the Church of England. The

2. Leland H. Carlson, ed., *The Writings of Henry Barrow, 1587–1590*, vol. 3 of *Elizabethan Non-Conformist Texts* (New York: Routledge, 2003), 331.
3. Carlson, *Writings of Henry Barrow*, 200.
4. Carlson, *Writings of Henry Barrow*, 211 (emend.).

warning to flee "Babylonish" churches echoed into early nineteenth-century American Christianity as the concept of apostasy and hope for restoration drove a growing community of Christians to search for the authentic church. A new class of reformers called on Christians to reject false doctrine and corrupt practices to rediscover the true and pure form of primitive Christianity found in the NT.

Restorationists like Alexander Campbell believed that "all christian sects are more or less apostatized from the institutions of the Saviour," and like the Separatists, he denied a total apostasy of the faith.[5] The church, not the gospel, suffered corruption and disunity. Christianity was fractured but not false because its authority, the Bible, ruled over an invisible class of true saints. The church, however, remained divided because it relied on the philosophies and traditions of men, especially ecumenical creeds, which obstructed the view of scripture. What the church needed was not another reformation, argued Campbell, but a "*restoration* of the ancient order of things."[6]

Restorationists envisioned a restored faith purged of all doctrine, practices, and missions not explicitly outlined in the NT. They called on every Christian to overcome sectarian divisions and pursue unity under the banner of a purely apostolic gospel. They employed a hermeneutic of commonsense rationalism coupled with salvific, biblical minimalism, concluding that the Bible's highest usefulness was its doctrine of salvation. So restorationists jettisoned the ecumenical creeds to take up their Bibles and judge matters of salvation for themselves.

Mormonism and the Great Apostasy

In many ways, early Latter-day Saints agreed with the restorationists; the church was established in purity but had "become corrupted every whit."[7] Initially, their concern focused on the lapsed morality among Christians, "a Crooked & a perverse generation" who wandered into a spiritual wilderness led by corrupt clergy.[8] As their movement grew, so did their understanding of the Great Apostasy, as they would come to call it. The falling away was worse than the Reformers and restorationists imagined.

Mormonism envisions human history unfolding in a series of eras or dispensations, each headed by prophets who act as chief stewards of God's power and authority. Adam, the first prophet, was followed by Noah, Abraham, Moses, and ultimately Jesus Christ. But each dispensation ends in tragedy, a story that repeats over and over: People rebel against and reject the prophets,

---

5. Alexander Campbell, "The Points at Issue," *The Christian Baptist*, August 6, 1827.
6. Alexander Campbell, "A Restoration of the Ancient Order of Things, No. 1," *The Christian Baptist*, February 7, 1825 (emphasis added).
7. MRB, 59 [D&C 33:4].
8. MRB, 59 [D&C 33:2].

God reduces or removes his power and authority from the earth, and the world becomes lost in a dark postlude of apostasy. Christianity was not merely corrupt and wayward, as the restorationists contended; instead, it became wholly inauthentic and powerless. It suffered an incredible loss of doctrinal clarity, scriptural purity, and church unity, which blunted the gospel's saving power.

After the apostolic era, humans blended the gospel with pagan philosophies to produce foreign doctrines, like original sin and Trinitarianism. They initiated unauthorized practices like asceticism, consubstantiation, and infant baptism. The church also forfeited genuine works of the Holy Spirit, like healing and speaking in tongues. This absence of charismatic signs was a strong indicator to Joseph Smith of "the apostacy there has been from the Apostolic platform."[9] Without unifying authorities and powers, the church was shattered, hopelessly "lost in a strife of words and a contest about opinions,"[10] said Smith, just as the Book of Mormon predicted: "They shall contend one with another; and their priests shall contend one with another" (2 Nephi 28:4). An early LDS apostle wrote that Christianity was doomed to disunity, becoming "disorganized and lost from among men."[11] All churches "deny the power of God" (2 Nephi 28:5). "When inspiration ceased," explained another apostle, "eve[r]y one went his own way & sung his own song" (cf. Judg 21:25).[12]

Unlike the restorationists, though, Latter-day Saints rejected the hope of retrieving truth by going back to the Bible. The problem, they claimed, was that the Bible itself was insufficient. Generations of transmission compromised the biblical manuscripts through the hands of careless and corrupt scribes who, according to the Book of Mormon, "transfigured the holy word of God" (Mormon 8:33). The negligence was so bad that LDS apostle Orson Pratt questioned whether "even one verse of the whole Bible has escaped pollution, so as to convey the same sense now that it did in the original?"[13] Consequently, "many parts which are plain and most precious" to the gospel and vital "covenants of the Lord" were "taken away" (1 Nephi 13:26). Universal apostasy followed, and with it the general downfall of humanity, citizens of an "unrighteous dominion" who oppress and are oppressed by wickedness, pride, and violence.[14]

But the most detrimental loss of all was the disappearance of divine power and authority on earth, or what Latter-day Saints call the priesthood (see question 18). One early LDS leader explained that, without the

9. JS to Noah Saxton, January 4, 1833, D2:352.
10. JS, H1:208 [Joseph Smith–History 6].
11. Parley P. Pratt, *A Voice of Warning to All People . . . Latter-day Saints*, 8th ed. (Liverpool: F. D. Richards, 1854), 20.
12. Orson Hyde, in JSJ, January 1, 1843, J2:208.
13. Orson Pratt, "Divine Authenticity of the Book of Mormon," in *A Series of Pamphlets by Orson Pratt . . . in the Year 1843* (Liverpool: R. James, 1851), 47.
14. Joseph Smith, History, 1838–1856, vol. C-1, *JSP*, 908 [D&C 121:39].

priesthood, Christians habitually rejected "immediate revelation from God to themselves."[15] So early Latter-day Saints looked for the return of the priesthood through supernatural means. Among these signs were the translation of the Book of Mormon, modern revelation from a living prophet, angelic appearances to ordain Joseph Smith and others, and the reinstitution of apostolic offices and ancient practices. Latter-day Saints hoped for the ancient church, in all its fullness and purity, to be miraculously resurrected in the latter days.

For the church to be restored, it needed the radical return of divine activity, a brilliant reopening of the heavens "to break forth through the dark atmosphere of sectarian wickedness," said Smith.[16] He added that the consequences of rejecting the restoration were severe. To deny latter-day "revelation and the oracles of God" was to choose apostasy over obedience and hell over heaven. "I tell you, in the name of Jesus Christ," Smith warned, "they will be damned."[17]

Contemporary Perspectives on the Great Apostasy

Contemporary Latter-day Saints generally hold more nuanced views of the Great Apostasy, absent the kind of polemics that often accompanied earlier LDS rhetoric. Of course, they still maintain that apostasy occurred; there would be no need for restoration without it. But they appreciate that ancient church history cannot be explained in the binary categories of either a state of depravity or one of total purity.[18] The Great Apostasy is less the sudden disappearance of all things good than it is the gradual loss of power due to a spiritual law of entropy.

Scholars recognize how early Latter-day Saints formulated their conception of the Great Apostasy during intense theological controversies and heightened millenarian expectations, convinced that Christ would return at any moment—all while enduring opposition and persecution. Undoubtedly, this context and the experiences of the early Church of Jesus Christ of Latter-day Saints affected how it viewed church history and its present state. Latter-day Saints would eventually frame their story within the popular myth of Western history as divided into three periods after the fall of the Roman Empire: the

---

15. Benjamin Winchester, *A History of the Priesthood . . . Now Extant* (Philadelphia: Brown, Bicking & Guilbert, 1843), 90.
16. JS to Noah Saxton, January 4, 1833, D2:352.
17. Joseph Smith, History, 1838–1856, vol. D-1, *JSP*, 5. Smith likewise warned that those who "reject the most glorious principle of the gospel of Jesus Christ"—i.e., "Prophets Apostles Angels Revelations Prophesyings, & visions &c."—"they will be damned" (JS, discourse, May 14, 1843, D12:305).
18. See Jason R. Combs et al., eds., *Ancient Christians: An Introduction for Latter-day Saints* (Provo, UT: Maxwell Institute, BYU, 2022).

so-called Dark Ages, Renaissance, and Enlightenment. This version of history harmonized nicely with the Mormon apostasy-restoration thesis.

But today many Latter-day Saints see genuine Christlikeness in the lives of Christians during and after the early church, despite it taking on forms they find objectionable.[19] And the Middle Ages were not a dark, backward era completely suppressed by apostasy. To adopt this view is to ignore the breathtaking beauty of the art, scholarship, and chivalry produced during the Middle Ages. Doing so concedes to the self-serving myth by Enlightenment elites that Western civilization was hopelessly lost in ignorance until their brilliance saved the day.

Latter-day Saints now also tend to place more emphasis on the restoration than apostasy, reorienting themselves toward a "future responsibility and potential rather than past loss," writes one LDS scholar.[20] Still, Mormonism maintains that after the apostolic era Christianity became incomplete in form, insufficient in power, and inauthentic in being. And while the apostasy was not terminal, it was pervasive enough to warrant the restoration (see question 6). Thus, the Great Apostasy is a "linchpin" doctrine of Mormonism, as one LDS historian argues.[21]

Traditional Christians are right to ask, did the Great Apostasy occur? While we can agree that apostasy occurs, it does not—and cannot—rise to a level at which the gospel, with its full power and authority to save, was or ever will be muted. Indeed, the wonder isn't how apostasy overwhelmed the church but how the church has overcome apostasy from its infancy to the present. This is not a victory of the church but of Christ, who has "overcome the world" (John 16:33). When he assured his disciples to "be of good cheer" (John 16:33) he did so because he would abide with them always (see Matt 28:20), this promise was not conditioned on the disciples' ability to remain faithful to Christ but on Christ's ability to remain faithful to his disciples, to "all that the Father giveth me" (John 6:37).

Christ's announcement that the "gates of hell" would not prevail against the church is prefaced by his prophetic promise that "I will build my church" (Matt 16:18). The life of the church throughout the ages is not the result of Christ's disciples but of Christ himself—"*I* will build *my* church" (emphasis added), not the disciples. The Great Apostasy suggests a great failure not of Christians but of their Christ. It assumes Christ failed to build his church like

19. See, for example, Gregor McHardy, *8 Myths of the Great Apostasy* (Salt Lake City: Signature Books, 2022).
20. Miranda Wilcox, "Narrating Apostasy and the LDS Quest for Identity," in *Standing Apart: Mormon Historical Consciousness and the Concept of Apostasy*, ed. Miranda Wilcox and John D. Young (New York: Oxford University Press, 2014), 118.
21. Eric R. Dursteler, "Historical Periodization in the LDS Great Apostasy Narrative," in Wilcox and Young, *Standing Apart*, 23.

he promised, which is a prospect no one—neither traditional Christian nor Latter-day Saints—should entertain.

Summary

The Bible warns that the church faces the threat of apostasy, a turning away from God. Protestant Reformers sensed apostasy in the Roman Catholic Church and advocated for returning to the Bible as a means to purify the church by the gospel. But the restoration movement of the nineteenth century contended that the Reformation had fallen short because Protestantism had adopted creeds and continued practices from Rome that were not explicitly found in the NT. As a result, restorationists called on Christians to transcend denominational division by uniting around the clear and common doctrines and practices of the NT. Latter-day Saints believed such a restoration was impossible because the Bible had become corrupted and was incomplete. What's more, they taught that the church, having lost its power and authority from God, had become so wayward that only the reopening of the heavens through a prophet could restore it. However, this Great Apostasy narrative calls into question the reliability of Christ's promise that he would build his church (see Matt 16:18).

REFLECTION QUESTIONS

1. Is Christian denominationalism a sign that a Great Apostasy has occurred? Why or why not?

2. How was Mormonism similar to Protestant restoration movements of Joseph Smith's day? How was it different?

3. Early Latter-day Saints believed that an *ad fontes* approach to reformation and restoration was insufficient because the Bible itself was corrupted. How might you respond to this claim?

4. Do you agree or disagree that the Great Apostasy is the linchpin doctrine of Mormonism? Why or why not?

5. Do you believe that a Great Apostasy of the church is incompatible with Christ's promise to build it (see Matt 16:18)? Why or why not?

QUESTION 7

What Is the First Vision?

"I had seen a vision; I knew it, and I knew that God knew it, and I could not deny it, neither dare I do it."[1]
~ Joseph Smith

Life in rural New York during the early nineteenth century was spiritually exhausting. Pulpit calls for repentance and Restorationist warnings to escape sectarian division were often tangled with intense apocalyptic anticipation, which created a pressing demand to recover Christ's primitive gospel before his imminent return. Revivals sprang up constantly, and no place was warmed more intensely by spiritual fire than the Burned-Over District of western New York.[2] People experienced conversion differently in this social milieu. Sometimes it was dynamic, with revival preaching and ecstatic worship spurring deep conviction as penitent sinners rushed to conversion.[3] At other times, personal transformation came through subtle contemplation and quiet prayer.[4] Practically all conversion was guided by meditation on the Bible, but some people's spiritual anxiety was so pronounced they had dreams and visions of hell, angels, and even of the Lord Jesus himself.[5] These experiences

1. JS, "History of Joseph Smith," *T&S*, April 1, 1842, 3:749.
2. Whitney R. Cross, *The Burned-Over District: The Social and Intellectual History of Enthusiastic Religion in Western New York, 1800–1850* (Utica, NY: Cornell University Press, 1950).
3. Michael Barkun, *Crucible of the Millennium: The Burned-Over District of New York in the 1840s* (Syracuse, NY: Syracuse University Press, 1986).
4. Richard E. Bennett, "Quiet Revivalism: New Light on the Burned-Over District," in *Joseph Smith and His First Vision: Context, Place, and Meaning*, ed. Alexander L. Baugh, Steven C. Harper, Brent M. Rogers, and Benjamin Pykles (Provo, UT: Brigham Young University, 2021), 89–108.
5. Ann Taves, *Fits, Trances, & Visions: Experiencing Religion and Explaining Experience from Wesley to James* (Princeton, NJ: Princeton University Press, 1999).

were especially common among those who found no solace in enthusiastic revivals or somber pews. Unsure where to turn for comfort and guidance, they appealed directly to heaven.

In this context, Joseph Smith claimed to have a vision of God, the moment Latter-day Saints would come to identify as among the most significant of his life.

Joseph Smith's First Vision

In the early 1820s, Smith retreated to a private grove near his home to pray.[6] "Information was what I most desired at this time," he said, but he also yearned deeply for grace.[7] "I became convicted of my sins," he confessed, worried no one could help him because in the marketplace of competing churches, it was difficult to know who held proper spiritual authority.[8] With so many conflicting voices, Smith did not know "who was right or who was wrong," especially pertaining matters of "eternal consequences."[9] After making an "intimate acquaintance" with various denominations and a thorough "searching [of] the scriptures," he concluded with the Restorationists "that mankind did not come unto the Lord but that they had apostatised from the true and liveing faith and there was no society or denomination that built upon the gospel of Jesus Christ as recorded in the new testament."[10]

If Smith were to receive wisdom and forgiveness, it must come by an authoritative and immediate experience rather than mediation from a wayward church. After heeding the advice of James 1:5, Smith went to God directly. He entered the privacy of a forest and quietly offered a prayer to cleanse his guilty conscience since "there was none else to whom I could go," he said.[11] Aside from finding divine mercy, Smith also hoped to learn "which of all the sects was right," if there was truth to be found in them at all.[12] This was the information he sought.

What followed would alter the trajectory of Smith's life. As he prayed for forgiveness and guidance, a "thick darkness" enveloped him.[13] Then, an unseen force muted his tongue and pressed him to feel "doomed to sudden destruction."[14] Suddenly, from high above, he witnessed "a pillar of light ex-

6. What follows is a matter of historical debate. To prevent telling this story in a cumbersome manner, I will avoid adding excessive caveats to the narration (e.g., "Smith *supposedly* saw" or "God *purportedly* said").
7. JSJ, November 9–11, 1835, J1:87–88.
8. JS, ca. 1832 history, H1:11 (emend.).
9. JSJ, November 9–11, 1835, J1:87.
10. JS, ca. 1832 history, H1:11–12.
11. JS, ca. 1832 history, H1:12.
12. JS, H1:214 [Joseph Smith–History 18].
13. JS, H1:212 [Joseph Smith–History 15].
14. JS, H1:212 [Joseph Smith–History 15].

actly over my head above the brightness of the sun," gradually descending toward him and freeing him from the dark oppression.[15] "I saw the Lord,"[16] he said, later clarifying the Lord appeared as "two personages,"[17] God the Father and Jesus Christ. In a moment reminiscent of the Mount of Transfiguration, the first personage pointed to the second and said to Smith, "This is my beloved Son, Hear him" (see Matt 17:5; Mark 9:7; Luke 9:35).[18] Smith listened as the second personage "spake unto me saying Joseph my son thy sins are forgiven thee."[19] Finally, Smith found absolution directly from salvation's pinnacle source.

With his soul forgiven, he then asked which church to join. The answer was startling: "join none of them" because "all their Creeds were an abomination in his sight."[20] A Great Apostasy ravaged the church; "the Everlasting covena[n]t was broken" as authority and authenticity were stripped from the faith (see question 6).[21] Smith, however, was promised "the fulness of the gospel should at some future time be made known unto" him.[22] That fullness would come through the Book of Mormon and other latter-day revelations. When the vision ended, Smith found himself lying on his back gazing into the sky.

The First Versions

Smith's vision comes to us mainly through a handful of primary accounts written by him or with his approval: a journal entry from 1835,[23] an account copied into a history record in 1838,[24] and a letter published in a newspaper in 1842.[25] These three accounts generally agree, with only minor differences in details between them. But a fourth account, written in 1832 and publicized in the 1960s, stands apart from the others in its details and voice.[26]

---

15. JS, H1:214 [Joseph Smith–History 16].
16. JS, ca. 1832 history, H1:12–13.
17. JS, H1:214 [Joseph Smith–History 17].
18. JS, H1:214 [Joseph Smith–History 17].
19. JS, ca. 1832 history, H1:13; cf. JSJ, November 9–11, 1835, J1:88.
20. JS, H1:214 [Joseph Smith–History 19].
21. JS, discourse, June 11, 1834, D12:389.
22. JS, "Church History," *T&S*, March 1, 1842, in H1:494.
23. JSJ, November 9–11, 1835, J1:87–88. For an introduction to the 1835 account, see Steven C. Harper, *First Vision: Memory and Mormon Origins* (New York: Oxford University Press, 2019), 31–34.
24. JS, H1:212–14 [Joseph Smith–History 13–20]. For an introduction to the 1838 account, see Harper, *First Vision*, 13–19.
25. JS, "Church History," *T&S*, March 1, 1842, in H1:492–94. For an introduction to the 1842 account, see Harper, *First Vision*, 37–43.
26. JS, ca. 1832 history, H1:10–13. For an introduction to the 1832 account, see Harper, *First Vision*, 23–27.

This earliest account is reminiscent of conversion testimonies in the early nineteenth century and is composed nearly entirely of biblical quotes, allusions, and language. Many biblical genres make an appearance, which demonstrates not only Smith's impressive familiarity with the Bible but also the Bible's impression on his early life.

He recalled how "a pillar of light above the brightness of the sun at noon day" (cf. Acts 22:6; 26:13) rested on him. Smith "saw the Lord" (cf. Isa 6:1; Ezek 1:1), who told him, "my son, thy sins are forgiven thee" (cf. Matt 9:2; Mark 2:5), and permitted him to "go thy way" (cf. Luke 17:19). But before he could leave, the vision continued. Smith was told how the "Lord of glory . . . was crucifyed for the world" (cf. 1 Cor 2:8; Jas 2:1; 1 John 2:2) so "that all those who believe on my name may have Eternal life" (cf. 1 John 5:13). The vision then confirmed what Smith already knew to be true: the church had fallen into apostasy. "None doeth good no not one" (cf. Rom 3:12), Smith was told, for they had rejected the gospel. "They draw near to me with their lips while their hearts are far from me" (cf. Matt 15:8), the vision continued, and God's anger would soon manifest against sin. Lo, "I come quickly" (cf. Rev 22:12), Smith was warned, and with that, the vision ended.

Smith founded the Church of Jesus Christ of Latter-day Saints some years later. He initially hesitated to share his vision, preferring to highlight his discovery and translation of the Book of Mormon as his primary credential.[27] But as his community grew, so did his desire for an origin story that paralleled Latter-day Saint ideas about the nature of their church and its God. So when Smith occasionally retold the First Vision, he sharpened its theological precision and widened the horizon of its meaning.

But some of the variations seem at odds with his earliest account. Was he fourteen or sixteen when the vision occurred? Were angels present or not? Did Smith determine Christianity had apostatized before or after the vision? Perhaps the most prominent question raised by the changes orbits the nature of God. In the earliest account, Smith recalled seeing only the "Lord," i.e., Jesus Christ, but in the subsequent accounts he described God the Father and Jesus Christ as two separate, embodied beings in sharp contrast to God's Trinitarian nature.

Critics of the LDS Church frequently question Smith's reliability due to these apparent contradictions. In response, Latter-day Saint apologists and scholars have offered explanations to synthesize and harmonize his memories. This conversation is important, but by focusing on the minutiae, we risk

27. Historian Steven Harper notes how "Smith appears not to have shared the vision until the 1830s" but that his "reluctance to tell of his first vision apparently ended in the early to mid-1830s" (*First Vision*, 51, 53). And historian Ronald O. Barney argued the "First Vision was generally unknown and irrelevant to church members until the early 1840s" (*Joseph Smith: History, Methods and Memory* [Salt Lake City: University of Utah, 2020], 145).

missing a significant development in Smith's self-identity during the earliest years of Mormonism.

The First Vision as Joseph Smith's Commissioning Authority

It is unlikely Smith intentionally revised his First Vision primarily to match his new ideas about God or to secure power, as some critics have suggested. The church's explanation is more convincing, which suggests differences between the accounts could be "read as evidence of [Smith's] increasing insight, accumulating over time, based on experience."[28] The explanation does not identify what, exactly, the insight and experience were, but they were obviously collected over the years Smith led the church. If this observation is true, then presumably the church means to say he received revelatory insight in the years following 1832 that prompted him to modify his earliest account. In other words, as Smith grew in his role as the church's prophet, his memory of the First Vision did, too.

But the modifications can also communicate something different: a fundamental change in Smith's posture toward the Bible when describing the First Vision after years of acting as a prophet. When the 1832 and later accounts are read side by side, there is an obvious difference: every account after 1832 used far less biblical content. Consider the abundance of biblical language Smith used to craft his 1832 account. He deferred to the Bible's language and symbols at nearly every turn. It's his vision, but he didn't describe it; the Bible did. Much of the 1832 account is a mosaic of direct citations from the Bible or allusions to and echoes of it.[29] He also implied it was an exhaustive study of the Bible that led him to discover for himself that no true church existed, so a biblical survey led him to the grove in the first place.

By 1838, however, a change occurred. The Bible's voice is replaced nearly entirely by Smith's voice. And his study of the Bible is no longer exhaustive. Instead, it terminates on a single verse, James 1:5, redirecting his quest for wisdom from the word to the woods. In this version, the Bible is less a primary source for revelation than a signpost to it. This change is itself a sign of Smith's advancing self-conception as a prophet. The more he saw himself as a prophet, the less he viewed the Bible as the primary conduit of revelation. The Bible complemented, rather than conducted, his prophetic mission.

Moreover, the later accounts evoke biblical events to explain Smith's commission as a prophet-apostle who was called to restore Christianity. In these accounts, Smith hints he would ascend to the status of Moses and Paul. For

---

28. "First Vision Accounts," 2013, accessed February 10, 2022, https://www.churchofjesus christ.org/study/ manual/gospel-topics-essays/first-vision-accounts?lang=eng.
29. Kyle Beshears, "'That Sacred Depository': Biblical Content in Joseph Smith's 1832 First Vision Account" in *Joseph Smith as a Visionary: Heavenly Manifestations in the Latter Days*, ed. Alonzo L. Gaskill, Stephan D. Taeger, Derek R. Sainsbury, and Roger G. Christensen (Provo, UT: Brigham Young University, 2025), 69–86.

example, according to Exodus, Moses was alone in the wilderness when he encountered a bush on fire, yet, mysteriously, "the bush was not consumed" (Exod 3:2). God spoke to Moses from the flames, commissioning him to "bring forth my people" (Exod 3:10) from their enslaved state in Egypt. Similarly, Smith reported being alone in the woods when he saw a personage "in the midst, of [a] pillar of flame which was spread all around, and yet nothing consumed."[30] God spoke from the flames, promising Smith the "fulness of the gospel"[31] would be made known to him, the message of restoration for a latter-day exodus of the church "called forth out of the Wilderness."[32]

And in the book of Acts, Paul was struck by "a light from heaven, above the brightness of the sun" (Acts 26:13) before hearing from Christ and being commissioned to the Gentiles. Smith sees his experience in similar terms. He recorded seeing a "pillar of light . . . above the brightness of the sun" before conversing with Christ, who later commissioned Smith to his service through the angel Moroni.[33] When the vision ends, Smith is "looking up into Heaven," the same posture as the disciples after Christ's ascension into heaven immediately prior to their apostolic careers (see Acts 1:11).[34]

These new details result, in part, from the changing relationship between Smith and the Bible. As a modern oracle of God, his revelations could match or even eclipse scripture. Consequently, his perception of the First Vision changed. It's no longer a story of personal conversion but divine commission, the beginning of a revelatory mission that would advance beyond what the Bible could offer the world.

Thus, the First Vision is the continental divide separating Mormonism from traditional Christianity, but not for intuitive reasons. That Joseph Smith claimed to have had a visionary experience is not incompatible with Christianity, nor can it be. We shouldn't restrict divine activity to meet our expectations. And the content of his vision per se is not what ultimately divides Salt Lake from Nicaea, although the LDS Godhead is fundamentally at odds with Trinitarianism (see question 24). The ultimate division between Mormonism and traditional Christianity in the context of the First Vision is Smith's declaration of authority: Who is God, and who gets to say so? Smith taught the Father and the Son were independent, embodied beings because he saw them with his own eyes.

30. JSJ, November 9–11, 1835, J1:88.
31. JS, "Church History," *T&S*, March 1, 1842, in H1:494.
32. MRB, 59 [D&C 33:5].
33. JS, H1:214 [Joseph Smith–History 16].
34. JS, H1:214 [Joseph Smith–History 16].

Summary

The First Vision is foundational to the LDS movement. The very origin of Mormonism has been traced to Smith's testimony of encountering God the Father and God the Son, whose message set Smith on a path toward establishing the Church of Jesus Christ of Latter-day Saints. While skeptics of the First Vision interpret its different versions as evidence of fraud, the versions chronicle a growing distance between Smith and the Bible over time as he grew more comfortable in his prophetic role. In the end, the most significant factor of the First Vision is not its doctrinal deviations from Christianity but the religious authority it provided Smith.

REFLECTION QUESTIONS

1. How significant is the First Vision to Mormonism? How does your understanding of the First Vision inform your view of the religion?

2. What do you make of Joseph Smith's visionary experience? How does this inform your view of Mormonism?

3. Do you believe visionary experiences like Joseph Smith described are possible today? Why or why not?

4. What do the various versions of Smith's First Vision suggest about his relationship to the Bible and spiritual authority, and why does this matter?

5. Do you agree that the continental divide between Mormonism and traditional Christianity is the First Vision? Why or why not?

QUESTION 8

How Did So Many Latter-day Saints End Up in Utah? (Part 1)

"From Zion's favoured dwelling The Gospel issues forth,
The covenant revealing To gather all the earth."[1]
~ William G. Mills, Latter-day Saint Hymnist

Most people think of Utah when they hear the word "Mormon," and vice versa. While Utah is known for its stunning national parks and superb skiing, it is more commonly associated with Mormonism. After all, Utah is the headquarters of the Church of Jesus Christ of Latter-day Saints and home to its most iconic temple. Brigham Young University, a well-known Mormon institution, is in Provo, which makes sense in a county where most of the residents identify as Latter-day Saints. Of course, not all Utahans are Latter-day Saints, and the percentage of LDS residents has declined over time. And Utah hasn't always been so Mormon. Native tribes, including the Utes, Shoshones, and Paiutes, first settled the deserts, plateaus, and mountains known as Utah today long before contact with European explorers in the late eighteenth century. But it wasn't until the mid-nineteenth century that Mormon pioneers began permanent settlement, forever changing Utah's history and culture.

Yet, as Mormon as Utah seems, those who are unfamiliar with the LDS story might be surprised to learn Joseph Smith, the founder of Mormonism, didn't necessarily envision his movement settling there. Smith never set foot in Utah. In fact, he never traveled farther west than Missouri. So how did so many Latter-day Saints end up in Utah? The next two questions are devoted to discovering the answer, and the story begins at a very unexpected place—theological speculation about the end times.

1. William G. Mills, "The City of Zion," *MS*, December 1, 1849, 11:368.

Zion and the New Millennium

The book of Revelation promises Christ's disciples' participation in a thousand-year reign of Jesus Christ on earth (see Rev 20:1–6), but the brevity and ambiguity of the text have led commentators throughout the centuries to speculate on its exact meaning. In the early nineteenth century, many Americans were captivated by premillennialism, the belief that the second coming of Christ, preceding the kingdom of God, could happen at any moment. This constant anticipation of the millennium led historian Nathan Hatch to wonder whether "the first generation of United States citizens may have lived in the shadow of Christ's second coming more intensely than any generation since."[2] Millenarians believed various signs would immediately herald Christ's return. They looked for the physical regathering of Israel in Jerusalem and terrible calamities everywhere else, such as war, famine, disease, natural catastrophes, and universal apostasy, cruelty, and persecution. At that dark hour, they hoped Christ would descend from the clouds to rescue his people and rule over the earth in its final dispensation.

Joseph Smith founded the LDS Church amid this apocalyptic excitement. Indeed, his followers viewed themselves mainly in terms of *when* they were in the grand scheme of history (i.e., the Church of Jesus Christ of *Latter-day* Saints). Smith's vision extended beyond a mere collection of congregants. He sought to build a society of communities and cities that could weather apocalyptic trials and purify his people prior to the second coming.

Smith believed God called him to build up a new Zion, a society of holy harmony (see D&C 6:6; 11:6; 12:6; 14:6). The Bible describes Jerusalem as *tsiyon*, the city of God (see Pss. 87:3; 132:13) where he desired to be, so he might care for the oppressed (see Isa 14:32) and defend and purify his people, the children of Zion (see Lam 4:2; Isa 4:4). Ancient Jerusalem struggled to be that city, and after seeing it conquered, OT prophets longed for its restoration (see Isa 51:1–6) while recognizing that the true Zion is God's people (see Isa 51:16). The NT describes Zion in terms of a partially realized kingdom of God on earth, which has been inaugurated by the work of Christ (see Heb 12:22) and will culminate in his second coming (see Rev 21:1–4). Believers look forward to the consummation of the "fulness of times" when God collects "in one all things in Christ, both which are in heaven, and which are on earth" (Eph 1:10).

Smith drew on biblical conceptions of Zion as a true community of people who "were of one heart and one mind, and dwelt in righteousness; and there was no poor among them" (Moses 7:18). It was both a people and a place, for "the Lord called his people ZION" (Moses 7:18) who dwelled in a righteous "City of Holiness, even ZION" (Moses 7:19). Smith began teaching

2. Nathan O. Hatch, *The Democratization of American Christianity* (New Haven, CT: Yale University Press, 1989), 184.

the need to build Zion just months after founding the LDS Church. Book of Mormon prophecy states the "New Jerusalem" (3 Nephi 21:23–24) would be built in the Americas as a gathering place for believing "Gentiles" (or non-Native Amerian Mormons) to live with displaced descendants of the ancient Hebrews, whom the Mormons believed were Native Americans. Zion would ultimately serve as a place of refuge, "built upon the American continent," to protect from the impending apocalypse and to prepare the worthy saints to receive Christ as their millennial king.[3] So for Latter-day Saints, the question wasn't *if* God would build Zion in America but when and where.

In the fall of 1830, Smith began to stress the importance of gathering God's elect "to prepare their Hearts & be prepared in all things against the day of tribulation & desolation," which was "soon at hand."[4] Over the years, building the utopia of new Jerusalem became one of his top priorities. Smith's followers were instructed to divert resources to support the poor and to purchase land for the "public benefit of the church."[5] Smith also prioritized proselytism early on, especially among indigenous people, whom early Latter-day Saints called "Lamanites" and identified as descendants of the Hebrews, according to the Book of Mormon. The missionary call came by a revelatory command to preach near the "borders by the Lamanites," just as the Indian Removal Act was prompting the US government to displace Native tribes west of the Mississippi River.[6] The Latter-day Saints found this timing opportune. All Native Americans who heard and accepted the Mormon gospel would be welcomed into the new Zion, an eschatological community of both "Jew" and "Gentile." And while no one knew where exactly new Jerusalem would be, one revelation offered a small clue, the same place where the earliest missionaries were called to preach: Zion "shall be on the borders by the Lamanites."[7]

Zion in Ohio

Although the LDS Church was founded in New York, the Mormons didn't remain there very long. Early missionary efforts in Ohio converted an entire congregation led by Sidney Rigdon, which prompted the church to relocate to Kirtland in the fall of 1830. There, Mormons began constructing their first temple, but not before receiving direction to settle Jackson County, Missouri, a divinely designated "place for the City of Zion."[8] The location seemed perfect: it had convenient access to the Missouri River and proximity to the Lamanite frontier, and it served as an economic hub at the eastern terminus

3. Articles of Faith 1:10.
4. JS, revelation, September 1830, D1:179 [D&C 29:8–9].
5. Minutes, November 10, 1837, D5:475 [D&C 42:35].
6. MRB, 601.
7. JS, H1:440 [D&C 28:9].
8. JS, revelation, July 20, 1831, D2:8 [D&C 57:2].

of the Oregon Trail. Little by little, Mormons began to arrive at the fledgling settlement.

Back in Ohio, new converts seemed to arrive daily. Missionary calls for gathering drew new converts like Brigham Young, who used his skills to help the growing community. A carpenter by trade, Young lent his hand to construct the first Mormon temple, which was dedicated in 1836. At the dedication, Latter-day Saints reported charismatic experiences and heavenly visitors. This high point would not last long, though, as external opposition and internal dissension dissolved the church's stability. Anti-Mormon neighbors were joined by disillusioned Saints who left the church and became sharp critics of Smith, accusing him of autocratic leadership, spiritual abuse, and immorality.

Tensions reached boiling point in the fall of 1837 after the failure of the Kirtland Safety Society, a frontier bank the Mormons established to raise capital in a vain attempt to prevent the economic collapse of their community. Mormons and non-Mormons alike lost investments as hundreds left the church. Kirtland was in an apostasy crisis, with three witnesses to the Book of Mormon plates, one of Smith's top leaders, and four LDS apostles numbered among the dissenters. In January 1838, Smith received a timely revelation to join the Mormons in Missouri as fast as possible.

Zion in Missouri

Smith saw firsthand how difficult the situation had become for Latter-day Saints in Missouri when he arrived in March 1838. By then, the church had weathered years of violent opposition from non-Mormons who would not tolerate their neighbors' religious, cultural, and political differences. Mormons stoked the embers by settling areas previously designated for non-Mormon use when Rigdon delivered a fiery speech on that fourth of July, which threatened retaliatory violence should the Gentiles attack. "It should be a war of extermination," he threatened.[9] Later that autumn, anger erupted into war. The governor issued an executive order to treat Mormons as enemies to be "exterminated"; in other words, to be "driven from the State."[10] The infamous command—described by Smith's wife, Emma, as the "ever to be remembered Governor's notable order"[11]—resulted in the violent expulsion by anti-Mormons of hundreds of Latter-day Saints from their settlements.

Smith wanted to build up Zion in Missouri despite the mounting hostility. Earlier, in 1831, Latter-day Saints had been promised by God that "the land

9. John Corrill, *A Brief History of the Church of Christ of Latter Day Saints*, 1839, in H2:169 (emend.).
10. Lilburn W. Boggs, letter to John B. Clark, October 27, 1838, The Missouri Mormon War Collection, Missouri State Archives, Jefferson City, Missouri.
11. Emma Smith to JS, March 7, 1839, D6:339.

of Missorie" was "appointed & consecrated for the gethering of the Saints."[12] The frontier town of Independence was chosen. Mormons were encouraged to acquire land at the very edge of Anglo-American civilization to build up the New Jerusalem, where the Latter-day Saints were also instructed to build a temple (see D&C 57:3).

The area held religious significance, too. Smith received a revelation naming Adam-ondi-Ahman (Daviess County)—"or the place where Adam dwelt"[13]—as the sacred location where Adam blessed his descendants before his death (see D&C 107:53–54). It was also to play a key role in the end of days as the site where the last Adam, Jesus Christ, would meet with the first Adam in the end times (see D&C 116). Missouri, then, was to be an important seat of millennial activity, which made leaving an extremely bitter experience for the Latter-day Saints. Authorities arrested Smith in December 1838, and in his absence, Brigham Young facilitated the Mormon exodus from Missouri to Illinois.

The city of Zion in Missouri was not meant to be, and the Latter-day Saints were learning that perhaps Zion was less about a place than it was about a people. Still, unlike Ohio, Missouri had been named explicitly in revelation through Smith as a place of sacred inheritance in anticipation of the millennium. Why, then, would God tolerate the Latter-day Saints being driven away? A later revelation explained how their work in Missouri was not in vain. The Latter-day Saints had diligently tried to obey the divine command "to build up a city, and an house unto my [God's] name" in Jackson County.[14] But after severe opposition, God no longer required the work and accepted anything completed to that point as an offering (see D&C 124:49, 51).

Their experience in Missouri broadened the Latter-day Saints' definition of Zion. It could no longer be contained in a small plot of land. Instead, the "whole of North and South America is zion," said Smith, and a temple would one day act as an epicenter from which congregations, like the stakes of a tent, would broaden the canopy of shelter for all God's gathered elect.[15] Despite their failure to build a city in Missouri, Latter-day Saints retained a strong sense of gathering as a people to a place and anticipated "Zion [would] be built upon this continent."[16] This impulse eventually led them to Utah.

Summary

Early Latter-day Saints were driven by a millennial expectation of Christ's imminent return. Revelation from Joseph Smith called for the building up of Zion on the American continent, a community made up of indigenous

12. JS, revelation, July 20, 1831, D2:7 [D&C 57:1].
13. JS to Stephen Post, September 17, 1838, D6:242. Elsewhere, Smith also identified "the land where Adam dwelt" as "Olea Shinihah" (JSJ, January 17, 1842, J2:25; see also D&C 117:8).
14. JS, revelation, January 19, 1841, D7:519 [D&C 124:51].
15. JS, discourse, April 8, 1844, *JSP*.
16. JS, "Church History," *T&S*, March 1, 1842, in H1:500.

Hebrew descendants (or "Lamanites") and Mormons. Yet internal dissension and persistent persecution frustrated the Church of Jesus Christ of Latter-day Saints as it attempted to create a new Jerusalem fit enough to receive the Son of God. Still, the Latter-day Saints persevered after their expulsion from Missouri to try, once more, to establish God's kingdom in Illinois and eventually Utah, the story of which is told in the next question.

REFLECTION QUESTIONS

1. How did early LDS eschatology stimulate their work of gathering and building up their first communities?

2. What is the biblical concept of Zion, and how does it relate to early Mormonism?

3. What role does America play in early LDS eschatology? How is this similar or different from ideas of the end times in Christianity?

4. Mormons faced violent opposition throughout their history. How do you imagine this persecution has shaped the Latter-day Saint identity?

5. LDS revelation specifically named Missouri as a sacred space for gathering, but Smith was unable to establish a permanent settlement there. What are the implications of this?

QUESTION 9

How Did So Many Latter-day Saints End Up in Utah? (Part 2)

> *"On this important day [July 24, 1847] . . . we came in full view of the great valley or Bason [sic] [of] the Salt Lake and land of promise held in reserve by the hand of GOD for a resting place for the Saints."*[1]
> ~ Wilford Woodruff, President of the LDS Church, 1889–1898

As the previous question explained, Joseph Smith called the first Latter-day Saints to gather in a millennial Zion, but opposition forced them to abandon settlements in Ohio and Missouri. After being driven from Missouri in 1838, they trekked eastward across the Mississippi River and found respite in Illinois.

Zion in Illinois

In the summer of 1839, the Latter-day Saints secured land along the banks of the Mississippi River and began building a new city, Nauvoo, from *na'a* (Heb.), meaning "beautiful." They worked quickly to build their urban Zion once again. Smith remarked how the Saints enjoyed "the most favorable auspices" (or favorable protection) during this period, a time when the Mormons experienced prosperity and peace as their community grew economically and the Church of Jesus Christ of Latter-day Saints grew in number, organization, and revelation.[2]

From 1839 to 1844, nearly every religious and civic enterprise was overshadowed by Smith's extensive leadership. Smith headed almost every aspect of Nauvoo life, from church and government to media and the militia. He

1. *WWJ* 2:229.
2. JSJ, January 6, 1842, J2:25.

served as mayor and judge of Nauvoo and editor of the church's main newspaper, the *Times & Seasons*. As the church's prophet, he advanced its doctrine and extended its canon. Smith introduced ideas like eternal progression and acknowledged the plurality of gods while also expanding on the origins of priesthood with the translation of the book of Abraham. Some Mormons also began to practice polygamy during this period.[3] As a member of the city's Masonic lodge, Smith aimed to purify and incorporate its elements in Mormon temple ceremonies (see question 34). And as lieutenant general of the Nauvoo legion, he commanded one of the most powerful military forces in the United States.[4] In 1842, Nauvoo boasted a population of "14 or 15,000,"[5] an incredible statistic compared to the city's intrastate neighbor Chicago, which had a population of only 6,248 the same year.[6]

The Nauvoo period represented the peak of Smith's power, but the moment would not last long. Moral, legal, and political controversies dominated the last few years of his life. Due to their experiences in Missouri, the Mormons grew wary of the government's ability to protect them from anti-Mormon hostility. On the one hand, they admired the Constitution of the United States, for it "provides the things which we want," but, on the other hand, it "lacks the power to carry the laws into effect."[7] Although religious freedom and property rights were enshrined in the Constitution, neither was secured for Mormons in Missouri. So while "Smith and other Latter-day Saints revered the founding," observed one LDS historian, "American institutions were not necessarily worthy of veneration."[8] Instead, they preferred a new government that blended democracy with divine law. Just as Smith had preferred to restore Christianity rather than reform it, now he desired not to rehabilitate the government but to *revolutionize* it with a new constitution for the literal kingdom of God.

---

3. See George D. Smith, Nauvoo Polygamy: "... *But We Called It Celestial Marriage*" (Salt Lake City: Signature Books, 2011).
4. According to one estimation, the Nauvoo Legion swelled from six hundred men just two months after its formation in February 1841 to as many as fifteen hundred by the end of the year. Benjamin E. Park, *Kingdom of Nauvoo: The Rise and Fall of a Religious Empire on the American Frontier* (New York: Liveright Publishing, 2020), 48–49, 56. Another estimate claimed, "the Nauvoo Legion contained about 2,500 men while the United States Army had a strength of approximately 8,500 men in 1845." John Lee Allaman, "Uniforms and Equipment of the Black Hawk War and the Mormon War," *Western Illinois Regional Studies* 13, no. 1 (1990): 11.
5. "Nauvoo," *T&S*, October 1, 1842, 3:936.
6. According to census reports, Chicago's population in 1839 was about 4,200 and grew to 12,088 by 1844, which was the approximate timeframe when Mormons resided in Illinois. Bessie Louise Pierce, *The Beginning of a City: 1673–1848*, vol. 1 of *A History of Chicago* (Chicago: University of Chicago Press, 1975), 44.
7. C:129.
8. Spencer W. McBride, *Joseph Smith for President: The Prophet, the Assassins, and the Fight for American Religious Freedom* (New York: Oxford University Press, 2020), 107.

In the spring of 1844, Smith formed a secret council to fix what they saw as flaws in government. Meanwhile, he ramped up an unlikely bid for the US presidency, desiring to secure civil rights for religious minorities until Christ returned to rule the whole world. He and the council also looked beyond the American frontier, imagining an "independent government" outside the United States and emphasizing its royal character. This kingdom of God, governed by the council of "The Kingdom of God and his Laws," with Joseph Smith as its earthly head, would ultimately answer to God.[9] The voice of the people, too, would have a say. Smith envisioned his kingdom as a theodemocracy.

The council considered western frontier lands, like Texas and Alta (or upper) California, which were not then part of the United States. One new convert, James J. Strang, recommended Wisconsin Territory, an intriguing proposal given its proximity to Illinois. In the end, however, Smith aimed to establish a Mormon nation—what Latter-day Saints would later call the State of Deseret—to ensure their community remained free from US government interference. He'd finally realize his dream of Zion.

But as Smith's plans for the kingdom of God unfolded, many lost confidence in his leadership. A band of dissenters formed a breakaway church, believing Smith had become a fallen prophet. They aired their grievances in a newspaper called the *Nauvoo Expositor*. After Smith ordered the press destroyed, he was arrested along with his brother, Hyrum. On June 27, 1844, a mob stormed the jail where the Smith brothers and two other Mormon leaders awaited trial. The attackers succeeded in their effort to assassinate Joseph and Hyrum. For the first time, the church was without a prophet.

Zion in the American West

Joseph Smith's death shocked the Mormon community. One woman, Eunice Kinney, described the church being like "sheep without a shepherd not knowing what to do."[10] Not only had he been taken from them suddenly, but with no clear order of succession in place, the beleaguered community was leaderless and confused, especially as several candidates vied for Smith's vacant office (see question 10). Brigham Young, who was ordained to his office in 1835, stepped forward to take the reins of leadership. He brokered a truce with anti-Mormons long enough for the Latter-day Saints to finish their temple, perform endowment rituals, and begin an arduous and grueling trek west to the Great Basin. In February 1846, the first LDS companies of evacuees marched 1,300 miles across the unsettled continent—wind, rain, snow, disease, privation, and starvation battered them the whole way. The journey

9. C:48, 95–96.
10. Eunice Ross Kinney, letter to Wingfield Scott Watson, May 18, 1891, typescript, LDS Church (Strangite) Archive, Burlington, Wisconsin.

felt like a new exodus for the thousands who undertook it. Latter-day Saints envisioned themselves as a new camp of Israel following their new Moses, Brigham Young, toward a new promised land (see D&C 136:22). They clung to the promise: "Zion shall be redeemed in mine own due time" (D&C 136:18).

On July 24, 1847, Young and his camp arrived in the Salt Lake Valley, declaring it the place where Mormons could finally rest from their trials. They proposed to create the US State of Deseret, the borders of which stretched from the Pacific coast to the Rocky Mountains, but ultimately Congress rejected the proposal as too ambitious. Outsiders believed the prospects for long-term settlement along the Wasatch front to be unlikely. The Mormons chose to settle an area straddling forested mountains and arid desert, nothing like the temperate woodlands they came from. Yet, despite the hardship, Mormons were willing to innovate through challenges and endure hardship in exchange for a season of isolation. During the mid-nineteenth century they colonized vast regions of the American West, from Salt Lake City to San Bernardino, California; Pueblo, Colorado; and even into Canada and Mexico.

The Mormon experience from New York to Utah deeply formed their identity as a unique religious community willing to sacrifice and suffer repeatedly to preserve and honor their beliefs. While "Gentile" society saw them as peculiar, Latter-day Saints viewed themselves as pioneers, having spiritually and literally blazed a trail for seekers to gather to Zion. Unlike many traditional Christians, whose identity is typically unmoored from their ancestral story, Latter-day Saints today are often keenly aware of their families' heritage, especially those who trace their lineage back along the Mormon Trail. To approach a Latter-day Saint as a traditional Christian is often to encounter a story we know little about but that means a great deal to that neighbor. As it was argued before, to love one's neighbor well means to understand them well (see question 1). Knowing the Latter-day Saints' history is a way to begin knowing them.

Summary

Having been expelled from one settlement to the next, the Latter-day Saints enjoyed a brief season of prosperity in Nauvoo. But dissension within and opposition outside the community led to the murder of Joseph Smith. Brigham Young led many Mormons on a grueling trek to the Great Basin where they colonized much of the American West. This historical narrative of persecuted pioneering continues to reverberate in the Mormon identity to this day.

REFLECTION QUESTIONS

1. Joseph Smith amassed incredible power during the Nauvoo period without jettisoning his self-description as a prophet-apostle. How does his rise to power compare with biblical prophets and apostles?

2. After Smith's death, the Mormons refused to evacuate Nauvoo until after they finished the temple. What does this communicate about the importance of temple ritual, at least for early Latter-day Saints?

3. How do you suppose the history of Mormonism has shaped LDS identity today?

4. How is the history of your faith important to you? How might this affect the way you interact with a Latter-day Saint for whom their religious history is very important?

5. Why is it important as a Christian to know the story of Mormonism when getting to know Latter-day Saints?

QUESTION 10

Are There Other Traditions That Claim to Be Mormon?

"Let no man presume for a moment that his [Joseph Smith's] place will be filled by another; for, remember he stands in his own place, *and always will."*[1]
~ Brigham Young, President of the LDS Church, 1847–1877

Schism within the LDS tradition should ideally not occur. Joseph Smith founded his movement, in part, to heal disunity within Christianity. The Great Apostasy had created divisive conditions so powerful that ever since the NT era, "not one solitary sample of a better state, or more perfect unity, of the church can be found upon the pages of history" (see question 6).[2] If authority were restored in the latter days and manifested in a central prophetic figure, then presumably the Church of Jesus Christ of Latter-day Saints would be less susceptible to the discord that partitioned other churches. Smith's success could be measured partly by the unity of the Latter-day Saint community. He emphasized the unity of Mormonism, both in confession and community, as he looked forward with millenarian hope to "when the Saints of God will be gathered in one."[3]

For Smith, the latter days represented a season of renewal from Christian plurality to unity. He hoped the dross of denominationalism would float atop the glowing heat of the eschatological restoration, purifying the church invisible from the imperfections that caused division in the first place. The gathering of people from across denominations into a new institution governed

1. BY, "An Epistle of the Twelve," *T&S*, August 15, 1844, 5:618 (emphasis original).
2. JS, ed., "Fallen Away," *T&S*, October 15, 1842, 3:955.
3. JS, "The Temple," *T&S*, May 2, 1842, 3:776 (cf. Eph 1:10).

by ancient powers renewed was a sign of Christ's return. Part of Mormonism's allure was its hope to unify Christian divisions because it was believed to hold the proper principles and authorities. So the succession crisis following Smith's death was more consequential than merely the question of ecclesiastical leadership. Schism within the religion undermines its mission, even its reason to exist.

When Smith died, Latter-day Saints strongly anticipated continuity of authority to preserve unity in the church and, consequently, the LDS restoration itself. But how would this continuity take place? Smith did not provide a clear succession plan, leaving a few possible scenarios that led to multiple factions.[4] Throughout the decades and up to the present day, dissenters have accused LDS leadership of apostasy and broken away to retrieve a "true" form of Mormonism. Since Smith's death, his tradition has splintered into hundreds of independent and networked congregations, becoming a refracted image of the denominationalism it aimed to repair.[5]

While all members of the Church of Jesus Christ of Latter-day Saints are "Mormon," not all Mormons are members of the Church of Jesus Christ of Latter-day Saints. This question will briefly explore five active Mormon traditions outside the Salt Lake City-headquartered church: Church of Jesus Christ (Monongahela, Pennsylvania), Church of Jesus Christ of Latter Day Saints (Strangite), Community of Christ, LDS fundamentalism, and a new movement led by Denver Snuffer.

The Church of Jesus Christ (Monongahela, Pennsylvania)

When Joseph Smith was murdered in the summer of 1844, Sidney Rigdon was the first contender for the prophet's office. He was the lone survivor of the First Presidency, the church's highest governing body, and had been in the religion's inner circle since nearly the beginning. On August 8, Rigdon publicly argued his case, claiming a revelation from God directed him to act as the church's guardian. Most Latter-day Saints were skeptical of his claim and opted to follow the LDS apostles instead. Rejected, Rigdon started his own church in Pittsburgh, though many followers abandoned him by 1847.

After Rigdon, his followers regathered under the leadership of William Bickerton, a convert of Rigdon's whose visionary experience eventually led to the organization of the Church of Jesus Christ in 1862.[6] Bickerton scaled back many of Smith's doctrinal innovations and restricted the scriptures to

4. Historian D. Michael Quinn discerned eight possible methods of succession that Smith had, in one way or another, recommended ("The Mormon Succession Crisis of 1844," *BYU Studies* 16, no. 2 [1976], 187–233).
5. For an exhaustive list, see Steven L. Shields, *Divergent Paths of the Restoration: An Encyclopedia of the Smith-Rigdon Movement*, 5th ed. (Salt Lake City: Signature Books, 2021).
6. See Daniel P. Stone, *William Bickerton: Forgotten Latter Day Prophet* (Salt Lake City: Signature Books, 2018).

the Bible and Book of Mormon, leading his church to reject practices like polygamy.[7] Bickerton's church would eventually be led by a quorum of twelve apostles rather than a prophet. The Church of Jesus Christ (Monongahela, Pennsylvania) is presently among the largest bodies within Mormonism not affiliated with the LDS Church.

The Church of Jesus Christ of Latter Day Saints (James J. Strang)

Rigdon's bid to replace Smith prompted the LDS apostles to reinforce their leadership. A week after publicly rejecting Rigdon, the twelve maintained their authority in an epistle to the church. "You are now without a prophet present with you in the flesh to guide you," they wrote, "but you are not without apostles."[8] Eventually, they would reorganize the church with Brigham Young as the prophet and a newly appointed Quorum of the Twelve Apostles. But not all Latter-day Saints were satisfied with this arrangement. Anti-polygamists rejected the apostles' authority outright because of the twelve's support for, and practice of, plural marriage. Others searched for signs God had ordained a new prophet in similar ways to Smith's story, like visions, angelic ordination, and bringing forth ancient records.

Thus, many Mormons took notice when an outspoken anti-polygamist, James J. Strang, began to publish supernatural evidence of his ordination to the prophetic office in the years immediately following Smith's death.[9] Even though he converted to the church mere months before Smith died, Strang nevertheless produced a letter purportedly from the prophet foreshadowing his death and appointing Strang as his successor. Strang also reported angelic visitations, a vision of the Saints gathering to him in Wisconsin, and the discovery of ancient plates, which he translated much the same way Smith had the Book of Mormon. Strang attracted Mormons seeking charismatic signs as evidence of God's approved successor. This was especially true among those who found polygamy to be unacceptable.

Strang called all Mormons to gather in Voree, Wisconsin, to build their new Jerusalem, yet again (see questions 8 and 9). Thousands heeded Strang's call, making him the primary competitor of Brigham Young for a short time. A subsequent revelation commanded his movement to colonize the Beaver Island archipelago of Lake Michigan, where Strang claimed to have translated the Book of the Law of the Lord. This ancient scripture effectively offered his followers a blueprint for the literal kingdom of God on earth. Then, in 1850,

---

7. Larry Watson, "The Church of Jesus Christ (Headquarters in Monongahela, Pennsylvania), Its History and Doctrine," in *Scattering of the Saints: Schism Within Mormonism*, ed. Newell G. Bringhurst and John C. Hamer (Independence, MO: John Whitmer Books, 2007): 190–205.
8. BY, "An Epistle of the Twelve," *T&S*, August 15, 1844, 5:618.
9. See Vickie Cleverley Speek, *"God Has Made Us a Kingdom": James Strang and the Midwest Mormons* (Salt Lake City: Signature Books, 2006).

Strang crowned himself king of God's earthly kingdom, which was a natural trajectory set earlier by the Council of Fifty (see question 9), but it raised concern among some Mormons (and non-Mormons) who worried Strang was amassing too much political power. Their fears were heightened after Strang was elected to the Michigan House of Representatives in 1852 and reelected in 1854. And although he once regarded his opinion on polygamy as "unchangeable," Strang experienced a change of heart.[10] Many followers of Strang became disaffected and abandoned their prophet after discovering his nephew and traveling companion was, in reality, Strang's first plural wife in disguise. Strang would marry an additional three women before he was assassinated in 1856, suffering the same fate as his predecessor.

Those who remained faithful to Strang struggled to keep his church together in the years following. Many of his followers joined with other Mormon churches, especially a new organization led by Smith's son, Joseph Smith III. But a core group of Strang's stalwart believers remained hopeful God would appoint the third latter-day prophet. A small remnant still exists today.

Community of Christ (Joseph Smith III)

Joseph Smith III was only eleven when a mob murdered his father, but some Latter-day Saints hoped he would pick up his father's baton one day.[11] Among them was Jason W. Briggs, an estranged member of Strang's church who left once it became clear he had abandoned his anti-polygamist convictions. In June 1852, Briggs and other like-minded Latter-day Saints called a special conference of disenfranchised Mormons in northeastern Illinois and southern Wisconsin. Attendees publicly rejected the "pretensions" of competing prophets and declared their belief that the only valid candidate to replace Smith would come by lineal descent. This announcement set into motion the eventual leadership of Joseph Smith III over the Reorganized Church of Jesus Christ of Latter Day Saints. This reorganization attracted many Mormons across the American Midwest, who coalesced around the reluctant son of a slain prophet. In 1860, Smith III was finally convinced to take his father's mantle as prophet and president after a series of quiet, spiritual "manifestations" led him to accept the roles.[12] The Reorganized Church quickly grew to become the second-largest Mormon organization, a status it holds to this day.

Early on, members of the Reorganized Church distinguished themselves from other Latter-day Saints by their fierce rejection of polygamy, an alternative scriptural canon, and the establishment of prophetic succession by

---

10. James J. Strang, "Official," *Zion's Reveille* (Wisconsin), August 12, 1847.
11. Quinn, "Succession," 222–23.
12. Joseph Smith and Heman C. Smith, eds., *History of the Church of Jesus Christ of Latter Day Saints*, 4th ed. (Lamoni, IA: Reorganized Church of Jesus Christ of Latter Day Saints, 1911), 247.

familial lineage. In addition to Briggs, all four men who ordained Smith III to the reorganized presidency were staunch monogamists, and Smith III went to great lengths to deny his father had participated in polygamy. Smith III argued the doctrine was introduced by the Twelve Apostles, not his father. The Reorganized church also did not adopt Smith's later teachings, such as the doctrine of eternal progression and baptism for the dead.

A direct descendant of Joseph Smith led the Reorganized Church until 1996. In recent decades, Community of Christ (Independence, Missouri), as it is now called, has moved toward a progressive Christian posture. The de-emphasis of its salvific exclusivity and the adoption of liberal theology have prompted a series of schisms within the movement.

Schisms in the Twentieth and Twenty-First Centuries

Not all groups who claim to be Mormon broke away from LDS communities in the years immediately following Smith's death. Many groups have formed in the twentieth and twenty-first centuries, typically prompted by dissatisfaction with the LDS Church. Fundamentalist dissenters, for example, have formed marginalized networks of independent communities that affirm tenets long abandoned by the LDS Church such as Brigham Young's Adam-God doctrine and polygamy. Fundamentalists commonly believe that Joseph Smith established a true priesthood and church, but subsequent leaders have forfeited their leadership. Among these groups are the Apostolic United Brethren and the Fundamentalist Church of Jesus Christ of Latter Day Saints, whose most infamous leader, Warren S. Jeffs, received a life sentence after being convicted of sexual abuse as leader of the Yearning for Zion Ranch.[13] Warren Jeffs's legacy cast a long, dark shadow over Mormon fundamentalism, but it is wrong to assume his abusive spirit haunts all forms of Mormon fundamentalism.

Not all contemporary dissenters leave mainstream Mormonism because of polygamy. Denver Snuffer, a staunch anti-polygamist, founded a Latter-day Saint restoration movement, a remnant community seeking to restore doctrine and practices they view as lost or compromised. Snuffer's movement is guided by a series of new revelations which aim to reestablish the LDS restoration, promising a return to an "original" Mormonism marked by speaking in tongues and other spiritual gifts. Snuffer's followers are perhaps best known within Mormonism for their belief in the possibility of receiving a personal visitation by the resurrected Jesus Christ.

Summary

Although most Mormons identify with the Church of Jesus Christ of Latter-day Saints (Utah), the church does not monopolize the Mormon identity against

13. See Cardell Jacobson and Lara Burton, eds., *Modern Polygamy in the United States* (New York: Oxford University Press, 2011).

those who claim a share in Joseph Smith's restoration tradition. After every split, each new group relies on a lineage of authority to demonstrate how their branch not only connects to the tree of Mormonism but is, in reality, its truest form. And they must. Yet without strong continuity, their movements are destined to suffer continued fracturing, which has occurred among the groups explored in this question. Today, the spiritual inheritors of Young, Smith III, Bickerton, and Strang join many other expressions, both extinct and extant, who trace their spiritual lineage back to Smith. The issue of authority is still contested and far from settled within the LDS restoration movement at large.

REFLECTION QUESTIONS

1. How do Christian and LDS visions of unity among churches differ? How might you discuss these differences with a Latter-day Saint?

2. How does schism within Mormonism undermine its restorationist goal? How does this contrast against the many denominations of Christianity?

3. What do you believe was a central cause of division within Mormonism after Joseph Smith's death? Does that cause matter to the LDS Church today?

4. Why is it important to parse out the different branches of Mormonism so as not to correlate them all to the LDS Church?

5. Do you believe the various Mormonisms are truly *Mormon*? Why or why not?

QUESTION 11

Is Mormonism Just an American Religion?

"Yea thou shalt have power to go from nation to nation & from Island to Island & proclaim my gospel in all the different languages & tongues of the earth."[1]
~ Early Latter-day Saint Missionary Blessing

Per capita, it is one of the most Mormon places on earth.[2] Latter-day Saint residents can trace their spiritual lineage back generations. In the town of Liahona—named after a sacred object in the Book of Mormon—members worship in their temple. At one time, it was a very Protestant place, the fruit of rich missionary activity reaching back centuries. But a monument now commemorates the work of the first Mormon missionaries who forever changed the community's religious path. A 2001 film, *The Other Side of Heaven*, explored part of their history. The place has been lauded for its persistent "display [of] enduring faith, an ideal not only for all members of the Church of Jesus Christ of Latter-day Saints but for Christians throughout the world."[3] I'm writing, of course, about the island nation of Tonga.

Some readers may be surprised to learn that one of the most Mormon places in the world is outside America. The perception of Mormonism as just an American religion is understandable. The religion began in New York, is headquartered in Salt Lake City, and is prominent in America's Great

1. Minutes, August 17, 1835, D4:390.
2. Riley M. Moffat, Fred E. Woods, and Brent R. Anderson, *Saints of Tonga: A Century of Island Faith* (Salt Lake City: Deseret Book, 2019), 378.
3. Moffat, Woods, and Anderson, *Saints of Tonga*, 379.

Basin. The American West is hard to imagine without Mormonism. Famous American figures from the Osmonds to the Romneys are well-known for their Mormon faith. In irreverent jest, the hit Broadway musical *The Book of Mormon* dedicated a song to the "All-American Prophet," Joseph Smith, the founder of Mormonism.

LDS Church statistics show that slightly more than half of all Latter-day Saints live in North America, reflecting the church's missionary zeal.[4] Indeed, Smith's vision for missions was global from the beginning, forbidding his apostles from letting "a single corner of the earth go without a mission."[5] Some of the earliest LDS missionaries were sent on international missions, laboring beyond the Euro-American ethnic and domestic borders. As early as the fall of 1830, just months after founding the church, Smith sent a few men to serve among American Indians living beyond Missouri's western border, then outside US territory (see D&C 28:8–9).

The first truly international mission began in the late 1830s when two LDS apostles began proselytizing in the United Kingdom, and with great success. LDS missionaries soon spread across continental Europe, but Europe was not their only mission field. In the spring of 1843, the church sent a small team from its headquarters in Illinois to the South Pacific, and by the early 1850s, Mormons could be found laboring in China, India, Chile, and South Africa. Mormonism has been an international religion from the beginning.

Mormonism Across the Globe

What follows is a brief history and present overview of Mormonism in Europe, the Pacific, Latin America, Africa, Asia, and the Middle East.

Mormonism in Europe

In 1837, Latter-day Saints began proselytizing among Protestant congregations in Great Britain. Their success opened the door for missionary work in Europe, especially among Scandinavian nations, leading to a wave of European Mormons emigrating to gather with American Mormons. By the 1890s, most Utah residents were European Mormon immigrants. Today, nearly half a

4. "2021 Statistical Report for the April 2022 Conference," The Church of Jesus Christ of Latter-day Saints, https://newsroom.churchofjesuschrist.org/article/2021-statistical-report-april-2022-conference; "Facts and Statistics," Worldwide Statistics, The Church of Jesus Christ of Latter-day Saints, https://newsroom.churchofjesuschrist.org/facts-and-statistics#. This number is likely inflated due to the inclusion of disaffiliated and inactive members in official tallies. Some scholars have suggested the number is much lower, perhaps as much as half. See R. T. Cragun, "Summing Up: Problems and Prospects for a Global Church in the Twenty-First Century," in *The Palgrave Handbook of Global Mormonism*, ed. R. Gordon Shepherd, A. Gary Shepherd, and Ryan T. Cragun (Cham, Switzerland: Springer Nature Switzerland AG, 2020), 833–34.
5. JSJ, April 19, 1843, J2:370.

million Latter-day Saints across Europe gather in hundreds of congregations and fourteen temples from Portugal to Ukraine. European Latter-day Saints differ from their American counterparts with smaller families, less active membership, and a more socially isolated posture.[6] European Mormonism is also shrinking. Lower birth rates, rising secularism, and mounting skepticism have contributed to decline, challenges that affect European Christianity in general. Still, a Mormon minority persists as a testament to the earliest international missionary efforts of the LDS Church.

Mormonism in the Pacific

Even as early as 1833, though the fledgling LDS Church numbered just a few thousand, Joseph Smith envisioned sending missionaries to all the nations of the earth, including "unto the islands of the sea."[7] His dream was realized after a new convert, Addison Pratt, expressed interest in missionary work throughout the South Pacific. By 1844, Pratt had opened the first chapter in a long history of LDS missions in the Pacific after laboring in Tubuai, an incredible accomplishment by any measure. To put this in perspective, LDS missionaries would not reach Florida until the following year. By the mid-1850s, thousands of Polynesians had converted to Mormonism. Within a century, LDS missionaries could be found across the islands of Micronesia and Melanesia. Today, members practice worship styles reflecting Western standards yet without totally sacrificing the unique cultural elements that set Pacific Mormonism apart from the wider religious community. Some examples of this are exhibited in the church-owned Polynesian Cultural Center in Hawaii, which is staffed with the help of LDS students from Brigham Young University-Hawaii.

Mormonism in Latin America

At first, LDS missionary work in Latin America was sporadic and sluggish. Missionaries toiled there as early as 1851, but their labor bore little fruit in cultural contexts steeped in Roman Catholicism. But Mormon interest in Latin America compelled them to keep trying. Latter-day Saints speculated the events described in the Book of Mormon may have taken place in Central America, which would mean the indigenous people there were descendants of Jews and a prime audience for the missionaries' message.[8] Their commitment to the region eventually paid off, particularly in the 1960s–1980s. Today, millions of Latin Americans are members of the LDS Church, making Latin America the most populous region for Mormonism outside the United States.

6. Wilfried Decoo, "Mormons in Europe," in *The Oxford Handbook of Mormonism*, ed. Terryl L. Givens and Philip L. Barlow (New York: Oxford University Press, 2015), 548–55.
7. MRB, 205 [D&C 133:8] (emend.).
8. See Matthew P. Roper, "Joseph Smith, Central American Ruins, and the Book of Mormon," in *Approaching Antiquity: Joseph Smith and the Ancient World*, ed. Lincoln H. Blumell, Matthew J. Grey, and Andrew H. Hedges (Salt Lake City: Deseret Book, 2015), 141–62.

Latin American Mormonism is concentrated in urban areas, where temples feature in most major cities.

Mormonism in Africa

Mormon missionary work in Africa initially focused on converting the descendants of European colonists, perhaps because at the time Blacks were restricted from the LDS priesthood (see question 20), even as some pleaded for communion with the church. In the mid-twentieth century, a group of Nigerian investigators acquired religious writings from the church, which prompted them to ask Salt Lake City to dispatch missionaries to western Africa. When their request was ignored, they formed unofficial congregations.[9] Since the late 1970s, however, ramped-up missionary efforts across the continent have led to many conversions, especially in western Africa. Still, the growth is modest in Africa when compared with traditional Christianity and Islam. Mormonism has lagged behind other religions because its late start has given the religion less than half a century to grow. The church also struggles to contextualize and adapt its message and practices in Africa. This challenge is shared with other religions but is especially true of Mormonism, which tends to emphasize—whether intentionally or not—narratives and norms more at home in an American context than in an African one.

Mormonism in Asia and the Middle East

Brigham Young sent the first LDS missionaries to Asia in the 1850s, with little success. Common barriers like language, cultural misunderstandings, and religious differences were amplified by a general skepticism toward Western influence among Asian nations. The church struggled to make inroads in Asia until after World War II, when pro-Western sentiment opened the door for LDS missionaries to reengage cultures previously suspicious of their presence. Still, growth has been minimal to nonexistent outside South Korea, Taiwan, Japan, and the Philippines. Today, a little over a million Latter-day Saints live in Asia, a number that appears impressive until juxtaposed against the billions of non-Mormons in the region. There are about three times the number of church members in Indiana (the seventeenth most populous state in the US) as there are in India (the most populous country in the world). Missionaries are effectively cut off from China, as is the case across the Middle East, especially in Israel, whose strict anti-proselytism laws forbid missionary activity despite the church's presence at an extension center of Brigham Young University outside Jerusalem. The Mormon population throughout the rest of the region is negligible and mainly constitutes small enclaves of expatriated Westerners.

9. James B. Allen, "Would-Be Saints: West Africa Before the 1978 Priesthood Revelation," *Journal of Mormon History* 17 (1991): 207–47.

Mormonism as a "World Religion"

Scholars debate Mormonism's status as a "world religion" even though Latter-day Saints dot the globe. For some, the rise of Mormonism is comparable to the rise of Sikhism and Bahá'í.[10] Although these religions are relatively small in population when compared with the likes of Hinduism and Islam, they are nonetheless marked by longevity and global distribution. Sociologist Rodney Stark famously argued in the early 1980s that Mormonism's consistent growth across the globe had placed it on a nearly inevitable path toward joining "dominant world faiths" and would be the first to earn such an achievement since Islam.[11]

But the breakneck speed at which Stark predicted Mormonism's growth—over 260 million by 2080—has slowed drastically; moreover, it's not clear how population constitutes a "world religion."[12] A truly global religion does not necessarily have a large quantitative presence but a strong qualitative presence, one that adapts to local norms of ritual and values without sacrificing social and religious distinctives that make it unique. Judaism is a good example of a small world religion.

From this perspective, one scholar argued Mormonism has yet to contextualize globally as a world religion in the same way as Buddhism and Christianity. To achieve this status, Mormonism must adapt to the cultural contexts in which it wishes to grow, demonstrating whether "it will prove possible for distinctive African, South American, Japanese, or any other regional forms of Mormonism to emerge."[13] As many Christian traditions have discovered, based on biblical examples, the proliferation of faith often relies on healthy indigenous leadership. But the LDS Church, as a hierarchical institution, has been reluctant to decentralize control, so it is uncertain Mormonism will ever experience the kind of rapid growth charismatic and evangelical movements have enjoyed in the Global South.[14]

LDS leaders are aware of these challenges, but their method of overcoming them has been to encourage uniformity. Since the mid-twentieth century, the church has emphasized its global identity as a universal institution, especially through correlation efforts that deliver religious resources to new converts in their native language. While this approach takes an essential step toward multiculturalism, it certainly does not guarantee it. As one scholar pointed out,

---

10. Eric Eliason, ed., *Mormons and Mormonism: An Introduction to an American World Religion* (Urbana, IL: University of Illinois Press, 2001), 15.
11. Rodney Stark, *The Rise of Mormonism*, ed. Reid L. Neilson (New York: Columbia University Press, 2005), 140. See also 139–46.
12. Stark, *Rise of Mormonism*, 141.
13. Douglas J. Davies, *The Mormon Culture of Salvation: Force, Grace, and Glory* (Burlington, VT: Ashgate, 2000), 258.
14. See Philip Jenkins, "Letting Go: Understanding Mormon Growth in Africa," in *From the Outside Looking In: Essays on Mormon History, Theology, and Culture*, ed. Reid L. Neilson and Matthew J. Grow (New York: Oxford University Press, 2016), 330–52.

"translating materials into a local language does not make a religion multicultural any more than translating the TV show *Friends* into Arabic makes it suddenly reflect Saudi Arabian values."[15] The curriculum and lessons still communicate Western norms, often in ways so subtle they escape their authors' attention. So when LDS missionaries are sent abroad to proselytize, they export norms more at home among the White middle class of the Mormon corridor than anywhere else. Perhaps this is to be expected from an institution whose highest-ranking officials are mainly elderly White men born in Utah. But the church signaled willingness to diversify leadership at its highest level when, in 2018, two non-White men were elected to the Quorum of the Twelve Apostles.

Summary

The Church of Jesus Christ of Latter-day Saints has leaned into its international presence and mission but still presents characteristics of the Mormon experience in the United States. As historian Colleen McDannell argued, while LDS leaders have become "more aware of their own American prejudices . . . points of tension within the global community persist."[16] Negotiating these tensions successfully will be a vital task for Mormonism moving forward. A religion that adapts too much to its surrounding culture loses its identity as a distinct community. Still, unless it discovers and implements strategies for the indigenization of its message, Mormonism will continue to struggle for world religion status.

REFLECTION QUESTIONS

1. Do you consider your faith tradition to be global, at least in the sense alluded to in this question? How is it different from or like Mormonism in this area?
2. What parts of the world where Mormonism is growing most surprised you, and why?
3. What global challenges to growth does your faith tradition share with Mormonism? How are the two different?
4. How do the doctrines and structures of the LDS Church help or hinder its growth across the globe?
5. Do you believe Mormonism is a world religion? Why or why not?

---

15. Cragun, "Summing Up," 823.
16. Colleen McDannell, "Global Mormonism: A Historical Overview," in *The Palgrave Handbook of Global Mormonism*, ed. Shepherd, Shepherd, and Cragun, 23.

PART 3

Authority in Mormonism

QUESTION 12

How Do Latter-day Saints View the Bible?

"Indeed, if the bible itself is true, it is but a portion of the inspired writings that God intended for the world."[1]
~ Benjamin Winchester, Seventy in the LDS Church, 1836–1844

Samuel H. Smith didn't believe his brother's message. The restoration of Christianity, angelic visitations, new scripture—could all this be true? It seemed like a bit much. Joseph Smith tried everything to convince Samuel of his doctrines, even reasoning "with him out of the Bible."[2] But no matter how much Joseph reasoned with his brother, he wouldn't budge. It wasn't until Samuel retreated to the privacy of a forest in prayer that he decided to accept his brother's message. In the end, the Bible didn't convince him—it was a spiritual experience.

Samuel's conversion to Mormonism foreshadowed the evolving relationship his new religion had with the Bible. It was foundational as an authority and necessary as a source of revelation, but it was not final. It needed to be reinforced by more revelation. This perspective contrasted sharply with the Protestant belief of Smith's day that regarded the Bible as the greatest and sufficient source for all faith and practice. But as one LDS scholar observed, early Mormonism "demoted scripture to the status of stream rather than fountain."[3]

1. Benjamin Winchester, "Introduction to the Subject of the Book of Mormon," *The Gospel Reflector* (Philadelphia), March 1, 1841.
2. H1:296.
3. Terryl L. Givens, *Wrestling the Angel: The Foundations of Mormon Thought: Cosmos, God, Humanity* (New York: Oxford University Press, 2015), 30.

The fountain, of course, was the reopened heaven pouring out new revelation in dynamic ways, especially through the mouth of a living prophet.

Still, traditional Christians mistakenly assume Latter-day Saints do not swim in a biblical stream. Three-fourths of LDS scripture is the Bible, which saturates the other texts with citations and allusions. Periodically, members of the Church of Jesus Christ of Latter-day Saints study the Bible collectively by following a church-wide curriculum. Brigham Young University leverages its ancient scripture department to publish its own commentary, and fortunate students can even study the Bible in the Holy Land at the university's Jerusalem campus. In terms of content, it's difficult not to find the Bible in Mormonism. LDS disagreement with the broader Christian community isn't whether the Bible is important, but *why* it's important.

So what is the Latter-day Saint view of the Bible? Before we can answer this question, we need to ask a more basic one: What is the Bible?

The Inspiration of the Bible

God delights to reveal himself in the handiwork of his creation (see Ps 19:1–6) and in the "divers manners" (Heb 1:1) he communicates. Theologians call these general and special revelation, respectively. It is *general* because God reveals himself generally through creation to all people across time and every culture, and *special* because he also reveals himself in more comprehensive, concrete, and clear ways than natural forms of revelation. At the core of God's divine revelation is Jesus Christ, the Word of God incarnate (see John 1:1, 14; Heb 1:1–3). All general revelation was "created by him, and for him" (Col 1:16), and all special revelation readies, reveals, and reminds us of him (see Luke 24:25–27, 44–49; John 5:39). Throughout centuries, Christians recognized this message in the special revelation of the Bible—the word of God proclaimed by his Spirit, penned by inspired writers, and providentially preserved by him who illuminates faithful reading in the hearts of all saints.

The Bible is a library of books collectively testifying of God's work to bring about redemption for his glory. The New Testament declares "all scripture is given by inspiration of God" (2 Tim 3:16) and every passage has the quality of being inspired, or God-breathed. The Old Testament is often self-consciously aware of its inspiration as a record of the very voice of God (e.g., "Thus saith the Lord"), recognizing prophecy did not come "by the will of man: but holy men of God spake as they were moved by the Holy Ghost" (2 Pet 1:21). The NT frequently draws upon the OT while recognizing its own content as being among "the other scriptures" (2 Pet 3:16).

Joseph Smith affirmed general revelation. He taught how all those of "common intellect" could gaze upward to see "the power of Omnipotence inscribed upon the heavens."[4] And he affirmed special revelation, believing

---

4. "Elders" (including JS) to the Church, ca. March 1834, D3:475.

all people can see God's "own hand-writing in the sacred volume."[5] Biblical material peppered Smith's writings, and throughout his life his sermons incorporated the Bible far more often than the Book of Mormon. For Smith, the Bible was an inspired text and prominent among LDS scripture.

Early Latter-day Saints were well-versed in the Bible and won converts from Protestantism primarily by arguing from their common holy text, as seen in Parley P. Pratt's influential *A Voice of Warning* (1837).[6] A Protestant minister in Smith's day remarked how impressed he was with the Mormons, "a people who read the Bible so much, and who could so readily quote any part of Scripture," that they put Protestants to shame.[7] From personal experience, I've found the same to be true of many Latter-day Saints today, who are grateful inheritors and students of this work of "divinely inspired authors."[8]

So, Latter-day Saints and traditional Christians agree the Bible is inspired, but they disagree about its sufficiency.

The Sufficiency of the Bible

Is the Bible sufficient special revelation from God? To answer this question, we must go back to the formation of the biblical canon. The Greek word *kanōn* refers to a measuring stick that provides the standard for an ideal length. Christians use the term as a metaphor to describe the list of texts recognized as scripture. Generally, early Christians adopted the Hebrew Bible while discerning the authenticity and recognizing the authority of the twenty-seven books of the NT by the late fourth century, although most NT texts functioned much earlier as scripture.[9] It's better to call the canon set, not closed, to recognize how Christians still believed God spoke, though he had chosen to do so through inspired texts about the Lord Jesus (see Heb 1:1–3). The living God does still speak—his gospel proclaims Christ's redemption, his Spirit testifies of Christ, and God whispers in his still, small voice to his saints in prayer. The Bible trains Christians how to recognize God's active voice.

Is the set canon truly sufficient, or may it be lengthened? Joseph Smith anticipated a skeptical reception of the Book of Mormon when he published it. The text itself told him what to expect, how "fools" would turn their noses up

5. "Elders" (including JS) to the Church, ca. March 1834, D3:475.
6. Although JS quibbled with Pratt's work, it nevertheless ranks among one of the most significant writings in early Mormon history. See JSJ, September 1–7, 1839, J1:351.
7. "Mormons and Mormon Tenets," *The Home Missionary and Pastor's Journal* 13 (New York: William Osborn, 1841), 38.
8. Andrew C. Skinner, "Bible," in *LDS Beliefs: A Doctrinal Reference*, ed. Robert L. Millet et al. (Salt Lake City: Deseret Book, 2011), 66.
9. See Michael J. Kruger, *Canon Revisited: Establishing the Origins and Authority of the New Testament Books* (Wheaton, IL: Crossway, 2012); Denis Farkasfalvy, *A Theology of the Christian Bible: Revelation, Inspiration, and Canon* (Washington, DC: The Catholic University of American Press, 2018).

at it, retorting: "A Bible! A Bible! We have got a Bible, and there cannot be any more Bible" (2 Nephi 29:3, 6). The Book of Mormon wondered why traditional Christians would not receive more from God and found the answer in disbelief. "Ye need not suppose that it [the Bible] contains all my words," cautions God in the text, "neither need ye suppose that I have not caused more to be written" (2 Nephi 29:10). In other words, traditional Christians would reject the Book of Mormon because they wouldn't lengthen the canon. Of course, such an argument for the Book of Mormon is necessary; the book forfeits its place among scripture otherwise. If the Bible is genuinely sufficient, then the Book of Mormon—and modern prophecy and other LDS scriptures—are canonical excess.

The issue of biblical transmission also bothered Smith, as it did some of his contemporaries. While many people believed in the Bible's inspiration, they wondered how the English Bible could be trusted if fallible or unscrupulous men controlled the translation process, let alone the degraded and corrupted state of biblical manuscripts. Discoveries like the Dead Sea Scrolls were generations away, and the rich manuscript evidence that provides witnesses to the NT was not as understood then as it is today.[10] Smith held the popular opinion that the original texts were inspired, but copies of the originals were corrupted—as a result of "ignorant translators, careless transcribers, or designing and corrupt priests"—rendering modern Bibles inaccurate.[11] LDS apostle Orson Pratt reflected this sentiment that biblical manuscripts had been so "mutilated, changed, and corrupted," that he wondered if anyone could be sure "that even one verse of the whole Bible has escaped pollution, so as to convey the same sense now that it did in the original?"[12] Even if it had, the Book of Mormon hints at the possibility of imperfection in scriptural source material (see 1 Nephi 19:6; 3 Nephi 8:1–2; Mormon 8:12; 9:31).

Still, Latter-day Saints considered the Bible essential; it was inspired but inadequate by itself. A self-stated mission of the Book of Mormon is to "establish the truth" (1 Nephi 13:40) of the Bible. Early LDS missionaries were frequently asked whether they believed the Bible. "If we do," they replied, "we are the only people under heaven that does. For there are none of the religious sects of the day that do."[13] In this sense, Latter-day Saints thought of themselves as *more* biblical than traditional Christians precisely because their movement sought to restore the plain and precious parts of the Bible they believed had been stripped out (see 1 Nephi 13:26–29, 32, 34) or to reveal the parts that had gone unseen due to spiritual blindness (see Jacob 4:14). They weren't rejecting the Bible; instead, they were restoring it. Through no fault of

10. See John D. Meade and Peter J. Gurry, *Scribes and Scripture: The Amazing Story of How We Got the Bible* (Wheaton, IL: Crossway, 2022).
11. Joseph Smith, History, 1838–1856, vol. E-1, *JSP*, 1755.
12. Orson Pratt, *Series of Pamphlets* (Liverpool: R. James, 1851), 47.
13. JS, *EJ*, July 1838, 1:42.

its own, the Bible could only offer a blurry vision for faith and practice, which explained to them why denominations disagreed at so many theological junctures. For these reasons, Smith believed "the bible to be the word of God as far as it is translated correctly."[14]

But from his prophetic vantage point, Smith viewed with skepticism any attempt to produce a correct translation. As he explained rather bluntly, there were "many things in the bible which do not, as they now stand, accord with the revelation of the Holy Ghost to me."[15] Only divine intervention could remedy the problem.

As early as 1830, Smith began working on a new translation for the church, although it was quite unlike actual translation. Smith was untrained in biblical languages and did not appear to have consulted linguistic tools available to him at the time.[16] Instead, he revised the King James Bible according to his decisions and revelations. As one LDS scholar explained, Smith's view "was not so much that his revelations needed to be tailored absolutely to biblical data but, rather, that an imperfect Bible ought to be conformed to his more current and direct revelations."[17] The Bible must conform to Smith, not the other way around because, he said, "I have [the] Key by which I understand the scripture."[18] Consequently, as another LDS scholar pointed out, "Smith understood his Bible rereading as revelation from God that superseded as necessary the printed text."[19]

Without the aid of lexicons and linguistic training, Smith began his revision with the book of Genesis and concluded the bulk of his project by 1833.[20]

---

14. JS, "Church History," *T&S*, March 9, 1842, 3:709. Traditional Christians can agree, in principle, with this position, as it reflects a surprisingly high view of the Bible. Smith did not say that the Bible merely contains the word of God; rather, he insisted that it *is* the word of God, with any defects attributed to imperfect translation rather than to the text's divine origin. This position dovetails the Chicago Statement on Biblical Inerrancy, which affirms that "copies and translations of Scripture are the Word of God to the extent that they faithfully represent the original." Thus, Smith's formulation places the Bible in an unmistakably positive light.
15. JSJ, June 11, 1843, J3:33 (emend.).
16. Smith would later be trained in Biblical Hebrew (1836) but not before he revised the Bible (summer of 1830 to July 1833).
17. Philip L. Barlow, *Mormons and the Bible: The Place of the Latter-day Saints in American Religion* (New York: Oxford University Press, 1991), 57.
18. JSJ, January 29, 1843, J2:252 (emend.).
19. Samuel Morris Brown, *Joseph Smith's Translation: The Words and Worlds of Early Mormonism* (New York: Oxford University Press, 2020), 165.
20. Smith was, however, aided by Adam Clarke's popular biblical commentary "less [as] a theological source than a practical resource." See Thomas A. Wayment and Haley Wilson-Lemmon, "A Recovered Resource: The Use of Adam Clarke's Bible Commentary in Joseph Smith's Bible Translation," in Michael Hubbard MacKay, Mark Ashurst-McGee, and Brian M. Hauglid, *Producing Ancient Scripture: Joseph Smith's Translation Projects in the Development of Mormon Christianity* (Salt Lake City: University of Utah Press, 2020),

But he died without publishing his translation. The manuscripts were delivered to the Reorganized Church (today, Community of Christ), which published the Inspired Version in 1867, but the LDS Church has never seriously considered replacing the KJV.[21] As a result, only portions from the book of Genesis and the Gospel of Matthew were canonized in LDS scripture, and those not until 1880.

The Authority of the Bible in Mormonism

Early Latter-day Saints esteemed the Bible as an inspired text but viewed it as insufficient because its source material was corrupted, and English translations lacked accuracy. Joseph Smith attempted to rehabilitate the Bible, according to his revelatory standards, but never finished. The church has not veered far from its earliest perspective on the Bible, continuing to regard it as inspired but insufficient. It is nestled among the three other standard works of the LDS scriptures: the Book of Mormon, Doctrine and Covenants, and the Pearl of Great Price. The church officially recognizes the KJV but also acknowledges other quality translations. LDS leaders encourage their members to study the Bible, especially when a four-year rotation through their scriptures focuses on the Old and New Testaments during two of those years. Latter-day Saints read the Bible in light of LDS scripture, aided by interpretations from their leaders and personal discernment.

Ultimately, the most significant difference between traditional Christian and LDS views on the Bible orbits its nature. Is the Bible a sufficient source of special revelation, or does it need supplementing by an extended canon? Of course, Latter-day Saints have long believed in the need for additional scripture. However, many traditional Christians view supplemental scripture with suspicion. For conservative Protestants, the denial of the Bible's sufficiency is tantamount to rejecting *sola scriptura* because the "authority of Scripture is inescapably impaired [if] total divine inerrancy is in any way limited or disregarded."[22] Worse yet, to tamper with the word of God is to jeopardize the gospel.

Summary

The Bible is foundational to Mormonism, but as an authority it is not final. The difference between Christians and Latter-day Saints concerning the Bible isn't whether it is important but *why* it is important. Mormonism denies the sufficiency of the Bible because it suffered corruption in its manuscript history, and God continues to speak through prophets today. This point is especially amplified on the nature of salvation. While Christians believe the Bible

21. The manuscripts were transferred from Community of Christ to the LDS Church in 2024.
22. Chicago Statement on Biblical Inerrancy, introduction.

contains all things necessary for salvation, Mormonism includes other texts, like the Book of Mormon.

REFLECTION QUESTIONS

1. What role of authority does the Bible play in your faith, and how is that different from or similar to Mormonism?
2. Do you agree the authority of the Bible is foundational but not final in Mormonism? Why or why not?
3. How do you understand the inspiration of the Bible? Does your understanding of inspiration diverge or converge with Mormonism? How might you discuss this with a Latter-day Saint?
4. How do you understand the sufficiency of the Bible? Does your understanding of sufficiency diverge or converge with Mormonism? How might you discuss this with a Latter-day Saint?
5. How would you converse with a Latter-day Saint about the differences between the Christian and LDS canons of scripture?

QUESTION 13

What Is the Book of Mormon?

"[W]e also believe in the ancient American Bible, called the Book of Mormon; which no other people do believe in, and hence, on this latter point we are regarded as very peculiar."[1]
~ Orson Pratt, Latter-day Saint Apostle, 1843–1881

The slender, compact book, embossed with bright gold letters against a deep sapphire background, is familiar to nearly everyone. Copies are often found tucked away in Marriott Hotel bedside tables and in the hands of missionaries from the Church of Jesus Christ of Latter-day Saints. Ridiculed on Broadway but revered by believers, its place among religious literature has straddled both criticism and devotion since its publication in the nineteenth century. It has been heralded as "the crowning gem in the diadem of our holy scriptures"[2] and dismissed as "chloroform in print."[3] I'm writing, of course, about the Book of Mormon.

What makes the Book of Mormon simultaneously cherished and critiqued, received and rejected? This question and the next will give us insight. This question will examine the purpose and content of the Book of Mormon before we explore its authorship and origin in the following question.

Overview of the Book of Mormon

The Book of Mormon is one of four standard works recognized by the LDS Church as scripture. First published on March 26, 1830, it emerged from a backdrop of incredible, supernatural tales. Earlier, in the spring of 1829,

1. "Discourse," *The Deseret News*, December 7, 1870.
2. Gary James Bergera, ed., *Statements of the LDS First Presidency: A Topical Compendium* (Salt Lake City: Signature Books, 2007), 50.
3. Mark Twain, *Roughing It* (Hartford, CT: American Publishing Company, 1872), 127.

scribes struggled to keep pace with the flurry of dictation by Joseph Smith, a poorly educated but talented imaginary who read from source material he claimed had been entrusted to him by an angel. Its stated purpose is simple: "To the convincing of the Jew and Gentile that Jesus is the Christ, the Eternal God."[4] The Book of Mormon is a saga that rehearses the rise and fall of a civilization in the Americas to whom Jesus Christ appeared and established his church. The Book of Mormon laid the foundation for what would arguably become the most successful new religious tradition in the history of the United States. Today, millions of members of the LDS Church, who have historically taken their namesake from its title (Mormons), are encouraged by their leadership to find within its pages the fullness of the gospel.

For traditional Christian readers, its style and content feel familiar. One could easily be forgiven for misidentifying its text with a passage from the Authorized Version, or King James Version (KJV), of the Bible. Written in Jacobean English, its pages are replete with familiar content: biblical phraseology, concepts, allusions, motifs, parallels, and quotations. One scholar noticed how even the appearance of the first edition mimicked the style of Bibles being printed by a domestic missionary agency in Smith's day.[5] The resemblance was intentional. Even though critics mocked it as the "Gold Bible"—so named for the gold plates from which Smith was said to have translated it—association with the Holy Bible was precisely the point.[6] Just as traditional Christians readily see the interplay and dialogue between the OT and NT, so Latter-day Saints see a similar relationship between the Book of Mormon and the Bible.

Purpose of the Book of Mormon

Toward the end of the Book of Mormon, its author issues a plea: "Come unto Christ, and be perfected in him" (Moroni 10:32). Perhaps no other command in the entire book captures its intended mission better than these closing words do. The reward in heeding its call is spiritual and mortal deliverance. Throughout the book, readers continually encounter precarious scenarios and potential catastrophes, both spiritual and temporal, that are avoided only by coming to Christ in faith, repentance, and obedience to his commands.

The Book of Mormon is written primarily to a future audience who would first see it in the last days before Christ's return. Its message concerns

---

4. JS, *The Book of Mormon: An Account Written by the Hand of Mormon, upon Plates Taken from the Plates of Nephi* (Palmyra, NY: E. B. Grandin, 1830), title page.
5. Paul Gutjahr, *The Book of Mormon: A Biography* (Princeton, NJ: Princeton University Press, 2012), 5.
6. Editors of *The Palmyra Reflector*, a newspaper located in the town where the Book of Mormon was first published, described the work as "that gross and bungling imposition the 'gold bible.'" See "The Marion Monk," *Palmyra Reflector* (New York), September 13, 1830.

the Lamanites—the "literal descendants of Abraham"[7] and ancestors of Native Americans—but also addresses Gentiles, or nonindigenous people (mainly traditional Christians), with the hope of conversion for both.[8] To the Lamanite, the Book of Mormon is a revelation about their "true" origin and redemptive story, and to the Gentile, it reveals the insufficiency of their traditions without the fullness of its gospel. Both are called to come to Christ, who was previously unknown by the former and unrecognized by the latter. In short, the Book of Mormon aims to offer spiritual and temporal mortal deliverance from sin and devastation via the evangelization of indigenous people and the rehabilitation of Christian readers who have strayed from its conception of authentic Christianity.

Latter-day Saints see an additional purpose of the Book of Mormon as "convincing evidence that Joseph Smith was a prophet and that the gospel of Jesus Christ has been restored."[9] For the earliest Mormons, the book was not merely a history of ancient people nor a theological text but also an artifact validating Smith's claim to divine authority. The greater meaning of the Book of Mormon was not what is *in* it but that *it is*. As one LDS scholar noted, "the 'message' of the Book of Mormon *was* its manner of origin."[10] Its content mattered deeply to early converts, but its very existence added an even deeper element to their faith.[11] They were not primarily convinced by its message—although that was very important—but they were more intrigued by "the very idea of a new revelation" apart from standard orthodoxy, argued one historian.[12] It was evidence to them that, for the first time since the apostolic era, God was speaking again through new scripture, a prophet, and personal revelation. This latter purpose of the Book of Mormon still rings true for many Latter-day Saints. For them, the coming forth of the Book of Mormon "set into motion the authority of subjective feeling as authentic revelation as a normative practice among Latter-day Saints for generations to come" (see question 38).[13]

---

7. JSJ, November 9–11, 1835, J1:88.
8. JS described the Book of Mormon as "a record of the forefathers of our western Tribes of Indians . . . containing the word of God, which was delivered unto them, By it we learn that our western tribes of Indians are desendants [*sic*] from that Joseph that was sold into Egypt, and that the Land of America is a promised land unto them" (JS to Noah C. Saxton, January 4, 1833, D2:354).
9. Bergera, *Statements of the LDS First Presidency,* 49.
10. Terryl L. Givens, *By the Hand of Mormon: The American Scripture That Launched a New World Religion* (New York: Oxford University Press, 2002), 84 (emphasis original).
11. Relatedly, one Protestant minister wondered whether there "would have been any permanent converts to Mormonism, had not this volume [the Book of Mormon] been ushered into existence." John A. Clark, "Gleanings By the Way. No. VII," *The Episcopal Recorder,* September 12, 1840.
12. Richard Bushman, *Joseph Smith and the Beginnings of Mormonism* (Urbana, IL: University of Illinois Press, 1984), 142.
13. Terryl L. Givens, *Wrestling the Angel: The Foundations of Mormon Thought: Cosmos, God, Humanity* (New York: Oxford University Press, 2015).

Content of the Book of Mormon

The Book of Mormon is an epic packed with narratives, prophecies, dreams, visions, sermons, and religious instructions. It generally follows the story of Hebrews who were divinely delivered from the impending destruction of Jerusalem and subsequent Babylonian captivity of the sixth century BC. Lehi, a descendant of the tribe of Manasseh (see Alma 10:3) and patriarch of his small clan, gathered his family and fled the Judean capital, trekking across land and sea to the Americas. The timeline of these Hebrews runs parallel with exilic and postexilic Israel. Upon arriving somewhere in the new promised land, the descendants of Lehi's sons became bitter rivals. Nephi, a faithful and stalwart leader, gathered a faction who are generally portrayed as righteous while the unrighteous followed Laman. The Nephites were nevertheless prone to episodes of prideful disobedience. In some cases, Lamanites are showcased as unexpected models of righteousness, especially seen in the Lamanite prophet Samuel, who preached repentance to the Nephites (Helaman 13–16).

These factions, the Nephites and Lamanites, carried out generational conflict despite continual calls for repentance and faith in the gospel. Still, the people of the Book of Mormon grew in culture and economy, even colonizing vast tracts of the Americas. The narrative climaxes with a New World visitation from the post-ascension Christ to the Nephites and Lamanites, where he ministered to his "other sheep" (3 Nephi 16:1; cf. John 10:16). As he did in the NT, Christ called disciples, performed miracles, taught people, and instituted sacraments. A subsequent time of peace between the Nephites and Lamanites was violently interrupted by relentless and devastating warfare, culminating in the annihilation of the Nephites at the beginning of the fourth century AD. The records of the Nephites were consolidated and abridged by a redactor, Mormon, after whom the book is named. Mormon's son, Moroni, assumed the narration, concluded the record, and buried it in a hill in modern New York for Joseph Smith to discover some fourteen centuries later.

It may surprise Christian readers to learn many of the hallmark doctrines of Mormonism are barely mentioned or wholly absent from the Book of Mormon, like temple ordinances, eternality of family, plurality of gods, premortal existence, exaltation, and plural marriage. In fact, theologically, little in the Book of Mormon sets it apart from the Protestantism (in both orthodox and heterodox forms) of nineteenth-century America. It speaks of revelation, scripture, and Zion with themes of atonement, faith, repentance, and grace prominent throughout. God is described as immutable, "unchangeable from all eternity to all eternity" (Moroni 8:18), omnipotent, having "all power" (Alma 26:35), and omniscient, having "all wisdom, and all understanding" (Alma 26:35). The love of God is praised as "the most desirable above all things" (1 Nephi 11:22), and the word of God is upheld as leading people to "the fountain of living waters" (1 Nephi 11:25). Readers are implored to repent and be "born again" (Mosiah 27:25; Alma 5:49; 7:14). They are warned against legalism, that "by the law no flesh is justified" (2 Nephi 2:5), for "it is only in and through the grace of God that ye are saved" (2 Nephi 10:24).

Granted, there are passages that, at face value, disturb traditional Christian sensibility. At times, the book seems to communicate a form of modalism,[14] but, at other points, it appears to champion Trinitarian thought in tandem with NT language.[15] And the notorious verse claiming it is "by grace that we are saved, after all we can do" (2 Nephi 25:23) could be understood as communicating salvation *despite* all we can do, when read in light of nineteenth-century use of the word "after" in similar phrases.[16] Perhaps the most concerning deviation from orthodoxy in the Book of Mormon is its apparent description of humanity's fall as a good event: "Adam fell that men might be; and men are, that they might have joy" (2 Nephi 2:25). Even this statement, however, could be interpreted at the frontier of orthodoxy. It may be read in loose parallel (although not identically) to the Roman Catholic concept of *felix culpa*, or "fortunate fall," in which God is celebrated for orchestrating a series of tragic events that nevertheless end with a joyful outcome by glorifying God for working all things together for good (see Rom 8:28). Indeed, many doctrinal positions in the Book of Mormon feel more at home among antebellum Christianity than modern-day Mormonism.

Again, as one LDS scholar argued, the "significance of the Book of Mormon has been almost entirely bound up not with its content but rather its manner of appearing; it has typically been judged not on the merits of what it *says*, but what it *enacts*."[17] What makes the Book of Mormon unique from traditional Christian belief is less its theological content than its claims to historicity and Smith's declaration of its divine origin, as will be discussed in the next question.

---

14. Modalism denies the permanent distinction between the Father, Son, and Holy Spirit, thereby collapsing the Trinity into one being who operates in three modes. See Mosiah 3:8; 16:15; Helaman 14:12; 3 Nephi 1:14; Mormon 9:12; Ether 3:14.
15. See 3 Nephi 11:5–8, cf. Matt 3:16–17; 3 Nephi 11:32, cf. 1 John 5:7–8; 3 Nephi 15:1, cf. John 6:39–40; 3 Nephi 18:27; 26:15, cf. John 20:17.
16. Daniel O. McClellan, "2 Nephi 25:23 in Literary and Rhetorical Context," *JBMS* 29 (2020):1–19. Stephen E. Robinson earlier suggested the same when he interpreted "after" as logical rather than chronological (i.e., that grace does not *follow* "all we can do" but comes *regardless* of "all we can do"). So Robinson: "I understand the preposition 'after' in 2 Nephi 25:23 to be a preposition of separation rather than a preposition of time. It denotes logical separateness rather than temporal sequence. We are saved by grace 'apart from all we can do' or 'all we can do notwithstanding,' or even 'regardless of all we can do'" (*Believing Christ: The Parable of the Bicycle and Other Good News* [Salt Lake City: Deseret, 1992], 91–92).
17. Terryl L. Givens, *The Book of Mormon: A Very Short Introduction* (New York: Oxford University Press, 2009), 105 (emphasis original).

Summary

The Book of Mormon is the foundational scripture of Mormonism. It promises readers deliverance through repentance to its portrayal of the person and work of Jesus Christ. For Latter-day Saints, it also serves as evidence that Joseph Smith was called by God to be his prophet. While the Book of Mormon plays a central role as LDS scripture, most of the unique Mormon doctrines Christians have come to associate with the LDS Church are largely absent from its pages.

REFLECTION QUESTIONS

1. What is it about the Book of Mormon that has made it both an object of scorn and devotion?

2. How might you explain the sufficiency of the OT and NT to a Latter-day Saint who contends for the addition of the Book of Mormon?

3. What does it mean the Book of Mormon is "another testament" of Jesus Christ?

4. What does it say about authority within Mormonism to learn the Book of Mormon is not the source for many of the religion's most unique doctrines?

5. Why do you suppose the content of the Book of Mormon is less important for a Latter-day Saint than what it establishes (e.g., restoration, living prophets, priesthood)? How is this different from a Christian's relationship to the Bible?

QUESTION 14

Where Did the Book of Mormon Come From?

"An angel from on high the long, long silence broke—descending from the sky, these gracious words he spoke: Lo! in Cumorah's lonely hill a sacred record lies concealed."[1]
~ Parley P. Pratt, Latter-day Saint Apostle, 1835–1857

The previous question examined the purpose and content of the Book of Mormon, which undoubtedly raised a host of questions regarding its authorship, historicity, and creation. Building on the previous question, we will now explore the authorship and origin of the Book of Mormon.

Authorship of the Book of Mormon

Joseph Smith envisioned himself as the translator of the Book of Mormon, not its author, despite its bearing his name as "author and proprietor" (a nineteenth-century legal formality for publications).[2] The Book of Mormon self-identifies as an ancient, composite library written and edited by prophet-historians who consolidated records, inscribed them onto gold plates, and buried the record for future posterity. Smith affirmed this position by claiming to have translated the record "by the gift and power of God,"[3] a supernatural ability early Latter-day Saints believed was closely linked to the spiritual gift of prophecy and tongues.[4] Skeptics, however, have been reluctant to accept his

1. Hymn 197, *A Collection of Sacred Hymns*, 2nd ed. (Manchester, UK: Parley P. Pratt, 1841), 218.
2. JS, *The Book of Mormon: An Account Written by the Hand of Mormon*, title page.
3. JS, *Book of Mormon*, title page.
4. Christopher James Blythe, "'By the Gift and Power of God': Translation among the Gifts of the Spirit," in Michael Hubbard MacKay, Mark Ashurst-McGee, and Brian M. Hauglid,

word. Even before it was published, critics denounced the Book of Mormon as a work of fraud and have continued to do so ever since. Because Smith largely grounded his prophetic authority in the coming forth of the Book of Mormon, to deny his account of its authorship is tantamount to rejecting his role as its translator and, subsequently, his authority.

Some see the question of authorship in binary terms. The Book of Mormon is either authentic scripture or a deceitful hoax; there is no middle ground. LDS apostle Bruce R. McConkie once argued that "[either] the Book of Mormon is true, or it is false; either it came from God, or it was spawned in the infernal realms."[5] There are, however, more nuanced possibilities that dismiss both ancient origin and Smith's intent to deceive.[6] Perhaps it is a work of fraud but a pious one (i.e., a modern work whose author intended it for good).[7] Or perhaps it is the product of the "energetic imagination" of Smith.[8] Another theory posits that Smith, with his associates, acquired a manuscript written by someone else—likely without its original author's permission or knowledge of what it would become—and massaged the text into LDS scripture. This theory was extremely popular with skeptics in Mormonism's earliest days, especially as rumors swirled at the possibility of a similar text written by a minister, Solomon Spaulding, which some believed was "unquestionably the ground-work" for the Book of Mormon.[9] Most scholars today reject this theory due to insufficient evidence, making it impossible to prove definitively.[10]

In any case, it's unlikely that Smith wrote the Book of Mormon. Examples of his writings contemporary to the creation of the Book of Mormon betray Smith's poor literacy, and he seems to have grown more familiar with the text over time, which is peculiar if he made it up. Despite its cumbersomeness, the Book of Mormon boasts a complicated narrative involving some two hundred named characters in many distinct places across the span of two thousand years. A complex matrix of stories and sermons with plots and themes is colored with

---

Producing Ancient Scripture: Joseph Smith's Translation Projects in the Development of Mormon Christianity (Salt Lake City: University of Utah Press, 2020), 27–53.

5. Bruce R. McConkie, "What Think Ye of the Book of Mormon?," Address to the 153rd Annual General Conference of the Church of Jesus Christ of Latter-day Saints, Salt Lake City, April 2–3, 1983.
6. Grant Hardy, *Understanding the Book of Mormon: A Reader's Guide* (New York: Oxford University Press, 2010), 6; Paul Gutjahr, *The Book of Mormon: A Biography* (Princeton, NJ: Princeton University Press, 2012), 45.
7. Jan Shipps, "The Prophet Puzzle: Suggestions Leading Toward a More Comprehensive Interpretation of Joseph Smith," *Journal of Mormon History* 1 (1974): 3–20; Dan Vogel, *Joseph Smith: The Making of a Prophet* (Salt Lake City: Signature Books, 2004), vii–xxii.
8. Robert A. Rees, "Joseph Smith, the Book of Mormon, and the American Renaissance," *Dialogue* 35, no. 2 (2002): 89.
9. John A. Clark, "Gleanings By the Way. No. VII," *The Episcopal Recorder*, September 12, 1840.
10. Spaulding's manuscript, titled "Manuscript Lost," was found in the late nineteenth century. It bore so little resemblance to the Book of Mormon that the theory deteriorated.

biblically inspired content that reveals an impressive awareness and comprehension of the Old and New Testaments. It also addresses pressing theological debates of nineteenth-century American Protestantism, suggesting whoever wrote it was keenly attuned to the religious *Zeitgeist* of the day. If Smith and ancient authors are both excluded from possibilities, then its authorship remains a mystery. Clues in the text, however, point to an author (or authors and editors) with an American Protestant background and immense creativity, capable literacy, and theological acumen. From this perspective, the Book of Mormon is American pseudepigrapha, and the most influential of its kind ever written.

Historicity of the Book of Mormon

The Church of Jesus Christ of Latter-day Saints maintains that the Book of Mormon represents ancient history, not merely theology. For this reason, corroborating evidence for or against its historicity has been the focus of apologists and skeptics seeking to verify or disprove its authenticity. Indeed, at times throughout the history of Mormonism, Latter-day Saints have been guilty of approaching the text primarily in an apologetic posture to prove, if possible, its historicity. It's important to note, then, how LDS apostle Neal A. Maxwell argued that the substance of the Book of Mormon is "basically spiritual, not historical" during a time of growing interest in its theological message.[11] Today, an enormous body of work ranging anywhere from lay devotionals to scholarly exegesis and commentaries is made available by Latter-day Saint scholars and authors.[12] Still, effort exists to discover both external and internal evidence of its historical nature.

Some Latter-day Saints take the position that the Book of Mormon is not a historical document but is still inspired.[13] Proponents of "inspired fiction" do not believe the Book of Mormon is a historical record but nevertheless argue that abandoning its historicity need not jeopardize its authority or veracity for the believing reader. Others, however, recognize the potential pitfalls of rejecting its historicity. Louis Midgley put it bluntly: "A true Book of Mormon is a powerful witness; a fictional one is hardly worth reading or pondering."[14] LDS scholar Stephen Smoot likewise argued that to read the Book of Mormon

11. Neal A. Maxwell, *Plain and Precious Things* (Salt Lake City: Deseret, 1983), 2.
12. See, for example, J. Spencer Fluhman and Philip L. Barlow, eds., *The Book of Mormon: Brief Theological Introductions*, 12 vols. (Provo, UT: Maxwell Institute, BYU, 2020).
13. Anthony A. Hutchinson, "The Word of God Is Enough: The Book of Mormon as Nineteenth-Century Scripture," in *New Approaches to the Book of Mormon: Explorations in Critical Methodology*, ed. Brent L. Metcalfe (Salt Lake City: Signature Books, 1993); Edwin Firmage Jr., "Historical Criticism and the Book of Mormon: A Personal Encounter," in *American Apocrypha: Essays on the Book of Mormon*, ed. Dan Vogel and Brent L. Metcalfe (Salt Lake City: Signature Books, 2002); Scott C. Dunn, "Automaticity and the Dictation of the Book of Mormon," in *American Apocrypha*, ed. Vogel and Metcalfe 17–46.
14. Louis Midgley, "The Challenge of Historical Consciousness: Mormon History and the Encounter with Secular Modernity," in *By Study and Also by Faith: Essays in Honor of Hugh*

as inspired fiction is to simultaneously "wrest it out of both its ancient and modern *Sitz im Leben*" and to "effectively neuter its theology."[15] He asked why anyone should "believe anything Joseph Smith claimed about God and the fate of the human soul if his foundational truth claims are fraudulent."[16] The answer, of course, is that they should not.

Traditional Christians rarely approach the Book of Mormon apart from criticism of its historicity, especially after learning of its incredible provenance and supernatural translation (see below).[17] The Bible boasts an extraordinary amount of archeological and textual evidence for its historicity. When Latter-day Saints curate the Book of Mormon alongside the Bible, Christians anticipate the same kind of evidence that shapes and solidifies their belief in the Bible as a work of ancient origin about real people in real places.

To date, no archaeological findings in the Americas have definitively established any connections between ancient ruins, like those of Mesoamerica, and the people and events described in the Book of Mormon. Granted, Old World discoveries like writing on metal plates and instances of demotic Egyptian make Smith's claims of gold ones written in "reformed Egyptian" plausible, but still very speculative.[18] And in the 1990s, when archeologists discovered an ancient altar in Yemen inscribed with a reference to *Nhm*, Latter-day Saints took notice.[19] The altar, they argue, is potentially located in a place the Book of Mormon called "Nahom" (1 Nephi 16:34), which is not something a nineteenth-century author could have known.[20] Latter-day Saints also point to internal evidences that suggest an ancient origin. Their scholarship has produced extensive work exploring the literary complexity, intertextual consistency, and apparent Hebraic elements to argue for the Book of Mormon's historicity.

W. Nibley, 2 vols, ed. Stephen D. Ricks and John M. Lundquist (Salt Lake City: Deseret Book, 1988), 2:525.

15. Stephen O. Smoot, "Et Incarnatus Est: The Imperative for Book of Mormon Historicity," *Interpreter* 30 (2018): 154.
16. Smoot, "Et Incarnatus Est," 157.
17. A notable exception is John Christopher Thomas, *A Pentecostal Reads the Book of Mormon: A Literary and Theological Introduction* (Cleveland, TN: CPT Press, 2016).
18. Demotic Egyptian is an ancient script derived from northern forms of hieratic writing used in ancient Egypt between the seventh century BC to the fifth century AD. The term is derived from the Greek *demotikos*, meaning "common," indicating the script's use among common Egyptians in place of hieroglyphs, which were reserved for religious and state texts. Demotic Egyptian bears no linguistic relationship to any extant evidence of the Book of Mormon characters. See Copies of Book of Mormon Characters, D1:353–367.
19. See Warren P. Aston, "A History of NaHoM," *BYU Studies* 51, no. 2 (2012): 79–98.
20. As one critic pointed out, however, it could just as easily be argued that Nahom is a variation of biblical names like Naham (1 Chr 4:19), Nehum (Neh 7:7), or Nahum (Nah 1:1). See Vogel, *Joseph Smith*, 609. Moreover, vowels were often omitted from ancient Semitic script, although they played a crucial role in phonology and grammar, so determining the exact pronunciation of *Nhm* is difficult, something like discovering the lone inscription "CT" without knowing whether the word means "cat," "cot," or "cut."

Still, external evidence for the Book of Mormon is very scant when placed next to the Bible. If it is possible to visit Jerusalem to learn about Hebrew history and culture, when will it be possible to visit Zarahemla to learn about Nephite history and culture? And the Book of Mormon's internal evidence has yet to prove its historicity conclusively. In light of these challenges, Book of Mormon evidence is often either the object of skeptical criticism or apologetic persuasion. More recently, however, scholars have begun to realize the importance of the Book of Mormon as a piece of American religious literature and its role in shaping beliefs and culture.[21] In specific, the Book of Mormon offers tremendous insight into nineteenth-century religious thought. Its value to our understanding of antebellum American Protestantism should not be ignored or overlooked. To read the Book of Mormon as American pseudepigrapha is to catch a glimpse of key theological and social issues that animated nineteenth-century American religion, especially regarding popular opposition to Catholicism, Calvinism, Universalism, cessationism, atheism, and monarchy, as well as other issues such as unholiness, pride, secret societies, and social corruption.

Translation and the Coming Forth of the Book of Mormon

According to Joseph Smith's mother, Lucy Mack Smith, the first time she laid eyes on the Book of Mormon source material was in September 1827, after her son burst through the door of their small cabin. The gold plates were wrapped in a linen frock, secured by Smith, who was "speechless from fright and the fatigue of running."[22] Breathlessly, he recounted being accosted by assailants who attempted to steal them for their commercial value after learning about his discovery of ancient artifacts.[23] But, for Smith, the plates were worth far more than the value of gold.

Four years earlier, in the dead of night on September 21, 1823, Smith was awakened by a strange light that grew brighter until it illuminated the entire room. Suddenly, there appeared a man, adorned in white clothing, standing, as it were, in midair.[24] The man, an angel named Moroni, told Smith how God had chosen him to "bring to pass a marvelous work and a wonder" involving the discovery of an ancient record.[25] Moroni was one of the prophet-historians mentioned earlier. The book, Moroni claimed, contained "the fullness of the everlasting Gospel as delivered by the Savior to the ancient inhabitants."[26] Over the course of a few years, Smith attended an annual *rendezvous* with

21. Gutjahr, *Book of Mormon*, 150–52.
22. Larry E. Morris, ed., *A Documentary History of the Book of Mormon* (New York: Oxford University Press, 2019), 185.
23. Morris, *Documentary History*, 185.
24. Joseph Smith–History 1:31–32.
25. Oliver Cowdery, "Letter IV," *M&A*, February 1835, 1:79, in H1:59.
26. JS, H1:223 [Joseph Smith–History 1:34].

Moroni near a hill called Cumorah at the burial site of the plates. Finally, he retrieved them on September 22, 1827.[27]

Buried with the plates were other artifacts, notably a device Smith called "spectacles"[28] and "Interpreters," or Urim and Thummim.[29] These were OT tools thought to have been consulted to determine the will of God (see Exod 28:30; Ezra 2:63; Neh 7:65). The Book of Mormon describes the interpreters as "two stones . . . fastened into the two rims of a bow" (Mosiah 28:13). Lucy Mack Smith similarly described them as "two smooth three-cornered diamonds set in glass, and the glasses were set in silver bows, which were connected with each other in much the same way as old-fashioned spectacles."[30] The Urim and Thummim enabled Smith to translate the text, which resembled a peculiar form of "reformed Egyptian" (Mormon 9:32).[31]

Smith was reluctant to offer more than scant details about the translation process, preferring to emphasize his revelatory principles rather than delving into specifics.[32] Eyewitness accounts, however, provide common details. Smith employed a series of scribes as he dictated the text. At times, in the vicinity of the plates, he utilized the Urim and Thummim by placing them into a hat and concealing them in darkness by burying his face in the hat.[33] Then, according to witness Joseph Knight, "he would take a sentence and it would appear in bright, Roman letters."[34] David Whitmer described it as "spiritual light" in the darkness of the hat.[35] Smith would then read aloud the sentence, "word for word," recalled his wife, Emma, "and when he came to proper names he could not pronounce, or long words, he spelled them out."[36] After returning from breaks, Emma said, Joseph "commenced again, [beginning] where he left off without any hesitation."[37] An error-proofing phenomenon prevented mistakes. Knight remembered how in the case of error, the bright translation "would not go away till it was right."[38] Smith's confidence in this work led him to assure pessimists that "the Book

27. Joseph Smith–History 1:59.
28. JS, ca. 1832 history, H1:15.
29. Oliver Cowdery to William W. Phelps, *M&A*, October 1834, 1:14, in H1:41.
30. Morris, *Documentary History*, 183.
31. Morris, *Documentary History*, 188, 231, 240, 245.
32. James E. Lancaster, "The Translation of the Book of Mormon," in *The Word of God: Essays on Mormon Scripture*, ed. Dan Vogel (Salt Lake City: Signature Books, 1990), 97.
33. Michael Hubbard MacKay and Gerrit J. Dirkmaat, "Firsthand Witness Accounts of the Translation Process," in *The Coming Forth of the Book of Mormon: A Marvelous Work and a Wonder*, ed. Dennis L. Largey et al. (Salt Lake City: Deseret Book, 2015), 68–70.
34. Morris, *Documentary History*, 79.
35. David Whitmer, *An Address to All Believers in Christ by a Witness to the Divine Authenticity of the Book of Mormon* (Richmond, MO: n.p., 1887), 12.
36. *EMD* 1:530.
37. *EMD* 1:530.
38. Morris, *Documentary History*, 79.

of Mormon was the most correct of any Book on earth & the keystone of our religion & a man would get nearer to God by abiding by its precepts than any other Book."[39]

Smith sometimes substituted the Urim and Thummim with a seer stone, a talisman used for scrying, the act of "seeing" supernatural visions through a medium.[40] He "was thought to be able to locate lost goods with a special seer stone and magical religious ceremonies," explained one historian.[41] The stone, Smith claimed, allowed him to see invisible things. According to Martin Harris, one of Smith's scribes, he used the seer stone in lieu of the Urim and Thummim for convenience.[42] Despite the different tools, the process was essentially the same. He translated "with his face buried in his hat, with the stone in it," said Emma, adding that he had "neither manuscript nor book to read from."[43] Sometimes, Smith separated himself from his scribe by a curtain to prevent them from seeing the plates.[44] At other times, however, "the plates often lay on the table without any attempt at concealment, wrapped in a small linen tablecloth."[45] "I once felt of the plates," Emma said. "They seemed to be pliable like thick paper, and would rustle with a metallic sound when the edges were moved by the thumb."[46] William Smith, Joseph's younger brother, also reported how some in his immediate family shared the same experience, having "handled them and hefted them while wrapped in a tow frock" but never seeing them uncovered.[47]

Some witnesses claimed to have seen the plates. At the end of the first edition of the Book of Mormon (and present in modern editions) were testimonies by two sets of witnesses. The first witnesses claimed to have "seen the engravings which are upon the plates" while the second witnesses said that they handled the plates, having "hefted" them. John Whitmer, one of the witnesses, maintained his testimony about the plates despite being excommunicated from the church, lending credence to his word. However, Martin Harris, another witness, complicated his testimony by having "repeatedly admitted the internal, subjective nature of his visionary experience," argued one

39. JS, remarks, November 28, 1841, *JSP*.
40. Some Latter-day Saints challenge Smith's use of a seer stone. See, for example, James W. Lucas and Jonathan E. Neville, *By Means of the Urim & Thummim: Restoring Translation to the Restoration* (Salt Lake City: Digital Legend Press, 2023).
41. H. Michael Marquardt and Wesley P. Walters, *Inventing Mormonism: Tradition and the Historical Record* (Salt Lake City: Signature Books, 1998), 63.
42. "One of the Three Witnesses," *Deseret Evening News*, December 13, 1881.
43. *EMD* 1:539.
44. Howe, Eber D., *Mormonism Unvailed* (Salt Lake City: Signature Books, 2015), 380.
45. Morris, *Documentary History*, 300.
46. Morris, *Documentary History*, 300.
47. "Another Testimony," *Deseret Evening News*, January 20, 1894.

historian.[48] When pressed by interrogators, Harris claimed to have seen the plates with his "spiritual eyes" or "the eye of faith."[49]

For traditional Christians, the translation methods of the Book of Mormon seem too unfamiliar and incredible to be considered akin to the work of biblical translation. The process Smith and witnesses described is better thought of as revelatory transcription than true translation.[50] LDS Church historians have described the Book of Mormon as the "most prominent among Joseph Smith's revelatory dictations" while acknowledging Smith "described [it] as a translation."[51] Smith had barely studied his native English, let alone an ancient, dead language with no corroborating evidence for its existence. There is no Rosetta Stone for reformed Egyptian, nor are there facsimiles of the text to study. And unlike biblical translation, images of Smith parsing verbs with lexicons strewn about a table are inaccurate.

Regardless of how it occurred, Smith and his scribes produced a manuscript by July 1829, and, as it was delivered for typesetting, the public buzzed with speculation and gossip about it coming forth. That summer, rumors of the new scripture circulated. In June, *The Wayne Sentinel*, a weekly newspaper in Smith's hometown, confirmed the dawn of the "*Golden Bible*."[52] The paper's editor, Egbert B. Grandin, also happened to be the Book of Mormon's publisher and bookseller. Smith secured publishing 5,000 copies in Palmyra for the sum of $3,000.[53] On March 26, 1830, a local newspaper published the title page of the Book of Mormon and advertised it was "now for sale . . . at the Palmyra Bookstore by Howard & Grandin."[54] From its initial publication to today, the Book of Mormon has been translated into many languages, distributed in nearly every nation, printed millions of times, and read by countless people.[55]

Summary

While Joseph Smith claimed to have miraculously translated the Book of Mormon from ancient sources, non-LDS scholars are reluctant to believe

48. *EMD* 2:254–55.
49. John H. Gilbert, "Memorandum," September 8, 1892, in *EMD* 2:548.
50. Scholars have offered an array of interpretive explanations to describe the translation process, both JS's activity and the materials involved. See Brant A. Gardner, *The Gift and Power: Translating the Book of Mormon* (Salt Lake City: Greg Kofford Books, 2011), 137–96; Samuel Morris Brown, "Seeing the Voice of God: The Book of Mormon on Its Own Translation," in MacKay, Ashurst-McGee, and Hauglid, *Producing Ancient Scripture*; Richard L. Bushman, *Joseph Smith's Gold Plates: A Cultural History* (New York: Oxford University Press, 2023), 8–26.
51. D1:xxviii.
52. Morris, *Documentary History*, 485 (emphasis original).
53. H1:352.
54. *The Wayne Sentinel* (Palmyra, NY), March 26, 1830.
55. Grant Hardy, ed., *The Annotated Book of Mormon* (New York: Oxford University Press, 2023), 785.

him. Moreover, skeptics reject the claims of Latter-day Saints regarding the historicity of the Book of Mormon due to a lack of convincing evidence. This rejection challenges a core element of Smith's claim to prophetic authority, making it a contentious issue between traditional Christians and Latter-day Saints. But the Book of Mormon holds tremendous value in understanding nineteenth-century American religion and Mormonism.

REFLECTION QUESTIONS

1. What, if any, are the limitations to viewing the Book of Mormon as only either divine scripture or a fraudulent hoax?

2. When read as American pseudepigrapha, how might the Book of Mormon help American Christians understand their own religious history?

3. What are your general impressions concerning the methodology of the translation of the Book of Mormon? How do these compare to your understanding of biblical translation?

4. Why do you suppose the authenticity of Joseph Smith's claims to divine authority are so closely linked to the Book of Mormon?

5. Given the contentious nature of rejecting Joseph Smith's account of the translation and coming forth of the Book of Mormon, how ought Christians approach the matter with Latter-day Saints?

QUESTION 15

What Is the Doctrine and Covenants?

"We'll praise him for a prophet's voice, His people's steps to guide:
In this, we do and will rejoice, Tho' all the world deride."[1]
~ Eliza R. Snow, Latter-day Saint Poet

The Doctrine and Covenants is an open collection of revelatory writings from LDS prophets bound by a general theme of building the eschatological Zion. It is perhaps the least familiar of all LDS doctrine to traditional Christians, and yet it is the scriptural origin of Mormonism's most unique practices like polygamy, temples, and baptism for the dead. Moreover, the scripture shows the radically unconventional and unparalleled authority Joseph Smith enjoyed as the spiritual leader of the Church of Jesus Christ of Latter-day Saints.

The Formation and Publication of the Doctrine and Covenants

The Doctrine and Covenants (D&C) opens with a proclamation: "Hearken, O ye people of my church, saith the voice of him who dwells on high" (D&C 1:1). "This is mine authority," God says, a "book of mine commandments" (D&C 1:6).

This 1831 record from Smith radically challenges established assumptions about the nature of divine revelation within Christianity. His revision of the Bible was well underway (see question 12), and the Book of Mormon had been in circulation for over a year. But the Doctrine and Covenants was different. The Bible and Book of Mormon were records of God's past revelation to former-day saints while the Doctrine and Covenants was God's present voice to Latter-day Saints. Smith wasn't merely extending the canon with newly discovered ancient scripture—he was expounding on the very nature of scripture per se, dictating divine commandments in the latter days. The church was like a new Israel and

1. Eliza R. Snow, "Praise Ye the Lord," *M&A*, August 1835, 1:175.

Smith their new Moses (see D&C 28:2). For them, God not only had spoken in scripture but also was speaking through new scripture written by Smith. No wonder his followers commissioned him "to receive and write Revelations & Commandments for this Church."[2] Unlike the ancient church of the former days, which discerned inspired texts over generations, the LDS Church commissioned a record of their new scripture from the very beginning.

With the help of scribes, Smith "began to arrange and copy the revelations which we had received from time to time," he said, which proved to be a challenging task.[3] He rejected verbal dictation—that God dictated new revelation word for word—and further denied his revelations were perfect even in final written form. Instead, Smith explained, God condescended to the church by giving his commandments "unto my Servents [*sic*] in their weakness after the manner of their Language,"[4] which was "crooked, broken, scattered, and imperfect."[5] Worse yet, Smith felt restricted in his ability to write, trapped in a "little narrow prison" of "paper, pen, and ink."[6] So, to ensure the integrity of God's message, Smith was tasked to "correct those errors or mistakes which he may discover by the holy Spirit while reviewing the revelations & commandments."[7] Edits and revisions of the text for the sake of accuracy and clarity were to be expected. And revelation would not come all at once. It would drip from heaven, little by little, as God's latter-day revelations were revealed "line upon line, precept upon precept" (2 Nephi 28:30; cf. Isa 28:10).

Smith recorded his revelations in a style that imitates the King James Bible. Perhaps this was inescapable. One historian noted "how biblically saturated the discursive culture of antebellum America was."[8] The Bible and its language inundated Smith's cultural context, so it's unsurprising his revelations "are suffused with the concepts, images, and language of the King James Version."[9] Still, Smith could have risen above the milieu to write in the vernacular of his nineteenth-century readers. Instead, he favored the KJV style to align his writings with scriptural material already esteemed by Latter-day Saints. If his revelations sounded biblical, it is because he believed they *were* "biblical" in the sense that they shared the Bible's inspiration and authority.

By 1831, church leaders decided to print Smith's revelations in a "Book of commandments," but plans were delayed after a mob sacked their printing

2. Minutes, September 26, 1830, D1:192.
3. JS, H1:424.
4. MRB, 225 [D&C 1:24].
5. JS to William W. Phelps, November 27, 1832, D2:320.
6. JS to William W. Phelps, November 27, 1832, D2:320.
7. Minutes, November 8, 1831, D2:123.
8. Grant Underwood, "The Dictation, Compilation, and Canonization of Joseph Smith's Revelations," in *Foundational Texts of Mormonism: Examining Major Early Sources*, ed. Mark Ashurst-McGee, Robin S. Jensen, and Sharalyn D. Howcroft (New York: Oxford, 2018), 108.
9. Underwood, "Joseph Smith's Revelations," 108.

press in 1833, just as the collection was nearing publication.[10] Two years later, the church published *Doctrine and Covenants of the Church of the Latter Day Saints*. As its title implies, the first edition of Doctrine and Covenants contained two sections: a doctrinal portion titled "Lectures on Faith" (i.e., Doctrine) and another section containing Smith's revelations (i.e., Covenants). Subsequent editions expanded the collection with more material from Smith and other LDS prophets. The second edition, published in 1844, featured a few additional revelations and Smith's eulogy; he was murdered the same year. An 1876 edition included over twenty additional revelations, among them a section on the nature of marriage (i.e., its eternality and potential for plurality; see D&C 132). The 1890 Manifesto prohibiting polygamy was added in 1908. Thirteen years later, the "Lectures on Faith" were removed, and by 1981 other canonical writings were added, including a second "Official Declaration" given in 1978 that revoked a priesthood ban against Black men (see question 20). The most recent edition features a total count of revelations of 138, the same amount since 1981.

The Content of the Doctrine and Covenants

The Doctrine and Covenants is dedicated to instructing Latter-day Saints on building their religious community. The first nineteen sections concern the organization of the early church, while sections 20–40 generally deal with ecclesiology and record early church activities. Sections 41–123 contain instructions on building up the new Jerusalem. Sections 124–135 feature many of the doctrinal hallmarks of Mormonism, such as building and operating a temple (124), baptism for the dead (127–128), the corporeal nature of God (130), and plural marriage (132). Much of its theological content is doctrinal clarification in light of LDS thought, especially through Smith's revelations.

Not all his revelations were published, though. Some were considered too mundane or personal to apply to the whole church.[11] Others, however, simply never rose to canonical prominence. Nevertheless, these revelations demonstrate Smith's self-perception as a prophet reaching into ancient mysteries to bring them to present-day light. For example, Zephaniah prophesied that in the latter days God would transform human speech into "a pure language, that they may all call upon the name of the Lord" (Zeph 3:9). Some commentators speculated God would miraculously turn back speech among Christians to the unified language humanity spoke before the confusion of Babel. Others wondered if the mysterious language was spoken in the garden of Eden, a precursor to Hebrew, or even Hebrew itself.[12]

10. Minutes, November 1–2, 1831, D2:97.
11. For a compilation of non-canonical revelations, see Stephen O. Smoot and Brian C. Passantino, eds., *Joseph Smith's Uncanonized Revelations* (Provo, UT: RCS, BYU, 2024).
12. Robert Wakefield, the first English Hebraist, argued Hebrew was the Edenic language and the *de facto* tongue until the confusion of Babel, and from then suffered corruption. See *On the Three Languages* (1524), trans. G. Lloyd Jones (Binghamton, NY: SUNY Binghamton

Smith held a similar view, believing the pure language was the tongue of Eden, and looked forward to a time when the Latter-day Saints "shall be endowed with a knowledge of hid[d]en languages."[13] As a seer, Smith believed that he held the power to retrieve this lost language. For him, rediscovering the Adamic tongue meant inching closer to the future new Jerusalem through the ancient garden of Eden.[14] He dabbled in speculative linguistics and claimed to have recovered some critical vocabulary. Smith believed, for example, that angels in the "pure Language" was "Awmen Angls-men," meaning God's "Ministerring [*sic*] servants."[15] A traditional interpretation of Zephaniah's prophecy suggests the "pure language" is best understood as "saving language," that God would enable people to "call upon the name of the Lord" (Zeph 3:9). As Paul proclaimed, "Whosoever shall call upon the name of the Lord shall be saved" (Rom 10:13).

The Importance of Doctrine and Covenants in Mormonism

Whether published or unpublished, Smith's revelations directed the church's theological and ecclesiastical development, a task that fell uniquely to him. That he believed his words were coequal in authority with scripture is self-evident. His revelations were not temporary nor meant for an elect few. Having been codified, Doctrine and Covenants is now one part of four in the standard works of Latter-day Saint scripture, available for all to read for generations to come.

For this reason, Doctrine and Covenants is, in a sense, a more extraordinary lengthening of the scriptural canon than the addition of the Book of Mormon. As argued earlier, the Book of Mormon could be considered American pseudepigrapha, so its relationship to the Bible parallels that of other pseudepigraphal texts (see question 14). While pseudepigrapha stand outside the canon, they are still valuable for communicating ideas about theological issues at the time of their writing. In this sense, Smith didn't author the Book of Mormon but merely contended for its status as scripture. Doctrine and Covenants, however, is Smith's explicit assertion of both; he is its primary author and advocate for its canonical status. "These words are not of man nor of men, but of me," wrote Smith in the voice of the Son of God.[16]

The Doctrine and Covenants is crucial for understanding Joseph Smith's evolving authority and the development of the church's distinctive practices.

Press, 1989). Others theorized similarly. See, for example, John Gill, *A Collection of Sermons and Tracts*, vol. 3 (London: George Keith, 1778), 449–50; and George Paxton, *Illustrations of the Holy Scriptures* (Edinburgh: Stirling and Kenney, 1825), 49.

13. JSJ, November 14, 1835, J1:100.
14. Samuel Morris Brown, *In Heaven as It Is on Earth: Joseph Smith and the Early Mormon Conquest of Death* (New York: Oxford University Press, 2012), 138–40.
15. MRB, 265.
16. JS, H1:458 [D&C 18:34].

While the Book of Mormon contains few uniquely Mormon doctrines, the Doctrine and Covenants introduces many of them, e.g., polygamy, baptism for the dead, temple rites. Yet even it does not represent the culmination of Smith's theological development. For that, we must turn to the Pearl of Great Price, where the most radical doctrinal expansions take shape.

Summary

The Doctrine and Covenants contains LDS revelations given from the earliest days of the Church of Jesus Christ of Latter-day Saints, most notably by Joseph Smith. Most of the work contains instructions for Latter-day Saints on forming and maintaining their community, but Doctrine and Covenants also codifies some unique Mormon beliefs, like baptism for the dead and the need for temples in the latter days. Not every revelation of LDS prophets is recorded in Doctrine and Covenants, but only those that have profoundly shaped the church's theological and ecclesiastical life.

REFLECTION QUESTIONS

1. In what ways is the Doctrine and Covenants different from the Book of Mormon? In what ways is it similar?

2. What is the Doctrine and Covenants, and what role does it play in the standard works of the LDS church?

3. It is possible the LDS Church could add sections to the Doctrine and Covenants, thereby extending Mormon scripture. How does this compare to your faith tradition?

4. Why do you believe not all of Joseph Smith's revelations were recorded in the Doctrine and Covenants?

5. Why is the Doctrine and Covenants critical to understanding Mormonism?

QUESTION 16

What Is the Pearl of Great Price?

"The PEARL OF GREAT PRICE will recommend itself to all who appreciate the revelations of truth as hidden treasures of Everlasting Life."[1]
~ Early Latter-day Saint Advertisement for *Pearl of Great Price*

The Pearl of Great Price (hereafter PGP) is a varied collection of writings by Joseph Smith, mainly revelatory translations and autobiographical material considered canonical by the Church of Jesus Christ of Latter-day Saints. In the same way Doctrine and Covenants provides a scriptural basis for unique practices in Mormonism, the PGP provides the foundation for many of the religion's distinctive doctrines, like polytheism, the premortal existence of humanity, and the positive quality to Adam's fall.

The PGP began as a pamphlet on the origins of Mormonism and its essential beliefs. Initially printed in 1851, the first edition was compiled by LDS missionary Franklin D. Richards, president of the British mission for the church. PGP enjoyed wide use in Great Britain as a convenient primer for theological and historical texts on par with the Latter-day Saint canon.[2] Richards's selections introduced readers to "comparatively unknown" revelations from Smith and detailed the church's origins.[3] The pamphlet included excerpts from Smith's revision of Genesis and Matthew, the book of Abraham (derived from Egyptian papyri) (see question 17), a brief autobiography of Smith highlighting the founding of the church, and a creedal formulation of

1. Franklin D. Richards, ed., "Etoile du Deseret . . . ," *MS*, July 15, 1851, 13:217.
2. Franklin D. Richards, ed., *The Pearl of Great Price: Being a Choice Selection from the Revelations, Translations, and Narrations of Joseph Smith, First Prophet, Seer, and Revelator to the Church of Jesus Christ of Latter-Day Saints* (Liverpool: Franklin Richards, 1851).
3. Richards, *Pearl of Great Price*, v–vi.

Mormon beliefs. Richards featured other material that the church removed by the time the PGP was canonized in 1880.[4]

The title *Pearl of Great Price* originates from a parable in the Gospel of Matthew. In it, Jesus likens one's reception of the kingdom of God to the discovery of a "pearl of great price" by a merchant, who then "went and sold all that he had, and bought it" (Matt 13:45–46). The lesson frames the pursuit of God's kingdom as sacrificial, requiring the forfeiture of something seemingly important for a joyous and greater good.[5] Early church father Augustine interpreted the pearl as godly wisdom.[6] The French Reformer John Calvin thought it was holy living.[7] Smith used the parable to encourage gathering in his latter-day Zion.[8] In what sense Richards had any of this in mind when naming his tract is unclear. Perhaps he chose the *Pearl of Great Price* to hint to readers that their quests for religious certainty were nearing the end, an implicit call to give up their former faith and embrace Mormonism. This could explain why Richards chose such exotic texts. For new converts, doctrines like human premortality and exaltation were not peculiarities; they were remedies. The PGP offered explanations to theological questions traditional Christian theologians could not—or would not—answer in a way that satisfied some seekers.

The Content of the Pearl of Great Price

Much of the PGP's content is covered throughout this book, either directly or indirectly. Smith's autobiographical material, for example, is sprinkled throughout the first section, as the Articles of Faith make appearances all throughout the next section. The book of Abraham is explored independently in the following question. For now, we will focus on two noteworthy sections of PGP: *Joseph Smith–Matthew* (JS–M) and the book of Moses.

In JS–M, Smith rearranged the verses of the Olivet Discourse (see Matt 23:39–24:51) to categorize Christ's teachings into two sections. The first, his teaching on the destruction of the temple, and the second, any sayings

4. Most texts removed from later editions were simply redundant because they also appear in Doctrine and Covenants (20, 27, 77, 87, and 107). However, the church deemed other material uncanonical, like Richards's short postlude, a poem titled "Oh Say, What Is Truth?" by John Jaques.
5. Barbara E. Reid, *The Gospel According to Matthew*, New Collegeville Bible Commentary (Collegeville, MN: Liturgical Press, 2005), 78–79; David L. Turner, *Matthew*, Baker Exegetical Commentary on the New Testament (Grand Rapids: Baker Academic, 2008), 352–53; Richard T. France, *The Gospel of Matthew*, New International Commentary on the New Testament (Grand Rapids: Eerdmans, 2007), 539.
6. Augustine, *Conf.* 8.1.2.
7. John Calvin, *Calvin's New Testament Commentaries*, ed. David W. Torrance and Thomas F. Torrance, trans. T. H. L. Parker, 12 vols. (Grand Rapids: Eerdmans, 1972), 2:82.
8. JS to the Elders of the Church, November 30–December 1, 1835, D5:99–100.

concerning the second coming.[9] Smith also clarified what he believed Christ meant by the prophecy, "This generation shall not pass, till all these things be fulfilled" (Matt 24:34). Did Jesus mean the generation of the disciples or some future generation who would experience the birth pains of the apocalypse? For Smith, these prophecies only apply to a future generation "in which these things shall be shown forth" (JS–M 1:34; cf. Matt 24:34).

If Smith aimed to clarify the Olivet Discourse, his goal with the book of Moses was far more ambitious. The book of Moses is a heavy revision of the creation narrative in the book of Genesis. The story holds an essential, yet mysterious, place in Christian theology. Within it, readers learn about the origins of the cosmos, especially the unique relationship humans enjoy with the Creator and the tragic fall from his glory. The language and form of the story have led to differing—and sometimes contradictory—interpretations. Contemporary readers debate their impressions of the text in the contested space of evolution versus creation, while the ancients wondered whether God created material already formed or potentially formable.[10] In the end, orthodoxy invites us to rest in the mystery of God's word by faith. "Whatever that great man had in mind when he uttered these words," wrote Augustine of Genesis's author, "I have no doubt . . . that he expressed it appropriately."[11]

For Smith, however, the latter days were marked by a time of supernatural retrieval of knowledge to answer the unanswerable. He appreciated the mysterious awe of the creation account but thought it ought not to be as puzzling as Christians assumed. Interpretive differences were not the result of limited imagination but lost information. Smith was not alone in thinking so. Eighteenth-century mystic Emmanuel Swedenborg explained how the ordinary reader was blind to arcane secrets in the creation narrative to which he was supernaturally privy. His interpretation of Genesis (*Arcana Coelestia*) posited a spiritual evolutionary process that enables humanity to achieve higher levels of existence through divine illumination.[12] Swedenborg thought each person was a divine embryo capable of staged development in spiritual knowledge to become "a celestial man."[13]

Smith held a similar anthropology but communicated it very differently. While Swedenborg relied on biblical texts, Smith believed the Bible itself had suffered attrition and required rehabilitation, especially the book of Genesis, which gave rise to his revision of the text in the book of Moses. Again, Smith

---

9. See Keith W. Perkins, "The JST on the Second Coming of Christ," in *The Joseph Smith Translation: The Restoration of Plain and Precious Things*, ed. Monte S. Nyman and Robert L. Millet (Provo, UT: RSC, BYU, 1985), 237–49.
10. *Conf.* 12.20.29.
11. *Conf.* 12.24.33.
12. Emanuel Swedenborg, *Arcana Coelestia*, ed. John Faulkner Potts, trans. John Clowes (West Chester, PA: Swedenborg Foundation, 2009), 11–12.
13. Swedenborg, *Arcana Coelestia*, 12.

is not unique in this belief. Numerous revisions and additions to Genesis have been written throughout the centuries, all seeking to clarify the text's meaning (e.g., The Book of Jubilees, Conflict of Adam and Eve with Satan, The Book of Jasher). Unlike these works, however, Smith's apparent purpose in revising Genesis was to resuscitate the primitive origins of the gospel in its purest form.

The book of Moses is a portion of Smith's revisions of the book of Genesis, which includes substantial additions to the Hebrew text. In the narrative, Moses was transfigured to commune with God and received a vision of creation, which occurred between God calling out from the burning bush (see Moses 1:17) and Moses's return to Egypt to lead the exodus (see Moses 1:26). Moses learned about the vast expanse of God's creation, "worlds without number" (Moses 1:33), and received divine insight into God's plan of redemption for this world (see Moses 1:32, 39). God explained the origins of Satan, who attempted to thwart God's plan by plotting "to destroy the agency of man" (*contra* Calvinism) but failed and was consequently "cast down" (Moses 4:3). God then created humanity, first in a spiritual premortality (see Moses 3:5) and then physically on earth through Adam and Eve, his image bearers (see Moses 2:27). After they exercised their agency to sin, the couple was expelled from the garden of Eden. God instructed Adam to offer sacrifices, which an angel explained is a foreshadowing of Christ's crucifixion (see Moses 5:5–8). Adam later learned how the Son's sacrifice "atoned for original guilt" (Moses 6:54), thus dissolving original sin, and was instructed on the need for faith, repentance, and baptism in the name of the "Only Begotten Son, which is Jesus Christ" (Moses 6:52).

Adam praised God for his fallen state as a blessing, not a curse. Because of his sin, Adam could experience the joy of salvation and generate humanity (see Moses 5:10). He and Eve encouraged their children in their faith, but not all believed (see Moses 5:15). This faithlessness became especially apparent in Cain, whose alliance with Satan earned him the apparently proto-masonic title "Master Mahan" (Moses 5:31), the steward of a treacherous secret: power is gained by murder. Generations passed until rebellion nearly overwhelmed humanity. To prevent total apostasy, God called the prophet Enoch to restore lost truth (see Moses 6:27–68), build up the city of Zion (see Moses 7:17–19), and expound Christ's eschatological mission with incredible clarity (see Moses 7:54–67). Still, rebellious humanity refused to listen and became subject to the watery judgment of a universal flood, except for Noah and his family (see Moses 8:17–30).

Looking Closer at the Book of Moses

Like the Book of Mormon, the book of Moses offered firm positions to some of the most pressing debates in Smith's day. It discouraged readers from engaging in Freemasonry because "secret combinations" (or secret societies) are associated with death and the devil. The text evidently assumed the mark of Cain was physiological to visually distinguish his descendants from others (see Moses 5:40; 7:22; cf. Gen 4:15). Calvinist doctrines of grace were rejected (see Moses 4:3) while Pelagianism was endorsed (see Moses 6:54). Smith also attempted to settle more complicated theological questions, like the apparent oddity of two separate accounts of creation. The first two chapters of Genesis are not slightly different versions of the same account; instead, they are a couplet describing two stages of creation with the spiritual preceding the physical (see Moses 3:5).

One of the most intriguing elements Smith injects into the story concerns humanity's procreation (or lack thereof) in Eden. In the book of Moses, Adam and Eve are commanded to "be fruitful and multiply" (Moses 2:28), just as they are in the Bible (see Gen 1:28), but readers of Genesis are not told whether children were born before the fall. Cain and Abel's births come after the fall (see Gen 4:1), as were their siblings' births (see Gen 5:4). Some theologians throughout church history have argued Adam and Eve's relationship was sexual and capable of procreation. Ambrosiaster,[14] Thomas Aquinas,[15] Martin Luther,[16] John Milton,[17] Herman Bavinck,[18] and C. S. Lewis[19] suggested intimacy in Eden was pure and lust-free, but sin perverted sexual desire into selfish and unbridled excess. Others, especially many patristic theologians, viewed sexual procreation as part of the fallen human experience. Smith sought to settle this debate. Adam and Eve would not procreate (nor enter mortal probation) until eating the fruit of the tree of knowledge of good and evil. Any chance of them procreating in Eden, then, is nullified. "Because that Adam fell," Smith explained, "we are" (Moses 6:48).[20] The Book of Mormon affirms this position. Had Adam not sinned, he and his wife would have remained in Eden forever and "they would have no children" (2 Nephi 2:22–23). It isn't until after the fall that "they began to multiply and replenish the earth" (Moses 5:2) because, as Eve explains, "were it not for our transgression we never should have had seed" (Moses 5:11). Indeed, for Mormonism, Eve's fall is not loss to be grieved but gain to be lauded. LDS apostle Dallin H. Oaks

---

14. David G. Hunter, "'On the Sin of Adam and Eve': A Little-Known Defense of Marriage and Childbearing by Ambrosiaster," *The Harvard Theological Review* 82, no. 3 (1989): 292.
15. Aquinas, *Summa Theologica* I–II.98.1.
16. *LW* 1:104, 168.
17. Matthew Stallard, ed., *Paradise Lost: The Biblically Annotated Edition* (Macon, GA: Mercer University Press, 2011), 145.
18. Herman Bavinck, *Sin and Salvation in Christ*, vol. 3 of *Reformed Dogmatics*, ed. John Bolt, trans. John Vriend (Grand Rapids: Baker Academic, 2006), 30.
19. C. S. Lewis, *Out of the Silent Planet* (New York: Macmillan, 1965), 72–74.
20. Scott H. Faulring, Kent P. Jackson, and Robert J. Matthews, eds., *Joseph Smith's New Translation of the Bible: Original Manuscripts* (Provo, UT: RSC, BYU, 2004), 101.

encouraged Latter-day Saints to "celebrate Eve's act and honor her wisdom and courage in the great episode called the Fall."[21]

But Smith's canonized interpretation creates interesting problems. To begin, it pits two commands of God against each other, forcing Adam and Eve to disobey one command to obey the other. On the one hand, the couple were commanded to "be fruitful and multiply" (Moses 2:28; cf. Gen 1:28). On the other hand, they were commanded not to eat from the tree of knowledge of good and evil (see Moses 3:16–17; cf. Gen 2:16–17). If Adam and Eve would not procreate prior to the fall, then they faced an impassible quandary—never to eat nor procreate or to eat and multiply. Aquinas imagined such a scenario and cautioned that unless one accepts the possibility of procreation in Eden, then "man's sin would have been absolutely necessary in order that such a great good might follow from it."[22] But this is precisely Smith's position. By divine design, Adam and Eve sinned against God to obey him. Such a conclusion renders divine command dysfunctional, especially considering Eve's punishment for sin.

In the wake of their rebellion, God issued the consequences of sin to Adam and Eve. Their punishments were different but united by the theme of hardship. They would find it difficult to perform tasks given to them by God. For Adam, who was placed in the garden "to dress it, and to keep it" (Moses 3:15; cf. Gen 2:15), his gardening labor (Heb. *'itstsabon*) in the soil would become sorrowfully toilsome (see Moses 4:23–25; cf. Gen 3:17–19). For Eve, who joined Adam as a "help meet" (Gen 2:18) in their duty to multiply, her delivery labor (Heb. *'itstsabon*) in child birthing would also become sorrowfully toilsome. More precisely, God says to her, "I will greatly *multiply* thy sorrow and thy conception" (Moses 4:22; cf. Gen 3:16, emphasis added). For something to increase implies its presence, as if until then Eve enjoyed less painful birth while Adam experienced less challenging gardening. Now, however, hardship would hinder their efforts to obey God.

Finally, if Adam and Eve were never to have borne any children pre-fall, then their first sin had less to do with fruit than it did with seed. By refraining from procreating, the original sin would have been one of omission, or not doing what they were commanded. In other words, Adam and Eve first disobeyed God when they refused to "be fruitful and multiply" in the garden. Instead, the Bible is clear that the first sin was one of commission, or doing what ought not to be done—eating the forbidden fruit. For this reason, the biblical text generously lends itself to the conclusion that Adam and Eve

21. Dallin H. Oaks, "The Great Plan of Happiness" (lecture, General Conference of The Church of Jesus Christ of Latter-day Saints, Salt Lake City, UT, October 3, 1993).
22. Thomas Aquinas, *Treatise on Human Nature: The Complete Text* (*Summa Theologiae I, Questions 75–102*), trans. Alfred J. Freddoso (South Bend, IN: St. Augustine's Press, 2010), 316.

either did, may have, or would eventually bear children in the garden without eating the fruit, contrary to Smith's interpretation. That Adam and Eve could never or would not procreate in Eden is an unviable interpretation, and even Smith's revision of the text retains enough of the original narrative to attest to this observation.

Summary

First published as a pamphlet to supplement LDS scripture, the Pearl of Great Price rose to canonical status with the Bible, Book of Mormon, and Doctrine and Covenants. It offers readers a glimpse into the origin of the Church of Jesus Christ of Latter-day Saints, according to Joseph Smith, while also providing the canonical foundation for many of Mormonism's distinct beliefs (e.g., plurality of gods, premortality, and a fortunate fall). The scripture also veers Mormonism away from traditional Protestant concepts like original sin and the bondage of the will.

REFLECTION QUESTIONS

1. What do you believe Christ meant by the "pearl of great price" in Matthew 13:45–46? How might a Latter-day Saint agree or disagree with you?

2. An apparent motivation for Smith to revise the Olivet Discourse was to explain what Christ meant by saying "this generation" would not pass until all things would be fulfilled (Matt 24:34). How do you interpret this text?

3. Concerning the fall of Adam, the Pearl of Great Price softens what traditional Christianity has long viewed as a catastrophic tragedy. What consequences do you believe follow from the LDS "fortunate fall" concerning sin and salvation?

4. What does it mean to you that Joseph Smith felt permission to revise the narratives of Genesis?

5. Do you agree or disagree with the possibility of procreation by Adam and Eve in the garden of Eden? Why or why not? How might your position shape conversation with a Latter-day Saint?

QUESTION 17

What Is the Book of Abraham?

"And they, that is the Gods, organized and formed the heavens and the earth."
~ Book of Abraham 4:1

The Church of Jesus Christ of Latter-day Saints considers the book of Abraham a translation by Joseph Smith of an ancient text that narrates the biblical patriarch's journey from Chaldea to Egypt and his reception of doctrine revealed by God. The text is small, roughly the length of the book of Hebrews, but its contribution to the development of Mormon doctrine is immense. Out of the book of Abraham emerges LDS doctrine on the eternality of human souls and their premortal experience, the plan of salvation by a savior from eternity past, and the material organization of creation by gods at the beginning of time. It is perhaps the most controversial scriptural text Smith ever created (so far as content is concerned), yet it is also the most crucial among his works to the development of Latter-day Saint cosmology, anthropology, and soteriology. Unlike the source material for the Book of Mormon—which Smith excavated from the earth and its whereabouts are now unknown—the book of Abraham was sourced from a collection of Egyptian antiquities, a portion of which presently resides with the Church History Library in Salt Lake City.

The Origin of the Book of Abraham

America was gripped with "Egyptomania" when Smith acquired a collection of Egyptian artifacts in 1835.[1] The young nation could not get enough

1. For a history of Western obsession with ancient Egypt, see Jasmine Day, *The Mummy's Curse: Mummymania in the English-Speaking World* (London: Routledge, 2006); Bob Brier, *Egyptomania: Our Three Thousand Year Obsession with the Land of the Pharaohs* (New

of ancient Egypt. Its history and culture mesmerized Americans, although myths and legends about pharaohs and gods formed their imagination more than the scholarly field of Egyptology we are familiar with today. In the nineteenth century, everyone from tots to tycoons crowded to hear lectures on archeological discoveries and to catch a glimpse of sarcophagi, mummies, and papyri covered in mysterious hieroglyphs. Antiquities dealers and itinerant showmen exhibited private collections for profit, rarely struggling to find an audience.

Egypt was seen as a mystical source of ancient power and wisdom, a depository of secrets waiting to be discovered. Christians were especially interested in the budding field of Egypt studies for its potential religious value. Though shrouded in mystery, the material culture of ancient Egypt offered them a tangible connection to their scriptural heritage. The Passover and Israel's exodus from Egypt are central and recurring themes throughout the Bible, especially for NT writers about Jesus Christ (see Matt 2:15; 1 Cor 5:7; 1 Pet 1:19; Jude 5). Biblical scholars in Smith's day busied themselves searching for scientific evidence among archeological discoveries that might verify the Bible. Buried in the sands of Egyptology might be evidence and answers waiting to be discovered. Smith viewed Egyptian antiquities a bit differently. He likely hoped for the potential of Egyptian artifacts to confirm literal readings of the Bible (i.e., a literal exodus), but he also believed the artifacts harbored the potential for restoring lost spiritual truth. Encrypted in hieroglyphs might be the residue of an ancient faith he sought to restore.

Thus, Smith was elated when he encountered antiquities dealer Michael Chandler in the summer of 1835, who showcased his collection, which included two papyrus scrolls and an assortment of fragments.[2] Chandler was equally excited to learn Smith's reputation for translating unknown languages. Although the Rosetta Stone had been discovered earlier, its role in deciphering Egyptian hieroglyphics was still coming to light. Smith purchased mummies and papyri from Chandler, and afterward revealed a significant discovery—a portion of the collection "contained the writings of Abraham."[3] According to LDS apostle Orson Pratt, Smith did not realize the significance of this collection until the "Lord told him they were sacred records, containing the inspired writings of Abraham when he was in Egypt."[4] Smith immediately attempted to translate some of its text, although he left little description of his technique. Presumably, Smith worked "by the gift and power of God," similar to how he translated the reformed Egyptian of the Book of Mormon plates (see Mormon

York: Palgrave Macmillan, 2013); Ronald H. Fritze, *Egyptomania: A History of Fascination, Obsession and Fantasy* (London: Reaktion Books, 2016).

2. See John Whitmer, 1831–ca. 1847 history, H2:86.
3. Joseph Smith, History, 1838–1856, vol. B-1, *JSP*, 596.
4. Orson Pratt, "Discourse by Elder Orson Pratt," *Deseret News* (Salt Lake City) 27, no. 40 (November 6, 1878).

9:32), and may have been aided by his seer stone.[5] Smith began drafting a pictographic alphabet either before or while attempting to translate hieroglyphs, but his efforts stalled by the fall of 1835.[6] In early 1842, however, Smith and his assistants finished a significant portion of their project, a text they published serially in the *Times and Seasons* titled "A Translation of some ancient Records . . . called the Book of ABRAHAM."[7] Two years after Smith's death, the surviving papyri came into the custody of his wife, Emma, while most of the translation manuscripts—including the handwritten texts produced during the book of Abraham project—remained with followers of Brigham Young.[8] The book of Abraham was subsequently printed in a pamphlet titled *The Pearl of Great Price* (1851), and canonized in 1880 (see question 16).

Critical Evaluation of the Book of Abraham

As early as 1860, Egyptologists disputed the biblical connection Smith believed was present in his papyri collection. Based on Smith's published facsimiles, Théodule Devéria argued the illustrations he relied on for translation were related to Egyptian funerary rites, not, as Smith claimed, scenes and revelations of Abraham.[9] Later Egyptologists shared Devéria's assessment, but their suspicions were impossible to verify without access to the original collection. After Smith's death, the papyri and mummies passed to his mother, Lucy Mack Smith. Upon her death in 1856, ownership of the collection transferred to Smith's widow, Emma, who sold the collection someone who, in turn, divided and sold the artifacts. One portion eventually made its way to a museum in Chicago, where it was presumably destroyed in the Great Chicago Fire of 1871. Another portion, however, passed down through the man's housekeeper and her family. In 1947, that set was sold to the Metropolitan Museum of Art. In 1967, the Met transferred ten surviving fragments to the LDS Church.[10] Though only a small part of the original 1835 collection survives, it includes the source material for what Smith published as "Facsimile No. 1" in *The Pearl of Great Price*.[11]

---

5. Stephen O. Smoot, "Did Joseph Smith Use a Seer Stone in the Translation of the Book of Abraham?," *Religious Educator* 23, no. 2 (2022): 64–107. See also Smoot et al., "How Did Joseph Smith Translate the Book of Abraham?," *BYU Studies* 61, no. 4 (2022): 29–43.
6. R4:xxiv–xxvi.
7. See JS, ed., "A Translation," *T&S*, March 1, 1842, 3:703–6; "The Book of Abraham," *T&S*, March 15, 1842, 3:719–22; and insert, *T&S*, May 16, 1842, 3:783–84. The Saints also called the collection "the Records of Abraham" (JSJ, February 25, 1842, J2:36) and "the Records of father Abraham" (JSJ, March 1, 1842, J2:39).
8. R4:xxviii.
9. Jules Remy and Julius Brenchley, *A Journey to Great Salt Lake City*, 2 vols. (London: W. Jeffs, 1861), 2:540–46.
10. R4:8.
11. "An Interview with Dr. Fischer," *Dialogue* 2, no. 4 (1967): 55; see also R4:xxix.

This rediscovery was significant because it represents the only extant sample of any original source for Smith's revelatory translative works. Unlike the Book of Mormon—the plates of which are inaccessible—the book of Abraham translation could, in part, be verified or refuted by scholars. Once the collection was evaluated and the relevant sections translated, Devéria's skepticism was confirmed; the fragments were sourced from Egyptian funerary material dating to the Greco-Roman period (322 BC to AD 284), many centuries after Abraham.[12] If Smith's work is still to be considered a translation of the text recovered in the 1960s, then it is, in the words of one Egyptologist, an "esoteric interpretation of hieroglyphics" that envisions the characters as symbolic rather than literal.[13]

Latter-day Saints who maintain the relationship between the papyri and book of Abraham have put forward theories to explain the linguistic distance between the original text and Smith's translation. Some have suggested the originals acted more like a catalyst to spur Smith's prophetic imagination. Others, like Egyptologist John Gee, tentatively posit that Smith translated the book of Abraham from non-extant papyri from the original collection but he cautioned that his theory is not "as neat or as compelling as one might wish."[14] Critics of Smith are quick to assume he fabricated the entire translation process, knowing all along there was never any relationship between what was written and what he was writing. But Smith and his scribes evidently attempted to develop grammatical tools to aid their translation, which, as one researcher argued, frames Smith's research of the Egyptian language as a sincere attempt to understand how it really worked.[15] Smith was not crafting a hoax; he believed his project

12. Marc Coenen, "The Ownership and Dating of Certain Joseph Smith Papyri," in *The Joseph Smith Egyptian Papyri: A Complete Edition*, ed. Robert K. Ritner (Salt Lake City: The Smith-Pettit Foundation, 2011), 57.
13. Lanny Bell, "The Ancient Egyptian 'Books of Breathing,' the Mormon 'Book of Abraham,' and the Development of Egyptology in America," in *Egypt and Beyond: Essays Presented to Leonard H. Lesko upon His Retirement from the Wilbour Chair of Egyptology at Brown University, June 2005*, eds. Stephen E. Thompson and Peter Der Manuelian (Providence, RI: Brown University Press, 2008), 30.
14. John Gee, *An Introduction to the Book of Abraham* (Salt Lake City: Deseret Book, 2017), 86. For recent scholarly engagement with the book of Abraham, see Terryl Givens, *The Pearl of Greatest Price: Mormonism's Most Controversial Scripture* (New York: Oxford University Press, 2019), 140–69; Brian M. Hauglid, "'Translating an Alphabet to the Book of Abraham': Joseph Smith's Study of the Egyptian Language and His Translation of the Book of Abraham," in Michael Hubbard MacKay, Mark Ashurst-McGee, and Brian M. Hauglid, *Producing Ancient Scripture: Joseph Smith's Translation Projects in the Development of Mormon Christianity* (Salt Lake City: University of Utah Press, 2020), 363–89; Dan Vogel, *Book of Abraham Apologetics: A Review and Critique* (Salt Lake City: Signature Books, 2021); and Stephen O. Smoot et al., "A Guide to the Book of Abraham," *BYU Studies* 61, no. 4 (2022).
15. See Brian M. Hauglid, "Translating an Alphabet" and "The Book of Abraham and the Egyptian Project: 'A Knowledge of Hidden Languages,'" in *Approaching Antiquity: Joseph Smith and the Ancient World*, ed. Lincoln H. Blumell, Matthew J. Grey, and Andrew H. Hedges (Salt Lake City: Deseret Book, 2015) 363–89, 474–511. Relatedly, Michael MacKay

was a genuine work of translation, likely due to his own self-identity as a seer and translator (see question 5). If the papyri served as the source material for the book of Abraham text, however, then Smith operated off the faulty assumption—apparently given by God—that the source materials were genuinely Abrahamic, which they were not. His unwillingness to consider them anything other than a record of Abraham set Smith on a trajectory to produce a translation sharing no linguistic relation to the source text.[16]

The Content of the Book of Abraham

The book of Abraham (Abr.) acts like a sequel to the book of Moses (see question 16), opening with God calling Abraham to a promised land (see Abr. 1:1; cf. Gen 12:1).[17] He is depicted as a righteous man who holds an ancient priesthood (see Abr. 1:2–3) in contrast to his idolatrous fathers (see Abr. 1:5), whose apostasy from God encouraged human sacrifice to Egyptian deities (see Abr. 1:9–11). Abraham himself was nearly sacrificed until God miraculously rescued him (see Abr. 1:12, 15). Famine in Chaldea prompted Abraham to migrate to Canaan (see Abr. 1:30, 2:3–4).[18] During the trip, God covenanted with Abraham (see Abr. 2:8–11; cf. Gen 12:2–3), and after his arrival, another famine pushed Abraham into Egypt (see Abr. 2:21; cf. Gen 12:10). God instructed Abraham to tell the Egyptians that his wife, Sarah, was his sister to prevent them from killing Abraham and stealing her (see Abr. 2:22–25; cf. Gen 12:11–13). Before entering Egypt, Abraham consulted the Urim and Thummim, which revealed a cosmology where time and space are relative to their proximity to God (see Abr.

---

and Daniel Belnap suggest this project was simply a continuation of an ongoing attempt to retrieve the lost "pure language" of antiquity and beyond ("The Pure Language Project," *Journal of Mormon History* 49, no. 4 [2023]: 1–44).

16. Some Latter-day Saint scholars suggested the possibility that Smith's translation is based on missing or non-extant papyri or is a stand-alone revelation. See Stephen O. Smoot et al., "The Relationship Between the Book of Abraham and the Joseph Smith Papyri," *BYU Studies* 61, no. 4 (2022): 50–55.
17. The book of Moses concludes with the beginning of God's call for Noah to construct his ark (see Moses 8:30; cf. Gen 6:13). While Smith continued to revise Genesis from 6:14 to 24:41, the book of Abraham injects substantive addition to the narrative.
18. A slight discrepancy between the book of Abraham and book of Genesis occurs here. Both accounts record God's command to the patriarch: "Abraham, get thee out of thy country, and from thy kindred, and from thy father's house, unto a land that I will show thee" (Abr. 2:3; cf. Gen 12:1). The book of Abraham situates this call in "the land of Ur, of the Chaldees" (Abr. 2:4), whereas the book of Genesis locates this event in Haran (Gen 11:32–12:1), where Terah had taken his family after departing from Ur (Gen 11:31) and subsequently died (see Gen 11:32). The Genesis narrative does not describe a return to Chaldea. In fact, after God's call to "Get thee out of thy country" (Gen 12:1), Abraham "departed out of Haran" as he and his family "went forth to go into the land of Canaan" (Gen 12:5). However, Acts 7:2–4 affirms that God appeared to Abraham while he was still in Mesopotamia, "before he dwelt in Haran," suggesting the book of Abraham's account may reflect greater familiarity with this New Testament framing.

3:1–16); the existence of an ungenerated, eternal divine intelligence and premortality of souls (see Abr. 3:17–19, 22–23); a creation from preexisting matter (rather than *ex nihilo*) by a council of eternal intelligences (see Abr. 3:23–24), the mortal probation of humanity (see Abr. 3:24–25), God's election of the Son of Man as his messiah (see Abr. 3:27); and the origin of Satan (see Abr. 3:28).[19] The book of Abraham concludes with an account of the gods' organization of creation according to the order found in Genesis 1–2 (see Abr. 4:1–5:21; cf. Gen 1:1–2:20).[20] Many of these concepts will be explored in subsequent questions. For now, we will consider the minor revisions Smith made to the book of Genesis, especially concerning the character of Abraham.

In many ways, the biblical story of Abraham is a parable for anyone who has ever struggled with faith and obedience. His life testifies of the transformative power of divine grace, which gradually reforms hearts through spiritual maturity. He is a faithful yet flawed man, so his story isn't clean. It wasn't meant to be. Abraham begins his walk with God by walking away from the "other gods" (Josh 24:2–3) with only God's promise to go on (see Gen 12:1–3). In this way, Abraham is an exemplar. "The right thing to do," commented Augustine, "is to believe God before he pays up anything, because just as he cannot possibly lie, so he cannot deceive. . . . That's how Abraham believed him."[21] But Abraham also sinned, most notoriously by exposing his wife to abuse not once but twice (see Gen 12:10–20; 20:1–7). In both instances, Abraham is portrayed as fearing powerful men he believed would murder him to steal his wife, so he convinced her to conceal their marriage by emphasizing their blood relation (see Gen 12:11–13; 20:1–2). Yet, each time, the faithlessness of Abraham is offset by the faithfulness of God, who rescued Sarah (see Gen 12:17; 20:6–7).

Abraham's polytheistic ancestry and bizarre exploitation of Sarah have long troubled and confused commentators. Throughout centuries, writers developed a tradition of expanding the narratives with "gap filling details and fullblown backstories" in part to help explain these difficulties.[22] Genesis isn't

---

19. Some LDS scholars see parallels and affinities between the book of Abraham cosmology and creation story and those of ancient Near East texts. See, for example, Stephen O. Smoot, "Council, Chaos, and Creation in the Book of Abraham," *JBMS* 22, no. 2 (2013): 28–39; Gee, *Book of Abraham*, 115–20, 129–42.
20. An interesting discrepancy from the book of Genesis in the book of Abraham describes Adam naming cattle, fowl, and beast before informing the reader "there was found an help meet for him" (Abr. 5:21). Here, the text ends. Genesis likewise describes Adam naming cattle, fowl, and beast before informing the reader "there was *not* found an help meet for him" (Gen 2:20, emphasis added), thus setting up the creation of Eve. Possibly, Abraham 5:21 may be read as a compression of Eve's creation account given the canonical status of Genesis in the LDS standard works.
21. Mark Sheridan, ed., *Genesis 12–50*, Ancient Christian Commentary on Scripture: Old Testament 2 (Downers Grove: IVP Academic, 2002), 2.
22. Barry Scott Wimpfheimer, *The Talmud: A Biography* (Princeton: Princeton University Press, 2018), 145.

clear about the patriarch's early relationship to idolatry (if any), but most ancient interpreters believed God singled out Abraham for blessing because he valiantly rejected his forefathers' idolatry.[23] The pseudepigraphic *Apocalypse of Abraham*, for example, portrays him as an active servant in an idolatrous cult before rejecting polytheism to embrace "the God of Gods and the Creator,"[24] a point with which the Qur'an quibbles, arguing that Abraham was never an idolater to begin with.[25] Josephus clarified how Abraham was banished from Chaldea because he was "the first boldly to declare that God, the creator of the universe, is one."[26] The books of Judith, Jubilees, and Jasher add how God miraculously rescued him from violent idolaters prior to his departure.[27]

The book of Abraham entered this debate by portraying the patriarch as a righteous monotheist, an heir to an ancient priesthood who lived in a violently pagan society. He was nearly murdered for his faith before God miraculously delivered him (see Abr. 1:15). In this sense, the book of Abraham sided with the Qur'anic suggestion that Abraham never indulged in polytheism while also agreeing with the pseudepigraphic tradition by framing his exit from Chaldea as an escape from violence. Abraham was always faithful to God from the beginning, even at the risk of his own life.

What to do with Abraham's treatment of Sarah has proven more challenging. Why would Abraham, the father of God's holy people, craft such an atrocious lie? Some writers simply denied the incident ever occurred, suggesting Sarah was taken by force from her distraught husband.[28] Others acknowledge Abraham's lie but frame it as a clever way to commit Sarah to God's protection.[29] Martin Luther disagreed: "Willingly and knowingly [Abraham] exposes his wife to the danger of adultery."[30] The book of Abraham attempted to solve this puzzle by explaining how God commanded Abraham to lie about his relationship with Sarah (see Abr. 2:22–24). This interpretation, though, creates a worse problem than denying the incident altogether because it makes God the source of a deception, implicitly declaring God guilty of lying to justify an innocent Abraham.[31]

23. James L. Kugel, *The Bible as It Was* (Cambridge, MA: Harvard University Press, 1998), 133–35.
24. *The Apocalypse of Abraham*, trans. George H. Box (New York: Macmillan, 1918), 43.
25. Qur'an 2:135; 3:95; 16:120.
26. Josephus, *Jewish Antiquities* 1:154–57. *Josephus*, vol. 4, *Jewish Antiquities, Books I–IV*, trans. Henry Thackeray (Cambridge, MA: Harvard University Press, 1961), 77.
27. Judith 5:8–9; Jubilees 12:6–7; Jasher 12:1–6, 21–35.
28. Jubilees 13:11–15; Genesis Apocryphon (1QapGen) col. 20.
29. Sheridan, *Genesis*, 7.
30. *LW* 2:291.
31. For a counterpoint, see Duane Boyce, "Why Abraham Was Not Wrong to Lie," *BYU Studies* 61, no. 3 (2022): 5–27. It is also possible that God commanded Abraham to express ambiguity about his relationship to Sarah. See Stephen O. Smoot et al., "Did Abraham Lie about His Wife, Sarai?" *BYU Studies* 61, no. 4 (2022): 125–28.

Summary

The book of Abraham is a foundational text to many distinctive aspects of Latter-day Saint theology. Although its relationship to its original sources is ambiguous, Latter-day Saints nevertheless consider the finished text canonical. Like many before him, Smith was distressed by the ungainly portrayal of Abraham in the Bible, which led him to protect the patriarch's image through biblical revision. His unnecessary revision assumes Abraham's integrity must be protected, that he must always have been an exemplary saint, an ever-devoted worshiper of God who is persistently righteous. In doing so, readers are robbed of a valuable spiritual lesson—God delights in using imperfect people to bring about his perfect will. In short, when considering its origin and content, the book of Abraham is best understood as a member of the pseudepigraphic library of the Abrahamic tradition, while Latter-day Saint scholars view the text as an authentic revelatory translation with deep connections to Abrahamic tradition and history.

REFLECTION QUESTIONS

1. What does the origin of the book of Abraham communicate to you about Joseph Smith?

2. Do you believe Smith sincerely attempted to translate the source material of the book of Abraham? Why or why not?

3. What LDS doctrines in the book of Abraham are most unique when compared to your faith tradition?

4. Why do you believe Smith and others have attempted to expand narratives about Abraham to make him seem more righteous than he appears in the Bible?

5. Do you agree the book of Abraham is best understood to be a pseudepigraphic work concerning the patriarch? If so, how might you discuss this portion of Mormon scripture with a Latter-day Saint?

QUESTION 18

What Is the Priesthood?

"Where the Christian priesthood is, there the Christian church is; and where the Christian priesthood is not, there the Christian church is not."[1]
~ John E. Page, Latter-day Saint Apostle, 1838–1846

When we hear the terms "priest" and "priesthood," what comes to mind depends on our theological backgrounds. At their most basic, priests are religious leaders authorized to perform sacred ceremonies, and priesthoods refer to the communities to which these leaders belong. For traditional Christians, the priesthood began in the OT with a class of Israelites who administered sacred duties and feasts for their nation. Priests offered up sacrifices to cleanse the sins of Israel, but their function ceased after the cross of Jesus Christ atoned for "the sins of the whole world" (1 John 2:2). Today, many churches evoke this intercessory imagery with ministers leading their congregations "in the priestly service of the gospel of God" as Christ's representatives (Rom 15:16 ESV).

In this sense, the concept of priesthood in the Church of Jesus Christ of Latter-day Saints is very similar to that found in most of Christianity. Latter-day Saints believe that God ordains certain people to specific functions within the church. The LDS priesthood, however, is much more than divine authentication. It is fundamental not only to the church's ecclesiology but also to its soteriology, cosmology, and theology proper. For traditional Christians, the LDS priesthood is perhaps the most essential yet least understood element of Mormonism. Priesthood in Mormonism is divine power and authority manifested in salvific work, the eternal principle by which God

1. John E. Page, "Treatise on the Spiritual Covenant Made with Abraham," *Zion's Reveille* (Wisconsin), August 19, 1847, 2:89.

wills and acts, which is extended to the church to authorize and organize its religious activity in every area. Wherever one looks in Mormonism, the priesthood is sure to be seen.

For this reason, the following three questions will explore the concept and development of the LDS priesthood, as well as its contemporary issues. Before doing so, however, it's important to consider the biblical and theological sources of the priesthood in traditional Christianity to recognize its continuities and contrasts with Mormonism.

A Biblical Theology of Priesthood

In the OT, priests were men who stood before God as mediators on behalf of Israel through priestly duties in the sanctuary. The priesthood "did not spring into existence as a brand new venture to surprise Israel."[2] There were antecedent types and scenes that paved the way.[3] The mysterious Melchizedek, a kingly priest of the "most high God" (Gen 14:18) from Salem blessed Abraham, whose ancestor, Noah, built an altar to offer a sacrifice of thanksgiving after being spared from God's judgment (see Gen 8:20). Even earlier, in the scenery of Eden, a garden separated from the world where God communes with Adam, stirs the imagination toward the future tabernacle, a sacred space separated from the world where God meets with his chosen people. But the Bible stops short of definitively identifying Adam, Noah, or Abraham as the first priest.[4]

After the exodus, God chose Aaron as the chief priest of Israel to sanctify and instruct the nation through ritual and teaching (see Exod 28:1–2; 1 Chr 6:49; Ezra 7:5). Admission into the Aaronic (or Levitical) priesthood was restricted to men from the tribe of Levi, and the chief priest, who headed the priesthood, was called only by divine appointment. Offering sacrifices was the most important of all Levitical duties, especially on Yom Kippur, the Day of Atonement, an annual cleansing of sin by the blood of a sacrifice to reconcile sinners to their holy God (see Lev 16). The priesthood developed to represent a conduit between the people and God. Priests held a unique role as God's "personal attendants" and Israel's pastoral mediators.[5]

But the Levitical priesthood was flawed from the beginning and would one day need to be replaced (see 1 Sam 2:35). In a sense, Aaron's construction of the golden calf was a prophetic warning of the priesthood's eventual failure in anticipation of a greater priesthood to come one (see Exod 32; Deut 18:15; cf. Acts 7:37–43). As OT prophets chastised corrupt priests

2. Andrew S. Malone, *God's Mediators: A Biblical Theology of Priesthood*, New Studies in Biblical Theology 43 (Downers Grove, IL: IVP Academic, 2017), 47.
3. Malone, *God's Mediators*, 47–67.
4. Malone, *God's Mediators*, 66.
5. Peter J. Leithart, "Attendants of Yahweh's House: Priesthood in the Old Testament," *Journal for the Study of the Old Testament* 24 (1999): 12.

(see Isa 28:7; Amos 5:21–27; Mal 2:1–9), they cast Israel's eyes forward to the future coming of an impeccable high priest who would lead a new priesthood of both Jew and Gentile (see Isa 56:6–7; 66:18, 21; Ps 110; Zech 6:12–13).

That future hope of the OT saints was a present reality for the NT ones. The distinction between the Old and New Testaments signifies Christ's priestly guarantee and administration over the "better" and "new testament" of God (Heb 7:22; 9:15), or his long-anticipated new covenant (see Jer 31:31; Luke 22:20). Although Jesus is never explicitly called a priest in the Gospels, his priestly function appears at nearly every turn of his ministry, especially in his teaching, healing, and self-sacrifice on the cross. Instructing people in God's will was a priestly duty, and Jesus was called "teacher" or "master" (see, e.g., Matt 22:36; Mark 14:14; Luke 20:21; John 3:2). His healing miracles were sometimes linked to priestly activity and the temple, which priests operated (see, e.g., Matt 8:1–4; 21:19). The Last Supper is replete with priestly language of sacrifice and covenant. According to John's gospel, Jesus self-sacrificed on the day of preparation when lambs were selected to be slain in the temple for Passover (see John 19:14–16).

The NT writers go to great lengths to present Christ as the greatest and final man to stand before God on our behalf. Like the Gospel writers, Paul never called Jesus a priest but taught explicitly how "Christ our passover is sacrificed for us" (1 Cor 5:7), a "propitiation" (Rom 3:25) for sins, and the "one mediator between God and men" (1 Tim 2:5). The power behind Christ's priesthood is love (see Gal 2:20) and joy (see Heb 12:2), which manifest obedience. Where love and joy are not, the priesthood of God is not. Revelation further depicts Christ as the spotless, slain lamb who has conquered sin and death, whose faithful church participates in his victory through priestly service (see Rev 1:6), song (see Rev 5:9), and sacrifice (see Rev 6:9–10).

But nowhere in the NT is the priestly description of Christ more explicit than in Hebrews. While Jesus was not a Levite, the author notes how his priesthood is after the order of Melchizedek (see Heb 5:6, 10; 6:20), the priest-king who presided over an earlier and greater priesthood than the Levitical one (see Heb 7:1–22). Jesus, then, is the antitype of Melchizedek, the greater high priest (see Heb 4:14–15) who offered himself as a once-for-all, unrepeatable sacrifice (see Heb 7:27; 9:11–12, 25–26; 10:10), mediated "by his own blood" (Heb 9:12; see also, 8:6, 9:15; 12:24) between God and "all that obey him" (Heb 5:9). As high priest, Jesus thus ushers the redeemed into the presence of God (see Heb 10:19–23) as they rely wholly on Christ's present and permanent intercessory work. In Christ, the purpose of the priesthood is not merely fulfilled but ultimately and finally realized in his self-sacrifice for reconciliation between God and sinners (see Heb 2:17; 10:10).

The effect of Christ's priestly work is astonishing. The cross nullifies the old covenant (see Heb 8:13) and dramatically expands priesthood members in the new covenant. Under the old covenant, the priesthood was insufficient. Generations of priests repeatedly offered God scant sacrifices at a distance. There was no finality to their offerings, there were only mere shadows and patterns of heavenly things. Under the new covenant, though, the priesthood is vibrant and abundant. Christ, the sinless high priest, offered himself as a perfect sacrifice once for all, forever collapsing the distance between God and his priesthood members, the beloved saints.

With the office of the high priest eternally occupied by the Son of God, no one could ever be called to usurp the priest-king's throne, who presently presides over his church, "a royal priesthood, an holy nation, a peculiar people" (1 Pet 2:9) of "ministers of a new covenant" (2 Cor 3:6 ESV) called to live differently from the world by priestly living for the Word through presenting their lives as "a living sacrifice, holy, acceptable unto God" (Rom 12:1).

The Latter-day Saint Priesthood Considering Church History

The early church maintained, as Origen did, that "to all of the Church of God and to the people of believers, the priesthood was given."[6] For patristic writers, the church is a priestly people in pursuit of holiness who offer their lives as sacrifices to God, a common priesthood of all the faithful saints, both male and female, who are "all one in Christ Jesus" (Gal 3:28).[7] Naturally, the early church rejected the idea that equality of membership in the church meant equity in function among its members. Bishops and deacons were called to servant leadership, especially for the sake of church unity. As the church grew, so did the priestly responsibilities of clergy. Aquinas stressed how Christ alone was the "true priest" and all others "only his ministers," but the gradual development of a special ministerial class of sacramental mediators within the common priesthood created a division between clergy and laity.[8] This division disturbed the Protestant Reformer Martin Luther, for whom "the priesthood is a kind of law of Christian community life."[9] According to Luther, such a division should not exist because "every Christian is someone else's priest, and we are all priests to one another."[10]

Entry into the priesthood does not come by ecclesiastical orders but rather by faith and baptism as the first steps of participation in the life of the church. Thus, the Reformers emphasized "the interior function of [Christ's]

---

6. Origen, *Homilies on Leviticus 1–16*, trans. Gary Wayne Barkley (Washington, DC: Catholic University of America Press, 1990), 177.
7. See Gerald O'Collins and Michael Keenan Jones, *Jesus Our Priest: A Christian Approach to the Priesthood of Christ* (New York: Oxford University Press, 2010), 68–104.
8. O'Collins and Jones, *Jesus Our Priest*, 114.
9. O'Collins and Jones, *Jesus Our Priest*, 129.
10. Timothy George, *Theology of the Reformers*, rev. ed. (Nashville: B&H Academic, 2013), 96.

priesthood over its public function in the sacramental life of the Church."[11] Protestantism, then, tends not to emphasize a priesthood distinction between clergy and members (i.e., it holds to a priesthood of all believers) but also resists atomized individualism, or what one theologian called "Christianity aloof from the church," though in practice churches often struggle with this tension.[12] Where all traditional Christians agree, however, is in Christ's victory over sin through his priestly self-sacrifice. His present priesthood—to which every Christian is anointed by faith and baptism—has faithfully endured through a succession of God's Spirit, who governs and guarantees its purity from generation to generation.

Mormonism retains enough priesthood theology from Protestantism to seem familiar at first, especially seen in the LDS Church's lack of a clerical class and its priesthood of all believers, at least among its male members when considering its offices. The Mormon priesthood hierarchy, however, resembles churches that employ episcopal polity like Roman Catholicism and Eastern Orthodoxy. But the LDS priesthood differs from traditional Christianity in significant ways, and chief among them is its association with the nature of God.

Some Latter-day Saints scholars argue that Joseph Smith did not necessarily *receive* something, as the language of priesthood "keys" and "ordinances" implies.[13] Rather, Smith *was received* into an eternal, cosmic economy of power and authority, ritual and relationship, as would all those who participate in its liturgies.[14] He viewed himself as joining a divine hierarchy of ministry in which God himself was a member. Consequently, Smith taught that the priesthood is coeternal with God, being "an everlasting principle & Existed with God from Eternity & will to Eternity, without beginning of days or end of years."[15] Here, Smith echoed the Book of Mormon's description of the "high priesthood" as eternally "without beginning of days or end of years" (Alma 13:8). Unlike the traditional Christian concept of priesthood, which God created as a gift for his people, Smith believed the priesthood was

---

11. O'Collins and Jones, *Jesus Our Priest*, 147.
12. Wolfhart Pannenberg, *Systematic Theology*, trans. Geoffrey W. Bromiley, 3 vols. (New York: T&T Clark, 2004), 3:126. See also Uche Anizor and Hank Voss, *Representing Christ: A Vision for the Priesthood of All Believers* (Downers Grove, IL: IVP Academic, 2016), 103–9.
13. For example, JS said he received "the keys of the gospel of repentance" from John the Baptist (JS, 1834–1836 history, H1:42). He also claimed to receive "the keys of the kingdom of God," perhaps meaning he received spiritual authority from Peter, James, and John (JS, ca. 1832 history, H1:10 [emend.]).
14. See, for example, Jonathan A. Stapley, *The Power of Godliness: Mormon Liturgy and Cosmology* (New York: Oxford University Press, 2018). Stapley argues the "cosmological priesthood," a "material network of heaven," is communicated to those who participate in rituals found in the "ecclesiastical priesthood," i.e., those found on earth. See Stapley, *The Power of Godliness*, 17–23.
15. JS, discourse, ca. June 26–August 4, 1839, D6:543. See also D&C 84:17.

associated with God's very nature, especially his divine attributes of omnipotence and sovereignty. For example, God acted with priesthood power when he created the universe, and the priesthood enables him to govern his creation. But the priesthood is not merely God's power—it is an *authoritative* power. As Latter-day Saint president John Taylor explained, the priesthood is "the government of God, whether on the earth or in the heavens" and it is "by that *power* that all things are upheld and sustained."[16] God's priesthood "governs all things—it directs all things—it sustains all things—and has to do with all things that God and truth are associated with," he said.[17] The LDS Church has not deviated far from this definition. It describes the priesthood as the very "power and authority of God" and teaches how "through the priesthood, God created and governs the heavens and the earth."[18]

But the priesthood is not restricted to God alone. It's something he participates in and shares with his creation, a principle that enables correspondence between heaven and earth, so what the priesthood is and does in heaven ought to be patterned on earth.[19] God's authoritative power is a gift available to all humanity, though its offices come only by the ordination of qualified men (and only men) who act as his representatives (see question 20). Smith taught that the "rights of the priesthood are inseparably connected with the powers of heaven, and that the powers of heaven cannot be controlled nor handled, only upon the principles of righteousness."[20] In other words, God's power authenticates righteous men through the priesthood—and by no other means—to act on his behalf. According to the Book of Mormon, men who are called to it and remain in it "become high priests forever" (Alma 13:9). Beginning with Adam, the priesthood "continueth in the church of God in all generations," said Smith, flowing uninterrupted throughout "all the generations of the Jews" from Adam to Melchizedek, whose ordination of Abraham continued to Moses.[21] This ancient priesthood, "which was in the beginning," would not remain there, and "shall be in the end of the world also" (Moses 6:7), connecting Adam to the saints of the latter days.

Smith also believed the priesthood is organized into two degrees. The Aaronic priesthood, the lower degree, was named after the high priest and

---

16. John Taylor, "On Priesthood," *MS*, November 1, 1847, 9:325 (emphasis added).
17. Taylor, "On Priesthood."
18. Gary James Bergera, ed., *Statements of the LDS First Presidency: A Topical Compendium* (Salt Lake City: Signature Books, 2007), 346.
19. Samuel Morris Brown argues that Smith viewed the transcendent and immanent cosmos as corresponding to one another in a metaphysical way, a principle that linked and reflected power and order "as it is above, so it is below," and (ideally) vice versa. Brown, *In Heaven as It Is on Earth: Joseph Smith and the Early Mormon Conquest of Death* (New York: Oxford University Press, 2012); idem, *JST*.
20. JS to Edward Partridge and the Church, ca. March 22, 1839, D6:393 (emend.).
21. JS, revelation, September 22–23, 1832, D2:293–95 [D&C 84].

identified with the Levitical priesthood. This "lesser Priesthood" equipped the Levitical priests with power and authority to administer "temporal matters and outward ordinances of the law and the gospel."[22] Smith explained how the Aaronic priesthood "holdeth the keys of the ministring [*sic*] of Angels and the preparitory gospel [of] repentance and of Baptism, and the remission of sins, and the Law of carnal commandments."[23] In other words, the Aaronic priesthood empowered the efficacy of the Levitical sacrificial system, thus offering Israel a degree of salvation. The Levites operated in this priesthood from Aaron to John the Baptist.[24] In the LDS Church, holders of this priesthood were enabled to administer "outward ordinances" (D&C 107:14) such as baptism.

The Melchizedek Priesthood, the higher degree, contains the very power of salvation. Therefore, one must hold the Melchizedek priesthood worthy to progress in salvation to celestial glory (see question 27). Through it the church "adminestereth the gospel and holdeth the key of the misteries [*sic*] of the kingdom, even the key of the knowledge of God [and] the authority of the Priesthood," according to Smith.[25] Without the Melchizedek priesthood, according to Smith, "the power of Godliness is not manifest unto man in the flesh"[26] because it "is the channel through which all knowledge, doctrine, the plan of salvation and every important truth is revealed from heaven."[27] In other words, Melchizedek priesthood holders may assume ecclesiastical offices and perform the duties to which they are called. When Christ came, he ordained his disciples to both the priesthoods, but they were both lost during the Great Apostasy (see question 6). The consequences of this loss and the restoration of the priesthood are discussed in the next question.

Summary

The LDS priesthood is similar and dissimilar to Christian views in significant ways. Both agree Jesus Christ is the great high priest whose once-for-all sacrifice on the cross brought an end to the Levitical system for atonement. Agreement is also found in the shared reception of Christ's priesthood among all his faithful followers. But LDS thought differs greatly from Christianity when it coalesces the priesthood to divine attributes. Furthermore, it is unique to LDS belief that the priesthood is an authority first given to Adam and passed along from generation to generation until Christ.

---

22. Andrew C. Skinner, "Aaronic Priesthood," in *LDS Beliefs: A Doctrinal Reference,* ed. Robert L. Millet et al. (Salt Lake City: Deseret Book, 2011), 5.
23. JS, revelation, September 22–23, 1832, D2:296 [D&C 84:26–27].
24. JS, revelation, September 22–23, 1832, D2:296 [D&C 84:27].
25. JS, revelation, September 22–23, 1832, D2:295 [D&C 84:19–21].
26. JS, revelation, September 22–23, 1832, D2:295 [D&C 84:21].
27. JS, Instructions, ca. October 5, 1840, D7:435.

REFLECTION QUESTIONS

1. What do the terms “priest” and “priesthood” mean to you? To your church?

2. How does the LDS priesthood differ from traditional Christian conceptions of priesthood?

3. Roman Catholic and Protestant concepts of the priesthood differ from one another, but what do they have in common compared with the LDS priesthood?

4. The LDS Church contends it is the truest form of Christianity in part because of its possession of the priesthood. How might you respond to this claim?

5. What are some theological issues (if any) with tying the priesthood to God’s attributes?

QUESTION 19

What Is the Origin of the Priesthood?

"On a sudden . . . the angel of God came down clothed with glory, and delivered . . . the keys of the gospel of repentance! What joy! what wonder! what amazement!"[1]
~ Oliver Cowdery, Latter-day Saint Apostle, 1829–1838

The previous question addressed similarities and dissimilarities of the priesthood with traditional Christianity and Mormonism. In this question, we will explore the origin of the LDS priesthood as it relates to the Great Apostasy (see question 6) as well as its organization and controversial exclusions.[2]

The Great Apostasy and the Priesthood

Many things distinguish the Church of Jesus Christ from Latter-day Saints from other churches, but to Joseph Smith, among the most significant were priesthood and prophecy. No other church had either of them. "All men are liars who say they are of the true church without the revelations of Jesus Christ and the priesthood of Melchizedek," he reportedly claimed.[3] His reason was simple: The priesthood is the eternal source of power and authority, and prophecy is the surest sign of their presence. Moreover, God himself acts in and through the priesthood, which brings about human salvation by governing divine activity, especially prophecy. Thus, an absence of the priesthood

1. Oliver Cowdery, letter to William W. Phelps, *M&A*, September 7, 1834, 1:15.
2. Portions of this question are based on my earlier writing on the history of the priesthood in "Wingfield Scott Watson and His Struggle to Preserve the Church of Jesus Christ of Latter-day Saints (Strangite) After the Death of Its Founder" (PhD diss., The Southern Baptist Theological Seminary, 2021), 61–77.
3. Joseph Smith, History, 1838–1856, vol. F-1, *JSP*, 104.

is tantamount to the absence of God's activity and voice, and vice versa; where the priesthood is, there God is also.

Smith believed the priesthood was present in the church. But how did Melchizedek's priesthood lineage trace from ancient Salem to Nauvoo, especially given Smith's insistence on a great apostasy?

Early Latter-day Saints believed that the priesthood had once orchestrated a symphony of order and righteousness in the apostolic church, but a terrible apostasy then caused God to withdraw his authority from the earth as the Christian faith descended into the cacophony of confusion and corruption. Perhaps this apostasy should have surprised no one. Early LDS writer Benjamin Winchester discerned a biblical pattern of rebellion among God's people who refused to sustain the authority of the priesthood.[4] Things began well. The Melchizedek priesthood passed faithfully from Adam to Moses, who, during his life, was its lone holder. Moses enjoyed meeting with God face-to-face in divine communion by "Urim and Thummim, through the agency of angels, by visions, and by the Spirit of God," explained Winchester.[5] But by the end of his life, Moses could not ordain a successor because of the "wickedness of the children of Israel."[6] Only the Aaronic priesthood of the Levites was carried forward, and even then prospects were bleak.[7] Throughout the OT, Levitical priests abused the lower priesthood so severely that they had "lost their efficacy; or in other words, were made void," teetering on the brink of total apostasy.[8]

But hope was on the horizon. At his first advent, Jesus Christ reorganized God's kingdom by ordaining his apostles to the higher priesthood. As members of the Melchizedek priesthood, the apostles advanced the authority of the kingdom of God throughout the world. The NT church was structured according to the priesthood's ecclesiastical offices and members enjoyed the spiritual gifts and signs attending them. The Book of Mormon describes how

4. Benjamin Winchester was an influential LDS missionary and writer, but his contributions were marked by controversy around the time he published *A History of the Priesthood* in 1843. JS remarked how church leaders "can never make any thing out of Benjamin Winchester," having silenced and then restored his ecclesiastical authority (JSJ, April 19, 1843, J2:367). He would eventually be excommunicated and affiliate with Sidney Rigdon's church after JS's death. Despite his provocative character, Winchester's *A History of the Priesthood* provides modern readers with keen insight into how early Mormons viewed their priesthood.
5. Benjamin Winchester, *A History of the Priesthood . . . Now Extant* (Philadelphia: Brown, Bicking & Guilbert, 1843), 35.
6. Winchester, *A History of the Priesthood*, 35.
7. Winchester offers a caveat that, on special occasions, the higher priesthood reappeared for a brief season and for a specific purpose. He hypothesized: "It is quite probable; that several of the Jewish prophets, by their faith received the Melchisedec [*sic*] priesthood from God, or an angel sent to confer it upon them. It is evident, that Samuel, David, Solomon, Elijah, Isaiah and others, received [the Melchizedek priesthood]" (Winchester, *A History of the Priesthood*, 36–37).
8. Winchester, *A History of the Priesthood*, 40.

Jesus duplicated these efforts in the Americas (see 3 Nephi 18:26–39). Only apostasy could have taken away the priesthood from the apostolic church. Yet, like the former-day saints of the OT, the ancient church incurred the same curse by their rebellion. The church tolerated "insubordinate apostates" who, acting in a foreign authority, disregarded priesthood law and manipulated the ordinance of baptism, which in turn broke the "everlasting covenant."[9] In place of Christ's church arose creedal churches, which became altogether "destitute of the holy priesthood."[10] When, precisely, the priesthood was lost is a matter of debate.[11] Perhaps, like an oscillating fan unplugged from its power source, the church waned for generations until coming to a complete stop. Doubtless, by that point, "God was disappointed that he could not function through a living church," wrote one LDS author.[12]

And how could he? The loss of the priesthood resulted in a corrupted church that bred generational apostasy by "supplanting primitive institutions of the kingdom," explained Winchester.[13] The list of evidence was long:

> the sale of indulgences, amalgamation of numerous pagan rites and ceremonies with those of the church, the worship of images, the celibacy of the clergy, monkery in all its horrid forms, the flagitious court of inquisition, exorcism, the nunnery system, and scores of other equally absurd notions and practices.[14]

Denominational fracturing after the Protestant Reformation served only to prove how disarrayed the church had become in the absence of priesthood. In 1830, God lamented through Smith about the sorry condition of Christianity: "My vineyard has become corrupted evry [*sic*] whit & there is none that doeth good save it is a few only," yet, even they "err in many instances because of Priest

---

9. Winchester, *A History of the Priesthood*, 84–86.
10. Winchester, *A History of the Priesthood*, 92.
11. A popular assumption is the priesthood was lost after the death of the last apostle (i.e., by the end of the first century). But some LDS scholars are unsure of when, exactly, the priesthood evaporated and wonder whether asking the question is helpful to begin with. It is sufficient to state that apostasy had so degraded the church after the NT period that God removed the fullness of his priesthood from the church, which required restoration in the latter days. See Miranda Wilcox and John D. Young, eds., *Standing Apart: Mormon Historical Consciousness and the Concept of Apostasy* (New York: Oxford University Press, 2014).
12. Gregor McHardy, *8 Myths of the Great Apostasy* (Salt Lake City: Signature Books, 2022), 45. McHardy further argued the priesthood was never fully removed from earth, and that a remnant persisted through the ages, which allowed Christian ministers to preach and administer ordinances that qualified the penitent for terrestrial glory (though not celestial glory) in the afterlife. See McHardy, *8 Myths*, 49–52.
13. Winchester, *A History of the Priesthood*, 86.
14. Winchester, *A History of the Priesthood*, 86–87.

crafts."[15] The church fell into the same tragedy of Israel, forcing God to repossess the priesthood from a wayward people. Like in the OT era, the Melchizedek priesthood vanished; but, unlike in the OT, the Aaronic priesthood disappeared, too. In one sense, the post-apostolic church was in a worse state than ancient Israel. The Great Apostasy evaporated God's power and authority from the earth and required an even greater event to restore it. Small remnants of the true faith survived through the ages, but without restoring the priesthood they would remain in a powerless and disoriented state.

The Restoration of the Priesthood

Joseph Smith explained how the priesthood was restored through his experiences during the "rise of the church of Christ in the eve of time."[16] First, he received testimony "from on high," presumably the First Vision. Second, he received "the ministering of angels," apparently named Moroni. Third, he received "the holy priesthood by the ministering of angels to administer the letter of the Gospel . . . and the ordinances," referencing John the Baptist. Fourth, he received "the high priesthood [and] the keys of the kingdom of God," perhaps alluding to Peter, James, and John.[17] Of these, the restoration of priesthood authority—first by John the Baptist and later through Peter, James, and John—deserve close attention.

Smith claimed to receive the priesthood by John the Baptist. While translating the Book of Mormon, Smith and his associate Oliver Cowdery read a portion of the text that prescribed the modes and means of proper baptism.[18] Cowdery wondered how any baptism before then could be effective if "none had authority from God to administer the ordinances of the gospel?"[19] Smith, who had yet to be baptized at all, was so concerned about the matter he stopped translating so he could pray for guidance. One historian noted how this event "proved a major transitional point, for it was the first time that Smith sought formal ordination, rather than acting under the implicit authority by which he published the Book of Mormon."[20] After consulting the Urim and Thummim, Smith and Cowdery were commanded to "repair to the water, and attend to the ordinance of Baptism," according to Smith's mother.[21]

15. JS, revelation, October 1830, D1:207 [D&C 33:4].
16. JS, ca. 1832 history, H1:10. I have modeled this short priesthood history based on Gregory Prince's reading of the same passage from Smith's history. See Gregory A. Prince, "Mormon Priesthood and Organization," in *The Oxford Handbook of Mormonism*, ed. Terryl L. Givens and Philip L. Barlow (New York: Oxford University Press, 2015), 167–77.
17. JS, ca. 1832 history, H1:10 (emend.).
18. This section was likely 3 Nephi 11:21–38.
19. JS, 1834–1836 history, H1:42.
20. Prince, "Mormon Priesthood and Organization," 170.
21. Lavina Fielding Anderson, *Lucy's Book: A Critical Edition of Lucy Mack Smith's Family Memoir* (Salt Lake City: Signature Books, 2001), 439.

She refrained from describing how the men were ordained, only that "they had now received authority to baptize" and performed the ordinance mutually.[22] Later accounts provide precise and astounding clarity.

According to Cowdery, he and Smith were praying when "the voice of the redeemer spake peace" and "the angel of God came down clothed with glory" to deliver the "keys of the gospel of repentance."[23] "Upon you my fellow servants," the angel said, "I confer this priesthood, and this authority."[24] Smith later identified the angel as John the Baptist glorified, who ordained them to "the priesthood of Aaron, which holds the keys . . . of baptism by immersion for the remission of sins."[25] It was the first time anyone had held the priesthood since the apostolic era and, for Smith, it was the first significant step in exercising his prophetic authority for restoring his vision of the true church.[26]

This point is vital for Smith's claim to authority. To him, all Christian clergy had to trace their ordination pedigree through a long, winding, and often convoluted succession from the apostles through a fallen church. His ordination, however, bypassed the Great Apostasy altogether, thereby retaining its purity and potency. Smith received his priesthood not through an illegitimate chain of corruption but directly from John the Baptist himself.

Following their ordination, Smith and Cowdery waded into the nearby Susquehanna River to baptize one another. John the Baptist promised a second authority, the Melchizedek priesthood, would be conferred to them later by Peter, James, and John.[27] The precise moment when this second ordination took place is unknown.[28] After receiving the priesthood and baptism, Smith donned the titles "apostle of Jesus Christ" and "the first Elder of this Church."[29] To Smith, centuries of corruption and confusion had ended; God's priesthood power and authority were restored.

---

22. Anderson, *Lucy's Book*, 439.
23. JS, 1834–1836 history, H1:42.
24. JS, 1834–1836 history, H1:43.
25. JS, H1:292 [Joseph Smith–History 69]. JS believed angels are not a different species of creature than humans but are the "spirits of just men made perfect" (JSJ, February 9, 1843, J2:258 [emend.]).
26. See Michael Hubbard MacKay, *Prophetic Authority: Democratic Hierarchy and the Mormon Priesthood* (Urbana, IL: University of Illinois Press, 2020), 24–36.
27. JS, H1:294 [Joseph Smith–History 72].
28. JS, 1834–1836 history, H1:39. Smith possibly referenced this event in a letter to the LDS Church dated September 6, 1842, in which he declared: "Glad tidings from Cumorah! . . . The voice of Peter, James, and John in the wilderness between Harmony, Susquehanna county, and Colesville, Broome county, on the Susquehanna river, declaring themselves as possessing the keys of the kingdom, and of the dispensation of the fulness of times" (D&C 128:20). Additionally, the glorified apostles are alluded to in a letter from Smith that promises Oliver Cowdery the reception of the "holy priesthood under the hands of they who had been held in reserve for a long season, even those who received it under the hand of the Messiah" (JS, blessing, October 2, 1835, D5:513–14). When this event occurred, however, is unknown.
29. JS, H1:336 [D&C 20:2].

The Organization of the LDS Priesthood

Priesthood functions expanded organizationally as the church grew. Initially, ordained men occupied one of only a few offices—deacon, teacher, priest, and elder—as they assisted Smith, the prophet-apostle.[30] The nascent priesthood was more of a flattened matrix of authority, a democratic body of believers through which church activity was "done by common consent."[31] It was patriarchal but not necessarily hierarchical. Over the years, however, church membership swelled from a handful to hundreds, necessitating more ordained offices as new quorums and councils networked geographically separated congregations to the central church. Challenges to Smith's authority prompted him to consolidate power in the office of the president of the high priesthood, which sat atop an ever-evolving hierarchy of elders, bishops, seventies, and apostles (see D&C 107:91–92).

Today, the priesthood is organized on the foundation of a massive volunteer laity with "a highly centralized, semiprofessional hierarchy at the top."[32] Beginning at the bottom, all active Latter-day Saints belong to a ward (at least 300 members) or branch (which is smaller), the most basic congregational units of the church. Ward membership is determined geographically, and wards are led by laity who serve their congregations in various callings.[33] Wards are organized into stakes (typically 1,000–2,000 members), and stakes into areas.[34] Each ward is presided over by a bishopric led by a bishop and his two counselors. Similarly, each stake is presided over and led by its own three-person stake presidency, consisting of a president and two counselors, assisted by a twelve-member high council, all of whom are men who lead voluntarily. Unlike many traditional Christian churches, there are no paid clergy in the lower levels of ecclesiastical leadership, although higher church authorities are sometimes compensated.

Above stake presidencies are the Area Authority Seventy (or Seventies). They continue working in their regular professions, live in their own homes, and serve within the geographic area to which they are assigned. Overseeing them is the seven-member Presidency of the Seventy. Alongside the Area Authorities are the General Authority Seventy (or Seventies), who serve full-time and are usually called until they are granted emeritus status, typically around the age of seventy,

30. Richard Bushman, *Joseph Smith and the Beginnings of Mormonism* (Urbana, IL: University of Illinois Press, 1984), 264.
31. JS, H1:424 [D&C 26:2].
32. Prince, "Mormon Priesthood," 167.
33. Only ordained priesthood holders may perform church liturgies (e.g., baptism and communion).
34. A parallel structure of missions, districts, and branches exists beneath the same governing authority of stakes and wards, each with their own presidencies (e.g., the mission president presides over his mission along with two counselors). The mission presidency is charged with facilitating and administrating the efforts of LDS missionaries. Latter-day Saints are also encouraged to participate in ancillary organizations like the Relief Society for women and associations for young men and women, which are governed by church authorities.

though there are occasional exceptions. General Authorities steward church-wide programs, such as education, poverty relief, or administration. Members of these authorities work with the Quorum of the Twelve Apostles, a council of lifetime-appointed men who are presided over by the First Presidency, a three-member office of the prophet-president and two counselors of his choosing. When a prophet dies, the senior-most apostle from the apostolic quorum assumes leadership of the church. While the First Presidency guides the church generally, the Quorum of the Twelve Apostles provides senior-level administrative oversight for the entire church—like the church's missionary program and educational system (e.g., Brigham Young University). Together, all members of these upper echelons constitute the General Authorities of the church.

Holding the priesthood is a prerequisite for each of these positions, and everyone from the president down to ward bishops must maintain personal worthiness to retain their position. Today, LDS males receive the Aaronic priesthood during the year they turn twelve or upon conversion, having been baptized and confirmed as members. At the age of eighteen, worthy men who have received the Aaronic priesthood are conferred the Melchizedek priesthood and become qualified to serve the church in various ecclesiastical callings and to impart spiritual gifts and blessings to their families, whom they guide as the spiritual leader. Not all church members, however, have been or are today privileged to receive callings into these positions due to restricted membership to the priesthood. Most notably, the church has barred Black people from the priesthood and presently restricts membership to males, a topic to be explored in the following question.

Summary

The LDS priesthood is like traditional Christian conceptions of priesthood as they reflect authority and hierarchy but different because it is the source of eternal and divine power. According to Mormonism, the priesthood is divided into two orders, the Aaronic and Melchizedek, and has been given and retrieved by God throughout human history. In the latter days, however, God has restored the priesthood through Joseph Smith, and the Church of Jesus Christ of Latter-day Saints is the only institution that enjoys God's special power and authority to act on his behalf.

REFLECTION QUESTIONS

1. How important to Mormonism do you believe is the narrative of the loss and retrieval of the priesthood?

2. What do you make of Joseph Smith's claims to have been ordained to the priesthood by glorified NT leaders?

3. What is the difference between the Aaronic and Melchizedek priesthood? Why do these differences matter to Latter-day Saints?

4. How does learning about the priesthood hierarchy help you to understand the LDS Church?

5. What is the relationship between God's power and worthiness in your faith tradition, and how does this compare to Mormonism?

QUESTION 20

Who Belongs to the Priesthood?

"[All] worthy male members of the Church may be ordained to the priesthood without regard for race or color."[1]
~ Spencer W. Kimball, president of the LDS Church, 1973–1985

The previous two questions explored the origin, formation, and organization of the Latter-day Saint priesthood. In Mormonism, the priesthood is more than a class of clergy; it is linked to the eternal power and authority of God. Members of the priesthood participate in God's power and authority to progress in salvation and act on his behalf. Historically and presently, however, not all Latter-day Saints have been permitted to hold the priesthood. In the past, Black men were segregated from the priesthood, and in the present, its offices are inaccessible to women.

The LDS Priesthood Segregated

Joseph Smith founded the Church of Jesus Christ of Latter-day Saints during intense racial discrimination in the United States. Although the Atlantic slave trade ended while he was a young child, slavery had not. The predominantly White nation struggled to recognize the intrinsic human value in people of color. Many people of African descent were enslaved while free Black people endured harsh marginalization, even within churches. White Christians generally believed the Bible sanctioned slavery, and many thought it specifically recommended Black people for enslavement. Racist rhetoricians, like Josiah Priest, argued falsely that God cursed Cain with dark skin. This curse was passed on to Noah's son, Ham, supposedly the progenitor of all Black people,

1. Doctrine and Covenants, Official Declaration 2.

whose race was designed and destined for slavery.[2] Other arguments were less oafish but no less prejudiced.[3] But over time, people began to see Black people as they truly are—human beings made in God's image worthy of dignity, respect, and love—and the once-unusual opinion that slavery is morally wrong became so commonly held by Americans that many believed enslaved people deserved freedom, giving rise to abolitionism and pitting abolitionists against pro-slavery kin and compatriots.

In this social context, Smith founded the church and published its scriptures, which can be read as reflecting (though certainly not endorsing) prejudice theories common in the day. The Book of Mormon, for example, theorized that "the skins of the Lamanites [i.e., Native Americans] were dark" (Alma 3:6) because they were "cut off from the presence of the Lord" (2 Nephi 5:20) and cursed by him. The Lamanites had been "white, and exceedingly fair and delightsome," but to become unenticing to their tribal kin, the Nephites, "the Lord God did cause a skin of blackness to come upon them" (2 Nephi 5:21), "which was a curse because of their transgression" (Alma 3:6).[4] Similarly, the book of Moses echoed the curse of Cain when it asserted that "the seed of Cain were black" (Moses 7:22). Even if these texts do not intend to communicate what they seem, as some apologists have suggested,[5] early Latter-day

2. Josiah Priest, *Slavery, as It Relates to the Negro . . . With Structures on Abolitionism* (Albany, NY: C. Van Benthuysen, 1843).
3. For an overview of the development and content of the divine race-curse and slavery, see Stephen R. Haynes, *Noah's Curse: The Biblical Justification of American Slavery* (New York: Oxford University Press, 2002); David M. Whitford, *The Curse of Ham in the Early Modern Era: The Bible and the Justifications for Slavery* (New York: Routledge, 2016); and David M. Goldenberg, *Black and Slave: The Origins and History of the Curse of Ham* (Boston: De Gruyter, 2017).
4. Latter-day Saints have advanced interpretations of these and related texts that the Lamanite's "darkness" was a spiritual, not physiological, feature or that their dark appearance is explained by clothing or self-applied markings, like animal skins, tattoos, or body paint. See, for example, Ethan Sproat, "Skins as Garments in the Book of Mormon: A Textual Exegesis," *JBMS* 24, no. 1 (2015): 138–65; Gerrit M. Steenblik, "Demythicizing the Lamanites' 'Skin of Blackness,'" *Interpreter* 49 (2021): 167–258; Clifford P. Jones, "Understanding the Lamanite Mark," *Interpreter* 56 (2023): 171–258. While the Book of Mormon is clear "that all are alike unto God" (2 Nephi 26:33) so far as human value is concerned, the text strongly indicates the Lamanite mark was neither metaphorical nor self-applied. Nephites were forbidden from mixing "seed" (2 Nephi 5:23; Alma 3:9) with the Lamanites, and some were warned that disobedience to God meant Lamanite "skins will be whiter than yours" (Jacob 3:8). Still, the Nephites were sternly warned against racial prejudice of their Lamanite kin, "that ye revile no more against them because of the darkness of their skins" (Jacob 3:9). Such a commandment makes less sense if the darkness was merely a non-visual spiritual status, dark outerwear, or tribal markings.
5. For example, see John A. Tvedtnes, "The Charge of 'Racism' in the Book of Mormon," Conference Proceedings, FairMormon, https://archive.bookofmormoncentral.org/sites/default/files/archive-files/pdf/tvedtnes/2016-03-16/john_a._tvedtnes_the_charge_of_racism_in_the_book_of_mormon_2003.pdf.

Saints interpreted them at face value, thus perpetuating the societal racism that dominated then.[6]

Even as the church reflected the culture, it also made strides toward justice. For example, Black men were ordained to the priesthood while Smith led the church, and Smith himself argued for gradual emancipation, advocating for an equal-but-separate social policy between Black Americans and all other citizens.[7] And the early church permitted Black people entry into temples, a policy that contrasted starkly against the segregationism that plagued many other churches in the antebellum period.[8] Smith set the church on a trajectory toward desegregation and inclusion, but leaders after him shifted course. His nephew and sixth president to succeed him, Joseph F. Smith, insisted the priesthood ban had always been in place, which it had not.[9] In fact, the church only began the ban under the leadership of Brigham Young in 1852, in addition to barring Black people entry into temples.

Young's decision was not based on revelation; rather, he built upon the popular conjecture that black skin was a curse from God.[10] Young concluded that any "man who has the African blood in him cannot hold one jot nor tittle of Priesthood,"[11] that is, at least, not until the end of days.[12] He reiterated that any man with "one drop" of Black blood "cannot hold the Priesthood, and if no other prophet spake it before," he emphasized, "I will say it now, in the name of Jesus Christ."[13] Young's successor, John Taylor, taught even more odiously that black skin was a necessary marker among people so that "the devil should have a representation upon the earth as well as God."[14]

Later doctrine reconciled Mormonism's emphasis on a person's moral agency with having no choice in the matter of being born to Black parents. After all, argued one LDS writer, it is "an affront to reasoning man and to the justice and mercy of God" if Black people bore the so-called penalty of

---

6. JS apparently believed Black people were descendants of Cain, having identified "the Negroes" as "Sons of Cain" (JSJ, January 25, 1842, J2:30). Brigham Young likewise taught that "the Lord had cursed Cain's seed with blackness" (*CDBY* 1:320).
7. So Smith: "Had I any thing to do with the negro—I would confine them by strict Laws to their own Species [and] put them on a national Equalization" (JSJ, January 2, 1832, J2:212). While this reads quite repulsively today, Smith's position was progressive for the time but was nevertheless legal segregation. Still, Smith refused to "vote for a Slave holder" and advocated giving Black people equal rights and education (JSJ, December 30, 1842, J2:197).
8. W. Paul Reeve, *Let's Talk About Race and Priesthood* (Salt Lake City: Deseret, 2023), 11–30.
9. Reeve, *Let's Talk About Race and Priesthood*, 85–86.
10. For a history of the so-called "curse" of black skin and its relationship to slavery, see David M. Goldenberg, *The Curse of Ham: Race and Slavery in Early Judaism, Christianity, and Islam* (Princeton, NJ: Princeton University Press, 2003) and idem, *Black and Slave*.
11. *CDBY* 1:468.
12. See also Reeve, *Let's Talk About Race and Priesthood*, 66–67.
13. *CDBY* 1:471.
14. *JD* 22:304.

their ancestors.[15] If Joseph Smith taught that "men will be punished for their own sins," not necessarily for their parents' sins, then why would God sustain a "curse" generation after generation?[16] There had to be another reason for being born with dark skin, and the doctrine of premortality offered an apparent solution: All Black people sinned in premortality, and their dark skin was proof.

According to the book of Abraham, God organized the earth with a council of spirits, or "good" souls (Abr. 3:23). Chief among them was one "like unto the Son of Man" (Abr. 3:27), whom God appointed the head of salvation. A second candidate, whom God rejected in favor of the Son, "was angry" and fell from God's presence as "many followed after him" (Abr. 3:28). Early Latter-day Saints wildly embellished this story, speculating how Lucifer, the rejected candidate, revolted against God in heaven, and those who "were too cowardly to be leaders in the rebellion . . . were cursed with blackness and became black spirits."[17] These black spirits were then matched with black bodies on earth to correspond with the color of their spirits and to mark their cowardice. When paired with the divine curse, ostensibly given to the biblical Cain and his descendants, this interpretation explained that "the Almighty cursed him [Cain] and put a mark on him, or rather turned him black to give the black spirits a chance to come and take bodies like themselves, and the black spirits taking the black bodies made the negroes."[18] This doctrine was developed and taught by LDS leaders for generations, although it was fortunately never codified and is soundly repudiated by the church today.

Still, the damage was done. Decades of LDS thought correlated race to spiritual worthiness and disenfranchised Black people from a full Mormon life. LDS leaders, like Bruce McConkie, clarified that this inequality did not originate with the church. "It is the Lord's doing," he insisted.[19] White LDS leaders in 1949 instructed Black people to hope for a future day when their race "will be redeemed and possess all the blessings which we now have."[20]

---

15. John J. Stewart, *Mormonism and the Negro* (Orem, UT: Bookmark, 1960), 45.
16. JS, "Church History," H1:500.
17. C:360.
18. C:360. These remarks were given in 1845 by LDS apostle Orson Hyde at the invitation of Brigham Young. While Young denied the idea of a black spirit curse in the premortal existence, he nevertheless maintained black skin was, in fact, the result of a curse in mortality. See W. Paul Reeve, *Religion of a Different Color: Race and the Mormon Struggle for Whiteness* (New York: Oxford University Press, 2015), 207–8.
19. McConkie added that Black people "are not equal with other races where the receipt of certain spiritual blessings are concerned, particularly the priesthood and the temple blessings that flow therefrom," but that this segregation was by divine mandate. Bruce R. McConkie, *Mormon Doctrine* (Salt Lake City: Bookcraft, 1958), 477. At the time he wrote this, McConkie served as a seventy and would go on to be appointed as an LDS apostle.
20. "The Negroes: A Proclamation to the World," statement of the First Presidency of the Church of Jesus Christ of Latter-day Saints, August 17, 1949.

Until then, they could take solace that, although Black people were prevented from entering the priesthood, they were unlikely to "become Sons of Perdition . . . as many of the Priesthood bearers [i.e., White Latter-day Saints] might become," explained one LDS writer.[21] In 1978, the priesthood ban was finally lifted in conjunction with new revelation and in the wake of the Civil Rights Movement.

The church has since taken steps in addressing the racism of its past, most recently by publishing an anonymous essay titled "Race and the Priesthood."[22] In it, the church admitted and repudiated its racist past, but the essay lacked an apology, as one scholar pointed out.[23] He praised it as "the best official expression to date concerning LDS racial teachings," but acknowledgment without apology has left many Latter-day Saints wounded, especially Mormons of color past and present.[24] A growing group of faithful Latter-day Saints has grown weary of carrying the burden of the church's past prejudice, "baggage we should have unloaded years ago," wrote one scholar.[25] Setting it down requires "acknowledgment, repentance, repair, and reconciliation," an admission that ought to echo among Christian traditions that share in similar guilt, including my own.[26] Another scholar noticed how uniquely equipped Latter-day Saints are to advocate for marginalized groups, having once been a persecuted people. "Rather than be hobbled by our past racism, what if we owned it and used our shared history to stand in places of empathy?" he wondered.[27]

---

21. Stewart, *Mormonism and the Negro*, 34.
22. The Church of Jesus Christ of Latter-day Saints, December 6, 2013, "Race and the Priesthood," Gospel Topics Essays, https://www.churchofjesuschrist.org/study/manual/gospel-topics-essays/race-and-the-priesthood?lang=eng.
23. Matthew L. Harris, "Whiteness Theology and the Evolution of Mormon Racial Teachings," in *The LDS Gospel Topics Series: A Scholarly Engagement*, ed. Matthew L. Harris and Newell G. Bringhurst (Salt Lake City: Signature Books, 2020), 276–77.
24. Harris, "Whiteness Theology," 279. For more on the topic of race and Mormonism, see Armand L. Mauss, *All Abraham's Children: Changing Mormon Conceptions of Race and Lineage* (Urbana, IL: University of Illinois Press, 2003); Russell W. Stevenson, *For the Cause of Righteousness: A Global History of Blacks and Mormonism, 1830–2013* (Salt Lake City: Greg Kofford Books, 2014); Matthew L. Harris and Newell G. Bringhurst, eds., *The Mormon Church and Blacks: A Documentary History* (Urbana, IL: University of Illinois Press, 2015); Reeve, *Religion of a Different Color*; Max Perry Mueller, *Race and the Making of the Mormon People* (Chapel Hill, NC: University of North Carolina Press, 2017); Newell G. Bringhurst, *Saints, Slaves, and Blacks: The Changing Place of Black People Within Mormonism* (Salt Lake City: Greg Kofford Books, 2018); Joanna Brooks, *Mormonism and White Supremacy: American Religion and the Problem of Racial Innocence* (New York: Oxford University Press, 2020); and Matthew L. Harris, *Second-Class Saints: Black Mormons and the Struggle for Racial Equality* (New York: Oxford University Press, 2024).
25. Patrick Q. Mason, *Restoration: God's Call to the 21st-Century World* (Meridian, ID: Faith Matters Publishing, 2020), 60.
26. Mason, *Restoration*, 60.
27. Reeve, *Let's Talk About Race and Priesthood*, 131.

While the priesthood today is no longer segregated, it is still separated. No woman in the LDS Church is presently permitted to hold the priesthood like her male counterparts.

The LDS Priesthood Separated

According to LDS thought, gender is linked to divine being. God the Father is an embodied male whose marriage to his wife, Heavenly Mother, forms the foundation of the celestial family from which all humans descend (see question 26). Church leaders maintain that every person, whether male or female, is a child of heavenly parents and enjoys a "divine nature and destiny." Consequently, "gender is an essential characteristic of individual premortal, mortal, and eternal identity and purpose," so that men and women are designed to complement each other not only in this life but also the one to come.[28]

As eternally gendered beings, women and men progress together in their salvation equally according to the power of the priesthood. All faithful members of the church are endowed with priesthood power, but only men are equipped with its ecclesiastical authority. Distinguishing between priesthood power and authority helps to clarify this point. All women may access priesthood power through ritual, and they maintain it through personal worthiness. And women are permitted, called, and encouraged to function in many roles within the church (e.g., missions, education, administration, temple work, and humanitarian ministries). But no woman may access priesthood authority by being called to a priesthood office or function. For example, they cannot serve as a bishop nor preside over the sacrament (see question 30). Any calling issued to a woman to serve in the church comes through men, who impart on women a measure of authority within the priesthood to perform their duties. Thus, while women are endowed by the priesthood, they are not entrusted to its offices. Why, then, can only men hold priesthood authority? The answer is simple: God has ordained it so.

This theological position has been a point of contention along a spectrum of critics and conservatives, especially since the rise of feminism in the late twentieth century.[29] For some, barring the priesthood from women is not only

28. Gordon B. Hinkley, "The Family: A Proclamation to the World" (Salt Lake City: LDS Church, 1995). For the development and place of this document in LDS Church and culture, see David W. Scott and Boyd J. Peterson, "Defending the Family, Defending the Faith: An Analysis of *The Family: A Proclamation to the World*, Religious Identity, and the Politics of Same-Sex Marriage in a Mormon Community," *Journal of GLBT Family Studies* 14, no. 3 (2018): 179–95.
29. For more on the topic of women and Mormonism, see Neylan McBaine, *Women at Church: Magnifying LDS Women's Local Impact* (Sandy, UT: Greg Kofford Books, 2014); Gordon Shepherd, Lavina Fielding Anderson, and Gary Shepherd, eds., *Voices for Equality: Ordain Women and Resurgent Mormon Feminism* (Salt Lake City: Greg Kofford Books, 2015);

misogynistic but also misrepresentative of Smith's original vision. Critics contend that Smith intended to open priesthood authority to women, which is best seen in his formation of the Relief Society. Established in 1842, the women's organization was designed to foster traditionally feminine attributes of nurture and care.[30] Smith told its earliest members they were being "ordained [and] set apart to administer in that authority which is confer'd on them" and that they would hold "the keys to this Society and to the church."[31] It is argued, then, that Smith intended to ordain women to priesthood authority.[32] After all, he promised those women spiritual authority in temple ritual that would be followed by miraculous signs of cleansing, anointing, and healing the sick. As Margaret Toscano has maintained, Smith placed the church on a trajectory toward female priesthood ordination, but later leaders deviated from his egalitarian vision.[33] It was only after Smith's death that any privilege women had slowly slipped away as ecclesiastical authority consolidated in the male-only priesthood.[34]

Additionally, other branches of Mormonism do not prohibit the ordination of women. In the mid-nineteenth century, female followers of James J. Strang enjoyed priesthood positions within his church, and Community of Christ has ordained women since 1985, some of whom serve in its apostolic ranks today. Among them is Stassi Cramm, the first woman ordained in 2025 to its highest office. Moreover, critics accuse the LDS Church of being formed more by social expectations of women in American and Mormon culture than their religious tradition.

Hollie Rhees Fluhman and Camille Fronk Olson, eds., *A Place to Belong: Reflections from Modern Latter-day Saint Women* (Salt Lake City: Deseret, 2019); Barbara Morgan Gardner, *The Priesthood Power of Women: In the Temple, Church, and Family* (Salt Lake City: Deseret, 2019); and Colleen McDannell, *Sister Saints: Mormon Women Since the End of Polygamy* (New York: Oxford University Press, 2019). McDannell's book concludes with exhaustive bibliographic essays that offer readers incredibly helpful insight into the topic.

30. For an introduction to the Relief Society, see Jill Mulvay Derr, Janath Russell Cannon, and Maureen Ursenbach Beecher, *Women of Covenant: The Story of Relief Society* (Salt Lake City: Deseret, 1992).
31. Jill Mulvay Derr, Carol Cornwall Madsen, Kate Holbrook, and Matthew J. Grow, eds., *The First Fifty Years of Relief Society: Key Documents in Latter-day Saint Women's History* (Salt Lake City: Church Historian's Press, 2016), 55–56.
32. See, for example, Jonathan A. Stapley, *The Power of Godliness: Mormon Liturgy and Cosmology* (New York: Oxford University Press, 2018), 83–85.
33. Margaret M. Toscano, "'Joseph Smith's Teachings on Priesthood, Temple, and Women': A Critique," in, *The LDS Gospel Topics Series*, ed. Harris and Bringhurst, 325–56.
34. Linda King Newell, "A Gift Given: A Gift Taken: Washing, Anointing, and Blessing the Sick Among Mormon Women," *Sunstone* 6, no. 4 (1981): 16–25. According to Newell, Smith considered the Relief Society as "parallel to the priesthood organization for men," whereas LDS Church leaders have traditionally maintained it is ancillary to the priesthood (Newell, "Gift Given," 17). See also Jonathan A. Stapley and Kristine Wright, "Female Ritual Healing in Mormonism," *Journal of Mormon History* 37, no. 1 (2011): 1–85.

But Latter-day Saint leaders adamantly maintain the male-female priesthood separation of authority, grounding their position in doctrine and dismissing historical arguments as groundless. They insist, for example, that the Relief Society has always been adjacent to the priesthood, serving it in auxiliary as an appendage organization. It is peripheral, not parallel, to the priesthood, and this is the way Smith intended. Their response so dissatisfied some members of the church that an activist movement formed in 2013 to petition leadership to address gender inequality by extending priesthood ordination to women. Around the same time, the church published an anonymous essay that sustained its stance.[35] But not all LDS women are bothered by the church's doctrine. In fact, they endorse it. Many women "have not demanded the priesthood," noted Catherine Brekus, "and most seem to value marriage and motherhood as their most important calling," so positional boundaries in the priesthood for them is not a serious issue.[36] If agency is at play, these women exercise it by choosing to live in traditional modes as LDS wives and mothers.[37]

Traditional Christian readers might wonder how to relate similar debates on the role of women in their own faith tradition. In one sense, there is an overlap of agreement between the official Latter-day Saint and traditional Christian positions. The Roman Catholic Church, for example, restricts priestly and episcopal offices to men, while Protestants who hold conservative views of gender do the same for pastoral positions. In this sense, conservative Christians and Latter-day Saints have a common friend, and progressives in those movements a common opponent. But traditional Christianity and Mormonism part ways when relating the priesthood to salvation. No traditional Christian church believes that gender determines anyone's role in any aspect of their salvation, particularly in how faithfully holding a church office might enhance one's potential standing before God. "There is neither male

35. The Church of Jesus Christ of Latter-day Saints, "Joseph Smith's Teachings About Priesthood, Temple, and Women," Gospel Topics Essays, October 23, 2015, https://www.churchofjesuschrist.org/study/manual/gospel-topics-essays/joseph-smiths-teachings-about-priesthood-temple-and-women?lang=eng. For a critical evaluation of the essay, see Margaret M. Toscano, "Joseph Smith's Teachings," 325–56.
36. Catherine A Brekus, "Mormon Women and the Problem of Historical Agency," in *From the Outside Looking In: Essays on Mormon History, Theology, and Culture*, ed. Reid L. Neilson and Matthew J. Grow (New York: Oxford University Press, 2016), 96.
37. For more on the topic of women and Mormonism, see Maureen Ursenbach Beecher and Lavina Fielding Anderson, eds., *Sisters in Spirit: Mormon Women in Historical and Cultural Perspective* (Urbana, IL: University of Illinois Press, 1992); Maxine Hanks, ed., *Women and Authority: Re-emerging Mormon Feminism* (Salt Lake City: Signature Books, 1992); Linda King Newell and Valeen Tippetts Avery, *Mormon Enigma: Emma Hale Smith*, 2nd ed. (Urbana, IL: University of Illinois Press, 1994); Dave Hall, *A Faded Legacy: Amy Brown Lyman and Mormon Women's Activism, 1872–1959* (Salt Lake City: University of Utah Press, 2015); and Kate Holbrook and Matthew Bowman, eds., *Women and Mormonism: Historical and Contemporary Perspectives* (Salt Lake City: University of Utah Press, 2016).

nor female," Paul taught, "for ye are all one in Christ Jesus" (Gal 3:28). No woman needs a husband to gain her greatest celestial glory.

Summary

The LDS priesthood has not always been available to every church member. In its past, the church has barred Black men due to prejudiced doctrine that promoted whiteness, but by reversing a ban, Black men have been qualified since the 1970s. Women, however, are not presently qualified to hold priesthood offices, which has created a contemporary controversy.

REFLECTION QUESTIONS

1. Most Christian denominations in nineteenth-century America taught and practiced racist doctrines and practices. In what ways did the LDS Church follow this pattern?

2. What does it mean that Mormon scripture contains echoes of racism during the time in which it was originally published (e.g., Book of Mormon and book of Moses)?

3. Why do you believe it took so long for the LDS Church to officially welcome Black men into the priesthood?

4. How does Mormon theology inform its separation of the priesthood between men and women?

5. Does your faith tradition presently restrict its clergy to men? If so, how is it different from or like Mormonism?

PART 4

The Beliefs of Mormonism

SECTION A

Key Doctrines

QUESTION 21

What Is the Latter-day Saint View of God?

"God himself, who sits enthroned in yonder heavens, is a man like unto one of yourselves, that is the great secret."[1]
~ Joseph Smith

Traditional Christians and Latter-day Saints share many of the same convictions about God. Most obviously, they reject atheism to affirm that God exists and that he is the highest object worthy of our worship. And they agree on many points about his character: God is good, righteous, and benevolent, and his love, mercy, and grace abound. But in other areas, the LDS doctrine of God ventures so far beyond the frontier of orthodoxy that traditional Christians struggle to recognize their God in Mormonism. How could God in the LDS tradition be so familiar yet so foreign to Christians? Let's consider two key areas of disagreement: God's immutability and incorporeality.

God as an Immutable Spirit

Traditional Christianity emphasizes the transcendence of God. It describes him as a being utterly distinct from his creation. Heavenly hosts sing about him, "Holy, holy, holy" (Isa 6:3; Rev 4:8), meaning that he is not only good and righteous but also independent and infinitely set apart from all things. His self-description from the burning bush as YHWH, or "I AM THAT I AM" (Exod 3:14), displays God's absolute self-dependence. As biblical scholar Richard Bauckham noted, the immolated-yet-unconsumed bush is a metaphor of God's self-determined being. All fires need fuel, but not God. He is

1. "Conference Minutes," *T&S*, August 15, 1844, 5:613.

a fire that burns as he chooses.[2] God is, according to theologian Karl Barth, "wholly and undividedly Himself," existing *a se* (of himself), and neither "divided or divisible."[3] God doesn't need anything to be. He simply is and always has been; he neither began nor can he ever end.[4] "Our God did not begin to exist in time," explained Tatian the Syrian to the Greeks. "He alone is without beginning, and he himself is the beginning of all things."[5] And even though his creation changes and ends, the psalmist recognized, "Thou art the same, and thy years shall have no end" (Ps 102:27; see also Heb 1:12).

Moreover, God's interaction with creation does not change his nature or character. He doesn't grow up or learn like a child maturing into adulthood. God has no unrealized potential in his being, character, and knowledge, nor has he ever been in such a state of deficiency. "For I am the LORD," he declared, "I change not" (Mal 3:6). Although things change around God, declared the psalmist, "Thou art the same" (see Ps 102:25–28). For this reason, James confidently affirms that God, the great giver of love's truest gifts, is one with whom there "is no variableness, neither shadow of turning" (Jas 1:17). Among most Christian writers from Athanasius to Aquinas to present day—and embedded in the historic creeds and confessions—is the conviction that God's nature is immutable. What and who God is cannot and does not change.[6] He is the unmoved Mover of all, acting not for gain but to *give*, because God has never lacked all that is good, true, and beautiful.

Traditional Christianity also emphasizes the incorporeality of God, that he exists without a bodily form. "God is a Spirit" (John 4:24), but unlike other spiritual beings (e.g., angels) he is not restricted to one location. Not even the heavens can contain him (see 2 Chr 2:6; 1 Kgs 8:27; Isa 66:1). God fills heaven and earth (see Jer 23:24) so that his presence is inescapable (see Ps 139:7–8), an impossible feat for beings who are bodily or spatially restricted. Although, at times, the Bible uses anthropomorphic language to communicate God's presence and

---

2. Richard Bauckham, *Who Is God? Key Moments of Biblical Revelation* (Grand Rapids: Baker Academic, 2020), 35–45.
3. Karl Barth, *The Doctrine of God: The Reality of God II*, vol. 2 of *Church Dogmatics*, ed. G. W. Bromiley and T. F. Torrance (London: T&T Clark, 2009), 6.
4. As Puritan theologian Stephen Charnock noted, "It is impossible for any to give a beginning and being to itself: if it acts, it must exist, and so exist before it existed. A thing would exist as a cause before it existed as an effect. He who is not cannot be the cause that he is; if, therefore, God does exist and has not his being from another, he must exist from eternity." (*The Existence and Attributes of God*, ed. Mark Jones, 2 vols. [Wheaton, IL: Crossway, 2022], 1:420).
5. Kevin Douglas Hill, ed., *Christianity in the First and Second Centuries: Essential Readings* (Dallas: Fontes Press, 2022), 267.
6. Immutability is among the attributes of God of classical theism, such as self-dependence, timelessness, simplicity, and impassibility. See James E. Dolezal, *All That Is in God* (Grand Rapids: Reformation Heritage, 2017); Matthew Barrett, *None Greater: The Undomesticated Attributes of God* (Grand Rapids: Baker Books, 2019); Craig A. Carter, *Contemplating God with the Great Tradition: Recovering Trinitarian Classical Theism* (Grand Rapids: Baker Academic, 2021).

activity—for example, the "hand of God" (Job 19:21)—it is a mistake to read such descriptions through a flat, biblicist lens. If God literally has arms and hands (see Jer 21:5), does he also have feathers and wings (see Ps 91:4)?

Moreover, God is not limited to bodily form, which is a point stressed in the prohibition against crafting idols, tangible images of an intangible God.[7] As theologian Thomas White noted, the Decalogue "underscores that God cannot be represented in an image, an ancient indication of the idea that God is not an embodied being."[8] Indeed, the Hebrews were prohibited from making images of God because they "saw no form on the day that the LORD spoke" at Horeb (Deut 4:15 ESV). It's impossible to make an idol of God because he has no body to model it after. Thus, although the Son of God "was made flesh, and dwelt among us" (John 1:14) and "in him dwelleth all the fulness of the Godhead bodily" (Col 2:9), the incarnation remains unique to him. The *corpus Christi*, or body of Christ, is not replicated across the divine nature that the Son shares with the Father and the Holy Spirit, who remain eternally unbodied.

Christians, then, have traditionally held that God is an incorporeal spirit who is ultimately independent, that he has neither cause nor need of anything outside himself, and that his nature and character are ultimate and unchangeable.

God as Changeable and Embodied

At times, LDS teaching appears to agree with traditional Christianity. The Book of Mormon, for example, described God as "unchangeable from all eternity to all eternity" (Moroni 8:18). Among Smith's earliest revelations is a description of God's nature that fits neatly into—or, perhaps more accurately, draws indirectly from—the creedal tradition: "There is a God in Heaven who is infinite & Eternal from everlasting to everlasting the same unchangeable God the Maker of Heaven & Earth."[9] But these bits of orthodoxy are scant. As Mormonism developed, so did its conception of God.[10] Such change is expected, after all, from a movement that saw itself restoring doctrinal purity out of a history of theological corruption. To outside observers, however, LDS doctrine has not restored ideas

7. On this point, scholar Brittany E. Wilson argues that the Decalogue's prohibition against idolatry is mainly concerned with "God's superiority in relation to other gods" ("Imaging the Divine: Idolatry and God's Body in the Book of Acts," *New Testament Studies* 65 [2019]: 356). However, God cannot be reduced to a material image precisely because his being transcends embodied reality. To Richard Lints's point on divine anthropomorphism, however, "undoubtedly these do not imply straightforwardly that God has a body, and must be viewed as consistent with the common claim in the canon that he cannot be seen or touched, because he is not a material being. The Creator is not to be confused with the creation" (*Identity and Idolatry: The Image of God and Its Inversion* [Downers Grove: IVP Academic, 2015], 38).
8. Thomas Joseph White, *The Trinity: On the Nature and Mystery of the One God* (Washington: Catholic University of America Press, 2022), 239.
9. MRB, 79 [D&C 20:17].
10. See Kurt Widmer, *Mormonism and the Nature of God: A Theological Evolution, 1830–1915* (Jefferson, NC: McFarland, 2000).

about the nature of God but has instead tumbled into familiar pitfalls of heterodoxies, past and present.

To begin, according to Joseph Smith, God *began.*[11] "We have imagined that God was God from all eternity," he said, claiming instead that "God came *to be* God."[12] God has a theogony, a moment of his beginning, because, Smith reasoned, God is described as Father—and no father ever became so without first being a son. Thus, God the Father must have once been born, reared, and matured from sonship to fatherhood.[13] There is "a God above the Father of our Lord Jesus Christ," he said.[14] In doing so, Smith read the human experience onto the nature of God when traditional Christianity has long argued for the opposite. Even the heresy of Arianism affirms that God is *anarchos*, having neither beginning nor first cause.[15] For Smith, however, God is immortal—he's forever unending—but not *anarchos* nor immutable, or unchanging. God will never end, but he did begin and does change. The only truly eternal thing to God is his intelligence and matter (attributes we share with him as humans), but God as he *is* has not always been so.

Smith speculated that God necessarily changes, having increased like a child to an exalted man, "from one small degree to another, and from a small capacity to a great one."[16] God's interaction with his environment developed and changed his nature. He learned, matured, and grew. And his growth has not yet culminated, meaning God's actions are motivated, in part, by the desire for gain, to complete some incompletion. God is a being whose perfection is unfinished, at least as it is measured against himself. God's progression is

---

11. By contrast, some LDS theologians contend for the eternality of God's divine nature. David Paulsen and Hal Boyd, for example, maintain that God the Father "has always existed and will always exist," further adding that God "is not dependent on anyone or anything other than His own nature for His existence" ("The Nature of God in Mormon Thought," in *The Oxford Handbook of Mormonism*, ed. Terryl L. Givens and Philip L. Barlow (New York: Oxford University Press, 2015), 247).
12. "Conference Minutes," *T&S*, August 15, 1844, 5:614 (emphasis added).
13. So Smith, in 1844: "If Jesus Christ was the son of God, and John discovered that God the Father of Jesus Christ had a Father, you may suppose that he had a Father also. Where was there ever a son without a father? and where was there ever a father without first being a son?" (Joseph Smith, History, 1838–1856, vol. F-1, *JSP*, 103). Earlier, in 1840, Smith delivered a public lecture primarily to non-Mormons in which he articulated a more traditional description of God's ungenerated eternality. "I believe that God is Eternal," he is recorded as saying, "that he had no beginning and can have no End" (JS, discourse, February 5, 1840, D7:178). But for Smith to be consistent, he likely meant that God is eternal in the sense that his intelligence is uncreated, just as the human soul is eternal, having "Existed from Eternity in the bosom of Divinity" (JS, discourse, February 5, 1840, D7:178).
14. JS, discourse, June 16, 1844, D15:268 (emend.).
15. Franz Dünzel, *A Brief History of the Doctrine of the Trinity in the Early Church*, trans. John Bowden (London: T&T Clark, 2007), 43.
16. Joseph Smith, History, 1838–1856, vol. E-1, *JSP*, 1971. This quote explains human progression into gods, but Smith hints that the same progressive activity was true for God, having ostensibly refuted "the Idea that God was God from all eternity" (JSJ, April 7, 1844, J3:218).

"continuously self-surpassing," explained LDS theologians.[17] Smith taught that God self-surpasses in the works of his creation and in his authority. Having once worked out "his kingdom with fear and trembling," God now awaits the kingdom of his son to enjoy "kingdom upon kingdom."[18] In doing so, God's glory would increase, taking on "a higher exaltation."[19]

The LDS nature of God aligns with open theism and is particularly akin to what theologian Brian Davies called "theistic personalism," in which God changes through personal interaction with his environment and creatures.[20] According to theistic personalists, God is the greatest intelligence among other beings, "a person like us only greater, older, wiser, more powerful, and immortal."[21] This is especially true of his creation, say open theists, with which God's relationship "is that of a most moved, not unmoved, Mover."[22] The aperture of God's intellect widens with experience, as does the progression of his being, principally as it relates to his loving relationships in triune communion and with humans.[23] God can—indeed, he *must*—change according to his dynamic affairs with principles, beings, and material creation. So it is with Mormonism. God's nature is in unending flux and process without aseity, or absolute independence. God is ever-progressing, and his progression depends on interactions outside himself.[24] "The God I serve is progressing eternally," said Brigham Young, and this progression often includes increase in knowledge

---

17. David L. Paulsen and Hal Boyd, *Are Christians Mormon?* (New York: Routledge, 2017), 116. Elsewhere, they clarified that in the absence of "a ceiling or upper limit" to divine perfection, "God the Father is eternally self-surpassing but unsurpassable by others" ("The Nature of God in Mormon Thought," 254).
18. "Conference Minutes," *T&S*, August 15, 1844, 5:614.
19. "Conference Minutes," *T&S*, August 15, 1844, 5:614.
20. Brian Davies, *An Introduction to the Philosophy of Religion*, 3rd ed. (New York: Oxford University Press, 2004), 9–15. Davies pointed out that advocates of theistic personalism argue that God cannot be taken seriously as a person if he is unchangeable and impassible, a concern shared by JS and his theological inheritors. Theistic personalism, however, is still far removed from LDS thought, especially regarding the incorporeality of God. While LDS doctrine affirms that God is embodied, Richard Swinburne, a theistic personalist, described a theist as someone who understands God as "something like a 'person without a body'" (*The Coherence of Theism* [New York: Oxford University Press, 1993], 1).
21. Carter, *Contemplating God with the Great Tradition*, 17.
22. Clark H. Pinnock, *Most Moved Mover: A Theology of God's Openness* (Grand Rapids: Baker Academic, 2001), 3.
23. Charles R. Harrell noticed that this view has been challenged by church leaders who advocate for a more traditional view of God's knowledge. As a result, the "coexistence of these two opposing traditions about God has led to conflicting views and confusing dialogue when discussing the nature of God" (*"This Is My Doctrine": The Development of Mormon Theology* [Salt Lake City: Greg Kofford Books, 2011], 130). This tension, however, is unlikely to be relieved without relinquishing some aspects of divine eternal progression. If God progresses in his nature, then he cannot be said to have infinite, or even unrealized, knowledge.
24. If this is the case, then the attributes of God progress with him, e.g., God's goodness increases as he grows in knowledge of good, desires more good, and acts out of greater goodness. His

and power, i.e., a qualitative progression in being.[25] His contemporary Orson Pratt, however, presented a more abstract view, suggesting that while a particular divine being might progress, God ultimately remains eternal and self-existent.[26] This debate reflects differing understandings of the nature and extent of God's progression, a discussion later framed by LDS scholars who distinguish between qualitative (gaining knowledge/power) and quantitative (increasing creations/dominions) models of divine advancement.[27]

But divine progression raises concerns from the perspective of traditional Christianity. If God's nature progresses, can it regress? If God can be added to, might he be subtracted from, and was he truly God before he was added to? Did God progress morally, and, if so, was he at any point able to sin? If he was able to sin, then God is not merely a passible being but also a peccable one (or, at the very least, was at one time peccable).[28] Traditional Christians are right to express concern here, leading some to wonder whether Mormonism could be considered, "even broadly, Christian," as one critic wrote.[29] This concern is not meant to slander Latter-day Saints; rather, it's an occasion to reflect together on the deep dependence our salvation has on God's nature. Open theism jeopardizes salvation itself, for our redemption depends on "the *immutability* of his counsel" (Heb 6:17, emphasis added). The unchanging promises of God are only possible if the promise-giver is unchanging, or immutable.

Smith also taught that God "the Father has a body of flesh & bones as tangible as mans," a radical departure from traditional Christianity.[30] He reiterated that "there is no other God in heaven but that God who has flesh and bones."[31] Perhaps Smith drew this conclusion from his early visionary experiences during which he claimed to have seen God the Father and Jesus Christ as two distinct and embodied personages (see question 7). Or perhaps Smith thought, as philosopher Thomas Hobbes did, that it was meaningless to imagine immaterial substance apart from a body, so God must be

---

goodness, therefore, is not perfect, as Paulsen and Boyd suggest, but *perfected*, which marks a significant departure from classic theism ("The Nature of God in Mormon Thought," 251).

25. *CDBY* 4:2396.
26. Orson Pratt, "Great First Cause" (Liverpool: R. James, 1851).
27. Matthew Bowman, "What Is the Nature of God's Progress?," *BYU Studies* 60, no. 3 (2021): 65–73.
28. Some readers might assume that Latter-day Saint teachings on divine progression imply that God the Father sinned at some point. JS taught, however, that the Son does only what he sees the Father do (see John 5:19), suggesting the Father as the standard of sinless behavior.
29. Richard Sherlock, "Becoming Like God: A Critique," in *The LDS Gospel Topics Series: A Scholarly Engagement*, ed. Matthew L. Harris and Newell G. Bringhurst (Salt Lake City: Signature Books, 2020), 52.
30. JSJ, April 2, 1843, J2:326 [D&C 130:22].
31. JS, discourse, January 5, 1841, D7:494. Smith also differentiated the corporeality of the Holy Spirit, who "is yet a spiritual Body," from the kinds of bodies had by the Son (Andrew F. Ehat and Lyndon W. Cook, eds., *The Words of Joseph Smith* [Provo, UT: RSC, BYU, 1980], 382).

embodied.[32] Certainly, Smith believed God the Father is an immortal and forever-gendered man, which implicitly opens the possibility of a divine feminine figure, a Heavenly Mother, who is an immortal and forever-gendered woman.[33] Brigham Young went so far as to suggest Adam was God the Father incarnate, a doctrine that Latter-day Saint leaders resisted during his life and rejected after his death.[34]

Even though at times Mormonism has emphasized God's corporeality as spiritual, Smith was adamant that the divine body is of a spiritual substance, something akin to the perfected body of Christ in his resurrected state. "If you were to see him today," Smith clarified, "you would see him in all the person, image and very form as a man."[35] For Smith, there was a distinction between "a body of flesh and blood, which is mortal and human, and a glorified body of flesh and bone, which is immortal and divine," explained one Latter-day Saint scholar.[36] But to affirm, as Tertullian did, that God the Father mysteriously exists in immaterial corporeality is very different from claiming that he dwells in a spiritual-material body as tangible as ours.[37] The former yields to Christ's definitive statement that "God is a Spirit" (John 4:24), while the latter is a Latter-day Saint revival of Audianism, the ancient belief that God exists in bodily form, after which the human body is modeled. The church has consistently rejected this position, which essentially recasts God as a great Aristotelian being composed of form and matter.[38] "God is Spirit," said Tatian the Syrian, "not pervading matter,

32. See Geoffrey Gorham, "The Theological Foundations of Hobbesian Physics: A Defence of Corporeal God," *British Journal for the History of Philosophy* 21 (2013): 240–61. If this concern bothered Smith, it has not concerned other theologians. As Katherine Sonderegger put it succinctly: "God is Object, yes, but not Body, most certainly not 'extended matter'" (*Systematic Theology*, vol. 1, *The Doctrine of God* [Minneapolis: Fortress Press, 2015], 491).
33. See Jill Mulvay Derr, "The Significance of 'O My Father' in the Personal Journey of Eliza R. Snow," *BYU Studies* 36, no. 1 (1997): 84–126; David L. Paulsen and Martin Pulido, "'A Mother There': A Survey of Historical Teachings About Mother in Heaven," *BYU Studies* 50, no. 1 (2011): 2–28; Blaire Ostler, "Heavenly Mother: The Mother of All Women," *Continuing Revelation: Essays on Doctrine*, ed. Bryan Buchanan (Salt Lake City: Signature Books, 2021), 141–50.
34. See Jonathan A. Stapley, "Brigham Young's Garden Cosmology," *Journal of Mormon History* 47, no. 1 (2021): 68–86.
35. "Conference Minutes," *T&S*, August 15, 1844, 5:613.
36. Terryl L. Givens, *Wrestling the Angel: The Foundations of Mormon Thought: Cosmos, God, Humanity* (New York: Oxford University Press, 2015), 95.
37. See Petr Kitzler, "Tertullian's Concept of the Soul and His Corporealistic Ontology," in *Tertullianus Afer: Tertullien et la littérature chrétienne d'Afrique*, ed. Jérôme Lagouanère and Sabine Fialon (Turnhout: Brepols Publishers, 2015), 43–62. For an LDS interpretation of Tertullian, see David L. Paulsen, "Divine Embodiment: The Earliest Christian Understanding of God," in *Early Christians in Disarray: Contemporary LDS Perspectives on the Christian Apostasy*, ed. Noel B. Reynolds (Provo, UT: Foundation for Ancient Research and Mormon Studies, 2005), 239–93.
38. Smith's nature of God appears farther from orthodoxy than Aristotle's theory of universal hylomorphism, the idea that natural, living beings consist of primary matter and substantial form existing in potentiality and actuality. See Robert Pasnau, "Form and Matter," in

but the Maker of material spirits and of the forms that are in matter."[39] This point is not trivial because a distinction must be made between worshiping things of matter and worshiping matter's Maker. "I do not worship matter," wrote John of Damascus, "I worship the Creator of matter, who became matter for my sake."[40] Paul praised the incarnation for making the unseen God seen, for Christ "is the image of the invisible God" (Col 1:15). As Catharina Regina von Greiffenberg reminded us, "Invisibility takes nothing from its reality."[41] All reality—even intelligence and matter—owes its total existence to the invisible God.

Summary

Joseph Smith set Mormonism's conception of God on an irreversibly separate trajectory from the traditional Christian faith. In Latter-day Saint thought, God is immortal but not eternal. He is spiritual but also material. He is neither omnipotent (all-powerful overall) nor omniscient (all-knowing overall). Instead, God is *maxipotent* (most-powerful over his creation) and *maxiscient* (most-knowing over his creation). For this reason, traditional Christians tend to keep the Latter-day Saint doctrine of God at arm's length, situating it outside of classical definitions and descriptions of his nature.

REFLECTION QUESTIONS

1. What are some important points of agreement about God between traditional Christianity and Mormonism?

2. Why does it matter that traditional Christianity teaches God is an immutable spirit?

3. Can God truly be *anarchos* (having neither beginning nor first cause) in Mormon thought? Why or why not?

4. What questions arise if God progressed morally to his exalted state? How might these questions be answered?

5. Read Exodus 20:4–6 and Deuteronomy 4:15–18. How does the Mormon view of a physically embodied God relate to biblical prohibitions against idolatry?

The Cambridge History of Medieval Philosophy, ed. Robert Pasnau and Christina Van Dyke, 2 vols. (Cambridge: Cambridge University Press, 2010), 2:635–46.

39. Hill, *Christianity in the First and Second Centuries*, 267.
40. Alister E. McGrath, ed., *The Christian Theology Reader, 5th ed.* (Oxford: Wiley Blackwell, 2017), 243.
41. Catharina Regina von Greiffenberg, *Meditations on the Incarnation, Passion, and Death of Jesus Christ*, ed. and trans. Lynne Tatlock (Chicago: University of Chicago Press, 2009), 180.

QUESTION 22

What Is the Latter-day Saint View of Jesus Christ?

"Jesus was a God in the pre-earthly existence. Our Father in heaven gave him a name above all other names—Christ."[1]
~ Ezra Taft Benson, President of the LDS Church, 1985–1994

When Jesus Christ asked Peter "Whom do men say that I the Son of man am?" (Matt 16:13), his question probed the heart of God's redemptive work. Answering incorrectly risks reducing Jesus to a mere prophet or moral teacher in the long tradition of God's representatives to Israel. Certainly, this was the case for those who equated him with John the Baptist or "one of the prophets" (Matt 16:14). To answer correctly, though, as Peter did, was to recognize not only that God sent his Messiah to secure our redemption, but that the Son of God himself was dwelling among us on earth, our Immanuel, God with us. So, Peter confessed, "Thou art the Christ, the Son of the living God" (Matt 16:16).

An early LDS revelation echoed Peter's confession, describing the Messiah as "Jesus Christ the Son of the living God," and signaling Joseph Smith's intent for his future church.[2] Jesus Christ would play the central role in what would become The Church of *Jesus Christ* of Latter-day Saints. Yet, as the revelation continued, it also promised the imminent restoration of "the fulness of [Christ's] gospel," implying the church he promised to build on Peter's confession was somehow incomplete (see Matt 16:18).[3] The Christ of traditional

1. Gary James Bergera, ed., *Statements of the LDS First Presidency: A Topical Compendium* (Salt Lake City: Signature Books, 2007), 233.
2. JS, revelation, June 1829, D1:68 [D&C 14:9].
3. JS, revelation, June 1829, D1:68 [D&C 14:9].

Christianity was insufficient; something more was needed, which latter-day revelation gradually supplied. Thus, the Jesus presented by Mormonism is both familiar and foreign to traditional Christians.

Claiming that Latter-day Saints worship an utterly different Jesus than traditional Christians is both rashly uncharitable and yet precisely true. On the one hand, it cannot be said that LDS theology teaches a Jesus who is totally foreign to the Christ of Christianity and completely devoid of any similarities whatsoever. Mormonism affirms that he was truly human, born of the Virgin Mary and raised in Nazareth. He gathered twelve disciples, performed miracles, and preached repentance. He lived sinlessly, setting the ultimate example of holiness and human flourishing. The object of Christ's life-giving ministry was paradoxically his sacrificial death for the atonement of the world's sin. After three days in the tomb, Jesus was resurrected and later ascended to the Father, where he awaits his return to judge the living and the dead. All these descriptions of Christ come from the Book of Mormon, which bears the subtitle "Another Testimony of Jesus Christ," and leads Latter-day Saints to envision him as "a shepherd, a comforter, an example for how to live their lives."[4]

On the other hand, the LDS view of Christ departs from traditional Christology in significant ways. According to Mormonism, Jesus is literally the Son of God, the firstborn child of God the Father and Heavenly Mother, making Christ our eldest spirit brother, whose membership in the Godhead is not timeless but began after his ascent to godhood by personal progression. These differences overshadow every shared conviction between traditional Christianity and Mormonism about the nature of the Son of God. Who is Jesus Christ according to Mormonism? To answer this question, we will consider two fundamental areas of disagreement: the nature of the Son and his relationship to the Father.

Christ's Nature According to Traditional Christianity

Jesus was truly human. Like all people, he was born, grew up, and increased "in wisdom and stature" (Luke 2:52). He traveled by foot, ate meals, and grew tired. He cried with his friends when one of them died. Sometimes he needed a break from the crowd and retreated to solitary rest. Jesus was even "in all points tempted like as we are, yet without sin" (Heb 4:15). Christ's humanity was never in question during the NT period. Instead, the earliest Christians were awestruck by his claims to deity. How could a human man, as great as he was, also be God? It's one thing to wonder whether "any good thing [can] come out of Nazareth" (John 1:46), but could *God* come from Nazareth, too?

The path to answering this question was long and winding, spanning over centuries and, at times, veering dangerously close to heresies that either refused to acknowledge Christ's full deity (e.g., Ebionism and Arianism), or oppositely,

4. John G. Turner, *The Mormon Jesus: A Biography* (Cambridge, MA: Belknap Press, 2016), 289.

highlighted his deity so brightly that one could barely see his humanity (e.g., Docetism and Apollinarianism).[5] To err in this area devastates Peter's confession that Jesus is the divine Son of God and the long-anticipated Messiah from among men. As Leo the Great contended, there is an "equal danger in believing the Lord Jesus Christ to be God only and not man also, or man only and not God," because Jesus would forfeit his unique role as mediator between both.[6]

The early church was particularly interested in understanding the Son's deity and his relationship to the Father. A fourth-century council in Nicaea recognized the both-and reality of the Son as a distinct person from the Father and of the same essence with the Father.[7] The Son is not merely like the Father; instead, the Father and the Son share the exact same divine essence—a concept also known as consubstantiation (or *homoousia*). These terms mean that both the Father and the Son share every attribute that is essential to God. Tertullian likened this relationship to a natural spring that produces a river.[8] Both are made of the same thing (water), but they are nevertheless distinguishable from each other as a spring is from a river. And as the only begotten of the Father, nothing of God's deity is diminished in the Son. Tatian the Syrian likened this phenomenon to lighting a torch with fire. The unlit torch receives its flames from the fire without taking away from the original fire's power, nor is it, the now-lit torch, a weaker form of the fire. The torch becomes fully lit, and the power of its flames is indistinguishable from its original source, even though the original fire and now-lit torch are distinguishable from one another.[9] So it is with the Father and the Son, who share

---

5. On the development of orthodox Christology, Latter-day Saints often assume a rather skeptical (and sometimes uncharitable) posture toward the ecumenical councils. Shadows of doubt are cast over the motivations of their participants, as the narrative is told against a backdrop of apostasy where the theological "losers" were often remnants of primitive Mormonism who were ostracized by politically motivated theological "winners." But the development of orthodoxy "should not really be thought of in terms of winners and losers," argued Alister E. McGrath; "it is better understood as a quest for authenticity" (*Heresy: A History of Defending the Truth* [New York: HarperCollins, 2010], 27). The councils' goals were to understand the mystery of faith, and once it was understood, to develop doctrinal matrices that best comport with revelation, "an intellectual scaffolding . . . to preserve the mystery, to safeguard what the church had discovered to be true" (McGrath, *Heresy*, 28). The framework that offered the superior interpretation of the scriptural witness of Christ led to the development of creeds.
6. *ACD* 2:166.
7. More could be written on the development of orthodox Christology, especially through the Nestorian and Eutychian controversies to the Council of Chalcedon. It is sufficient to say, however, that LDS Christology departs from Nicaea by claiming the Son to be *homoiousios* with the Father, so Mormon thought does not fit neatly into post-Nicene dialogue.
8. Tertullian, *Against Praxeas* VIII.
9. Tatian the Syrian, "Address to the Greeks," in Kevin Douglas Hill, ed., *Christianity in the First and Second Centuries: Essential Readings* (Dallas: Fontes Press, 2022), 267–69. The analogy here breaks down, however. There was never a time when the Son was an "unlit torch" because the Light of the World has always been so and never began to be so.

the same essence and yet are distinctly identifiable persons. As the gospel of John declares, "The Word was with God, and the Word was God" (John 1:1), and this Word, the eternal Logos of God, mysteriously "was made flesh, and dwelt among us" (John 1:14). Thus, while the immutable Son of God is an unmoved Mover, Jesus of Nazareth is our most moved Messiah.[10] Caricatures of a cold, austere God must yield to the incarnation, when the immutable God—in whom "we live, and move, and have our being" (Acts 17:28)—truly experienced the human condition. This is a paradox, a great mystery that surpasses human reason without opposing or dismissing it. We receive the incarnation itself just as we receive the incarnate one—by faith. Appealing to mystery is not a cop-out but a confession, a recognition that our finite comprehension can only take us so far until all we can do is worship the sheer grandeur of the Lord Jesus Christ.

So, why did early Christians come to these conclusions? The Bible consistently forbids creaturely association with the Creator. No attribute of God may be attributed to anything or anyone beside God, nor may they share in his works, name, or worship.[11] To associate anything with what God *does* is to equate it with who God *is*. It's shocking, then, for the earliest Christians—mainly monotheistic Jews—to believe what they did about Christ. Jesus is one in whom "dwelleth all the fulness of the Godhead bodily" (Col 2:9). He is the one through whom all things were created (see John 1:3; Col 1:16–17). Christ sustains the cosmos by presently "upholding all things by the word of his power" (see Heb 1:3; cf. Rom 11:36; Col 1:15–19). Like God, Jesus is called Lord, Holy One, Savior, and even shares in the holiest name, YHWH, but is mysteriously distinct from him (see Exod 3:14; John 8:58; cf. John 1:1). God's name and redemptive work collide in Jesus when the apostle Paul promises "whosoever shall call upon the name of the Lord shall be saved" (Rom 10:13). Here, Paul attributes to Christ what Joel first attributed to YHWH (see Joel 2:32). No wonder Jesus not only directs worship to himself but also receives it (see John 5:22–23; 20:27–29; Rev 5:11–12). The Son of God is the immutable creator who was made flesh, died for the forgiveness of sins, and is "the firstborn from the dead" (Col 1:18), the first among many to resurrect into eternal life.

While Mormonism shares many of these same convictions, it also teaches that Jesus Christ is literally the firstborn son of God, who ascended to his glorified position within the Godhead. From a traditional Christian perspective, then, it is more useful to ask how, instead of whether, Mormonism affirms the deity of Christ.

---

10. K. Scott Oliphint, *God with Us: Divine Condescension and the Attributes of God* (Wheaton, IL: Crossway, 2012), 124.
11. See Richard Bauckham, *Jesus and the God of Israel* (Grand Rapids: Eerdmans, 2008); Gerald O'Collins, *Christology: A Biblical, Historical, and Systematic Study of Jesus*, 2nd ed. (New York: Oxford University Press, 2009), 141–57.

Christ's Nature According to Mormonism

Like traditional Christianity, Mormonism affirms that the Son of God came to earth in the flesh, having dwelt among his own "in a tabernacle of clay" (Mosiah 3:5). And he is divine, the Firstborn of the Father, an instinctively familiar title to Christians, but one that carries with it different meaning. The Bible frequently uses the plain meaning of "firstborn" to describe order of birth, while at other times "firstborn" indicates a unique status with God (see Exod 4:22; Ps 89:20, 27–29; Jer 31:9). It is in this second sense, for example, that Christ is understood to be the firstborn of creation, preeminent over the universe (see Col 1:15), and the firstborn among those who would share in his resurrection (see Rom 8:29). Christ as firstborn, then, does not necessarily describe his origin but rather his status, one of absolute supremacy and glory.

When applied to Christ, Mormonism interprets "firstborn" in both senses simultaneously. As one LDS theologian explained, "Jesus was the firstborn spirit child of God the Father and thus the recipient of the birthright of the royal family."[12] Jesus, then, is the "only begotten" Son of the Father who became so—but was not always so—by virtue of being born first and achieving exaltation prior to us, his spiritual younger siblings, who receive glorified states through our elder brother. Thus, the glorified nature of the Son is not truly eternal (having no beginning), and neither is his membership in the Godhead. Instead, the Son joined his Father, *elohim*, as his divine council, becoming YHWH, "the Great Jehovah of the Old Testament," the creator of this cosmos and object of our worship.[13] And in his subordinated status, the Son, having learned about the Father's past redemptive work (i.e., death and resurrection), emulated the Father because, as Christ taught, "the Son can do nothing of himself, but what he seeth the Father do" (John 5:19).[14]

In this way, LDS Christology departs significantly from orthodox Christology. While Christians have traditionally believed the Son to be eternally same-in-essence with the Father, Mormonism understands the Father and Son to be *similar* in essence. They are essentially of the same species of being but do not share the same being. The LDS position genuinely

12. Robert L. Millet, *A Different Jesus?: The Christ of the Latter-day Saints* (Grand Rapids: Eerdmans, 2005), 20. Relatedly, Mormonism also acknowledges (but has no official doctrine) concerning a divine feminine figure, Heavenly Mother, the godly Eve of all souled beings.
13. "The Living Christ: The Testimony of the Apostles," cited in Terryl L. Givens and Reid L. Neilson, eds., *The Columbia Sourcebook of Mormons in the United States* (New York: Columbia University Press, 2014), 50.
14. Latter-day Saints interpret this passage to mean the Son bore the cross and resurrected for salvation, in part, because the Father had also done so, and the Son was faithfully following the Father's example. Yet the present tense of the passage renders a past-tense interpretation untenable, pointing instead to the inseparable operations of the Father and the Son presently. In other words, the Son cannot do anything other than what the Father does because their redemptive works are unified and undivided.

appreciates the holy grandeur of the Son's glorified nature distinct from the cosmos he created (*contra* Ebionism or Arianism). When compared to orthodoxy, however, Mormonism minimizes the Son's timeless and immediate sharing in God's glorious nature.[15] The Son is very much 'like' God but lacks eternal equality with God. To recall Tertullian's imagery, sometime in eternity past, the Father was a river-less spring.

For traditional Christians, then, LDS Christology teaches a Jesus who is not eternally God, and if so, then not truly God. He is only ever a God-like being who became a member of the Godhead. It is true that Mormonism teaches an eternality to the Son, owing to Smith's teaching that the only uncreated things are minds and their ideas, or "intelligence," from which all rational beings ultimately originate.[16] As with the Father, the Son is, in a sense, eternal insofar as his intelligence is without beginning or end. But so are all intelligences for that matter; every reader of this book is co-eternal with God in this sense. What is at issue is not whether the Son had some ideal premortal existence that he shared with other intelligences. At issue is whether the Son is ungenerated and eternally personal and complete. To affirm the latter is to confess that his divine nature is uncreated and timeless.[17] And while traditional Christianity affirms with the Bible that Jesus is the only begotten Son of God, it understands this title to mean that the Father is eternally the Son's Father, not by sourcing the Son's essence, but by mutual loving relationship that communicates essence.[18] As Augustine explained, the Father did not at some point in time begin to beget the Son, for "the life which the Father gave to the Son by begetting is co-eternal with the life of the Father who gave."[19]

---

15. Here, LDS Christology is and is not like Arianism. On the one hand, both Arianism and Mormonism affirm that the Son achieved his exalted status through obedience and self-sacrifice. On the other hand, Arianism prefers adoptive language to describe the relationship between Father and Son, not literal descriptions like Mormonism. See Rebecca Lyman, "Arius and Arians," in *The Oxford Handbook of Early Christian Studies*, ed. Susan Ashbrook Harvey and David G. Hunter (New York: Oxford University Press, 2008), 237–57.
16. So Smith: "Intelligence exists upon a self existent principle. . . . The first principles of man are self existent with God" ("Conference Minutes," *T&S*, August 15, 1844, 5:615).
17. For discussion in the preexistence of the Son, see Simon J. Gathercole, *The Preexistent Son: Recovering the Christologies of Matthew, Mark, and Luke* (Grand Rapids: Eerdmans, 2006).
18. See Fred Sanders and Scott R. Swain, eds., *Retrieving Eternal Generation* (Grand Rapids: Zondervan, 2017); Steven J. Duby, *Jesus and the God of Classical Theism: Biblical Christology in Light of the Doctrine of God* (Grand Rapids: Baker Academic, 2022), 51–96. So Duby: "This eternal generation involves the Father sharing or communicating the divine essence and life to the Son so that the Son has and is all that the Father essentially has and is. Eternal generation entails that the Son is personally distinct from the Father (since he receives from the Father the divine essence, while the Father receives it from no one) and essentially one with the Father (since the Son does indeed receive the fullness of the essence)." Duby, *Jesus and the God of Classical Theism*, 61.
19. Augustine, *On the Trinity: Books 8–15*, ed. Gareth B. Matthews, trans. Stephen McKenna (Cambridge: Cambridge University Press, 2002), 219.

So, why does this matter in the end? Because one's understanding of the nature of Jesus underpins Peter's salvific confession, "Thou are the Christ, the Son of the living God" (Matt 16:16). And as Jesus taught elsewhere, "He that seeth me seeth him that sent me" (John 12:45). To know the Son of God, then, is to know God. So, whom do we see when we look at Jesus Christ; the eternal Son *of* God himself or a generated Son *from* God? The answer to this question is not trivial, for when we see the Son truly, Jesus says, we see the living God truly, too.

Summary

Traditional Christian and LDS convictions about Jesus Christ overlap in many significant ways. They disagree sharply, however, over the nature of the Son of God and his relationship with the Father. While traditional Christianity teaches that the Son is eternally same-in-essence with the Father, Mormonism teaches the Son to be similar-in-essence with the Father. And where traditional Christianity sees Christ as the firstborn of God in a metaphorical sense, Mormonism believes the Son is literally the first spirit child born of God. These differences effectively create two familiar yet distinct visions of Jesus Christ and God's means of salvation. Perhaps, then, it's best not to talk of a *different* Jesus in Mormonism, given the similarities. There is, after all, only "one Lord" (Eph 4:5), not two or three. Yet, given the dissimilarities, Mormonism does put forward *another* vision of Jesus described by *different* authorities (i.e., LDS scripture and living prophets). In the end, our mutual goal must be the true and earnest pursuit of Jesus Christ amid our agreements and despite our disagreements, for he bids all people, "Come unto me" (Matt 11:28).

REFLECTION QUESTIONS

1. What is the problem (if any) in elevating either Christ's humanity or deity over the other?

2. Why did early Christians believe that Jesus Christ was truly divine and yet truly a man?

3. How does Mormonism differ from traditional Christianity on the nature of Jesus Christ?

4. How does Mormonism differ from traditional Christianity on the relationship between the Father and the Son?

5. Why is the Son's nature and relationship to the Father important to salvation?

QUESTION 23

What Is the Latter-day Saint View of the Holy Spirit?

"I know by the manifestations of the Holy Ghost that Jesus is the Christ and that Joseph was a prophet by revelation."[1]
~ Brigham Young, President of the LDS Church, 1847–1877

Brigham Young could have chosen from any number of topics when he addressed the Latter-day Saints in 1844. It was the first time he spoke as their prophet in General Conference, just four months after Joseph Smith's assassination. Young used the speech to encourage his followers to continue "building up the kingdom of God," especially by completing the unfinished temple in Nauvoo, which he promised would be "where the power of God shall be made known."[2] It was a privilege to be called to such a task, he said, one that was only made possible by the power of the Holy Ghost. "All saints male and female have the privilege of revelation, of inspiration, the spirit of God the Holy Ghost."[3]

To Young, and numerous Latter-day Saints before and after him, the Spirit of God is the divine revelator, an accessible avenue for every sincere believer who yearns for knowledge, a privilege given only "after one repents and becomes worthy."[4] This emphasis on the Spirit's revelatory mission is prevalent in Mormon theology of the Holy Spirit (or pneumatology), but it is not the only divine activity Latter-day Saints anticipate from the third member of the Godhead. And while Mormonism speaks of God's Spirit in ways that seem

1. *CDBY* 2:808.
2. George D. Smith, ed., *Brigham Young: Colonizer of the American West*, 2 vols. (Salt Lake City: Signature Books, 2021), 1:106.
3. *CDBY* 1:55.
4. Gary James Bergera, ed., *Statements of the LDS First Presidency: A Topical Compendium* (Salt Lake City: Signature Books, 2007), 207.

familiar to traditional Christianity, there are also important differences. Who, then, is the Holy Spirit according to Mormonism? To answer this question, let's first consider the Holy Spirit in traditional Christianity and then compare his person and work against LDS pneumatology.

The Holy Spirit in Traditional Christianity: Our Comforter and Sanctifier

As the third person of the Trinity, the Holy Spirit shares every divine attribute that is essential to God. The Bible uses titles to associate the Spirit with God, like "the Spirit of the Lord God" (Isa 61:1; cf. Luke 4:18), "the Spirit of our God" (1 Cor 6:11), and "the Spirit of his Son" (Gal 4:6). And like the Son, the Spirit shares the same essence with the Father, proceeding from them as the loving Comforter and Sanctifier of faith.[5] The title "Holy" is less a description of the Spirit's nature than it is of the Spirit's mission and work. That the Spirit of God is holy ought to be apparent, for nothing that is of God or proceeds from him is unholy. What makes him the *Holy* Spirit is the holy work that he does.[6]

Symbols vividly describe the Spirit's work, like the wind (see John 3:8), fire (see Acts 2:1–4), and a dove (see Luke 3:22). Jesus taught that just as the "wind bloweth where it listeth" (John 3:8), so the Spirit moves as he pleases. The Spirit acts personally yet invisibly, so that, like the wind, he is only seen by his effects and not his body, for he is an unembodied being.

The Spirit is also like a fire that burns and melts away impurities, refining souls into a purity untainted by sin. And like a dove sent from heaven to rest on Christ at his baptism (see John 1:32), so the Holy Spirit searches for our souls. Unlike a punishing hawk that hunts sinners, the Spirit rests gently on us, hovering over our chaotic hearts to bring about holy order, just as he did over the dark and formless primordial earth (see Gen 1:1–2).

Of all the Spirit's titles, perhaps none is more cherished by Christians than Comforter (Gk. *paraklētos*), or the promised Counselor sent by the Father and the Son (see John 14:26; 16:7). The term describes someone who is "called alongside" another to aid them, and the Holy Spirit does so by testifying of Christ and advocating for him to the sinner (see John 15:26).[7] This is an especially precious doctrine for Christians because it reinforces Christ's promise to his disciples that the Holy Spirit would "come unto you" and "reprove the world of sin" (John 16:7–8), not avoid sinners in their fallenness. The Holy Spirit does not depart the saint when they sin, as if he were "weak

5. The procession of the Spirit is debated between Eastern and Western Christianity. For a concise overview of this debate, see Thomas Joseph White, *The Trinity: On the Nature and Mystery of the One God* (Washington: Catholic University of America Press, 2022), 481–504.
6. The Holy Spirit is portrayed in the Bible as acting personally, which is why traditional Christians commonly refer to the Holy Spirit as "he" rather than "it" (see John 14:26; 15:26).
7. Sinclair B. Ferguson, *The Holy Spirit: Contours of Christian Theology* (Downers Grove: InterVarsity Press, 1996), 36–38.

and ill-inclined and a deserter, standing far off and watching for us to repent from our sin, and then, once we are in a state of justification again, return to dwell within us."[8] What good would it do for us if the Holy Spirit fled when we needed him the most? "Does a doctor leave a patient the moment he sees that he has fallen into some illness?"[9] Of course not. The doctor remains and presses in because that is precisely when his skills are needed the most. So it is with the Comforter of God. Personal qualification or worthiness neither invites nor maintains one's companionship with the Holy Spirit; instead, it is the Spirit's love for sinners, shared with the Father and the Son, that keeps his residence in our hearts. We do not make ourselves worthy to receive the Holy Spirit; rather, the Holy Spirit is received by faith as a gift to make us worthy. The only reason we can repent is because of the Holy Spirit's presence. No wonder an early theologian rejoiced that the Comforter came "not only to relieve the sadness of the faithful but also to fill them with unspeakable joy."[10]

As theologian Jonathan Edwards taught, the saints of God find blessed joy in holiness, in the power of God to "bring grace to perfection, in making the soul completely amiable in Christ's glorious likeness."[11] This is, after all, what it means to be a "saint" (Gk. *hagios*). To be *hagios* is to be called a "holy one," not holy by our own means but by the critical mission of the Holy Spirit to make sinners holy, sanctifying them by his power for the glory of God. The Spirit does so in many ways. First, he effectually calls sinners to repentance through the gospel (see 1 Thess 1:5) and then empowers their conversion by causing them to be born again (see John 3:3–8). He fastens God's saints to Christ in an inseparable union (see John 6:37; 1 Cor 6:17), cleanses, justifies, and sanctifies them (see 1 Cor 6:11), and produces in them spiritual fruit (see Gal 5:22–23). He happily gives them spiritual gifts (see Isa 11:1–2; 1 Cor 12:8–11; Rom 12:6–8), indwells them to enable a life of holiness (see 1 Thess 4:7–8), and offers them assurance of faith and seals them (see Eph 1:13; 1 Thess 1:5). The Spirit also plays a revelatory role, guiding the saints "into all truth" (John 16:13), testifying of Jesus Christ (see John 15:26), and inspiring the word of God (see 2 Tim 3:16).

In short, traditional Christianity recognizes the Holy Spirit as God, coequal with the Father and Son in their divine essence, who glorifies God as his sent Comforter and Sanctifier, who testifies of Jesus Christ to the world.

The Holy Ghost in Mormonism: The Revealer and Sealer

Mormonism describes the Spirit of God in ways familiar to traditional Christianity. The Spirit is a witness of God (see 2 Nephi 31:18) and the

8. *ACD* 4:35.
9. *ACD* 4:35.
10. *ACD* 4:19.
11. Jonathan Edwards, *The Sermons of Jonathan Edwards: A Reader*, ed. Wilson H. Kimnach, Kenneth P. Minkema, and Douglas A. Sweeney (New Haven, CT: Yale University Press, 1999), 72.

Comforter (see D&C 88:3) who inspires scripture and faith (see D&C 20:35; 21:2), authenticates church leadership (see D&C 20:60; 1 Nephi 12:7), guides congregational life (see D&C 20:45; 46:2), and prompts and empowers personal obedience to God (see D&C 45:57; 121:43, 46). But LDS pneumatology is distinct in portraying the Holy Ghost's nature and role as a divine revealer. The shift in the Spirit's name here is intentional; although "Holy Spirit" and "Holy Ghost" are used interchangeably in LDS scripture (see D&C 121:26), the latter is commonly favored. Relatedly, LDS language oscillates between calling the Holy Ghost "it" and "he," apparently not because of any theological rationale but likely a habit learned from their preferred translation of the Bible, the King James Version, which sometimes refers to the Spirit as "it," (e.g., "the Spirit *itself* beareth witness with our spirit," Rom 8:16, emphasis added). It is generally the LDS conviction that the Holy Ghost is a "male spirit personage," although this is challenged in Mormonism (as it is in traditional Christianity) by those who advocate for neutral or feminine renderings of the Holy Spirit for a variety of reasons.[12]

What is meant by "personage," though, reveals a doctrinal distinctive. According to Smith, the Holy Ghost is a personage like the Father and the Son but differs from them in its embodiment. While the Father and Son are embodied in "flesh & bones as tangible as man[']s," the third member of the Godhead is "a personage of Spirit."[13] "Were it not so," Smith explained, "the Holy Ghost could not dwell in us."[14] He underlined his point by also teaching that the Spirit can "descend upon" a person "but not to tarry with him" (i.e., to stay and lodge within a person).[15] He believed that the Spirit cannot take up residence within someone because the "Holy Ghost is a personage, and a person cannot have the personage of the Holy Ghost in his heart."[16] This assertion stands in contrast to God's promises to place his Spirit within us (see Ezek 36:27; 1 Cor 6:19–20). Jesus Christ promised the "Spirit of truth" will "dwelleth with you, and shall be *in* you" (John 14:17, emphasis added), that he would descend upon *and* tarry with us. Smith speculated the Holy Ghost would eventually receive a tangible body, which is perhaps why he struggled with the doctrine of the Spirit's indwelling.[17] For him, the Holy Ghost already

---

12. Robert L. Millet, "Holy Ghost," in *LDS Beliefs: A Doctrinal Reference*, ed. Robert L. Millet et al. (Salt Lake City: Deseret Book, 2011), 307. One LDS president clarified further that the Holy Ghost "is one of the sons of our Father and our God and he is that man that stood next to Jesus Christ" in the beginning (Heber C. Kimball, "Discourse," *Deseret News* [Salt Lake City] 7, no. 28 [September 16, 1857]).
13. JS, instruction, April 2, 1843, D12:144–145 [D&C 130:22].
14. Joseph Smith, History, 1838–1856, vol. D-1, *JSP*, 1511 [D&C 130:22].
15. JS, instruction, April 2, 1843, D12:145 [D&C 130:23].
16. JS, instruction, April 2, 1843, D12:141 (emend.). See also D&C 130:3.
17. So Smith: "The God & father of our Lord Jesus Christ was once the same as the Son or Holy Ghost both having redeemed a world became the eternal God of that world he had a son Jesus Christ who redeemed this earth the same as his father had a world which made them

inhabits a spatially restricted spirit body, being "a personage in the form of a personage," and can, on occasion, manifest this and other forms before us (see 1 Nephi 11:11).[18] But apparently two personages cannot inhabit the same metaphysical, corporeal space. This seeming discrepancy is possibly due to the LDS distinction of the Holy Ghost as a divine personage and the Holy Spirit as divine presence.

As a revealer, the Holy Ghost "takes of the Father, and of the Son, and shows it to the disciples," taught Brigham Young. "It opens the vision of the mind, unlocks the treasures of wisdom, and they begin to understand the things of God."[19] Smith explained this role more succinctly: "No man can receive the Holy Ghost without receiving revelations" because the Spirit is "a revelator."[20] Generally, according to LDS thought, God gifts all people with the light of Christ, a basic moral sense capable of recognizing divine calling and works, something akin to John Calvin's "sense of divinity" (Lat. *sensus divinitatis*), an internal awareness of God that is common in all people. But the Holy Ghost adds to this sense, especially as he authenticates the validity of the Latter-day Saint restoration with its scriptures and prophets. Oliver Cowdery, one of Smith's earliest converts, once asked if he could join the translation work on the Book of Mormon, even as he apparently harbored uncertainty. Smith's reply came in a revelation, promising Cowdery that God would give him "a knowledge concerning the engraveings [*sic*] of old Records."[21] This knowledge would come "by the Holy Ghost" to inform Cowdery's mind and indwell his heart, God's "spirit of Revelation."[22] Here, Smith drew heavily from the Protestant tradition of how God confirms the truth of scripture, echoing the Reformer John Calvin's assessment that "God alone can properly bear witness to his own words," so that the Bible "would not obtain full credit in the hearts of men, until they are sealed by the inward testimony of the Spirit."[23] Of course, Calvin would have strongly objected to Smith and the Book of Mormon, as he did a group of radical spiritualists in his day.[24] But where the

---

equal & the Holy Ghost would do the same in his turn" (JS, discourse, January 30, 1842, D9:129 [emend.]). Also Smith: "But the holy ghost is yet a Spiritual body and waiting to take to himself a body" (JS, discourse, June 16, 1844, *JSP*).

18. JSJ, January 29, 1843, J2:251.
19. *CDBY* 2:693.
20. JSJ, October 15, 1843, J3:114 (emend.).
21. JS, revelation, April 1828, D1:46 [D&C 8:1].
22. JS, revelation, April 1828, D1:46 [D&C 8:1].
23. Calvin, *Inst.* 1.7.4.
24. Calvin, *Inst.* 1.9.1. Among Calvin's fiercest opponents in Geneva were the Libertines—the "giddy men [of] madness"—whose hyper-charismaticism led them to an inflated view of personal revelation over established canonicity. They favored the "living spirit" over the "written word" of revelation, to which Calvin strongly objected in his treatise *Against the Libertines*.

Reformers would refrain, Smith advanced his new scripture by appealing to old ways of supernatural confirmation.

Cowdery was given a caveat to his request, though. The Holy Ghost would only confirm the Book of Mormon's veracity so long as Cowdery's prayer was sincere. "Ask with an honest heart believing that ye Shall receive" confirmation, he was commanded.[25] The Holy Ghost would then confirm the authenticity of the Book of Mormon material, apparently by religious experience. This confirmatory role is still prevalent today, as investigators (or seekers) of the LDS Church are commonly asked to do likewise—to pray sincerely whether the Book of Mormon is true (see question 38). Thus, in Mormonism, the Holy Ghost works, in part, to reveal the wills of the Father and the Son to genuine seekers, constantly reorienting their minds and hearts back to the Godhead through the church and its canonical tradition, especially the Book of Mormon.

Converts are then baptized, having placed their confidence in the Latter-day Saint gospel, and shortly thereafter receive the ordinance known as confirmation by the laying on of hands by authorized priesthood holders. In this ordinance, the convert is confirmed a member of the church and invited to receive the Gift of the Holy Ghost (see D&C 20:43; 76:52). This reception is essential because, as Brigham Young taught, "you cant [*sic*] get into the celestial kingdom" without the Holy Ghost, a gift that seals to individuals certain promises and covenants of God "for time and for all eternity" (D&C 132:7, 18–19, 26).[26]

Mormonism draws an important distinction between the influence of the Holy Ghost and the gift of the Holy Ghost. The Spirit's influence is available to all people across all time, and may guide, comfort, and prompt them toward truth. The gift of the Holy Ghost, however, is the privilege of the Spirit's constant companionship—granted conditionally, dependent on one's continued worthiness—and is conferred only after baptism and confirmation by priesthood authority. While traditional Christians may experience the *influence* of God's Spirit, Latter-day Saints believe those people are not recipients of his constant companionship.

Mormonism also teaches that the Holy Ghost serves as a moral agent and protector from spiritual and physical harm. It aids in guiding a person's decision-making and moral development yet without interfering with personal agency. It is possible to see this blessing diminished, however, as members must seek God and personally qualify for companionship with the Holy Ghost, or his influence will evade them. "Breaking covenants [with God] may remove the sealing," explained Latter-day Saint leaders.[27]

---

25. JS, revelation, April 1828, D1:46 [D&C 8:1] (emend.).
26. *CDBY* 1:358.
27. Bergera, *Statements of the LDS First Presidency*, 205.

Summary

The Holy Spirit is the third person of the Trinity who comforts and sanctifies according to traditional Christianity. By contrast, in Mormonism, the Holy Ghost is the divine witness of the Godhead who reveals and seals. It is not a matter of pitting one doctrine against the other, for traditional Christian and Mormon doctrines of the Holy Spirit include comforting, sanctifying, revealing, and sealing. But Latter-day Saints and traditional Christians tend to place difference emphases on the Spirit's work in their pneumatology. Mormonism also teaches that the Holy Ghost is an embodied spirit person in contrast to the bodiless Holy Spirit of traditional Christianity.

REFLECTION QUESTIONS

1. What are some similarities between traditional Christian and Mormon views of the Holy Spirit?

2. What do biblical descriptions of the Holy Spirit communicate about his nature and work?

3. What does it mean that the Holy Spirit is the Comforter and sanctifier?

4. Mormonism teaches that the Holy Ghost is a male spirit person. How is this different (if at all) from traditional Christianity?

5. How did early Latter-day Saints envision the role of the Holy Ghost? Does Mormonism still emphasize this role today?

QUESTION 24

What Is the Latter-day Saint View of the Trinity?

"I say, that is a strange God anyhow—three in one, and one in three! It is a curious organization."[1]
~ Joseph Smith

One of Mormonism's earliest doctrinal statements about God sounds mundanely Trinitarian, even Nicene: the "Father & Son & [Holy Ghost] which is one God Infinite & eternal World without end."[2] But over the years, Mormonism dissented from creedal orthodoxy. Joseph Smith thought it was odd how Christians worshiped a triune God, which directly conflicts with his visionary experience of the Father and Son as two distinct and embodied gods, accompanied by an immaterial personage, the Holy Ghost (see question 23). Instead of being one God, "infinite and eternal," the Father, Son, and Holy Ghost are three beings united in affectionate purpose "as the hearts of three men who are united in all things," explained Brigham Young.[3] While the differences between traditional Christian and LDS views of the Trinity seem semantic, a closer examination reveals meaningful differences that lead to drastically divergent visions of God.

What Is the Trinity?

Latter-day Saints often hesitate to use the term "Trinity," opting instead for "Godhead" to differentiate their position from traditional Christianity. This is not to say that Latter-day Saints wholly reject the term. After all,

1. Joseph Smith, History, 1838–1856, vol. F-1, *JSP*, 103 (emend.).
2. MRB:9 [D&C 20:28].
3. *CDBY* 3:1377.

LDS authorities throughout the church's history have used it to describe the God of three persons.[4] Still, Latter-day Saints sometimes express concern that because the term *Trinity* is not found in the Bible, it is therefore unscriptural and should not be used. Moreover, many find the Trinity to be "a concept that is at odds with human reason and in many cases downright confusing or misleading," in part because it reflects the early church fathers' employment of Platonism as an intellectual framework to describe the nature of God.[5] Latter-day Saints wonder whether early Christians committed a serious error in melding Christian theology with Greek philosophy, of which the Trinity is a prime example (see question 37). What, then, is Trinitarianism?

Trinitarianism is the doctrine of the nature and economy of God, describing how God is one in nature but not in number. Traditional Christians believe there is only "one LORD" (Deut 6:4), *contra* tritheism, or the belief in three distinct gods. Yet they also believe that God is always three persons—Father, Son, and Holy Spirit—*contra* modalism, or the belief that God manifests himself as one of three persons at different times. In other words, God is one when counting gods, but God is three when counting persons. Trinitarianism, then, is more than a mere abstract description of God or human analysis of his being. The Holy Trinity is God himself, revealed by the Bible, and deserving of our most profound awe and childlike wonder, for it is the triune God who wills and works to create, sustain, and redeem humanity. Indeed, the Trinity is not at odds with human reason; the Trinity is the object of human worship. "God in three persons," we sing, "blessed Trinity!"[6]

Traditional Christianity did not reach these conclusions by combining scripture with Greek philosophy but by inference of God's self-revelation across all the Bible. Why do Christians believe in the Trinity? "Because God has so revealed Himself in His Word."[7] The Bible unwaveringly proclaims God's oneness. He alone is Lord, "and there is none else, there is no God beside me" (Isa 45:5), God declared. God's oneness is where proper reflection about him begins.[8] But as the narrative of redemptive drama unfolds, God's

4. Daniel C. Peterson, "Notes on Mormonism and the Trinity," *Interpreter* 41 (2020): 89–90.
5. Robert L. Millet and Gerald R. McDermott, *Claiming Christ: A Mormon–Evangelical Debate* (Grand Rapids: Brazos, 2007), 80. For an excellent survey of Christian Platonism, see Alexander J. B. Hampton and John Peter Kenney, eds., *Christian Platonism: A History* (Cambridge: Cambridge University Press, 2021).
6. "Holy, Holy, Holy! Lord God Almighty!" by Reginald Heber (1826).
7. See Herman Bavinck, *The Wonderful Works of God*, trans. Henry Zylstra (Glenside, PA: Westminster Seminary Press, 2019), 128–29.
8. For God's oneness as the proper starting point for the Trinity, see Katherine Sonderegger, *The Doctrine of God*, vol. 1 of *Systematic Theology* (Minneapolis: Fortress Press, 2015), 3–45.

mysterious plurality becomes undeniably apparent: Father, Son, and Holy Spirit act in distinct roles to advance God's covenant promises. The Trinity is not found in "scattered verses here and there that tell us of an esoteric teaching at the margins of the faith," explained one theologian.[9] Instead, the Trinity is revealed as the primary point of the Bible when read along its whole canon with an eye toward God's activity, especially his redemptive actions.[10] God acts in a threefold way because he *is* triune; he can't act in any other way. In short, Trinitarianism teaches:

1. There is only one God.
2. God is a Trinity of Father, Son, and Holy Spirit.
3. The Father, Son, and Holy Spirit are not the same persons.
4. The Father, Son, and Holy Spirit are of the same divine Being.
5. The Trinity is bound by common essence or nature.

On God's nature, the Trinity describes what he is apart from creation. Before the cosmos sprung into existence by the power of God's word, long before he uttered "Let there be," there was the Father, Son, and Holy Spirit. All three were ungenerated and eternal, having never come to be. They always *were* because God always *is*, for "I AM THAT I AM" (Exod 3:14) is who he is. The Trinity has no starting point: no birth, no growth, no progression. The Son and Holy Spirit are consubstantial with the Father, meaning they equally and eternally share their being from the same divine essence without any diminishment and are thus coessential with God, sharing in all God's attributes. Whatever the Father possesses in being, so do the Son and Holy Spirit. Is the Father holy? So is the Son, and so is the Spirit. Is the Son faithful? So are the Father and Spirit. Is the Spirit wise? The Father and the Son are, too. And because God is immutable—neither changeable nor subject to sequential moments—there was never a time when God the Father began to communicate his essence to the Son and Spirit. They are not merely like the Father in their nature. No, all three are God because they share the exact same Being. Theologians describe this as the immanent Trinity.

On God's economy, the Trinity describes what God does outside himself; in other words, the external operations of God, especially in creation and redemption. The Father's operations are inseparable from those of the Son and Spirit, so that whatever the Father does, he does so with and through the Son and Spirit. Their desire to create and redeem is not born out of three independent, synchronized wills but from a commonly sourced desire from which they will not dissent. Each person, however, acts in unique roles. For example,

9. Fred Sanders, *Fountain of Salvation: Trinity and Soteriology* (Grand Rapids: Eerdmans, 2021), 17.
10. Sanders, *Fountain of Salvation*, 16–17.

the Son, not the Father, was crucified on the cross. And it is a mistake to assume an eternal hierarchical relationship simply because the Father sends and the Son and Spirit are sent and act in obedience to the Father.[11] The activity of the Trinity reveals things about the immanent Trinity but is not equated with it. Theologians call this the economic Trinity.

For some theologians, however, the distinction between the immanent and economic Trinity is unhelpful. If God's being and doing are indistinguishable, any distinction between the two should be collapsed.[12] Consequently, we ought to be more concerned with God's activity among the three Persons to understand his nature. This perspective has given rise to social Trinitarianism, a way of viewing the Trinity that prioritizes God's relationships to explain his nature, describing the Trinity as "a kind of divine society in which the divine persons have priority over the unity of essence."[13] The social Trinity is like a divine communion, akin to a small society or family of deities with personal knowledge and wills whose being is not sourced from a common nature, yet they are bound together essentially by love, cooperation, and joint purpose.[14] They aren't together because their nature requires them to be; instead, they eternally choose to be together in love.[15]

---

11. This assumption leads to the view of Trinitarian relationships as eternal authority-submission relationships (e.g., an eternal functional subordination [EFS] of the Son to the Father). See, for example, Wayne Grudem, *Systematic Theology: An Introduction to Biblical Doctrine* (Grand Rapids: Zondervan, 1994), 251; Bruce Ware, *Father, Son, and Holy Spirit: Relationships, Roles, and Relevance* (Wheaton, IL: Crossway, 2005), 50–57, 71; and John Frame, *Systematic Theology: An Introduction to Christian Belief* (Phillipsburg, NJ: P&R Publishing, 2013), 500–502. Relatedly, EFS commonly serves as a prototype for social paradigms (i.e., natural hierarchies between men and women). For critiques of EFS, see D. Glenn Butner Jr., "Eternal Functional Subordination and the Problem of the Divine Will," *Journal of the Evangelical Theological Society* 58, no. 1 (2015): 131–49; Stephen R. Holmes, "Classical Trinitarianism and Eternal Functional Subordination: Some Historical and Dogmatic Reflections," *Scottish Bulletin of Evangelical Theology* 35, no. 1 (2017): 90–104; Michael F. Bird and Scott Harrower, *Trinity Without Hierarchy: Reclaiming Nicene Orthodoxy in Evangelical Theology* (Grand Rapids: Kregel Academic, 2019).
12. See Karl Rahner: "The 'economic' Trinity is the 'immanent' Trinity and the 'immanent' Trinity is the 'economic' Trinity" (*The Trinity*, trans. Joseph Donceel [New York: Continuum, 1970], 22). For a concise critique of Rahner's Rule, see D. Glenn Butner, *Trinitarian Dogmatics: Exploring the Grammar of the Christian Doctrine of God* (Grand Rapids: Baker Academic, 2022), 164–68.
13. Frederick Christian Bauerschmidt, "The Trinity and Politics," in *The Oxford Handbook of the Trinity*, ed. Gilles Emery and Matthew Levering (New York: Oxford University Press, 2011), 534.
14. For example, J. P. Moreland and William Lane Craig argue that "[in] God there are three distinct centers of self-consciousness, each with its proper intellect and will" (*Philosophical Foundations for a Christian Worldview*, 2nd ed. [Downers Grove: IVP Academic, 2017], 582).
15. Moreover, this divine society offers us a model for ecclesiastical life and reforming society that leads to human liberation and flourishing. See Miroslav Volf, *After Our Likeness: The*

Even within traditional Christianity, there are different understandings of the Trinity. What all of these approaches (immanent, economic, and social Trinitarianism) have in common is their belief that God has one nature, even though that nature is expressed in three distinct ways through God the Father, God the Son, and God the Holy Spirit. Latter-day Saints, however, do not share this general view.

What Is the Latter-day Saint View of the Trinity?

Early Mormon descriptions of the Godhead emphasized divine oneness.[16] The 1830 charter for the LDS Church affirmed that "the Father and the Son, and the Holy Ghost is one God, infinite and eternal, without end."[17] An early LDS theology text, *Lectures on Faith* (1834), sustained this belief by describing the Son as possessing "the same mind with the Father, which mind is the Holy Spirit, and these three are one [and] constitute the Godhead, and are one."[18] As LDS doctrine developed—perhaps in light of Joseph Smith's First Vision—plurality became the preferred starting point for understanding God's nature, so much so that Mormonism developed a theological allergy to Trinitarianism.[19] Smith dismissed the Trinity as a God of "three Heads & but one body,"[20] a "giant" Cerberean "monster" of three persons "crammed into one God."[21] Smith's solution was to view God as a fellowship of "three distinct personages, and three Gods."[22]

Mormonism has since expanded on this description. LDS theologians envision the Godhead as "comprising three physically separate and distinct individuals, who together constitute the presiding council of the heavens."[23] The Godhead is "three separate beings who are one in thought, will, action, and love"[24] or "a unity of purpose and understanding."[25] God is three separate instances of

---

Church as the Image of the Trinity (Grand Rapids: Eerdmans, 1998); and Leonardo Boff, *Trinity and Society*, trans. Paul Burns (New York: Orbis, 1988).

16. While early LDS concepts of God at times evoke Trinitarianism, Dan Vogel is right to argue that "Mormonism was never trinitarian but consistently preferred heterodox definitions of God" ("The Earliest Mormon Concept of God," in *Line upon Line: Essays on Mormon Doctrine*, ed. Gary James Bergera [Salt Lake City: Signature Books, 1989], 17).
17. JS, Articles and Covenants, ca. April 1830, D1:122 [D&C 20:28].
18. Doctrine and Covenants (1835), 53. The Father and the Son also possessed the same "wisdom, glory, power and fulness" (Doctrine and Covenants [1853], 54).
19. See Kurt Widmer, *Mormonism and the Nature of God: A Theological Evolution, 1830–1915* (Jefferson, NC: McFarland, 2000).
20. JS, discourse, ca. February 16, 1841, D8:47.
21. Joseph Smith, History, 1838–1856, vol. F-1, *JSP*, 103 (emend.).
22. Joseph Smith, History, 1838–1856, vol. F-1, *JSP*, 101.
23. James E. Talmage, *Jesus the Christ* (American Fork, UT: Covenant Communications, 1915), 31.
24. David L. Paulsen and Hal Boyd, "The Nature of God in Mormon Thought," in *The Oxford Handbook of Mormonism*, ed. Terryl L. Givens and Philip L. Barlow (New York: Oxford University Press, 2015), 253.
25. James E. Faulconer, *Thinking Otherwise: Theological Explorations of Joseph Smith's Revelations* (Provo, UT: Maxwell Institute, BYU, 2020), 59.

the divine nature expressed as three distinct centers of affection, intellect, and action in perfect harmony of purpose. Each member is an individual instance of a common genus whose unity is bound not by nature but by love.

Some Latter-day Saints see social Trinitarians (ST) paralleling and mirroring Joseph Smith.[26] But they point out that "none of the modern proponents of [social Trinitarianism] credit Joseph Smith of Mormonism in any way for their views," and rightly so.[27] ST doesn't owe its origin to Smith or his religion because, upon close examination, Mormonism does not espouse ST.

The God of ST has always been so. There was never a time when the Son was not nor was there ever a time when the Son was welcomed into the divine council of the Godhead after progressing to the position. The God of ST is also not materially embodied like the LDS Godhead. ST upholds God's immateriality as a divine attribute. To call the LDS Godhead socially Trinitarian requires radical modification to ST's affirmation that "God is a Spirit" (John 4:24). And while ST and Mormonism both emphasize the three-ness of God, going so far as to identify three distinct wills, ST nevertheless seeks to maintain the one-ness of God's being while Mormonism does not. LDS scholars explain how the "Father, the Son, and the Holy Ghost are three separate persons who constitute a perfectly harmonious social unit but are not one metaphysical substance or essence."[28] The persons of the Godhead "*have* the divine essence, though none *is* the divine essence."[29] Their unity is due to cooperation, not consubstantiation.[30] Perhaps, as it has been suggested, the LDS Godhead may be described as "liberal social trinitarianism,"[31] a form of ST that treks far beyond orthodoxy's frontier due to Mormonism's intense amplification of God's—or, better, the *Gods'*—plurality, materiality, and progression.

In short, Trinitarianism distinguishes the immanent and economic Trinity, ST collapses the immanent and economic Trinity, and Mormonism maximizes the economic Trinity. Thus, Mormonism teaches:

1. There is only one Godhead.
2. The Godhead is a divine council of Father, Son, and Holy Ghost.
3. The Father, Son, and Holy Ghost are not the same personages.
4. The Father, Son, and Holy Ghost are not consubstantial.
5. The members of the Godhead are bound by mutual love and harmonized wills.

---

26. David L. Paulsen and Hal Boyd, *Are Christians Mormon?* (New York: Routledge, 2017), 51–52.
27. Paulsen and Boyd, *Are Christians Mormon?*, 53.
28. Roger R. Keller, "Response to Professor McKim," in *Mormonism in Dialogue with Contemporary Christian Theologies*, ed. Donald W. Musser and David L. Paulsen (Macon, GA: Mercer University Press, 2007), 39.
29. Keller, "Response," 41 (emphasis added).
30. Paulsen and Boyd, "The Nature of God in Mormon Thought," 253.
31. Peterson, "Mormonism and the Trinity," 118.

Latter-day Saints, then, tend to begin with plurality and work toward unity, holding that the persons of the Godhead are genuinely distinct from one another.

What's at Stake?

The question deserves to be asked whether these theological distinctions matter. After all, "a social Trinity is still a Trinity," said an LDS scholar, and to press the point further, the Mormon Godhead still describes deity in terms of Father, Son, and Holy Ghost.[32] Therefore, does maintaining or minimizing their consubstantiality really make a difference? Perhaps the question could be asked a different way: Could God the Father exist without the Son or the Spirit in eternity past, long before the foundation of the world?

According to LDS theology, the Father did exist without the Son and Spirit (in their present form), for he is their paternal source having literally sired them sometime before the creation of the cosmos. Mormonism teaches there was a time when the Father *was* but the Son and Holy Spirit *were not* yet. It is difficult, though, to conceive that the Father's divinity would be fully actualized in total isolation, especially love. As Richard of St. Victor argued, the sharing of love cannot exist among fewer than three persons, since it is only with a third that relational fullness and the delight of shared charity are complete.[33] In the Mormon theological system, however—one in which God develops and progresses—the God who emerged from that process prior to his creative work is the one who has revealed himself and, consequently, is of our only concern.[34] Still, it stands to reason that if there is never "a father without first being a son," then God experienced sonship and bachelorhood before becoming a father and, eventually, *the* Father.[35] Consequently, there was a time when the Son and Holy Spirit were not yet.

For Trinitarians, however, such a scenario is impossible because if the Father, Son, and Holy Spirit are consubstantial—if they find their being in the same divine source equally and eternally—then God could not exist without the Son and Spirit any more than the sun could exist without emanating rays

32. Kevin Christensen, "Eye of the Beholder, Law of the Harvest: Observations on the Inevitable Consequences of the Different Investigative Approaches of Jeremy Runnells and Jeff Lindsay," *Interpreter* 10 (2014): 198.
33. Richard of St. Victor argued that while love can exist between two persons, it reaches perfection only with a third, since true charity delights not only in loving and being loved, but in seeing the beloved loved by another; thus, a third person completes the fullness of relational sharing. See *De Trinitate*, III.14.
34. Some Latter-day Saints have posited from this doctrine an infinite regression of gods, that "there has been and there now exists an endless line of Gods, stretching back into the eternities, that had no beginning and will have no end. Their existence runs parallel with endless duration, and their dominions are as limitless as boundless space." See Brigham H. Roberts, *A New Witness for God* (Salt Lake City: Cannon & Sons, 1895), 466.
35. Joseph Smith, History, 1838–1856, vol. F-1, *JSP*, 103.

of light or giving off heat. The Father has never existed—and *could* never exist—without the Son or the Spirit. If it were otherwise, then there would be a deficiency in God's being, a gap that could only be filled by adding to himself.[36] Is God *truly* Father, Son, and Holy Spirit if he was not *always*, *fully*, Father, Son, and Holy Spirit? If there was a point at which the Father waited (so to speak) for the Son and Spirit to join him in Trinity, then was God eternally triune and complete in his nature? For traditional Christians, the answer is obvious: No. So, they affirm that God, from the very beginning (if such a thing could be said of him), has always been Father, Son, and Holy Spirit. But for Mormonism, God the Father was *joined* by the Son and Spirit at some point, to complete an incompletion, and so gained a relational status that completed the Godhead.

Summary

Trinitarianism holds that God is a Trinity of three consubstantial persons—Father, Son, and Holy Spirit. The Mormon Godhead is a divine community of three independent personages—Father, Son, and Holy Ghost. Mormonism resembles Social Trinitarianism but cannot be equated with it. According to Mormonism, the Father can (and has) existed without the Son and Holy Spirit in their present forms, which contrasts sharply against the eternality of the persons of Trinitarianism.

REFLECTION QUESTIONS

1. How might you respond to a Latter-day Saint who is skittish about the term "Trinity"?

2. What does it mean for the Father, Son, and Holy Spirit to share the same essence or being (to be consubstantial)?

3. The immanent Trinity describes the inner life and relationships of the Father, Son, and Holy Spirit, while the economic Trinity describes their roles and functions. Why are these important distinctions to make for Trinitarianism?

---

36. This is Athanasius's argument for the deity of God the Son in *Against the Arians*. More recently, Keith Yandell has argued for the same, describing the Trinity as a "logically inseparable triad" whose unity dissolves in the absence of one or more persons. Keith E. Yandell, "The Doctrine of the Trinity: Consistent and Coherent," in *Building on the Foundations of Evangelical Theology: Essays in Honor of John S. Feinberg*, ed. Gregg R. Allison and Stephen J. Wellum (Wheaton, IL: Crossway, 2015), 162.

4. Social Trinitarianism describes God as a perfect community of Father, Son, and Holy Spirit who share equal fullness of divine being. How is it different from and akin to descriptions of the LDS Godhead?

5. Could any person of the Trinity exist without another in eternity past, prior to the world's creation? How does your answer to this question reveal similarities or differences with the LDS Godhead?

QUESTION 25

What Is the Latter-day Saint View of Creation?

"What now, ye learned ones . . . What of God?
'God?—Mystery incomprehensible; All things made He from nothing'—
Hold, enough! Night and gross darkness—darken it no more."[1]
~ Orson F. Whitney, Latter-day Saint Apostle, 1906–1931

"The heavens 'declare the glory of God!'" (Ps 19:1) cried the psalmist, his joy for the Creator overflowing. The beautiful grandeur and incredible artisanship of God's creation transform our hearts into fountains of praise. "The firmament sheweth his handywork" (Ps 19:1), continued the psalmist, because rightly seeing creation opens our eyes to the God who reveals himself through it. It is this sort of confessional praise that prompts traditional Christians and Latter-day Saints alike to sing "All Creatures of Our God and King," and it's no wonder why. There are many points of noteworthy agreement between our views of creation.

Neither traditional Christianity nor Mormonism believes God *is* creation; we both affirm that God is distinct *from* creation, rejecting a cosmological model like pantheism. And both reject strict naturalism without room for supernatural activity or nonnatural beings. Instead, we believe that the cosmos is the result of God's handiwork and that our beautiful world is a gifted resource to steward, yet it suffers from the effects of sin as creation "groaneth and travaileth in pain" (Rom 8:22). "Every thing has become degenerated from what it was in its primitive state,"[2] an early LDS leader taught,

1. Orson F. Whitney, *Elias: An Epic of the Ages* (New York: Knickerbocker Press, 1904), 49.
2. Hyrum Smith, "The Word of Wisdom," *T&S*, June 1, 1842, 3:799.

so we "look for new heavens and a new earth" (2 Pet 3:13) in hopeful anticipation of God's new creation (see Isa 65:17; Rev 21:1–2).

But what is creation? What is it made from, and how did God create it? Exploring these questions from both perspectives reveals the different metaphysical realities inhabited by traditional Christians and Latter-day Saints. Traditional Christianity has long believed that God created everything from nothing and that matter had a definite beginning as a creation of God. Latter-day Saints, however, inhabit a quasi-materialist cosmos, one in which all of nature—spiritual and physical—is made from eternal matter so that God formed everything that *is* out of *all that* already *was*.

So, what exactly is the LDS view of creation? To answer this question, let's contrast the traditional Christian and LDS views of creation.

Creation *ex nihilo*

God is the Creator who "maketh all things" (Isa 44:24), and he did so from nothing (Lat. *ex nihilo*), having called "into existence the things that do not exist" (Rom 4:17 ESV). No preexisting material was necessary for this creation because God, through his divine Word, "is before all things, and by him all things consist" (Col 1:17), wrote the apostle Paul. He also declared that "by him [Christ] were *all things* created, that are in heaven, and that are in earth" (Col 1:16; see also Eph 3:9). In other words, all that is depends on God and owes its creaturely worship to him, "for thou hast created all things, and for thy pleasure they are and were created" (Rev 4:11). Creation *ex nihilo*, then, is less a statement about the nature of the cosmos than it is about the nature of its Creator. Only a genuinely omnipotent, sovereign, and independent God could have said to nothingness, "Let there be," so that "there was." This early Christian conviction became consensus by the fourth century and was codified in the ecumenical creeds.[3] Creation *ex nihilo* is not, as some dogmatically suggest, "a reflective innovation"[4] or "a postbiblical intrusion into Christianity,"[5] nor is it without biblical warrant.[6] As one theologian rightly argued, not only is *creatio ex nihilo* the

3. As theologian Craig Carter has shown, even pre-Nicene theologians—Justin Martyr, Irenaeus, and Theophilus of Antioch—read the Bible in supporting creation *ex nihilo*, "and as soon as they were confronted with a denial of creation *ex nihilo*, whether from heretical Christian teachers, Greek philosophers, or Gnostics like Marcion, they immediately affirmed" the doctrine (*Contemplating God with the Great Tradition: Recovering Trinitarian Classical Theism* (Grand Rapids: Baker Academic, 2021), 251; see also 243–53).
4. Daniel O. McClellan, *YHWH's Divine Images: A Cognitive Approach*, Ancient Near Eastern Monographs 29 (Atlanta: SBL Press, 2022), 202.
5. David L. Paulsen and Hal Boyd, "The Nature of God in Mormon Thought," in *The Oxford Handbook of Mormonism*, ed. Terryl L. Givens and Philip L. Barlow (New York: Oxford University Press, 2015), 250.
6. See Gary A. Anderson and Markus Bockmuehl, eds., *Creation* ex nihilo*: Origins, Development, Contemporary Challenges* (South Bend, IN: University of Notre Dame Press, 2018), 1–171.

"central metaphysical doctrine generated by the Christian doctrine of God as the transcendent creator," but to deny this belief risks yielding to neopaganism.[7]

Creation *ex materia*

Joseph Smith taught an alternative cosmogony to traditional Christianity, one in which God did not create all things from nothing (Lat. *ex nihilo*) but instead organized the universe out of preexisting matter (Lat. *ex materia*), which is uncreated and incapable of being destroyed.[8] Granted, caution is needed when discussing Smith's cosmology; he did not live long enough to develop it. In fact, early Mormonism appears to have initially supported creation *ex nihilo*.[9] For example, Smith believed he discovered God's personal name, "Awman," which means "the being which made *all things* in all its parts."[10] But as Smith's nature of God materialized, so did his cosmology (see question 21).

According to Smith, there are three eternal components of being (i.e., things that are ungenerated and endless). The first, intelligence, or "the Light of truth,"[11] is the cradle of agency and moral progression that grows along the trellis of an everlasting priesthood "without beginning of days or end of years" (see question 18).[12] Intelligence is the ungenerated, fundamental antecedent for the will to "act for itself."[13] The second eternal component, elements, are the materials God used to frame and fill the cosmos. All matter is composed of elements that have "had their existence in an elementary state from Eternity."[14] Smith further denied any essential difference between physical and spiritual matter, suggesting the substance of spirit "is material, but that it is more pure, elastic, and refined matter than the body—that it existed before the body."[15] He also believed elements "may be organized and re-organized; but not destroyed."[16] If "elements are

7. Carter, *Contemplating God*, 238.
8. So Smith: "God had materials to organize the world out of chaos; chaotic matter, which is element." Element, Smith wrote, "had an existence from the time he [God] had" and "can never be destroyed." Elements "may be organized and re-organized," he clarified, "but not destroyed" ("Conference Minutes," *T&S*, August 15, 1844, 5:615). For creation *ex materia*, see Tzvi Novick, "Creator, Text, and Law," in Anderson and Bockmuehl, *Creation* ex nihilo, 195–211.
9. Charles R. Harrell, *"This Is My Doctrine": The Development of Mormon Theology* (Salt Lake City: Greg Kofford Books, 2011), 231–34.
10. MRB, 265 (emphasis added).
11. JS, revelation, May 6, 1833, D3:89 [D&C 93:29].
12. JS, discourse, ca. June 26—ca. August 4, 1839, D6:544 (emend.).
13. JS, revelation, May 6, 1833, D3:89 [D&C 93:30]. Here, Smith sounds a bit like George Berkeley, who affirmed the necessity of "spiritual substances, because he believed it was unintelligible to believe that there could be ideas that did not inhere in a mind," explained one philosopher. "Hence Berkeley accepted both a divine mind and finite minds, as spiritual substances" (C. Steven Evans, *A History of Western Philosophy: From the Pre-Socratics to Postmodernism* [Downers Grove: IVP Academic, 2018], 350).
14. JS, discourse, ca. June 26—ca. August 4, 1839, D6:543.
15. JS, "Try the Spirits," *T&S*, April 1, 1842, 3:745.
16. "Conference Minutes," *T&S*, August 15, 1844, 5:615.

eternal, and spirit and element, inseparably connected," then spirit is co-eternal with element, making spirit a third eternal component of being.[17] These components—intelligence and matter, in physical and spiritual forms—are the fundamental building blocks of Mormon metaphysics, a kind of substance monism.[18] All things, including God himself, are composed of ungenerated and eternal elemental-intelligence, but all things are not God (*contra* pantheism).

This raises an important question: How can matter be eternal and yet also said to have been created, especially in LDS canonical creation texts?[19] It appears Smith thought "matter *as we know it* has a beginning, an origin," one scholar suggested.[20] The present state of matter, then, started when God began to organize the world. Yet, because matter is eternal, it existed in an unorganized or chaotic form prior to creation. Thus, God is "the creator from chaos, not from nothing."[21] God's plan for matter is one of perfection so that "matter *as it can be*, in its perfected form, is eternally an attribute of the divine" so far as its eternality is concerned.[22] Because God is made from matter, and that in its perfected form, Mormonism teaches "matter can come from God without compromising God's nature."[23] There is a matter perfected and a matter unperfected, "and matter at its lowest form has the potential to become more than 'mere matter.'"[24] A fundamental purpose for human glorification is to receive a perfected, material body like the one God inhabits. For Smith, matter is eternal and exists in three forms: the primordial tumult, a present imperfection, and a future perfection.

Thus, elements (i.e., physical and spiritual matter) are uncreated and co-eternal with intelligence, meaning the creation was "a divinely managed organization of matter that had always existed."[25] Smith's cosmology may be described as a form of eternalism, "the belief that the content of the universe is uncreated and unending,"[26] so whatever now exists always has existed.[27]

---

17. JS, revelation, May 6, 1833, D3:89 [D&C 93:33].
18. For a counterpoint, see Samuel M. Brown, "Mormons Probably Aren't Materialists," *Dialogue* 50, no. 3 (2017): 39–72.
19. See Gen 1–2; Ps 33:6; Prov 8:22–31; Jer 10:12; John 1:1–3; Heb 1:10; 11:3; Col 1:16; Rev 4:11; Mosiah 3:8; Helaman 14:12; 3 Nephi 9:15; Mormon 9:11; D&C 14:9.
20. Stephen Webb, "Godbodied: The Matter of the Latter-day Saints," *BYU Studies* 50, no. 3 (2011): 94 (emphasis added).
21. Paulsen and Boyd, "The Nature of God in Mormon Thought," 250.
22. Webb, "Godbodied," 94 (emphasis added).
23. Stephen H. Webb, *Jesus Christ, Eternal God: Heavenly Flesh and the Metaphysics of Matter* (New York: Oxford University Press, 2012), 251.
24. Stephen H. Webb, *Mormon Christianity: What Other Christians Can Learn from the Latter-day Saints* (New York: Oxford University Press, 2013), 34.
25. Brent L. Top, "Creation," in *LDS Beliefs: A Doctrinal Reference*, ed. Robert L. Millet et al. (Salt Lake City: Deseret Book, 2011), 139.
26. Terryl L. Givens, *Wrestling the Angel: The Foundations of Mormon Thought: Cosmos, God, Humanity* (New York: Oxford University Press, 2015), 53.
27. LDS theologian B. H. Roberts coined the term "eternalism" to describe Mormon cosmology. See David L. Paulsen, "Theology," in B. H. Roberts, *The Truth, The Way, The Life:*

Considering the LDS View of Creation

Mormonism's rejection of creation *ex nihilo* stems partly from Smith's reading of biblical creation narratives, especially Genesis 1, which he interpreted as God forming the cosmos out of a preexisting, formless material in dark chaos (see Gen 1:1–2). "God had materials to organize the world out of chaos," Smith explained.[28] "God spake, chaos heard, and worlds came into order."[29] Smith interpreted the word *bara'* (Heb. "to create") in Genesis as "to *organize*." Certainly, *bara'* "does not mean to create out of nothing," he claimed.[30]

Here, Smith parted ways with other interpreters who understand "the matter out of which God formed the world as itself a work of God," explained one scholar.[31] When read this way, "the most immediate problem with the formlessness, the darkness, and the void is not that they are coeval with God but that they are ugly, unsightly."[32] In other words, God didn't create out of a preexisting matter because the void *itself* was dependent on God, one that needed to be formed by him from void to "very good" (Gen 1:31).[33] "As [God] is the Creator of light," theologian Karl Barth added, "darkness, too, is not without but through Him."[34]

But Barth was quick to clarify that no biblical texts permit a scenario where God "positively willed, created and posited darkness in the same positive way as light or evil as peace, as an independent goal and event of His plan."[35] Even

---

An Elementary Treatise on Theology, 2nd ed., ed. John W. Welch (Provo, UT: BYU Studies, 1996), 619–22. LDS apostle John A. Widtsoe defined eternalism in salvific terms, describing how "the Gospel is founded on tangible and eternal things and relationships" (*A Rational Theology*, 4th ed. [Salt Lake City: Deseret, 1937], 15).

28. Joseph Smith, History, 1838–1856, vol. E-1, *JSP*, 1973.
29. R2:318.
30. Joseph Smith, History, 1838–1856, vol. E-1, *JSP*, 1973.
31. Novick, "Creator, Text, and Law," 197.
32. Novick, "Creator, Text, and Law," 197.
33. If it seems strange that God would create something that would involve darkness (Heb. *hoshek*), consider God's explicit statement, "I form the light, and create darkness" (Isa 45:7), and his use of darkness to execute judgment over Egypt (see Exod 10:21–22). Even so, Karl Barth is right to say that darkness in Gen 1:2 "cannot possibly be regarded even as a potentially positive magnitude" (*The Doctrine of Creation: The Work of Creation*, vol. 3 of *Church Dogmatics*, ed. G. W. Bromiley and T. F. Torrance [New York: T&T Clark, 2009], 105). "[N]othing that is good can come out of darkness," he wrote (p. 105). And yet the point of Genesis is to assert God's sovereignty over both the darkness and the light, contrasting the brilliance of God's holiness and light, the Lord Jesus (see John 1:4–5), which darkness cannot abide (see John 12:46). Interestingly, Smith's own revision of Gen 1:2 hints that he also wrestled with darkness in the early creation. Genesis simply states that "darkness was upon the face of the deep" without offering an explanation why, but Smith has the text state that God "*caused* darkness" to cover the waters (Moses 2:2, emphasis added). Perhaps Smith initially interpreted darkness as God's shadow, for in the third verse, God's Spirit "moved upon the face of the water" (Moses 2:3; cf. Gen 1:2).
34. Barth, *The Doctrine of Creation*, 105.
35. Barth, *The Doctrine of Creation*, 105.

so, Barth said, the creation narrative is not primarily concerned with the world's origin and composition. Rather, the text communicates how God sustains and governs the world, and his grand purpose for it, beginning with Israel.[36] From day one, God desired to see his will done on earth as it is in heaven (see Matt 6:10). Genesis presents the chaotic earth not in a state of formless confusion but lost in an abyss that separates the light and orderly heaven from a dark and disordered earth. It is an earth "in supreme antithesis" to heaven, wrote Barth.[37] The message of Genesis is less about origins than it is about making earthly life look celestial because the end purpose of God's creation is the merging of earthly and heavenly realities to his eternal glory (see Rev 21:1–5).

To hold Smith's interpretation is to assume God is not the uncaused generator of all things, nor can it be said that he truly "calls things into existence that do not exist" (Rom 4:17 CSB). Instead, Brigham Young taught that God constructs things into forms as a "supreme Architect," a superbeing "who organized the world."[38] Creation is an evolutionary work of God, progressing matter forward from simplicity to complexity. Moreover, God was not alone. The scope of Smith's creation account widened to include countless worlds formed by the Godhead in council with a host of heavenly agents (see Abr. 4–5). And because God is a physically embodied personage, he abides in physical space, dwelling on a celestially glorious planet "like crystal, and like a sea of glass"[39] and is seated on "the blasing [*sic*] throne of God."[40] LDS revelation locates this world near a great celestial body, Kolob—perhaps from the Hebrew "star" (Heb. *kokav*)—which was God's "first creation."[41] From his celestial throne, God rules a massive universe filled with habitable and inhabited worlds, an "immencity [*sic*] of space"[42] where "there is no space in which there is no Kingdom."[43]

A God who creates *ex materia*—or, better, a Godhead that constructs in community—depends on material for his own being and the formation of his creation. This contrasts starkly to a being who creates *ex nihilo*, relying only on

---

36. Barth, *The Doctrine of Creation*, 102–9. See also Gary A. Anderson, "*Creatio ex nihilo* and the Bible," in Anderson and Bockmuehl, *Creation* ex nihilo, 15–35; Ian A. McFarland, *From Nothing: A Theology of Creation* (Louisville: Westminster John Knox, 2014); Ernan McMullin, "Creation *ex nihilo*: Early History," in *Creation and the God of Abraham*, ed. David B. Burrell et al. (Cambridge: Cambridge University Press, 2010), 11–23; and Janet M. Soskice, "*Creatio ex nihilo*: Its Jewish and Christian Foundations," in *Creation and the God of Abraham*, ed. Burrell et al., 24–39.
37. Barth, *The Doctrine of Creation*, 103.
38. *CDBY* 1:530.
39. JS, instruction, April 2, 1843, D12:140 [D&C 130:7].
40. JSJ, January 21, 1836, J1:167.
41. R4:331.
42. MRB, 293 [D&C 88:12].
43. MRB, 297 [D&C 88:37]. Charles Harrell noticed how Smith's cosmology resembled speculations of his day about the possibility of inhabited worlds and the design of the universe ("*This is My Doctrine*," 238–41).

his own will to bring about all things.[44] As Augustine clarified, "It is true that [God], from whom all things exist, made not only what is created and formed but also whatever is creatable or formable," even intelligence and spirit.[45] After all, if "what is external to God is contingent and dependent upon God," then nothing can be unconditionally independent of him, not even intelligence or spirit.[46] Otherwise, God is like a human craftsman "who decides to shape a material thing."[47] To do so, the craftsman needs matter to form, but this is not how God created things. The craftsman was himself made by God and "imposes a form on something that already exists and has being," like stone, wood, or metal.[48]

As Augustine confessed:

> You made the craftsman's body. You made the soul that commands his bodily members. You made the matter out of which he makes something. You made the talents by which he grasps his art and sees within himself what he will make outside himself. You made the bodily sense by which he translates his work from mind into matter and then reports back to the mind what he has made, so that he may take counsel with the truth the presides within him to see whether the work has been made well.[49]

Were God a craftsman—even a *cosmic* craftsman—he would depend on a greater being or eternal principle for generating his own body and mind in addition to the material needed for forming the world. But God is YHWH, the Great "I AM THAT I AM" (Exod 3:14), and is not dependent on anyone or anything, so "how, God, did you make heaven and earth," asked Augustine? It was not by something his hands held, "for where would this thing have come from—this thing that you did not make—from which you would make something?"[50] Augustine found the answer in the opening scene of the Bible: "[God] spoke and they were made; and in your word you made them" (see Gen 1:3; John 1:1–3).[51]

This is why the suggestion that a carpenter-God is somehow preferable to the One who simply says, "Let there be," falls apart under the weight of scripture.

---

44. On this point, as Janet M. Soskice argued, early Christians considered the "Neoplatonic conviction that 'being necessarily proceeded from the One,' an assertion entirely at odds with the idea that God creates freely," and so rejected it as "unacceptable" ("*Creatio ex nihilo*: Its Jewish and Christian Foundations," 33).
45. *Conf.* 12.19.28.
46. Richard C. Barcellos, *Trinity and Creation: A Scriptural and Confessional Account* (Eugene, OR: Resource Publications, 2020), 28.
47. *Conf.* 11.5.7.
48. *Conf.* 11.5.7.
49. *Conf.* 11.5.7.
50. *Conf.* 11.5.7.
51. *Conf.* 11.5.7.

The craftsman depends on something beyond himself, like raw materials, tools, and time. But the God of the Bible depends on nothing. God does not shape what is given; rather, he summons what was not. To favor the carpenter over the Creator is to prefer contingency over self-existence. Only the God who needs no thing, no space, no help—only his will—can rightly be called the Maker of all.

Moreover, traditional Christianity does not lack intimacy or nearness in God. In fact, it affirms the opposite: that the very God who said "Let there be light" became flesh and dwelt among us (see John 1:1–3, 14). This God did not begin as a carpenter; rather, he condescended to carpentry. The Son of God took up wood not to build a cosmos, but to redeem it, from a manger to a cross. Unlike a cosmic carpenter who depends on the world to act within it, the Christian God freely enters what he made—not out of need but out of love—because he alone made absolutely everything: intelligence, spirit, matter, time, all of it.

This is why traditional Christianity finds it difficult to reconcile how, according to Mormonism, "all things were made by him; and without him was not any thing made that was made" (John 1:3) unless "all things" excludes the preexisting elemental-intelligence from which God's being is sourced. But then "all things" wouldn't truly be all things but all *other* things beside elements and intelligence.[52] God, then, is not the creator of "all things" because he did not create elements or intelligence; instead, he depends on the latter to form the former. For this reason, the Mormon doctrine of creation evokes—but is certainly not equivalent to—Neoplatonic theories of creation from preexisting materials. But scripture leaves no room for such dependence. God is not *of* it all; all of it is *of God*.

Summary

Traditional Christianity has long taught that God, an infinite and completely independent being, created all things *ex nihilo*. By contrast, Mormonism teaches that God formed all other things *ex materia*. He depended on preexisting matter and relied on ungenerated things, like intelligence and matter, for his existence. In this way, Mormonism blurs the Creator-creation distinction and holds to a radically different metaphysical reality from that of traditional Christianity. God did not merely create the worlds and all that is in them. He created the cosmos and all things in it, above it, around it, and beyond it, including intelligence and pure matter. God did not organize us; he made us from nothing. He is not our architect; he is our Creator.

---

52. Top, "Creation," 138. The Book of Mormon describes the Son of God as being the creator of "all things from the beginning" (Mosiah 3:8; Helaman 14:12), leaving an interpretive possibility that "all things" is a description limited to things created *at* and *after* the formation of this world, but not things prior. Still, God cannot be said to be the Creator of "all things," only the organizer of "all things" at the point when he caused the cosmos to be.

REFLECTION QUESTIONS

1. What are some shared convictions between traditional Christians and Latter-day Saints about creation and God's relationship to it?
2. What are the major differences between creation *ex nihilo* and creation *ex materia*? Why do they matter, if at all?
3. Does creation *ex nihilo* have biblical support? Why or why not?
4. Why does it matter that God created all things from nothing?
5. Why did Augustine reject the idea of God as a cosmic craftsman? Do you agree or disagree with his rejection?

QUESTION 26

What Is the Latter-day Saint View of Humanity?

"Our earthly bodies are framed in the image of God; they are framed to fit our spirits which are the offspring of God, which are therefore in His image, according to the law that every seed brings forth its own kind."[1]
~ Charles W. Penrose, Latter-day Saint Apostle, 1904–1925

The Bible opens with a spectacular narrative of cosmic creation. The heavens, the earth, and all that fill them are brought into existence by an incredibly powerful Creator. The pace of the story is fast. Days unfold rapidly as stars, oceans, plants, and animals burst into being. But the narrative lingers a bit when it arrives at the creation of humanity, drawing our attention not only to the origin of human beings but also to our purpose and value. Unlike the other creatures, humans were created by God in his image and likeness, animated by his breath. Theologians have long pondered what it means to be made in the *imago Dei*, or the image of God. Is this language allegorical, meant to communicate humanity's special status as God's image bearers? Is it literal, meaning humans are facsimiles of their embodied creator? Or, perhaps, could it be both?

Humans as a Creation of God

Every human being is a creation of God, made from earthly "dust" and divine "breath" (Gen 2:7), a material body and immaterial soul. We are incomplete without both.[2] That humans are composed of material bodies is self-evident,

1. "Remarks by Elder Chas. W. Penrose," *The Deseret News*, July 19, 1882.
2. A question arises: Are we a trichotomy of "spirit and soul and body" (1 Thess 5:23), as Irenaeus proposed, or a dichotomy of body and soul, as Tertullian believed? For an overview

a topic the Bible seems less interested in arguing than it does the implications of our spiritual dimension. It often draws the reader's attention to spirituality, to the immaterial "soul" (Heb. *nephesh* and Gk. *psyche*), though it is silent on how exactly God enjoins body and soul.[3] This silence has prompted theologians to articulate a few potential options. Patristic theologian Origen posited the premortal existence of souls, and with them, the premortal human experience in heaven.[4] Long ago, God created human souls in heaven, where they waited for assignment to physical bodies on earth. But the early church father Tertullian dissented, suggesting that the body and soul are products of earthly procreation.[5] He believed that God generates souls in the same way he generates bodies—through the natural process of conception. Other theologians, however, envision God tailoring our souls the very moment our bodies are conceived in wombs and then enjoining them by supernatural means.[6] While the formation of the body is a natural process, God intervenes supernaturally at conception by adding a soul.

Augustine provided a unifying baseline amid these diverse opinions. In the end, the soul must be a work of the God who created all things *ex nihilo*, even spiritual things.[7] Affirming this point protects against the assumption that souls are fashioned from ungenerated spirit matter that is co-eternal with God or that he somehow sired spirits by an act of procreation. As John Calvin summarized, each human being "consists of a body and a soul" and is "an

---

of this debate, see Gregg Allison, *Historical Theology: An Introduction to Christian Doctrine* (Grand Rapids: Zondervan Academic, 2011), 322–27.

3. For a brief history of the soul in Christian thought, see Anthony C. Thiselton, *The Thiselton Companion to Christian Theology* (Grand Rapids: Eerdmans, 2015), 784–87.
4. Origen found in the Platonic conception of preexistent souls "a way to explain apparent injustice in the way providence operates" (Joseph W. Trigg, *Origen* [New York: Routledge, 1998], 28–29). For Origen, the distinction between the elect and nonelect was not based on the seemingly arbitrary decisions of God but rather "on the basis of those souls' behavior before they were conceived in the womb" (Trigg, *Origen*, 29). Origen's idea was rejected by Constantinople II in the mid-sixth century. It does, however, dovetail with Latter-day Saint concepts of premortality. Origen, however, would disagree sharply with Mormonism that human souls are of the same essence as God.
5. Tertullian "argued that the human soul was not derived from pre-existent matter but from the breath of God," created simultaneously in the procreative act of parents (Geoffrey D. Dunn, *Tertullian* [New York: Routledge, 2004], 26). Gregory of Nyssa, Martin Luther, and Jonathan Edwards affirmed this position called *traducianism*.
6. Methodius, for example, thought the soul was "sown" by God along with the physical body, which harmonized with Lactantius's thought, who argued that "the soul comes directly from God, while the body is derived from physical material" (Allison, *Historical Theology*, 325). Jerome, Anselm, Aquinas, and John Calvin followed this *creationist* view of the soul.
7. So Augustine: "I can affirm nothing about the human soul . . . except that it comes from God in such a way as not to be part of God's substance but yet still incorporeal, that is to say, it is not a body but a spirit. It was not begotten from the divine substance, nor does it proceed from it, but it was made by God. It was not made out of any corporeal or irrational nature, but out of nothing" (*ACD* 1:123).

immortal though *created* essence."[8] Souls are apparently endless but certainly not beginningless.

At first glance, Joseph Smith appears to have favored Origen's perspective. Smith's revision of Genesis narrated God spiritually creating "men before they were in the flesh" (Moses 6:51), possibly to clarify humanity's place within the spiritual creation God made prior to the physical one. Smith clarified elsewhere that spirits "have no beginning; they existed before, they shall have no end, they shall exist after, for they are *gnolaum*, or eternal."[9] All spirits are eternal because their nature constitutes "intelligence," an ungenerated, everlasting component of creation. Similar to Platonic ideas, which suggest that each human soul lived in the world of ideas of the premortal state, Smith perceived a timeless connection between the soul and mind. He explained to Latter-day Saints that, like the Son of God, "ye were also in the beginning with the Father," explaining that "intelligence or the Light of truth was not created or made neither indeed can be."[10] It has "no beginning, neither will it have an end," he clarified.[11] Humanity is, in this sense, beginningless and endless because all intelligence is eternal, and humans, as conscious and rational agents, source their most fundamental being from this uncreated and everlasting font.[12] And because the building blocks of our spiritual and material being—elements or matter—are ungenerated and eternal, and God is constituted from these same materials, humans are eternally coexistent with God. As Smith said, "The mind or the intelligence which man possesses is coequal with God himself."[13]

At some point in eternity past, though, every human was spiritually begotten, birthed into a spirit body by heavenly parents, God the Father and

8. Calvin, *Inst.* 1.15.2 (emphasis added).
9. See Abraham 3:18. "Gnolaum" is an old English transliteration of the Heb. *olam*, meaning "perpetual" or "everlasting." Smith was tutored in Hebrew during early 1836, less than a year after acquiring the source material for the book of Abraham. Relatedly, the Book of Mormon is as relatively silent on premortality as the Bible, giving only sparse hints, like describing Christ's mission as bringing humanity "back into the presence of the Lord" (Helaman 14:17). But the Book of Mormon neither elaborates on nor develops this doctrine.
10. JS, revelation, May 6, 1833, D3:88–89 [D&C 93:23, 29] (emend.).
11. Joseph Smith, History, 1838–1856, vol. E-1, *JSP*, 1974.
12. Whether humans are eternally independent intelligences or are sourced from intelligence at spirit birth is undecided in LDS thought. Either way, the point remains that intelligence is eternal, and because humans are intelligent, their being shares in eternity.
13. Joseph Smith, History, 1838–1856, vol. E-1, *JSP*, 1973. An alternative version of this text suggests Smith said that "the mind of man is as immortal as God himself," suggesting length and not level of existence (JS, discourse, April 7, 1844, reported by Thomas Bullock, *JSP*). Three other records of this sermon, however, have "coequal" or "co-equal." See JS, discourse, April 7, 1844, reported by Wilford Woodruff; reported by Willard Richards; reported by William Clayton, *JSP*. See also *WWJ* 1:630.

Heavenly Mother.[14] But this birth moment "does not mark the beginning of consciousness," clarified LDS philosophers, "rather, it constitutes a transformation or enlargement of the uncreated 'intelligence.'"[15] This enlargement continues when the spirit body enjoins a physical one in the womb, forming the essential being of humanity, or the soul. Smith taught "the spirit, and the body is the soul of man."[16] Thus, "the Spirit of Man is not a created being," he believed; "it existed from Eternity & will exist to Eternity."[17] As one LDS theologian summarized, "Just as Christ had an existence before mortality, so did all humanity."[18]

For the earliest Latter-day Saints, this doctrine was more than the solution to an age-old theological conundrum; it was "a way to understand themselves, their origins and endings, or more properly, the fact that they had neither."[19] But there is a reason why orthodoxy dismisses the eternality (but not immortality) of the soul. This belief doesn't elevate humanity to a higher status of dignity, as perhaps Smith hoped it would. Instead, it diminishes God to a lower status of a demiurgical being who depended on something before and beyond himself to create all *other* things beside intelligence and matter (see question 25).[20] Even Origen, who believed in souls' premortal existence, denied they are co-eternal with God in their nature.[21] Moreover, humanity doesn't share the same kind of premortal existence as Christ. Even if the Son and our souls awaited their incarnations, the Son was not created like our souls were. There was a time when souls were not, but never a time when the Son was not. It was through him all souls were created, for "all things were created by him, and for him" (Col 1:16), even souls.

Still, Latter-day Saints see the soul's premortal existence as a helpful explanation for humanity's deep yearning for the transcendent, as if we long to return to a place we've already been and to reunite with a family we already

14. For a doctrinal survey of Heavenly Mother, see David L. Paulsen and Martin Pulido, " 'A Mother There': A Survey of Historical Teachings About Mother in Heaven," *BYU Studies* 50, no. 1 (2011): 71–97.
15. David L. Paulsen and Hal Boyd, *Are Christians Mormon?* (New York: Routledge, 2017), 66.
16. JS, revelation, December 27–28, 1832, D2:337 [D&C 88:15].
17. JS, discourse, ca. June 26–August 4, 1839, D6:543.
18. Samuel Morris Brown, *In Heaven as It Is on Earth: Joseph Smith and the Early Mormon Conquest of Death* (New York: Oxford University Press, 2012), 249.
19. Brown, *In Heaven as It Is on Earth*, 252.
20. LDS scholar Terryl L. Givens noticed the orthodox anxiety on this point since "the extension of divine attributes to brute matter" leads to the "destruction of God's monopoly on eternal existence" (*When Souls Had Wings: Pre-Mortal Existence in Western Thought* [New York: Oxford University Press, 2010], 214). Givens acknowledges that to pivot away from the orthodox position is to turn toward Gnostic and Platonic ideas on the preexistence (*When Souls Had Wings*, 217; see also 214–20).
21. Origen thought it ungodly to say, "Matter is uncreated and co-eternal with the uncreated God." Saying otherwise is to be "altogether ignorant of the power and intelligence of uncreated nature" (*ACD* 1:96).

know but have long forgotten. Yet, a premortal experience is unnecessary to explain this longing if, as Genesis tells us, humans were created in the image and likeness of God (see Gen 1:27). It's not a place our souls pine after. Instead, it is a *person* for whom our souls long, our Creator, the one we were designed to reflect.

In the Image of God and Gods

Augustine noticed this yearning when he described humanity as being made *toward* God, unlike other creatures. Humans are embodied rational souls "whose being and well-being consists in turning to God in order to be what it was created to be."[22] For Augustine, humans "are not God, but they are intrinsically ordered toward him."[23] We were created to love, believe, and know God, and we discover our completion in emulating the glory of his nature, but never to become it. Our likeness is not found in our nature nor our personal potential to achieve god-likeness but by divine mercy and grace, which gift us with partaking in the divine nature with the Father, Son, and Holy Spirit. "What is common to them by nature," explained one theologian, "is and will become common to us by grace."[24] To "be partakers of the divine nature" (2 Pet 1:4), then, is not about human potential; it's about our participation. We will never comprehend, let alone apprehend, God's nature. "Our union with God—real as it is—is one in which we are always on the receiving end. Our being is accidental."[25] It is forever contingent on the only self-existent One.

What led to these conclusions? The Bible describes humans as a special creation of God distinct from other creatures because he "created man in his own image" (Gen 1:27).[26] Christianity affirms that every human bears the image and likeness of God, but defining the *imago Dei* with precision is difficult. The doctrine is like a fine jewel, impossible to describe from only one angle, so a pattern of faceted explanations is to be expected. Popular interpretations commonly fall into one of two categories: the ontological and the operational. In other words, being made in the image of God is a statement

22. Jared Ortiz, *"You Made Us for Yourself": Creation in St. Augustine's* Confessions (Minneapolis: Fortress Press, 2016), 31.
23. Ortiz, *"You Made Us for Yourself,"* 32.
24. Christopher R. J. Holmes, *A Theology of the Christian Life: Imitating and Participating in God* (Grand Rapids: Baker Academic, 2021), 26.
25. Holmes, *A Theology of the Christian Life*, 31.
26. Genesis also explains that humans were made in the likeness of God, leading some to speculate the relationship between "image" and "likeness." Some interpreters, like Irenaeus, distinguished the two, having believed Adam's fall caused humanity to retain its likeness to God but not God's image. See Robert M. Grant, *Irenaeus of Lyons* (New York: Routledge, 1997), 38. John Calvin, however, thought it absurd to bifurcate "image" (Heb. *tselem*) and "likeness" (Heb. *demuth*) and assign them different meaning (*Inst.* 1.15.3). Modern interpreters largely agree, seeing in them as a "synonymous parallelism" common to Hebrew writing (Anthony C. Thiselton, *Systematic Theology* [Grand Rapids: Eerdmans, 2015], 137).

about what humans *are* (i.e., the nature of our being, or ontology) and what humans *do* (i.e., our activities and capabilities).[27]

Ontologically, the *imago Dei* offers the most basic answer to what it means to be human. If everything owes its existence to God, how are humans distinct in creation? Unlike animals, God created humanity with "an exclusive kind of dignity," explained one scholar, "a dignity rooted in their roles as image bearers" and shared equally as male and female.[28] Humans are the only living creatures that God intimately animated with "the breath of life" (Gen 2:7). They are also "like" God in that they are rational and affectionate moral agents who were created to desire holiness and community. But the *imago Dei* is not merely "a generic account of natural human attributes."[29] It also speaks to human identity, "not in an abstract sense but in the concrete relationship to [God]."[30] For this reason, the concept also describes human meaning—*why* we are *what* we are—and the activity God enables and expects. God created humans in his image "in order that [we] might be fit for the presence of God" and fellowship among creation.[31] In this vein, it's better to think of humans created *as* the image of God. We are created as an image of God for the world.[32] And as image bearers, humanity is designed to operate "as representative of one who is really or spiritually present, though physically absent."[33]

Humans are visible images of God precisely because he is invisible, which is why he abhors idols of his image. "The only physical image with which God is represented is the human being—the one who can hear,

27. For a history of interpretations of the *imago Dei*, see Stanley J. Grenz, *The Social God and the Relational Self: A Trinitarian Theology of the* imago Dei (Louisville: Westminster John Knox Press, 2001), 141–222. For a survey of recent interpretations, see Ryan S. Peterson, *The* imago Dei *as Human Identity: A Theological Interpretation* (Winona Lake, IN: Eisenbrauns, 2016), 5–16.
28. Abigail Favale, *The Genesis of Gender: A Christian Theory* (San Francisco: Ignatius Press, 2022), 36.
29. Lints, *Identity and Idolatry*, 35.
30. Lints, *Identity and Idolatry* 35.
31. Charles Octavius Boothe, *Plain Theology for Plain People* (Bellingham, WA: Lexham Press, 2017), 25.
32. David J. A. Clines, "Humanity as the Image of God," in *On the Way to the Postmodern: Old Testament Essays, 1967–1998*, 2 vols. (Sheffield: Sheffield Academic Press, 1998), 2:470–71.
33. Clines, "Humanity," 482. Furthermore, to be made "in the image of God" leaves open the possibility of being an individual icon of an embodied being, which is contrary to the OT tradition that resists the notion that YHWH is embodied ("Humanity," 468–75). For an overview of Clines's interpretation as related to LDS theology, see Jim W. Adams, "The God of Abraham, Isaac, and Joseph Smith? God, Creation, and Humanity in the Old Testament and Mormonism," in *The New Mormon Challenge: Responding to the Latest Defenses of a Fast-Growing Movement*, ed. Francis J. Beckwith, Carl Mosser, and Paul Owen (Grand Rapids: Zondervan Academic, 2002), 171–73.

understand, speak, and embody the divine Word."[34] Thus, the image of God is not merely a statement about our *being* but also our *doing*, a description of identity and vocation, "a special commission, for a special relationship with God."[35] We are meant to embody his heart, to imitate his actions, and symbolize him to the world.

Sin, however, complicated the matter. Herman Bavinck noted how "a human being does not *bear* or *have* the image of God but that he or she *is* the image of God."[36] So, since it is something humans *are* and not something they *have*, it is impossible for humanity to lose the image of God. Still, the image was tragically defaced by sin. John Calvin rightly contended that the *imago Dei* was not "utterly effaced and destroyed" in Adam's fall but was instead "so corrupted, that any thing which remains is fearful deformity" in desperate need of godly renovation.[37] Our hearts were "seized by legions of vile affections," taught John Wesley.[38] So the renewal of the *imago Dei* comes by conformity to the sinless Image of God, the Lord Jesus Christ (see Rom 8:29). By God's grace alone is his image restored in humanity. For traditional Christianity, then, the *imago Dei* communicates human attributes and purpose in relation to God.

Mormonism affirms many of these ideas about the *imago Dei*, a doctrine that explains our inherent value and worth,[39] rationality and agency,[40] affections and senses,[41] and even our creativity.[42] And the Book of Mormon seems to interpret the *imago Dei* as a moral quality lost at the fall but regained at conversion (see Alma 5:13–14, 19). Being made in God's image and likeness is more than an allegory for human identity, however; it's a literal description of the human form. When God created us, he did so "in the image *of his own body*" (Moses 6:9, emphasis added), distinguishing the Mormon *imago Dei* from any kind of "incorporealist construction."[43] "Adam was created in

34. Daniel J. Treier, *Introducing Evangelical Theology* (Grand Rapids: Baker Academic, 2019), 150.
35. Michael Horton, *The Christian Faith: A Systematic Theology for Pilgrims on the Way* (Grand Rapids: Zondervan Academic, 2011), 381.
36. Herman Bavinck, *God and Creation*, vol. 2 of *Reformed Dogmatics*, ed. John Bolt, trans. John Vriend (Grand Rapids: Baker Academic, 2004), 554 (emphasis original).
37. Calvin, *Inst.* 1.15.4.
38. Thomas C. Oden, *God and Providence*, vol. 1 of *John Wesley's Teachings* (Grand Rapids: Zondervan Academic, 2012), 175.
39. David Alton, *Inspiring Service*, ed. Andrew Teal (Salt Lake City: Deseret Book, 2019), 11–12.
40. Ernst W. Benz, "*Imago Dei:* Man in the Image of God," in *Reflections on Mormonism: Judaeo-Christian Parallels* (Provo, UT: RSC, BYU, 1978).
41. Parley P. Pratt, *Key to the Science of Theology* (London: F. D. Richards, 1855), 98.
42. Truman G. Madsen, "The Latter-day Saint View of Human Nature," in *On Human Nature: The Jerusalem Center Symposium*, ed. Truman G. Madsen, David Noel Freedman, and Pam Fox Kuhlken (Ann Arbor, MI: Pryor Pettengill, 2004), 104.
43. David Paulsen, "The Doctrine of Divine Embodiment: Restoration, Judeo-Christian, and Philosophical Perspectives," *BYU Studies* 35, no. 4 (1995): 21.

the very fashion and image of God," said Joseph Smith, and if Adam, so all humanity.[44] The Book of Mormon affirms Smith's position, teaching that "all men were created in the beginning after [God's] own image," not merely to reflect his character but also his body, for "man have I created after the body of my spirit" (Ether 3:15–16; cf. Mosiah 7:27).[45] Thus, for Smith, God is less anthropomorphic than humans are theomorphic, or having physical God-like characteristics.[46]

Smith isn't alone. Some biblical scholars argue that the terms *image* (Heb. *tselem*) and *likeness* (Heb. *demuth*) "pertain specifically to the physical contours of God," so that humans are made after God's (and the gods') "form" and "shape."[47] "At some level," concluded one scholar, "humans belong to the divine class or species" but are nevertheless "not divine, nor are they members of the heavenly host."[48] Such interpretations favor *image* and *likeness* as concrete terms, although this view is not the scholarly consensus. Rather, abstract readings are "contextually defensible," as one scholar noted, and for good reason.[49] The *imago Dei* speaks not to humanity's form and physique but to our function and purpose. In other words, we fill and subdue the earth as God's authoritative agents (see Gen 1:28). Furthermore, the OT is replete with warnings against fashioning idols in the image of God because he is immaterial, which is why, from its earliest days, Christianity has repeated the constant refrain "that the image of God is to be found in man's soul and not in his body,"[50] especially the soul in synchrony with the Spirit of God. What matters is not whether we are of the divine nature but whether we are nearest to God, for true divine likeness "is unison or unity with God in will."[51] We are not divine because we resemble God's body; rather, we are like God when our will mirrors his. That is the image that counts.

44. "Conference Minutes," *T&S*, May 1, 1844, 5:613.
45. In this passage, Jesus Christ is described as "the Father and the Son," and not the Son only, so it is reasonable to assume the author's intention is to teach on the *imago Dei* rather than the image of Christ alone. Also, here the book of Ether reverses the order of images in the book of Hebrews, which states that the Son of God incarnate was "made like unto his brethren," and not *vice versa* (Heb 2:17).
46. Madsen, "The Latter-day Saint View of Human Nature," 104.
47. Benjamin D. Sommer, *The Bodies of God and the World of Ancient Israel* (Cambridge: Cambridge University Press, 2009), 69.
48. Catherine L. McDowell, *The Image of God in the Garden of Eden* (Winona Lake, IN: Eisenbrauns, 2015), 133.
49. Sommer, *Bodies of God*, 70.
50. Walter J. Burghardt, *The Image of God in Man According to Cyril of Alexandria*, Studies in Christian Antiquity, ed. Johannes Quasten (Woodstock, MD: Woodstock College Press, 1957), 18–19.
51. C. S. Lewis, *The Four Loves* (London: Geoffrey Bles, 1960), 14.

Summary

Traditional Christianity and Mormonism affirm that humanity is created in the image and likeness of God, a special feature among all creation that endows us with intrinsic value and commissions us with a purpose to "live, and move, and have our being" (Acts 17:28) in him. While being made in God's image is commonly understood to define human nature and responsibility, Mormonism also interprets the Bible literally to express that humans are facsimiles of an embodied God, who is an exalted man. Our physical form resembles the body of God, so to be made in God's image and likeness is to be replicas of his material form.

REFLECTION QUESTIONS

1. How do you believe that God enjoined body and soul?

2. How does Joseph Smith's theory of the soul's origin differ from Origen's idea?

3. What convictions are shared about the *imago Dei* by traditional Christianity and Mormonism?

4. What are the differences between how traditional Christianity and Mormonism view the *imago Dei*?

5. How might you respond to a Latter-day Saint who draws on non-LDS scholarship that affirms the physical form of God?

QUESTION 27

What Is the Latter-day Saint View of Salvation?

"God restored his ancient gospel to Joseph Smith, giving him revelation, opening the heavens to him, and making him acquainted with the plan of salvation and exaltation of the children of men."[1]
~ John Taylor, President of the LDS Church, 1880–1887

When the Philippian jailer asked his prisoners "Sirs, what must I do to be saved?" (Acts 16:30), the answer he received from Paul and Silas was perhaps not what he expected. There was nothing he could do except to "believe on the Lord Jesus Christ" (Acts 16:31). Faith alone in Christ alone saves sinners because we are not worthy of celestial glory, but he is, and by faith in his atoning work alone, he gifts us complete and total celestial salvation (see Eph 2:8–9; 1 Tim 2:5; Titus 3:5). Their response cut to the heart of the Christian gospel: that mere faith in the Son of God is sufficient to save and sustain the sinner through the transformative sanctification of their souls toward a future glorification in resurrected and eternal life. Mormonism, too, affirms faith in Jesus Christ, especially the centrality of his atonement, the power that liberates us from original sin and aids us in overcoming temptation and trials on the long journey of eternal progression. Yet theological additions, deviations, and inflection points differentiate traditional Christianity and Mormonism concerning salvation, causing tension between two historically missional communities.

1. "Discourse by Elder John Taylor," *The Deseret Evening News*, February 28, 1847.

In this question and the next two questions, we will consider these similarities and differences concerning the nature of salvation by examining the grand redemptive narrative of the plan of salvation according to Mormonism.[2]

The First Estate: Premortality

Long ago, before the creation of the world, God the Father and Heavenly Mother conceived every human soul. We were spirit children who endlessly worshiped God as "intelligences who surround the throne of Jehovah," said Joseph Smith, while growing in the knowledge of holiness in our first estate.[3] God's offspring were like him, spiritually embodied moral agents with divine potential for celestial glory. We were, in effect, embryonic gods.[4] Fatherly affection toward his children moved God to conceive a plan in which he could gift all his progeny the potential of progressing toward an exaltation like his own, although we would never—nor *could* ever—match his greatness. This plan of salvation was announced in heaven after God called together the heavenly hosts and "sat in grand council to bring forth the world," Smith explained.[5] During the council, however, confrontation erupted over competing visions for the plan's execution. In the end, Jesus Christ, God's firstborn son and our eldest brother, was elected to redeem the world, a prospect Lucifer would not accept, so he "was thrust down from the presence of God & the Son."[6] The Holy Ghost, as the third member of the Godhead, would aid the Father and Son in executing God's redemptive plan.

The Second Estate: Creation

Physical creation inaugurated the plan's first phase, providing a second estate in which humanity could obtain physical bodies and gain experiences on their way toward perfection. Being sent from heaven above to earth below into a physical body is, ironically, a higher state of being than merely spiritual embodiment

---

2. For an in-depth analysis of this narrative with visual aids, see Tyler J. Griffin and Donald B. Anderson, "The Great Plan of Happiness: A Christ-Centered Visual Approach," *Religious Educator* 18, no. 1 (2017): 12–31. See also Tad R. Callister, *The Infinite Atonement* (Salt Lake City: Deseret, 2000); Terryl and Fiona Givens, *The Christ Who Heals: How God Restored the Truth That Saves Us* (Salt Lake City: Deseret, 2017); idem, *All Things New: Rethinking Sin, Salvation, and Everything in Between* (Meridian, ID: Faith Matters, 2020); Adam S. Miller, *Original Grace: An Experiment in Restoration Thinking* (Salt Lake City: Deseret, 2022).
3. JS to Orson Hyde and John E. Page, May 14, 1840, D7:282 (emend.).
4. Paulsen and Boyd identified at least six significant LDS leaders who have used this metaphor (David L. Paulsen and Hal Boyd, *Are Christians Mormon?* (New York: Routledge, 2017), 84).
5. Joseph Smith, History, 1838–1856, vol. E-1, *JSP*, 1972.
6. MRB, 245 [D&C 76:25]. Smith relayed how Lucifer "rebelled against the only begotten Son, whom the father loved" and was consequently cast out of heaven and called "perdition" as a result (MRB, 245 [D&C 76:25]). Smith rooted Satan's error in pride, the kind that manifests in open oppression by those who "put their foot on the necks of others" (C:92).

because God, in his exalted state, "has flesh and bones."[7] To become like their Heavenly Father, his spirit children require material bodies. But more than this, they need to collect experiences that would form, reform, and perfect their moral agency. To aid in this process, some spirits were foreordained or predestined for special tasks, like apostolic or prophetic roles, but all were given the necessary conditions to choose good or evil in the wake of premortality.

God formed the first man and woman, Adam and Eve, through whom all humanity would eventually receive their bodies by earthly parents. Humankind's first parents were then placed in the garden of Eden.[8] There, in the paradisiacal garden, God planted the tree of life and the tree of knowledge of good and evil, encouraging Adam and Eve to enjoy the first tree but forbidding them from partaking in the second. The consequence for disobeying God was dire, "for in the day that thou eatest thereof," he warned Adam, "thou shalt surely die" (Gen 2:17). But Smith caveated this instruction: "Nevertheless, thou mayest choose for thyself, for it is given unto thee" (Moses 3:17). The choice was Adam's to make, and he chose to sin. Smith resisted labeling Adam's action sin, arguing instead that his transgression was a divinely decreed choice.[9] Adam and Eve could have either remained in a paradisal-yet-progression-less state by themselves or they could progress to celestial glory through death, and with them, the whole human family. They chose the latter.

The Forward Fall of Humanity

With bite marks in the fruit, God's plan of happiness pressed onward. Not only had Adam and Eve grown in moral knowledge, but also the floodgate of spiritual children gaining bodies was now opened through earthly procreation. Reflecting on this moment, LDS apostles have lauded Adam and Eve as "the great hero and heroine of human history"[10] and their the fall the result of wisdom and courage.[11] But this is a far cry from the universal Christian lament of Adam's sin as corrupt,[12] criminal,[13] inexcusable,[14]

7. JS, discourse, January 5, 1841, D7:494. Smith also differentiated the corporeality of the Holy Spirit, who "is yet a spiritual Body," from the kinds of bodies had by the Son (JS, discourse, June 16, 1844, reported by George Laub, *JSP*).
8. Smith speculated the garden of Eden was located near the ancient valley of Adam-ondi-Ahman in present-day Missouri.
9. So Smith: "Adam did not commit sin in eating the fruit, for God had decreed that he should eat and fall" (JS, discourse, ca. February 9, 1841, D8:30 [emend.]).
10. John A. Widtsoe, *Rational Theology* (Salt Lake City: General Boards of the Mutual Improvement Association, 1915), 47.
11. Dallin H. Oaks, "The Great Plan of Happiness," *Ensign*, November 1993, 72–75.
12. *ACD* 3:69.
13. Calvin, *Inst.* 2.1.4.
14. John Dagg, *A Manual of Theology* (Greenville, SC: The American Baptist Publication Society, 1857), 146.

darkened,[15] disobedient,[16] disastrous,[17] disruptive,[18] and tragic,[19] a reckless surrender to the serpent who "whispered that [Adam and Eve] could become as gods," explained C. S. Lewis.[20] The serpent's lie was subtle; disobedience led to divinization, not death. The apostle Paul warned against imitating Eve for this very reason (see 2 Cor 11:3). She's no role model to emulate but a cautionary tale to flee. For it wasn't bravery that led our first parents into obedience and life; rather, as Lewis noted, it was selfishness that drove them to sin and death. "They wanted some corner in the universe of which they could say to God, 'This is our business, not yours.'"[21]

For traditional Christianity, the fall deformed humanity into a "lost mass," as Augustine described, living selfishly toward oneself (Lat. *incurvatus in se*) and away from God (Lat. *aversio a Deo*). Adam's motivation was not courageous. He didn't selflessly set aside his life by stepping bravely into the dark unknown of death so that God's spirit children could begin their journey of mortal probation. Nor was his decision wise, for it is impossible to describe disobedience to God as wisdom. It's the fool who does what is "right in his own eyes" (Prov 12:15), for the height of foolishness is to disobey and be deceived, as Adam and Eve did and were (see Titus 3:3). Adam's sin was cowardly and motivated primarily by pride "to take for himself what he had not received, so that he might be like his own creator and maker, so that he might claim divine honor."[22] "Nothing necessitated the fall of humanity," opined John Wesley. "It was absurdly chosen."[23] The fall of humanity is the true Great Apostasy.

For Mormonism, however, Adam's transgression was less a fall *downward* into the pit of death than it was a fall *forward* into the messiness of mortality. Granted, in yielding to temptation, our first parents "became subject to the will of the devil" and set a tragic example for their offspring that led to the disharmony and disarray of this fallen world.[24] But Adam's sin was his alone and not communicable to those under his federal headship. Smith rejected,

---

15. Herman Bavinck, *Sin and Salvation in Christ*, 35.
16. Dietrich Bonhoeffer, *Creation and Fall: A Theological Exposition of Genesis 1–3*, ed. John W. de Gruchy, trans. Douglas Stephen Bax (Minneapolis: Fortress, 1997), 68.
17. Andrew Louth, *Introducing Eastern Orthodox Theology* (Downers Grove: IVP Academic, 2013), 69.
18. Francis, Encyclical Letter *Laudato Sì ("Praise Be to You") of the Holy Father Francis, On Care for Our Common Home* (Vatican City: Vatican Press, 2015), no. 66.
19. Bruce Demarest, *The Cross and Salvation: The Doctrine of Salvation* (Wheaton, IL: Crossway, 1997), 73.
20. C. S. Lewis, *The Problem of Pain* (New York: HarperCollins, 2015), 75.
21. Lewis, *The Problem of Pain*, 75.
22. *ACD* 5:238.
23. Thomas C. Oden, *John Wesley's Teachings*, vol. 2, *Christ and Salvation* (Grand Rapids: Zondervan, 2012), 223.
24. MRB, 49 [D&C 29:40].

as Pelagius did, that humanity is born under the Adamic curse of original sin, utterly incapable of holy loving and living because of pervasive depravity.[25] In other words, we become sinners because we sin; we do not sin because we *are* sinners (*contra* Augustine). The human spirit, then, is untested and unperfected, having yet to be refined through mortal probation. And because we live in a world in which the devil "as a roaring lion, walketh about, seeking whom he may devour" (1 Pet 5:8), moral failure by temptation is as inevitable as a kindergartner's failure to pass the bar exam.[26] Sin prevents us from living up to our divine potential because we violate our covenants with God, deny spiritual truth from the Holy Ghost and modern prophets, and fail to make the best use of Christ's atoning work in our lives. Thus, moral perfection is a standard too high for any of God's children with only one exception: Jesus Christ, the Son of God before creation, who stepped into the world to repatriate into God's kingdom every soul alienated from him and to offer to those who believe and obey the potential of participating in an exalted state.

Christ's Vicarious Atonement

Jesus accomplished this feat through his atonement, with its blood-sweat prelude in the garden of Gethsemane to his excruciating and alienating death on the cross of Golgotha. Christ's atonement is less a substitutional payment for the penalizing debt of sinners tainted by original sin and more a vicarious remedy that rectifies the consequences of poor moral choice while simultaneously healing the injuries inflicted by acting contrary to the will of God. We are forgiven and healed from our sin by "relying alone upon the merits of Christ" (Moroni 6:4) through faith, and then we enter a "saving partnership," one in which sinners are joined to Christ by repentance, enveloped in divine grace, grown by God's mercy, and sustained by Christ's suffering with us in our sins.[27]

For Mormonism, the atonement is the power of God that heals the effects of sin, erases the penalty of sin, and enables Saints to grow distant from the presence of sin. To believe in the atoning work of Christ is to be justified, or to be "*made* perfect through Jesus the mediator of the new Covenant."[28] The convert receives a state of justification as a gift and retains that status through the outworking of practices, like repentance, baptism, reception of the Holy Ghost, and fidelity to covenants. Failure to do so jeopardizes one's pursuit of worthiness because "there is a posibility [*sic*] that men may fall from grace

25. Smith's position seemed to be that humans die because of Adam's first sin, but we are judged and punished for our actual sin, inherited by no one.
26. Even this analogy is too generous, for if we were "*dead* in trespasses and sins" (Eph 2:1, emphasis added), then outside of Christ, we are as hopeless as a corpse to pass the exam of righteousness.
27. Miller, *Original Grace*.
28. MRB, 249 [D&C 76:69] (emphasis added).

& depart from the living God."[29] Yet, through consistent demonstrations of dependence, God restores the sinners as they remain in a justified state by "the assisting grace of the Savior," one of many gifts of grace that are requisite to salvation.[30] It is less a matter of *if* Mormonism teaches grace than it is *how*.[31] Grace is the unprompted, default disposition of God's loving kindness toward sinners and the underpinning of his plan of salvation for them; yet, it is not unconditionally effective (*contra* Reformation soteriology) and is capable of being diminished and even lost through sin.

Moreover, the effects of the atonement are available to all people for all eternity. The Book of Mormon describes the atonement as "an infinite and eternal sacrifice" (Alma 34:10), an intercession that is universally available to every person and endlessly powerful, securing resurrection from death for all and affording a portion of salvation for humankind *in toto* while also enabling greater degrees of glory for those who believe and keep covenantal promises.[32] So while death ushers souls into a postmortem spirit world of prison or paradise, all people will be resurrected in the end for judgment and entrance into degreed heavens.

Degrees of Glory

But what kind of heaven awaits the righteous? This question has long perplexed theologians, especially speculation around the possibility of degreed glory in heaven based on Paul's discourse of the resurrection (see 1 Cor 15:35–49). The apostle wrote about the nature of the resurrection body, teaching that just as the luminosity of the sun, moon, and stars differ in brilliance, so the resurrection body would differ in "glory," which Paul hoped would stir up the believer's wonder of "what beauty, what splendor, what brightness the spiritual body will have," explained Tertullian.[33] Augustine augmented this text

29. MRB, 79–80 [D&C 20:32].
30. JS to Oliver Cowdery, December 1834, D4:215.
31. For a survey on this point, see John Anthony Dunne and Logan Alexander Williams, "A Perplexing Gift: Toward Clarity in the Evangelical-Mormon Interfaith Dialogue on Grace," *Journal of the Evangelical Theological Society* 60, no. 2 (2017): 349–76.
32. On the infinite atonement of Mormonism, Charles Harrell noted that early Latter-day Saints viewed the *quality* of the atonement as infinite (i.e., sourced from an infinite being), while contemporary Mormonism tends to view the atonement as infinite in *quantity* (i.e., given to all people) (*"This Is My Doctrine": The Development of Mormon Theology* [Salt Lake City: Greg Kofford Books, 2011], 285–86).
33. Tertullian, *1 Corinthians: Interpreted by Early Christian Commentators*, ed. and trans. Judith Kovacs (Grand Rapids: Eerdmans, 2005), 271. See also Gordon D. Fee, *The First Epistle to the Corinthians*, New International Commentary on the New Testament (Grand Rapids: Eerdmans, 1987), 775–78; Raymond F. Collins, *First Corinthians* (Collegeville, MN: Liturgical Press, 1999), 562–68; Anthony C. Thiselton, *The First Epistle to the Corinthians*, New International Greek Testament Commentary (Grand Rapids: Eerdmans, 2000), 1276–80; Craig S. Keener, *1–2 Corinthians*, New Cambridge Bible Commentary (Cambridge: Cambridge University Press, 2005), 129–35.

to include not only a description of resurrection bodies but also the spaces in which those bodies would dwell. Perhaps, he thought, "like the stars in heaven, the saints have been allotted lodgings of varying glory in heaven."[34] John Calvin, too, rejected absolute equity among the elect in heavenly glory, arguing rather "that to each is promised that degree of honour to which he has been set apart by the eternal purpose of God."[35] Still, all souls occupy the same heavenly mansion, living under the same roof. No partition divides them from full access to the triune God of their salvation. All saints, no matter their brightness, will access the Father, Son, and Holy Spirit to become "partakers of the divine nature" (2 Pet 1:4).

Smith posited a similar idea, though he claimed it was revelatory rather than interpretive. Similar to Augustine, he parsed out differing degrees of glory in the afterlife. But unlike Augustine, Smith believed that heaven is not a single space inclusive of all saved souls. Instead, it is a segregated continuum of three states of glory, from greatest to least: the celestial, terrestrial, and telestial.[36] The telestial realm is the ultimate end for unrepentant sinners "who will not be gathered with the saints" but, having passed through suffering on earth and judgment in hell, will resurrect to the lowest degree of glory.[37] The population of this degree is practically innumerable, like "the sand upon the sea shore," and although it is the least glorious kingdom, the telestial existence will "surpasseth all understanding."[38] Still, telestial members forfeit the company of the Father and the Son since only the Holy Ghost's presence will be felt there. Smith hinted at the possibility of members from higher degrees visiting and aiding occupants of the telestial kingdom, similar to the way the angel Moroni condescended from celestial glory to minister to Smith (see question 14).

Above the telestial realm is the terrestrial glory, the heavenly home of "honorable [people] who were blinded by the craftiness of men" or those who lacked valiancy in their testimony.[39] They are moral people who either did not participate in the LDS tradition or whose participation was unsatisfactory to God. Members in this kingdom will enjoy the "presence of the son but not of the fulness of the father," whose throne is established in the highest realm of glory, the celestial kingdom.[40] This highest degree is reserved for those who

---

34. *ACD* 5:191.
35. John Calvin, *Commentary on a Harmony of the Evangelists, Matthew, Mark, and Luke*, trans. William Pringle, 3 vols. (Grand Rapids: Eerdmans, 1965), 2:422.
36. A helpful, albeit silly, mnemonic device to remember this order is "sea turtle," where "sea" corresponds to celestial, "tur-" to terrestrial, and "-tle" to telestial. Smith hinted that these three realms may be further subdivided into "12 from the abode of Devils to the Celestial glory" (JS, discourse, January 30, 1842, D9:129).
37. JS, revelation, February 16, 1832, D2:191 [D&C 76:102].
38. JS, revelation, February 16, 1832, D2:190 [D&C 76:89].
39. JS, revelation, February 16, 1832, D2:189 [D&C 76:75].
40. JS, revelation, February 16, 1832, D2:189 [D&C 76:75].

were received into the Church of Jesus Christ of Latter-day Saints, faithful members who received priesthood ordinances, made and kept covenants with God, and grew in moral maturity to become "Gods even the sons of God."[41] Also eligible are those who had died in innocent ignorance but would have otherwise received salvation and acted faithfully "if they had been permited [*sic*] to tarry," especially children who die before the age of accountability.[42] Members of the celestial kingdom will enjoy living "where God, and Christ is, and where they will be for eternity."[43] This highest of the three degrees requires strict obedience to all priesthood laws, so entry into this kingdom is reserved for those who have proven their willingness and ability to abide there. If a person cannot abide what celestial law offers, then "he can't obtain it."[44]

Thus, each degree is like a kingdom governed by laws that increase in moral intensity the closer one comes in proximity to God. Only those who can "abide the law of a celestial kingdom" are permitted entry there, the same being true for the other degrees.[45] It is up to each person "to enjoy that which they are willing to receive," meaning the degree of glory one receives directly correlates with their willingness to accept and obey the moral expectations of each degree, with the highest expectation at the top and lowest at the bottom.[46] For those eternally unwilling whatsoever to obey, even to confess the lordship of Christ, a bleak outer darkness awaits.

In short, telestial glory is universal for nearly all, terrestrial glory is inclusive of many, and celestial glory is particular to some.[47] Entry into the telestial glory is by God's mercy while entry into the terrestrial by his mercy and grace, but citizenship in the celestial kingdom comes by faith, mercy, grace, and good works, which will be explored in the next question.

---

41. JS, revelation, February 16, 1832, D2:188.
42. JSJ, January 21, 1836, J1:168. Relatedly, Smith taught that "God judgeth men according to the light he gives them" (JSJ, May 21, 1843, J3:20).
43. William W. Phelps, "To Man," *EMS*, June 1832, 1:6.
44. JS, instruction, May 16, 1843, D12:309 (emend.).
45. JS, revelation, December 27–28, 1832, D2:338 [D&C 88:22].
46. JS, revelation, December 27–28, 1832, D2:338 [D&C 88:32].
47. Joseph Smith thought it ridiculous that God would judge non-Christians based on Christian standards, especially in its state of apostasy. So Smith: "To say that the heathen would be damned because they did not believe the gospel would be preposterous; and to say that the Jews would all be damned that do not believe in Jesus, would be equally absurd . . . neither Jew, nor heathen, can be culpable for rejecting the conflicting opinions of sectarianism, nor for rejecting any testimony but that which is *sent* of God," that is, the restored gospel (JS, "Baptism for the Dead," *T&S*, April 15, 1842, 3:760, emphasis original). Smith's solution was to shrink hell and expand heaven, relegating only the very worst to outer darkness. Those ignorant of God's law would receive mercy, a universal assignment to telestial glory. Those near the gospel yet without its restored ordinances would receive mercy and grace, an inclusive welcome into terrestrial glory. Those worthy few among the Latter-day Saints, whose faith and obedience to covenants prevailed, would be ushered into celestial glory.

In the end, Smith taught God will judge all people "according to the desires of their hearts," a point he perhaps made to assuage anxiety about our eternal fate but one that is very sobering to consider, and a position traditional Christians may get behind.[48] In the end, the only hope for sinners is God's faithfulness to his covenant promise: "A new heart also will I give you, and a new spirit will I put within you: and I will take away the stony heart out of your flesh, and I will give you an heart of flesh" (Ezek 36:26). We are only given two options: (1) to be judged by the desires of a stony heart, or (2) to trip over the stumbling stone of Jesus Christ (see Rom 9:32–33) and break into pieces of repentance before a merciful and gracious God. Only the latter choice ends with a shattered heart of stone miraculously replaced with a regenerated heart of flesh that beats with affection for God and in sync with his will for eternity.

"You never knew my heart," Smith told a crowd near the end of his life.[49] While the outward life is how people judge one another, "the Lord looketh on the heart" (1 Sam 16:7). What God saw in Smith's heart, and what he sees in all the hearts of every person, is what matters most in the end.

Summary

According to Mormonism, God announced his plan of salvation for enabling his spirit children to progress to an eternal state of glory through mortal probation by the atoning work of Jesus Christ. While life on earth in our second estate is wrought with sin and plagued by death, Christ's death and resurrection secured for all humanity the ability to live faithfully for God and to walk in obedience of his ordinances, thus preparing them for reception into varying degrees of glory in the afterlife. These ordinances are explored in the subsequent questions.

REFLECTION QUESTIONS

1. Why do you think Mormonism has developed a narrative about the plan of salvation in premortal existence?

2. While Christianity has long lamented the fall of Adam, Mormonism views it as a somber, though welcomed, development of/for the plan of salvation. How do these two views compare to your own?

3. The atonement in Mormonism is central to its soteriology. How is it similar or different from your understanding of Christ's sacrificial work?

---

48. JSJ, January 21, 1836, J1:168.
49. JS, discourse, *T&S*, August 15, 1855, 5:617.

4. Based on 1 Corinthians 15:35–49, Joseph Smith envisioned heaven as a partitioned space of glory. Does this passage suggest such an interpretation? Why or why not?

5. In the end, Joseph Smith believed God will judge us by our hearts. Do you agree or disagree? Why or why not?

QUESTION 28

What Are Common Terms About Salvation Shared by Traditional Christians and Latter-day Saints?

"For salvation cometh to none such except it be through repentance and faith on the Lord Jesus Christ."
~ Mosiah 3:12

Traditional Christians and Latter-day Saints view themselves as members of a community God is saving, and they draw language from the Bible to describe that process. Both speak of salvation by faith and repentance and hope for a future resurrection. We communicate this experience in "salvation language," or words drawing primarily from biblical sources to describe salvation. Yet even though we share many salvation language terms, we often mean very different things, which leads to misunderstanding and frustration. It's often said that traditional Christians and Latter-day Saints share different dictionaries. That may be true, but perhaps it's more precise to say that common terms carry distinct theological freight.

For example, reread the epigraph to this question from the Book of Mormon to notice three key salvation language terms it uses: "salvation," "repentance," and "faith." The meanings of these terms for Latter-day Saints are similar to traditional Christians in some aspects, yet they significantly differ in others.

This question will offer definitions of common terms for traditional Christians and Latter-day Saints to discover the similarities and dissimilarities of our salvation languages.[1]

1. I do not intend to suggest the ordering of these terms represent a necessary progression inherent to each side's soteriologies. And admittedly, these definitions skew Protestant,

Traditional Christian Salvation Language

Regeneration is God's gift of new life (or being "born again") to those he calls through the Holy Spirit, by whom he revives their hearts to respond positively to divine love and commands (see Ezek 36:26–27; John 3:3; Eph 2:4–5). Just as we experienced a genesis of life as image bearers of God at conception and birth, we are "re-genesised," or re-created, to experience a new birth, a complete renewal "to form in us anew the image of God, which was sullied, and all but effaced by the transgression of Adam," taught John Calvin.[2] Regeneration is "a spiritual resurrection," wrote Presbyterian theologian Charles Hodge, "the beginning of a new life."[3]

Election is God's choosing a people for redemption, not based on their merit but wholly rooted in his unconditional love and divine will for them (see Deut 7:7–8; John 6:44; Rom 9:9–13; Eph 1:4–5; 1 Pet 2:9). God chose his people "not because we have believed," clarified Augustine, "but that we might believe" (see John 15:16).[4] His choice was made without regard to any foreseen work on our part because "foreknowledge of merits is not the cause or reason of predestination," wrote Thomas Aquinas; it is only ever by the will of God.[5]

Calling is God's divine summons to his chosen people for redemption, especially through the gospel (see Hos 11:1; Rom 8:30; 2 Thess 2:13–14; 1 Pet 2:9). As with election, God is not motivated to call people based on any merit in them. God calls us not because of the good we have done but so that he might do good in and for us. He calls us with "an holy calling, not according to our works, but according to his own purpose and grace, which was given us in Christ Jesus before the world began" (2 Tim 1:9; see also Titus 3:5).

Justification is God's reconciliation of sinners to himself by declaring a state of righteousness over anyone who believes the gospel, aligning themselves with Jesus Christ, and being recognized as a member of his kingdom. Christ the King pardons them from the penalty of sin, gifting them a status that is not earned by their merits but is freely given by God's grace and received through

---

though I broadly center them in Christian orthodoxy. I recognize readers may nuance some terms (e.g., a Roman Catholic reading of the term "justification" and a Pentecostal reading of "sanctification") but recommend focusing on the similarities and dissimilarities of one's own definitions with those of Mormonism.

2. Calvin, *Inst.* 3.3.9.
3. Charles Hodge, *Systematic Theology*, 3 vols. (New York: Scribner, Armstrong, and Company, 1873), 3:5.
4. Augustine, "On the Predestination of the Saints," in *The Fathers of the Church: A New Translation*, trans. John A. Mourant and William J. Collinge (Washington: Catholic University of America Press, 1992), 86:265.
5. Thomas Aquinas, *Summa Theologica*, vol. 1 (New York: Benziger Brothers, 1947), 128.

faith alone, "not because of works done by us in righteousness, but according to his own mercy" (Titus 3:5 ESV; see also Gen 15:6; Hab 2:4; Rom 3:28; Gal 2:16; Eph 2:8; 2 Cor 5:21).

Adoption is God's free gift of childship in God's covenant family through the Holy Spirit to those he justifies, by which they become joint heirs with Jesus Christ, the Son of God (see Gal 3:26–27; Rom 8:15, 17). Through this gracious adoption we become children of God, not by nature but by the grace of our heavenly Father (see 1 John 3:1).

Sanctification is God's work of love and holiness in his saints (or "holy ones") by which he frees them from the power of sin through enabling and empowering their obedience through the Holy Spirit, thereby making actual what was accounted to them by faith, according to his holy will (see Eph 2:10; 2 Cor 3:18; 1 Thess 4:3; Heb 12:14; 1 Pet 1:15–16; Jas 2:17). While sanctification is "in some degree the immediate fruit of justification," argued John Wesley, it is nevertheless "a distinct gift of God, and of a totally different nature."[6] Justification is what God does for us in the Son while sanctification is the work God does in us by the Holy Spirit.

Perseverance is God's gracious sustainment of his saints in the process of their sanctification to its final end, ensuring that they will never fall away nor be lost in the end (see John 10:28; Rom 8:39; Phil 1:6; 1 John 2:19). Christians persevere because God preserves them, not by their own efforts or merit but by his free grace and mercy.

Resurrection is God's merciful act of "re-rising" (Lat. *resurrectionem*) the dead to life through the transforming power of Jesus Christ, the firstfruits of resurrection, and the Holy Spirit, who gifts the saints with glorified bodies like the body of the risen Lord (see Rom 6:10–11; 1 Cor 15:20–22; Phil 3:20–21). This future gift from God reframes Christian understanding of the body in the present while also giving hope for the future. As N. T. Wright noted, because of resurrection, "the present bodily life is not valueless just because it will die."[7] We have hope that our lives are not in vain and that death, as painful as it is, will one day yield to life forever.

Glorification is God's work of redemption to bring about complete holiness in all his saints, whereby his image is completely restored in them and they dwell

6. John Wesley, *The Works of the Rev John Wesley: Sermons*, vol. 1, ed. John Emory (New York: The Methodist Book Concern, 1916), 47.
7. N. T. Wright, *Surprised by Hope: Rethinking Heaven, the Resurrection, and the Mission of the Church* (New York: HarperCollins, 2008), 193.

eternally in the direct presence of the Father, Son, and Holy Spirit, forever partaking of God's divine nature and free from the presence of sin, suffering, and death (see Rom 8:29; 2 Pet 1:4; 1 John 3:2; Rev 21:4). God's people will be wholly, perfectly, and forever conformed to the image of Christ. It is the final chapter in the grand redemptive narrative of heaven.

Salvation is the whole work of the Father, the Son, and the Holy Spirit to save God's people from sin and death to holiness and eternal life with the triune God forever.

These are not the only vocabulary of traditional Christian salvation language, but they are common terms often shared with LDS salvation language, to which we now turn.

Latter-day Saint Salvation Language

Before defining LDS salvation language, it's important to note how doctrine and theology tend to be dynamic and fluid in LDS thought. Latter-day Saints often prioritize covenantal practices over theological precision, making exact definitions variable even within their own tradition. What follows is a traditional Christian's good-faith attempt to describe how Latter-day Saints tend to use these terms.

Election, related closely to calling, is God's choosing people to fulfill certain roles or responsibilities that advance his plan of salvation (see 2 Cor 6:1; 2 Pet 1:10–11; D&C 84:33–41). The elect are the pre-called of premortality, "certain spirits [who] are ordained to certain callings before they tabernacle in the flesh," explained LDS apostle Orson F. Whitney.[8] They are not individuals chosen by God for salvation; rather, they are individuals tasked by God for salvation-related works (e.g., prophets and apostles).

Regeneration, or being born again, is the spiritual transformation that occurs when a person places their faith in the Lord Jesus Christ, repents from sin, is baptized by immersion, and receives the Holy Ghost by laying on of hands by a proper priesthood holder (see John 3:3; Mosiah 27:25; Alma 7:14). As Joseph Smith explained, "Being born again comes by the Spirit of God through ordinances."[9] It is a process that brings about "a change in one's beliefs, heart, and life to accept and conform to the will of God," explained LDS apostle David A. Bednar.[10]

8. Orson F. Whitney, *Gospel Themes: A Treatise on Salient Features of "Mormonism"* (Salt Lake City: LDS Church, 1914), 78.
9. JS, discourse, summer 1839, D6:548.
10. David A. Bednar, "Converted unto the Lord," *Ensign*, November 2012, 107.

Justification is God's mercy to pardon the sinner's guilt by making them innocent when they experience regeneration, a state that is made possible by Jesus Christ through the Holy Ghost and is manifested in obedience to covenants and ordinances (see Jas 2:14–26; D&C 20:30–31; 76:69; Moses 6:60). Justification "removes the punishment for past sin,"[11] explained LDS apostle D. Todd Christofferson, though not necessarily the punishment for future sins, so that the state of one's justification is sustained through faith, repentance, obedience to covenants, and participation in ordinances.

Covenant is a binding agreement between God and people in which they agree to the conditions, standards, privileges, and blessings that fosters and seals their relationship to him (see D&C 84:39–41; 128:4; 132:7). Because covenants are "a sacred promise with God," taught LDS president Russell M. Nelson, it is God alone who "fixes the terms," not us, though continuation in a covenant partly depends on us.[12] As another LDS president, Spencer W. Kimball, explained, "When we make a covenant or agreement with God, we must keep it at whatever cost."[13]

Ordinance is a ritual commanded by God and performed by proper authorities that is either salvific (e.g., baptism, endowment) or non-salvific (e.g., sacrament, patriarchal blessings), in which the power of godliness is manifested (see Ezek 11:20; D&C 84:21). It is an act by which we respond to God's commandments by making covenants with him according to his terms and obtain blessings if the terms are met.

Adoption is the covenant status of people who, by regeneration and justification, are made members of the house of Israel, are considered sons and daughters of the Lord Jesus Christ, and become beneficiaries of joint heirship with him (see Rom 8:15–17; Gal 4:4–7; Mosiah 5:7–8).

Sanctification is the process in which a person becomes freed from the effects of sin by the aid of the Holy Ghost, whereby that person is made holy by participating in ordinances and obedience to covenants through the atonement of Jesus Christ (see D&C 20:30–33; Moses 6:60). It is the gradual process that "removes the stain or effects of sin," taught Christofferson, ever purifying the heart and soul to prepare a person to dwell in the holy presence of Heavenly Father forever.[14]

---

11. D. Todd Christofferson, "Justification and Sanctification," *Ensign*, June 2001, 22.
12. Russell M. Nelson, "Covenants," *Ensign*, November 2011, 86.
13. Spencer W. Kimball, *Teachings of Presidents of the Church: Spencer W. Kimball* (Salt Lake City: LDS Church, 2006), 126.
14. Christofferson, "Justification and Sanctification."

Perseverance, or enduring to the end, is the faithful obedience to commandments and covenants throughout a person's life that results in that person receiving divine blessings and attaining exaltation by the strength received from God (see Matt 24:13; 2 Nephi 31:19–20; D&C 14:7). "For perish they must who can not abide a celestial Law, and endure to the end," taught LDS apostles.[15]

Resurrection is God's merciful act of physically raising the dead to life through the sanctifying power of Jesus Christ, the firstfruits of resurrection, and the Holy Ghost, whereby all people are gifted with glorified bodies to varying degrees of glory (see Rom 6:10–11; 1 Cor 15:20–22; Phil 3:20–21).

Exaltation is the culmination of God's plan of salvation for humankind to bring about complete holiness in his faithful and righteous saints, whereby they are completely transformed to be like him through sealing ordinances, especially marriage, and to dwell eternally in the direct presence of the Father, Son, and Holy Ghost, forever participating in God's divine nature and free from the presence of sin, suffering, and death (see D&C 76:58–59; 88:107; 132:19–20). Exaltation is the highest goal of Latter-day Saints, an eternal state of divinity and experiences like God.

Salvation is God's gifted reward to all humankind for resurrection from death by the power of the atonement of Jesus Christ alone, the fullness of which is obtained through one's faith in the Lord Jesus Christ, repenting from their sin, being baptized by immersion, receiving the Holy Ghost by laying on of hands by a proper priesthood holder, and enduring to the end (see Articles of Faith 1:3). As Joseph Smith taught, "To get salvation we must not only do some things but everything which God had commanded to get salvation."[16]

Summary

Traditional Christians and Latter-day Saints speak about salvation in similar ways with terms like *regeneration, election, calling, justification, covenant, ordinance, adoption, sanctification, perseverance, resurrection,* and *glorification* or *exaltation.* At times the definitions overlap, but at other points they depart in important ways. It is crucial for traditional Christians to first understand their own salvation language before exploring the salvation language of Latter-day Saints. Doing so provides both sides with clarification in communicating the gospel.

15. "An Epistle of the Twelve," *T&S*, April 1, 1842, 3:738.
16. JSJ, February 21, 1844, J3:181.

REFLECTION QUESTIONS

1. What are some key terms in your faith tradition's salvation language? Are those terms also used in the LDS tradition?

2. Describe the challenges of discussing the gospel with Latter-day Saints if we use the same salvation language vocabulary with different dictionaries?

3. What similarities between traditional Christian and LDS salvation languages stood out to you?

4. What differences between traditional Christian and LDS salvation languages stood out to you?

5. How does understanding those similarities and differences help you understand the LDS faith?

QUESTION 29

What Is the Latter-day Saint View of Baptism?

"As 'twas said to Nicodemus, So I must be born again;
'Tis by water and the Spirit I the promise may obtain."[1]
~ William W. Phelps, Latter-day Saint Hymnist

When the Lord Jesus emerged from the waters of the Jordan River, he modeled and initiated one of the most recognizable rites of the Christian faith. Baptism is so important to Christ that he paired it with his final charge to make disciples among the nations (see Matt 28:19–20; Mark 16:15–16). Baptism by water is an initiatory act that identifies a believer with the saving work of Christ (see Rom 6:3; Col 2:12) and binds them to his body, the church, and to fellowship with the Holy Spirit (see 1 Cor 12:13, 27).[2] Just as the church is united under "one Lord" and by "one faith," so are its members united through "one baptism" (Eph 4:5).

It is a great tragedy that Christians have allowed the ordinance to become a marker of division. Debate over its purpose and customs has fragmented the "one body" (Eph 4:5) baptism meant to unite. Already in the NT era, the Corinthian church segregated into quarreling cliques that aligned with either Paul, Apollos, or Cephas (see 1 Cor 1:10–13). Apparently, baptism played a role in their dysfunction (see 1 Cor 1:14–15). Similarly, the diverse state of

1. William W. Phelps, "For Baptism," *EMS*, April 1833, 1:11 (emend.).
2. For Christian views on baptism, see Everett Ferguson, *Baptism in the Early Church: History, Theology, and Liturgy in the First Five Centuries* (Grand Rapids: Eerdmans, 2009); David F. Wright, ed., *Baptism: Three Views* (Downers Grove: IVP Academic, 2009); John S. Hammett, *40 Questions About Baptism and the Lord's Supper* (Grand Rapids: Kregel Academic, 2015); and Isaac Augustine Morales, *The Bible and Baptism: The Fountain of Salvation* (Grand Rapids: Baker Academic, 2022).

Christianity in early nineteenth-century America prompted questions about baptism. Who has the right to baptize? Who ought to be baptized? How should baptism be performed? These questions were hotly disputed during Joseph Smith's formative years, but the argument was off-putting for many, a divisive distraction from pure worship and Christian unity.[3] One newspaper in Smith's day complained that preachers "have made the *mode of Baptism* their grand engrossing subject," which tended "to grieve the Holy Spirit, and to divert the attention of saints and sinners from the one thing needed."[4] Partly to avoid controversy, the Quakers refused to practice baptism altogether, arguing instead that the "one baptism" of those who worship "in spirit and in truth" (John 4:24) was a purely spiritual, not ritual, experience.[5]

But the Quaker position was the minority. Smith himself rejected this view, recognizing that baptism is an indispensable ordinance to the Christian faith. When he established the Church of Jesus Christ of Latter-day Saints, Smith faced the same theological quandary over baptism as countless others before him but with one key difference: a radical hope to end the debate once and for all. What was his solution, and how does it inform the LDS view of baptism?

Baptism in Early Mormonism

Smith was dictating the Book of Mormon when he began to reflect on baptism. The text warned "there shall be no disputations among" Christians concerning the meaning and mode of baptism (3 Nephi 11:22). But as Smith looked around him, this was certainly not the case. Congregationalists, Presbyterians, and Methodists were united in their dissent from Roman Catholicism that baptism communicated God's grace by the very act (Lat. *ex opere operato*), but they all disagreed with Baptists and Restorationists that full immersion was the only proper way to baptize. For a rite meant to unify the church, Smith thought baptism was anything but unifying. Debate about the ordinance was a "great strife and noise" among clergy. He reasoned that

3. For example, see the widely published debate between Alexander Campbell and William Latta MacCalla, held October 15–21, 1823 in Washington, Kentucky. This debate reverberated throughout the young nation and echoed across the Atlantic two decades later. Restorationist Campbell argued for full immersion of believers only while Presbyterian MacCalla contented for sprinkling and pouring for children of believers. Alexander Campbell, *A Debate on Christian Baptism* (Buffalo: Campbell & Sala., 1824); William Latta MacCalla, *The Unitarian Baptist* (Philadelphia: John Young, 1826); Alexander Campbell, *Facts and Documents* (Bethany, VA: Alexander Campbell, 1828); William Latta MacCalla, *A Discussion of Christian Baptism* (Philadelphia: George McLaughlin, 1831); Alexander Campbell, *A Public Debate on Christian Baptism* (London: Simpkin and Marshall, 1842).
4. "Lectures on Infant Baptism," June 27, 1828, *Vermont Chronicle* 3, no. 26 (emphasis original).
5. David L. Johns, "Worship and Sacraments," in *The Oxford Handbook of Quaker Studies*, ed. Stephen W. Angell and Ben Pink Dandelion (New York: Oxford University Press, 2013), 271–72.

baptism was in such disarray because "none had authority from God to administer the ordinances of the gospel," and like everything else in the church, it needed to be restored.[6]

Smith later claimed that God restored the necessary authority to baptize through John the Baptist, who delivered "the keys of the gospel of repentance," enabling Smith to unlock the ordinance.[7] In 1830, Smith organized the LDS Church and reiterated that baptism must be performed by those with proper authority. Christian converts were rebaptized because their first baptism was unauthorized and, consequently, unrecognized by God (see D&C 22). The church also followed baptism instructions "written in the Book of Morman [*sic*]," which answered many burning theological questions about the ordinance.[8] Indeed, early Latter-day Saints rejoiced that, for them, "the doubtful points of doctrine, in the bible, which left one sect to immerse for baptism; a second to sprinkle; a third to pour, and a fourth to do without either, were cleared up by the book of Mormon."[9]

First, and most fundamentally, the Book of Mormon rejected the Quaker position that baptism is merely a spiritual experience. Christ began his ministry with baptism, setting a precedent that his followers are encouraged to follow (see Matt 3:13–17; Mark 1:9–11; Luke 3:21–22; John 1:29–34), whether they are in the Old or New World (see 3 Nephi 11:21). Jesus commanded his disciples to "teach all nations, baptizing them" in God's triune name (Matt 28:19), and his disciples in the Americas began to baptize immediately after Christ's ascension (see 3 Nephi 19:11–12).

Second, the Book of Mormon based the effect of baptism in identity with Christ (see Mosiah 26:22; 2 Nephi 31:13). The book rejected baptismal regeneration, or the removing of the guilt of original sin, partly because it not only denied *ex opere operato* and insisted that baptism followed forgiveness (see Moroni 6:1–3) but also because Christ's atonement universally purged original sin, so there was no Adamic stain on the sinner's soul to wash out (see Moroni 8:8). Brigham Young reflected on this point. "Has water, in itself, any virtue to wash away sin? Certainly not," he said, adding that "keeping the commandments of God will cleanse away the stain of sin."[10] But baptism is not merely symbolic. The Book of Mormon saw baptism as less a proclamation about the recipient than a promise *from* its recipient. Baptism is a necessary waypoint as the sinners transition from their old life, death in sin, to a new life in the Holy Spirit. The ritual is a testimony of one's entry into covenant

6. JS, 1834–1836 history, H1:42.
7. JS, 1834–1836 history, H1:42.
8. Articles and Covenants, ca. April 1830, D1:125; see also 3 Nephi 11:21–28.
9. "The Book of Mormon," *EMS*, January 1833, 1:113.
10. *CDBY* 2:729.

relationship with God (see Mosiah 18:13) and his covenant community (see Alma 4:5; Helaman 3:26).

Therefore, the only proper candidates for baptism are those "willing to take upon them the name of thy Son, and always remember him, and keep his commandments" (Moroni 4:3), so infants and small children are not baptized. The Book of Mormon dismissed infant baptism as "solemn mockery before God" (Moroni 8:9). The atonement of Christ, not the waters of baptism, cleansed original sin from the souls of children. There is no need to baptize infants because "little children are alive in Christ" (Moroni 8:12). Smith explained that baptism was only necessary for children who "have arriven to the years of accountability," later approximating the age to eight years old.[11] Children need baptism only after becoming "accountable and capable of committing sin" (Moroni 8:10). In the interim, families were commanded to bring their young children before the church so that the elders could "lay hands on them in the name of the Lord, and bless them in the name of Christ."[12] This ritual is still performed today.

Third, the Book of Mormon affirmed full immersion rather than affusion, or pouring water over a convert's head. People were instructed to "go down and stand in the water" (3 Nephi 11:23) to be immersed (see 3 Nephi 11:26) or "buried in the water" (Mosiah 18:14; see also Col 2:12). Smith affirmed full immersion, having taught that the "Gospel requires Baptism by immersion for the remission of sins, which is the meaning of the word in the original language viz to bury or immerse."[13] Baptismal candidates in the Book of Mormon were baptized into the Trinitarian name of God (see 3 Nephi 11:25; see also Matt 28:19), although the text left open the possibility of being baptized "in the name of Jesus" only (Mormon 7:8; see also Acts 2:38). The baptized then received "the baptism of fire and of the Holy Ghost" (2 Nephi 31:13; 3 Nephi 19:11–14; Mormon 7:10), which enabled speaking in "a new tongue" (2 Nephi 31:14), or "the tongue of angels" (2 Nephi 31:13). This point was stressed by early Latter-day Saints who viewed the act of immersion as incomplete on its own. "Baptism by water is but half a baptism," said Smith, "and is good for nothing without the other half, that is the baptism of the Holy Ghost."[14]

In short, from its earliest days, the LDS Church taught that all converts must be baptized in water "by immersion for the remission of sins," reception of the Holy Ghost, and inclusion into the community.[15]

---

11. JS, revelation, June 1829, D1:73 [D&C 18:42]; discourse, February 5, 1840, D7:178.
12. Articles and Covenants, ca. April 1830, D1:125.
13. Joseph Smith, History, 1838–1856, vol. E-1, *JSP*, 1666.
14. Joseph Smith, History, 1838–1856, vol. E-1, *JSP*, 1666–67.
15. JS, "Church History," *T&S*, March 1, 1842, in H1:500. Early Latter-day Saints also baptized for "the healing of the sick" ("An Epistle of the Twelve," *T&S*, January 15, 1845, 6:779).

The Effect and Purpose of Baptism in Modern Latter-day Saint Thought

Aside from the issue of authority, early LDS thought on baptism thus far appears related to modern Pentecostal theology. What sets LDS baptism apart today is the power of its effect and purpose.

Effectually, baptism is a salvific ordinance. It is the capstone of repentance, prerequisite for receiving the Holy Ghost, and the gateway into God's covenant family. Smith made a distinction between actual and formal remission of sins, or the act of God's forgiveness. God *actually* forgives sinners when they "truly repented of all their sins."[16] Then, God *formally* remits their sin after they are "received by baptism into his [Christ's] church."[17] Remember, too, that Mormonism teaches everyone is a literal child of God (see question 26). Baptism, then, is a sign of rejoining God's family, a "re-incorporation into heirship with heavenly parents, with Christ as spiritual father."[18] Baptism is a covenantal sign of return, symbolizing the power that prompts a prodigal child's journey home.

Today, baptisms are performed by authorized priesthood holders, typically in meetinghouses—although any body of water deep enough for full immersion and clean enough for good health may be used. Baptisms for the dead are performed exclusively in temples (see question 35). Prior to baptism, candidates are reviewed by church leadership to ensure that they understand the ordinance and are personally prepared to participate in it. Immediately following baptism, priesthood holders lay their hands on the new member for their reception of the Holy Ghost.[19] Baptism is performed only once, although converts who received baptism in an organization other than the church are required to be rebaptized.

Summary

Baptism is the primary initiation ordinance of the Christian faith. Regardless of their disagreements on modes and means, traditional Christian denominations recognize baptism as central to the faith. The Book of Mormon serves Latter-day Saints as a definitive guide to baptism. It prescribes full immersion for repentant people of an accountable age. Joseph Smith further described baptism as a power to remit sins and gateway into the covenant community of God. Considering Mormon views of human origins, and because baptism is the first ordinance of the gospel, Mormonism also envisions baptism as a sign of God's family being regathered.

---

16. JS, H1:342.
17. JS, H1:342.
18. Terryl L. Givens, *Feeding the Flock: The Foundations of Mormon Thought: Church and Praxis* (Oxford: Oxford University Press, 2017), 155.
19. For more on LDS baptism, see Craig J. Ostler, "Baptism," in *The Book of Mormon and the Message of the Four Gospels*, ed. Ray L. Huntington and Terry B. Ball (Provo, UT: RSC, BYU, 2001), 139–57; Noel B. Reynolds, "Understanding Christian Baptism through the Book of Mormon," *BYU Studies* 51, no. 2 (2012): 5–37; Givens, *Feeding the Flock*, 149–66.

REFLECTION QUESTIONS

1. What are your beliefs about baptism? Who ought to be baptized, how, and when?
2. People debated the modes and means of baptism in Joseph Smith's day. Are those debates still alive today? If so, how do you account for your beliefs about baptism?
3. Baptism is required for salvation in Mormonism because it is seen as being regenerative. Do you agree or disagree? Why or why not?
4. Joseph Smith distinguished between actual forgiveness of sin through repentance and formal remission of sin through baptism. Do you agree with this distinction? Why or why not?
5. The LDS Church requires converts to be rebaptized upon joining. Do you believe rebaptism is necessary? Why or why not?

QUESTION 30

What Is the Latter-day Saint View of the Lord's Supper?

"The sacrament & every other institution that [God] has planted in the church is to bless the Saints."[1]
~ Brigham Young, President of the LDS Church, 1847–1877

The disciples were very familiar with the Passover supper, which Jesus Christ led on the night before his crucifixion. They had celebrated it from childhood, as was the custom of every Jewish family. This time was different, though. Rather than remembering what God had done to redeem Israel from Egypt, Jesus directed the focus of the supper toward himself, celebrating what God was about to accomplish for the redemption of sinners from death, ironically by his own death. His body, given to the disciples, and his blood, shed for them (Luke 22:19–20), foreshadowed how Christ's sacrificial death on the cross would make possible the forgiveness of sins. Just as the blood of the Paschal lamb allowed death to pass over Israel in Egypt, the blood of the "Lamb of God, which taketh away the sin of the world" (John 1:29), would also do the same for all who believe. It is a "propitiation for our sins," wrote the apostle John, "and not for ours only but also for the sins of the whole world" (1 John 2:2). "For even Christ our passover is sacrificed for us," said the apostle Paul (1 Cor 5:7).

To commemorate this event, Christ invited his disciples to receive the Passover bread and wine "in remembrance of [him]" (Luke 22:19), a practice the early church carried forward as a regular and regulated ordinance, or sacrament (see Acts 2:42; 20:7; 1 Cor 11:17–34). It is "the Lord's supper" (1 Cor 11:20), a thanksgiving meal (Gk. *eucharistia*) for the church to "proclaim the

1. JS, *Brigham Young*, *JD* 2:259.

Lord's death until he comes" (1 Cor 11:26 NIV) together in communion.[2] The Lord's Supper is a powerful image: forgiven saints united in Christ's atonement and public confession of the gospel's power. While Christian churches differ on its theological meaning, nearly all affirm that the Lord's Supper is a critical—if not *the* central—act of worship. Unsurprisingly, Latter-day Saints have carried on this ancient tradition.

Development of the Mormon Sacraments

In early Mormon worship, communion was an important rite. It was not, however, as prominent as baptism or preaching, nor was it practiced regularly.[3] In April 1830, at the inaugural meeting of the Church of Jesus Christ of Latter-day Saints, the first act of corporate worship was the Lord's Supper, or what Latter-day Saints simply call the sacrament (see D&C 20:46). Members "took bread, blessed it, and brake it with them, also wine, blessed it, and drank it with them" immediately after affirming Joseph Smith's leadership over the church.[4] The first temples were designed, in part, to be spaces where the Saints could give their "Sacrament offerings."[5] This was among the first acts of worship when the Kirtland temple was opened in 1838, offering the Mormons dedicated space to take the ordinance more regularly. The sacrament was also distributed during meetings of the School of the Prophets, an early Mormon seminary, and at times was met with charismatic experiences and heavenly visions. Even the last Latter-day Saints to leave Nauvoo, before their western emigration, gathered in the temple for "administering the Sacrament, and speaking in Tongues."[6]

Early Mormonism envisioned the sacrament much in the same way as their low-church, Protestant contemporaries. Latter-day Saints rejected the Roman Catholic view of transubstantiation, which Brigham Young called "preposterous,"[7] echoing the concern of John Calvin, who thought it was "an error not to be tolerated."[8] Both men denied Christ's body is objectively present in the Supper. But unlike Calvin and other Reformers, Mormons viewed the elements as merely emblematic or symbolic of Christ's body and blood, a position

2. The word *Eucharist* comes from the Greek word *eucharistia*, meaning "thanksgiving." Christians began to describe the Lord's Supper this way by the turn of the second century.
3. See Justin R. Bray, "The Lord's Supper in Early Mormonism," in *You Shall Have My Word: Exploring the Text of the Doctrine and Covenants*, ed. Scott C. Esplin, Richard O. Cowan, and Rachel Cope (Salt Lake City: Deseret, 2012).
4. JS, H1:366.
5. MRB, 341. Latter-day Saint president Joseph F. Smith later analogized the sacrament to Levitical sacrifices. "Therefore this law [i.e., the sacrament] is to us, what the law of sacrifice was to those who lived prior to the first coming of the Son of Man, until he shall come again" (*JD* 15:327).
6. Devery S. Anderson, ed., *The Development of LDS Temple Worship: 1846–2000* (Salt Lake City: Signature Books, 2011),3.
7. *CDBY* 5:2645.
8. Calvin, *Inst.* 4.17.33.

reminiscent of the one taught by Ulrich Zwingli, the radical Reformer whose memorial view of the ordinance contrasted sharply against real or spiritual presence. The elements are "tokens of the love of the Redeemer," explained Brigham Young, and by extension signs of fellowship with God and the congregation.[9] Latter-day Saints, however, developed unique practices and distinct theological emphases, setting the LDS sacrament apart from memorialism.

The first converts to Mormonism were mainly from Protestant churches, each with their own way of celebrating communion. Some denominations refrained from instructing congregations on proper manner, like the United Brethren, who recommended "no prescribed form of words used at the administration of the Holy Communion."[10] Other denominations gave exact guidelines, like Anglicanism's Book of Common Prayer. It's easy to imagine confusion about communion in the early LDS Church largely populated with former Protestants, each with their own expectations for how sacraments are performed.

As with baptism, Latter-day Saints were instructed to administer the sacrament "as [it] is written in the Book of Morman [*sic*],"[11] which described how Christ instituted the sacrament among his ancient American disciples "in remembrance of my body" (3 Nephi 18:7) and "in remembrance of my blood, which I shed for you" (3 Nephi 18:11). The purpose of the sacrament is deeply Trinitarian (see 3 Nephi 18:7, 11; see also 1 John 5:6–7). Participants are called to remember the Son of God's atonement, a "ransom" (Matt 26:22 JST) sacrifice Smith clarified elsewhere. In doing so, they testify as witnesses to the Father of his life-giving gift and receive the Spirit. The Lord's Supper is a sacramental reaffirmation by the congregation that "thou art the Christ, the Son of the living God" (Matt 16:16), a point made clear by Christ: "If ye shall always do these things [i.e., sacrament] blessed are ye, for ye are built upon my rock" (3 Nephi 18:12). Anything added beyond this instruction, like Roman Catholic transubstantiation, or subtracting from the sacrament, like Quaker abstinence, risked nothing short than "the gates of hell open[ing] to receive them" (3 Nephi 18:13).

The Book of Mormon also detailed the exact procedure for administering the sacrament. A threefold distinction was made between the sacrament's originator, officiants, and participants. The originator, of course, is Jesus Christ, who first blessed and distributed the elements (see 3 Nephi 18:3; see also 20:3–4).[12] Christ then ordained officiants who would continue giving the

---

9. *CDBY* 2:728–29.
10. *A Collection of Hymns, For the Use of the Protestant Church, of the United Brethren* (Manchester: R&W Dean, 1809), xxvii.
11. Articles and Covenants, ca. April 1830, D1:125; see also Moroni 4:1–5:2.
12. Interestingly, Christ only blesses the bread, not the wine (see 3 Nephi 18:3, 8; 20:3–4). In doing so, the author of the Book of Mormon follows the Synoptic tradition of Christ blessing only the bread (see Matt 26:26–27; Mark 14:22–23) and giving thanks (Gk. *eucharistia*) for the wine, a point that readers are apparently meant to infer in the Book of

sacrament in his physical absence to those who are worthy, baptized believers (see 3 Nephi 18:5; Mormon 9:29). Smith warned the Church to take the "ordinance with pure hearts" and "with acceptance to the Lord," lest God withdraw his spirit from them.[13]

The officiants were given explicit guidance for communion. In a knelt posture, they offer a Trinitarian, eucharistic prayer over both elements for their consecration (see Moroni 4:3; 5:2). The benediction outlines the purpose of the sacrament to the participants: first, to remember the body and blood of Christ, "which was shed for them" (Moroni 5:2, see also D&C 27:2); second, to witness, or reaffirm, their willingness to take on the name of Christ (see Mosiah 18:10); third, to prove their desire to "keep his commandments" (Moroni 4:3; see also 3 Nephi 18:10–11); and finally, to sustain fellowship with the Spirit of Christ. Thus, while the elements retain their material characteristics, a mystical blessing is given to participants, for the one who eats and drinks the elements does so "to his soul" (3 Nephi 20:8).

The Sacrament Today

Today, Latter-day Saints celebrate the sacrament weekly, following revelation instructing "that the Church meet together often to partake of bread and wine in remembrance of the Lord Jesus," though Latter-day Saints ceased using wine long ago.[14] Traditional Christians witnessing a sacrament meeting might find it strange that water is substituted for wine or grape juice, and so would their ancestors. Early Mormons used wine, as was the common practice, preferably made by vintners within the church (see D&C 89:5–6). But the types of elements used were irrelevant to the sacrament itself. Revelation given to Smith explained how "it mattereth not what ye shall eat or what ye shall drink when ye partake of the sacrament if it so be that ye do it with an eye single to my glory."[15] Frequency was the greater concern (see D&C 59:7–9, 12). John Calvin was similarly unconcerned about the "external form of the ordinance," like the type of bread and wine used, believing it was of "no consequence." "These things are indifferent, and left free to the church," he said.[16] Still, early Mormons used wine during Smith's life, although "they prefer[ed] the pure juice of the grape when they can get it."[17] Perhaps they used alcohol-free grape juice to maintain the aesthetic relationship between the dark liquid and the blood it represented. Latter-day Saints only began to sporadically substitute

---

Mormon. Later, however, readers are told explicitly to bless both the bread and the wine (see Moroni 4:3; 5:2), a deviation from Christ's example earlier in the text. It is common practice today for Latter-day Saints to bless both elements.

13. JS, discourse, March 1, 1835, D4:265.
14. JS, H1:350.
15. MRB, 34 [D&C 27:2].
16. Calvin, *Inst.* 4.17.43.
17. John Corrill, *A Brief History of the Church of Christ of Latter Day Saints,* 1839, H2:195.

colorless water for wine after the church migrated west. By 1893, however, wine was formally banned.[18] That same year, Charles Edgar Welch established his grape juice company "to serve God by helping His Church to give its communion 'the fruit of the vine,' instead of the 'cup of devils.'"[19] The LDS Church, however, declined to follow other churches' substitution of non-alcoholic grape juice for wine, opting instead for water. The practice continues to the present day.

Elements aside, the sacrament was originally taken in temple worship but is now observed on Sundays during sacrament meetings. Indeed, the title of Sunday services itself indicates the centrality of the Lord's Supper for Latter-day Saints. It is, perhaps, the holiest ordinance that takes place outside the temple, one that Latter-day Saints "must honor and keep sacredly," explained one LDS prophet.[20] And although some Latter-day Saints have suggested the sacrament is non-salvific, others see it as adding "to our acceptance before God, or to our condemnation."[21] Brigham Young went further, calling the sacrament "the only legal way to obtain salvation, and an exaltation in the presence of God."[22]

Perhaps this is because of the sacrament's deep connection to the ordinance of baptism, which which also may help to explain the use of water rather than wine. At baptism, converts repent from sin and covenant with God to take on the name of Jesus Christ and to keep his commandments, obedience that leads to exaltation. If communion is a time for reaffirming one's commitment to taking Christ's name and obeying his commands (see Mosiah 18:10; Moroni 4:3; 5:2), then it is reasonable to envision the sacrament within a rebaptismal, and thus salvific, framework.

But for traditional Christians, the Lord's Supper is less about renewing our commitment to Christ than it is about remembering Christ's commitment to us. By receiving the elements, we are reminded that Christ's work alone—and not ours—is sufficient to forgive all our sins, and that he, being "the true bread from heaven" (John 6:32), is more than enough to fill and sustain the hunger of our souls. Communion is a corporate confession that Christ is faithfully committed to us, even to the point of death on a cross (see Phil 2:8), and that by feasting on his sacrifice in faith, we live by Christ forever (see John 6:57–58).

---

18. Terryl L. Givens, *Feeding the Flock: The Foundations of Mormon Thought: Church and Praxis* (Oxford: Oxford University Press, 2017), 203–4. Other researchers place the date later, in 1906, based on Thomas G. Alexander, "The Word of Wisdom: From Principle to Requirement," *Dialogue* 14, no. 3 (1981): 79. Alexander only tentatively suggested this date.
19. William Chazanof, *Welch's Grape Juice: From Corporation to Co-operative* (Syracuse, NY: Syracuse University Press, 1977), 1, 31–34.
20. *JD* 15:327.
21. *JD* 15:324.
22. *CDBY* 2:730.

Summary

The Book of Mormon deeply informs the purpose and practice of the LDS sacrament, the central ordinance of non-temple worship. Members of the Church of Jesus Christ of Latter-day Saints gather to eat and drink blessed emblems, bread and water, to remember Christ's sacrifice, display their willingness to carry his name obediently, and sustain fellowship with Christ's Spirit. In doing so, Latter-day Saints reaffirm their covenantal commitments made at baptism, although the Lord's Supper is perhaps better understood as a reminder of Christ's covenantal commitment to his church.

REFLECTION QUESTIONS

1. What is the significance of the Lord's Supper originating in the Passover meal? Does your church emphasize this Old Testament connection?

2. Traditional Christians celebrate the Lord's Supper in obedience to Jesus Christ, to remember his atonement in thanksgiving, and to collectively proclaim his second coming. How do these reasons for celebrating inform your view of the Lord's Supper?

3. The Lord's Supper in Mormonism is only delivered by authorized (priesthood) holders. How is this different or similar to your faith tradition?

4. Latter-day Saints receive bread and water as the elements for the Lord's Supper. What are your thoughts on substituting water for wine (or grape juice)?

5. Christianity generally views the Lord's Supper primarily as a reminder of Christ's commitment to the church, not as the church's commitment. What is the relationship between these two views?

QUESTION 31

What Is the Latter-day Saint View of Marriage and Family?

"Among all the duties devolving upon mortal man there is none of more importance than that of marrying in righteousness."[1]
~ Orson Pratt, Latter-day Saint Apostle, 1843–1881

I once attended a public event in Utah that featured a popular evangelical filmmaker. He was interviewed on stage before a largely Latter-day Saint audience. During the interview, the filmmaker pointed out a disparity between the large size of LDS families when compared with smaller evangelical families. The interviewer, a Latter-day Saint, took slight umbrage in a bit of friendly banter. "We're not *all* like that," he said as he began to ask questions sent in from the audience. "This one comes from Kayla. 'Hi, I'm a Latter-day Saint mother of . . .'" The interviewer paused. His eyes were fixed on his tablet as a thin smile played across his face. He continued. "I'm a Latter-day Saint mother of *nine*." The audience burst into laughter. The filmmaker didn't say a word. He didn't have to. Kayla made the point for him. Latter-day Saints tend to have larger families and marry much younger than their non-LDS peers, although the Church of Jesus Christ of Latter-day Saints is not immune to the demographic changes in America that are trending toward later marriages and smaller families.[2]

Even those Latter-day Saints who do not marry, have smaller families, or have no children at all are still part of a religion that values marriage and

1. Orson Pratt, ed., "Celestial Marriage," *The Seer*, September 1853, 1:139.
2. See Jana Riess, *The Next Mormons: How Millennials Are Changing the LDS Church* (New York: Oxford University Press, 2019), 71–90.

family. The LDS tradition is formed by a theology of family that compels its members to marry and rear children so that families might contribute to and join an eternally expanding kinship network. While this position might not sound very different from traditional Christianity, what distinguishes the LDS view of marriage and family? Let's begin with shared convictions.

Common Convictions on Marriage and Family

Traditional Christianity has long regarded marriage as a covenantal institution established by God. Evangelical theologians Timothy and Kathy Keller noted how marriage is "the most deeply covenantal relationship possible between two human beings" because it "has both strong horizontal *and* vertical aspects to it."[3] When a couple enters into marriage, one spouse joins a horizontal covenant with the other spouse and both commence a joint vertical commitment with each other to God. At its core, marriage is a declaration of the gospel. It is a living icon of Christ, the husband, joined to his church, his bride, in true love, mutual self-giving service, and exclusive fidelity, a covenantal relationship between the lover and the beloved (see Eph 5:22–33; cf. Gen 2:24). To see marriage in its ideal is to be reminded of the covenant God made between himself and his people (see Ezek 16; Hos 1–3; Mal 2:14). Latter-day Saints affirm this vision of marriage, a covenantal bonding of "the *Me*, *We*, and *Thee*," or "a triangle, with God, their spouse, and themselves connected through a covenant relationship."[4]

Marriage was also the first human institution ordained by God. Long before societal institutions like schools, businesses, and governments existed, Adam and Eve were joined together by marriage when they became "one flesh" (Gen 2:24; cf. Moses 3:24). Indeed, marriage is "*the foundational divine institution* for humanity," explained one evangelical theologian, a point with which many Latter-day Saints would agree.[5] And because marriage was established by the will of God, it is defined by him. For much of traditional Christianity, humanity does not own the copyright to marriage. We are merely its recipients and beneficiaries. God established marriage as an exclusive relationship between a man and a woman to enjoy a consummate oneness, equal co-operation, and friendship (see Gen 1:27–28; 2:24). Their sexual differences complement the mission to which they were mutually called, to "be fruitful" in childbearing and "subdue" the earth (see Gen 1:28; cf. Moses 2:28) as God's stewards of creation, working in mutual co-operation. Of course, the fallen state of nature complicates childbearing for some couples,

---

3. Timothy and Kathy Keller, *The Meaning of Marriage: Facing the Complexities of Commitment with the Wisdom of God* (New York: Penguin, 2011), 86 (emphasis original).
4. Debra Theobald McClendon and Richard J. McClendon, "Bringing God into Our Marriage," *Religious Educator* 20, no. 1 (2019): 62.
5. Andreas J. Köstenberger and David W. Jones, *God, Marriage, and Family: Rebuilding the Biblical Foundation*, 2nd ed. (Wheaton, IL: Crossway, 2010), 52 (emphasis original).

so adoption—another picture of the gospel (see Eph 1:5)—is encouraged. Regardless, erotic love consummates marriage and ought to be confined to the "marriage bed" (Heb 13:4 ESV), not as an arbitrary restriction but as a blessed consent to enjoy "cleaving" in the best of all possible relational spaces. After all, behind the negative prohibition "Thou shalt not commit adultery" (Exod 20:14) is the positive permission "Thou shalt enjoy marriage." And considering the present controversies surrounding definitions of marriage, sexuality, and identity, traditional Christians and Latter-day Saints generally share ethics and ideals for family life, like refraining from sexual activity prior to marriage, disdain for adultery, lamenting over divorce, upholding the sanctity of pre-born children, and rejoicing in childbearing and adoption.

On the surface, it's difficult to discern what differentiates the Latter-day Saint vision of marriage and family from traditional Christianity. There are, however, theological departure points that help to explain why Latter-day Saints uphold marriage and family as near-pinnacle vehicles for human flourishing.

Departure Points on Marriage and Family

According to Mormonism, God is married, and necessarily so for our sake. If each human being is "a beloved spirit son or daughter of heavenly parents,"[6] then "apparently, neither of them alone could beget our spirit bodies."[7] Moreover, God's exaltation to his celestial station depended, in part, on his marital status.[8] Presumably having once been a mortal man and woman, the beings who would become Heavenly Father and Heavenly Mother mutually experienced a probationary period of trials and growth that blossomed into divinity. At one point, they began to procreate spirit children (see question 27). Thus, for God to be a father, there needs to be a mother; otherwise, God is not who he has revealed himself to be (i.e., the Father).

To become like God, his children must be married as he is. They need to be married eternally. Joseph Smith taught that "except a man and his wife enter into an everlasting covenant and be married for eternity," then they will "cease to increase when they die" as celestial bliss forever eludes them.[9] The church denies that marriages last only "till death do us part." Faithful LDS couples who marry in a temple are bound together through ritual that seals the man and woman for eternity (see question 28). But only those who are married by proper priesthood authority "will continue to increase & have children in the celestial

---

6. "The Family: A Proclamation to the World," *Ensign* 25 (November 1995): 102.
7. David L. Paulsen and Martin Pulido, " 'A Mother There': A Survey of Historical Teachings About Mother in Heaven," *BYU Studies* 50, no. 1 (2011): 76.
8. Speculation on the marital status of the Son of God is an open debate in current Mormon discussion. For a thoughtful treatment on how Latter-day Saints have approached this question, see Christopher James Blythe, "Was Jesus Married?" *BYU Studies* 60, no. 3 (2021): 75–84.
9. JS, instruction, May 16, 1843, D12:308.

glory," just as God the Father and Heavenly Mother have increased and multiplied to bring the human family into being.[10] For Smith, marriage is among the most important covenantal relationships to remain intact when crossing from life to death.[11] Children are likewise sealed to their parents' marital sealing or by subsequent temple rituals. Marriages, then, are hubs of an eternally expanding kinship network of families sealed for time and eternity.

If residents of the celestial kingdom are like God—a glorified spouse and parent—then singleness is antithetical to the end of God's plan of salvation. In this sense, marriage in Mormonism not only sanctifies couples—it not only makes us holy through love, humility, and sacrifice—but it also plays a role in glorifying them, exalting their status beyond what they could have achieved in an unmarried state. Consequently, marriage is prerequisite for Latter-day Saints who desire the fullest celestial exaltation. This emphasis on the eternality of family fosters in Mormon culture the ideal norm for the man as husband and father and the woman as wife and mother.

Relatedly, early Latter-day Saint leaders taught that a woman must be covered by her husband's priesthood authority to enter celestial glory. It's what one scholar described as "salvific coverture," the idea that celestial salvation for a woman comes "through the husband to whom she was sealed, that husbands were salvifically responsible for their wife or wives, and/or that a woman could rely on her husband for salvation."[12] But such an idea chafes against the apostle Paul's insistence that salvation comes not through marriage but through putting on Christ, which is an equal invitation to all people, for "there is neither male nor female: for ye are all one in Christ Jesus" (Gal 3:28). In fact, Paul himself was a single man who wished that "all men were even as I myself" (1 Cor 7:7). To the unmarried and widows, he commended singleness: "it is good for them if they abide even as I" (1 Cor 7:8). Paul's recommendation is odd if he believed in the importance of marriage for celestial glory. Perhaps he signaled that singleness is not a discriminator for celestial bliss in Christ. After all, "if marriage shows us the shape of the gospel, singleness shows us its sufficiency."[13]

Moreover, the Lord Jesus made clear that in the resurrection we "neither marry, nor are given in marriage" (Matt 22:30). The institution of marriage—at least *our* marriages—yields to the greater marriage of Christ and church. Smith countered this interpretation, arguing that Christ was warning people

10. JS, instruction, May 16, 1843, D12:308.
11. See Samuel Morris Brown, *In Heaven as It Is on Earth: Joseph Smith and the Early Mormon Conquest of Death* (New York: Oxford University Press, 2012), 232–36.
12. Brooke R. LeFevre, "'I Would Not Risk My Salvation to Any Man:' Eliza R. Snow's Challenge to Salvific Coverture," *Journal of Mormon History* 47, no. 2 (2021): 52. As LeFevre points out, despite her leader's teaching salvific coverture, Eliza R. Snow, a nineteenth-century Relief Society president, openly advocated against this notion.
13. Sam Allberry, *7 Myths About Singleness* (Wheaton, IL: Crossway, 2019), 120.

to get married "in view of eternity" during this life while they still can, "otherwise they must remain as angels, or be single in heaven."[14] "Those who have not secured their marriage for eternity in this life can never have it attended to hereafter," clarified an LDS apostle.[15] This point is confusing within Smith's cosmology, in which angels are exalted people. For example, if Peter was married in mortality (see Luke 4:38) and was a Melchizedek priesthood holder ordained by Christ, and then in his glorified state as an angel Peter ordained Smith to the Melchizedek priesthood, then is Peter presently single in heaven because he is an angel?

At any rate, Smith's reading of Matthew 22:30 misses the forest for the trees. Eugene Peterson's translation captures Christ's point well.

> Marriage is a major preoccupation here, but not there. Those who are included in the resurrection of the dead will no longer be concerned with marriage nor, of course, with death. They will have better things to think about, if you can believe it. All ecstasies and intimacies then will be with God. (Luke 20:34–38, MSG)

Yet, again, according to Mormonism, "marriage between man and woman is *essential* to [God's] eternal plan."[16] Without marriage, human beings cannot reach their greatest potential. No wonder one Latter-day Saint leader called marriage "the crowning ordinance of the Gospel."[17] Traditional Christianity retreats from this point, however, not to dissent from the importance of marriage per se but to remind us how marriage is meant to imitate the never-ending covenant between Christ and his church. The theological intention of marriage is iconic, and as with any icon, we risk turning marriage into an idol if we focus too much on it rather than the thing it represents. Our marriages are not the crowning ordinance of the gospel; rather, *the* Marriage is—"the marriage of the Lamb," Jesus Christ, to his bride, the church, who "hath made herself ready" (Rev 19:7). Of course, all Christians are susceptible to idolizing marriage. Latter-day Saints are not unique in this regard. But the salvific emphasis and theological function of marriage in Mormonism makes it even more tempting. Whom do we look forward to being with the most in the afterlife? Our spouse and families, or God? If the answer is not the latter, then marriage and family have become an idol. "For those who love anything alongside you," Augustine prayed, "unless they love it for your sake, love you

---

14. Joseph Smith, History, 1838–1856, vol. F-1, *JSP*, 81.
15. Pratt, "Celestial Marriage," 43.
16. "The Family," 102 (emphasis added).
17. Quote from Joseph Fielding Smith. Leo Perry, "Lay Cornerstone at Provo Temple," *Deseret News*, May 22, 1971, 2B.

too little."[18] It's possible to love families more than God, but we are called to love our families *because* of God.

This point gets to the heart of the matter. The core importance of marriage is not what it accomplishes but what it communicates. Ultimately, marriage is a dress rehearsal for the big one, the Lamb's wedding to his church-bride. To bring our marriages into the resurrection Marriage is to tote along types and shadows to the real thing. We might say that marriage is "a shadow of good things to come, and not the very image of the things" (Heb 10:1) because, in the heavenly Marriage, all the beauties and mysteries of our earthly marriages will be realized.

A Note About Polygamy

Readers may wonder why a question discussing marriage and Mormonism does not focus on polygamy. The answer is simple: the Church of Jesus Christ of Latter-day Saints upholds monogamy, marriage between one man and one woman, as the ideal marital state. True, its founders and past members introduced and practiced polygamy, and some communities of people today who identify with Mormonism continue to practice plural marriage.[19] But studying polygamy is not particularly helpful in understanding Mormonism beyond its historical narrative or present-day forms of fundamentalism. Your Latter-day Saint neighbor is not a polygamist. But to satisfy curiosity, I briefly address some common interests in this area.

While not all Mormons practiced polygamy, early Latter-day Saint leaders did.[20] They viewed polygamy as a divine duty to raise up a righteous population who could receive the coming kingdom of God. To them, plural marriage wasn't a barbaric deformity of the norm. Instead, it was a righteous retrieval

18. *Conf.* 29.40.
19. For a historical survey of polygamy in American culture and politics, see Sarah M. S. Pearsall, *Polygamy: An Early American History* (New Haven, CT: Yale University Press, 2019). For more on polygamy in Mormonism, see Todd Compton, *In Sacred Loneliness: The Plural Wives of Joseph Smith*; Brian C. Hales, *Modern Polygamy and Mormon Fundamentalism: The Generations after the Manifesto* (Salt Lake City: Greg Kofford Books, 2006); B. Carmon Hardy, ed., *Doing the Works of Abraham: Mormon Polygamy; Its Origin, Practice, and Demise* (Norman, OK: University of Oklahoma Press, 2007); Newell G. Bringhurst and Craig L. Foster, *The Persistence of Polygamy*, 3 vols. (Independence, MO: John Whitmer Books, 2010–15); Laurel Thatcher Ulrich, *A House Full of Females: Plural Marriage and Women's Rights in Early Mormonism, 1835–1870* (New York: Alfred D. Knopf, 2017); Laura Parson, *Polygamy, Women, and Higher Education: Life After Mormon Fundamentalism* (Cham, Switzerland: Springer Nature Switzerland AG, 2019); and Brittany Chapman Nash, *Let's Talk About Polygamy* (Salt Lake City: Deseret, 2021).
20. See Compton, *In Sacred Loneliness*; Brian C. Hales, *Joseph Smith's Polygamy*, 3 vols. (Salt Lake City: Greg Kofford Books, 2013); Brian C. and Laura H. Hales, *Joseph Smith's Polygamy: Toward a Better Understanding* (Salt Lake City: Greg Kofford Books, 2015); Todd Compton, ed., *In Sacred Loneliness: The Documents* (Salt Lake City: Signature Books, 2022).

of an ancient practice that led to eternal blessing. But their view neglected to acknowledge that, since the beginning, God ordained marriage between one man and one woman, so that in their union, "they are no more *twain*, but one flesh," said the Lord Jesus (Matt 19:6, emphasis added; see also Gen 2:24). Christ offered no room for any other arrangement beyond the twain-turned-one. It's unsurprising that polygamy was the first distortion of marriage after the fall, when "Lamech took unto him two wives" (Gen 4:19), and that OT men who took multiple wives suffered negative consequences (e.g., Abraham's split household [see Gen 16] and Solomon's spiritual downfall [see 1 Kgs 11:4]). Biblical kings engaged in polygamy despite being forbidden by divine law to "multiply wives" (Deut 17:17). Those who took mother-daughter pairs risked being "cut off from among their people" by the death penalty (Lev 18:17, 29). "It is wickedness," the Torah states bluntly (Lev 20:14). These examples of polygamy are not simply unauthorized plural marriages, as some LDS apologists occasionally frame them, because monogamy is always the ideal norm. The NT and the Book of Mormon make this point clear in their rejection of polygamy, especially among spiritual leadership (see Mark 10:7–9; 1 Tim 3:2; Titus 1:6; Jacob 1:15; 2:23, 24, 27; Mosiah 11:2–6).[21] Ultimately, polygamy fractures the image of the gospel present in marriage (see Eph 5:31–32). Christ did not come to join himself to many *brides* but to one bride alone, his beloved church.

After publicly staying the practice of polygamy in 1890 and gradually refraining from it in the early twentieth century, the LDS Church has since advocated for a universal fidelity to traditional marriage.[22] And while specters of polygamy continue to haunt the church to this day, any of its critics who have yet to retire the tired accusation that Mormonism *is* polygamous risks bearing false witness against their neighbor. Joseph Smith was right to instruct the men in his early church: "Thou shalt love thy wife with all thy heart, and shalt

21. The earliest published version of Doctrine and Covenants likewise described marriage as "ordained of God unto man: wherefore it is lawful that he should have one wife, and the twain shall be one flesh" (Doctrine and Covenants 1835, 192). Polygamy, however, was introduced to the standard works through Doctrine and Covenants 132, a revelation used by leaders, like Brigham Young, to formally permit plural marriage in the LDS Church.
22. On this point, critics of the LDS Church argue that the Latter-day Saints only reluctantly stayed the practice of plural marriage in exchange for Utah statehood in the decades following federal prohibition of polygamy in the United States. Yet as early as 1858—just six years after the LDS Church publicly announced their practice of polygamy—one apostle reasoned that Latter-day Saints ought not to practice polygamy under any state or territory that forbade it (Pratt, "Celestial Marriage," 1:111). Still other leaders, like Wilford Woodruff, openly advocated for defying federal law. In 1870, he warned the Saints how God re-instituted "the Patriarchal order of Marriage," or polygamy, and "said if we do [not] obey it we shall be damned," but that the US Congress prevented them from doing so. "Now, [w]hich shall we obey God or Congress[?]" he blustered. "The assembly shouted in By acclimation we will obey God" (*WWJ* 4:189).

cleave unto her and none else."[23] This is the call the LDS Church issues to its husbands. Instead of badgering Latter-day Saints about their polygamist past, traditional Christians would do well to encourage the church's present emphasis on marriage while speaking to the theological concerns raised in this question.

Summary

Mormonism recognizes marriage as a God-ordained covenantal institution that forms an exclusive relationship for the purpose of companionship, family rearing, and imaging the gospel. Unlike traditional Christianity, however, Mormonism extends marriage to God and, consequently, considers matrimony essential to becoming like him. Christians traditionally recognize marriage as a temporal institution that points toward the greater eschatological marriage of Christ and his church. And while early Latter-day Saints practiced polygamy, plural marriages were stayed by the church in the late-nineteenth century.

REFLECTION QUESTIONS

1. At what points do Latter-day Saint and traditional Christian views of marriage overlap? Where do they depart?

2. What is the theological reason for the LDS belief that God is married? What does it mean for God the Father to be called "father" according to traditional Christianity?

3. How does singleness and marriage relate to one's salvation in Mormonism and in traditional Christianity?

4. According to traditional Christianity, what is the ultimate (i.e., eschatological) purpose of marriage?

5. Do you agree or disagree that it is unhelpful to study polygamy beyond the interest of historical Mormonism or contemporary LDS fundamentalism? Why or why not?

---

23. Joseph Smith, History, 1831–ca. 1847, H2:25.

SECTION B

Unique Doctrines

QUESTION 32

What Is the Doctrine of Eternal Progression?

"God is thus glorified and exalted in the salvation and exaltation of all his children."[1]
~ Joseph Smith

King Follett died tragically while digging a well. Those who knew him best, his fellow Latter-day Saints, remembered Follett's insatiable curiosity about religion and his stalwart devotion to the answers he found in the Church of Jesus Christ of Latter-day Saints. He was among the most loyal in his community, so to his loved ones it must have seemed like a very unceremonious way to pass into eternity after being crushed "by the falling of a tub of rock on him."[2] To Joseph Smith, though, death wasn't Follett's abrupt end, but neither was it a new beginning. Instead, his passing was a painful—albeit necessary step—in an ongoing process of progression "from one small degree to another, and from a small capacity to a great one."[3] Follett's potential reward was not merely to be received into the celestial kingdom of God, as many Christians supposed, but also to potentially *receive* a kingdom of his own as a god. Smith wished to console mourners with his theologically unorthodox message, so during a spring church conference—being "inspired by the Holy Spirit," he said—Smith delivered what would become one of his most paradigm-shifting theological discourses.[4]

1. Joseph Smith, History, 1838–1856, vol. E-1, *JSP*, 1971.
2. JSJ, April 7, 1844, J3:217.
3. Joseph Smith, History, 1838–1856, vol. E-1, *JSP*, 1971. One of Smith's scribes dictated this statement as "from grace to grace" and "from exaltation to exaltation."
4. Joseph Smith, History, 1838–1856, vol. E-1, *JSP*, 1968.

King Follett Discourse

On the morning of April 7, 1844, Smith rose before "the largest congregation ever seen in Nauvoo" to address a community in mourning.[5] Mortality was on their mind, as was the question of what happens when souls pass through the veil of death. Smith took the occasion to comfort his congregation. But his funerary homily quickly pivoted into a treatise on the nature and potential of humanity, which was the consoling Smith wished to convey. King Follett hadn't experienced his end—nor should anyone for that matter—because all humans are immortal spirits, sourced from uncreated intelligence, an essence that is "coequal with God himself."[6] And this eternal intelligence is neither static nor unchanging but is "susceptible to enlargement," continuous development and progress, thus implying humanity's immortality.[7] As an eternal intelligence, God himself progressed "from grace to grace, from exaltation to exaltation" until arriving at his present gloriously divine state, having "worked out his kingdom with fear and trembling" (see Phil 2:12).[8] The Son of God, too, followed in the Father's footsteps. As Jesus said (according to Smith), "I do the things I saw my Father do when worlds came rolling into existence" (cf. John 5:19), words that Smith believed meant the Son would obtain a kingdom just as his Father had and implies that even though the Father had a mortal existence, he (like his Son) never sinned.[9] For just as the Father had

---

5. JSJ, April 7, 1844, J3:216 (emend.). The King Follett Discourse ranks among Smith's most influential lectures. In it he expands the horizon of LDS doctrine in the areas of God's nature, premortality, salvation for the dead, and eternal progression. While the discourse presently does not rank among LDS scripture, its concepts are certainly present. The King Follett Discourse acts supplementally to canonical material, especially on the nature of God and human potential. Christians, then, ought to approach the discourse with caution, rightly recognizing it as subordinate to the standard works but nevertheless extremely influential. Some Latter-day Saints express additional caution when approaching the Discourse, arguing its non-canonical status is compounded by the unreliability of its record. I would not go this far. As Stan Larson long ago noticed, there is a "high degree of agreement and harmony" among the different accounts of the sermon, which enjoys "the greatest contemporary manuscript support" of all Smith's other speeches ("The King Follett Discourse: A Newly Amalgamated Text," *BYU Studies* 18, no. 2 [1978]: 194). Importantly, the sermon was delivered at the April 1844 general conference, not at a funeral, though it responded to Follett's death and is often called a funerary address. See also William V. Smith, *The King Follett Sermon: A Biography* (Newburgh, IN: Common Consent Press, 2023).
6. Joseph Smith, History, 1838–1856, vol. E-1, *JSP*, 1973.
7. Joseph Smith, History, 1838–1856, vol. E-1, *JSP*, 1974.
8. Joseph Smith, History, 1838–1856, vol. E-1, *JSP*, 1971.
9. JS, History, 1838–1856, vol. E-1, *JSP*, 1971. Here, Smith calls on John 5:19, "The Son can do nothing of himself, but what he seeth the Father do: for what things soever he doeth, these also doeth the Son likewise." Smith's interpretation relies heavily on the past-tense sense of Christ's words (i.e., that the Son does *presently* what he witnessed the Father do in the *past*). But the text gives very little permission to be read this way. The Son does what he *presently* and *actively* "seeth" the Father do, not what the Son *saw* Father did in eternity past. Jesus's

"redeemed a world [and] became the eternal God of the world," so too would the Son redeem the earth to become its God.[10] Once the Son was exalted, as the Father was before him, the Father became even more exalted than before. After all, Smith argued, it's a great glory to obtain a kingdom as its king, but it's even more glorious to be the Father of a Son who has a kingdom as well, to be a King of a King. The Father and the Son have experienced the *telos* of the eternal priesthood—attaining glory through exaltation.

In his affectionate kindness, the Father desired the same progression for his other children, so that he "saw [it] proper to institute laws whereby the rest could have a privilege to advance like himself."[11] These laws, tied as they are to the priesthood, provided the salvific framework for the mission of the Son, whose life, death, and resurrection would neutralize the effects of sin to enable his spirit siblings the opportunity to advance toward godhood as he had. This idea wasn't necessarily new to Smith. Some twelve years earlier, he had described the celestial kingdom as filled with "Gods even the sons of God," so some sort of deification was expected.[12] How, exactly, celestial citizens became gods LDS leaders and writers developed over time, much of which will be explored in the subsequent questions (e.g., ordinances, temple ritual, marriage). During a church conference, Smith issued an invitation for his followers to keep pace with the developments and to "learn how to be Gods yourselves, and to be Kings and Priests to God, the same as all Gods have done before you."[13] Such progress is not aimed at self-exaltation but serves as an act of worship, one whose ultimate end is the magnification of the glory of the Son and the Father, who *is* and is *becoming* a King of a King of kings.

The audience was clearly interested in immediately learning more. The very next day, they petitioned Smith to elaborate his new doctrine. But he declined, promising to "continue the subject of my discourse some other time" because his lungs were "worn out," having projected over the wind to thousands the day before.[14] But he would breathe his last breath just two months later. Smith would never get an opportunity to clarify his teachings, thus relegating eternal progression to doctrinal mystery. As a result, "the principle of eternal progression cannot be precisely defined or comprehended, yet it is fundamental to the LDS worldview."[15] Indeed, as one scholar noted, there is

---

words speak directly to the present reality of his synchronized will with the Father rather than to some learned behavior earlier in life.

10. JS, discourse, January 30, 1842, D9:129.
11. JS History, 1838–1856, vol. E-1, *JSP*, 1974.
12. JS, revelation, February 16, 1832, D2:188.
13. Joseph Smith, History, 1838–1856, vol. E-1, *JSP*, 1971.
14. Joseph Smith, History, 1838–1856, vol. E-1, *JSP*, 1981.
15. Lisa Ramsay Adams, "Eternal Progression," in *Encyclopedia of Mormonism*, ed. Daniel H. Ludlow, 5 vols. (New York: Macmillan, 1992), 1:465–66. For development of the doctrine immediately after Smith's death, see Boyd Kirkland, "Eternal Progression and the Second Death

"an apotheosis, a making of gods, at the heart of LDS spirituality."[16] And at the core of this heart lie the ideas Smith presented in the King Follett Discourse.

Even though Smith's life was cut short, speculation on his enigmatic doctrine was not. Later church presidents and apostles have advanced personal perspectives on the matter, and there remains a degree of diversity in how the specifics of eternal progression are understood and articulated among Latter-day Saints today. For example, while Smith's discourse emphasized progression in terms of growth, later Saints theorized that human progress also incorporates growth in divine attributes. We progress in power and being as all people are "capable, by experience through ages and aeons, of evolving into a God."[17] In this vein, one scholar defined eternal progression as "a quality of experience and not exclusively a duration of experience," further arguing that God lives in a continual increase of "power, thought, and experience."[18] Divine progression is not static but eternally dynamic, one that offers each person "radical ontological transcendence," a transformation inconceivably beyond our mortal comprehension.[19] To become a god is to experience progression like God has experienced, increasing in knowledge, power, wisdom, status, and life. This divine sameness—not merely ontological likeness but shareable experiences—best describes the doctrine. According to Mormonism, it is a given that we are like God in our nature, but Smith's discourse revealed to Latter-day Saints that they might be like God in his experiences, too.

To be clear, Mormonism vehemently denies anyone can take God's place, that they may "unseat or oust God."[20] Aside from myriad other reasons, it's impossible to become God in the same way one person can't become another. I cannot, no matter how hard I try, become my father or take his place as my father. I can become *a* father, but not my own father. So humans can grow through experience just as God has, and this growth is potentially endless. Thus, as LDS president Lorenzo Snow explained, it is possible to become "as great as you will

---

in the Theology of Brigham Young," in *Line upon Line: Essays on Mormon Doctrine*, ed. Gary James Bergera (Salt Lake City: Signature Books, 1989), 171–81. For a general LDS assessment on the doctrine in relation to Christian "becoming like God," see David L. Paulsen and Hal Boyd, *Are Christians Mormon?* (New York: Routledge, 2017), 65–96. For a concise rationale for traditional Christianity's rejection of *apotheosis*, see Douglas J. Davies, *An Introduction to Mormonism* (Cambridge: Cambridge University Press, 2003), 79–80.

16. Davies, *An Introduction to Mormonism*, 79.
17. Heber J. Grant, Anthony W. Ivins, and Charles W. Nibley, "'Mormon' View of Evolution," First Presidency statement, September 1925, *Improvement Era* 28:1091.
18. James R. Harris, "Eternal Progression and the Foreknowledge of God," *BYU Studies* 8, no. 1 (1968): 43, 46.
19. Jacob Baker, "'The Grandest Principle of the Gospel': Christian Nihilism, Sanctified Activism, and Eternal Progression," *Dialogue* 41, no. 3 (2008): 71.
20. Robert L. Millet, "Becoming as God," in *Talking Doctrine: Mormons and Evangelicals in Conversation*, ed. Richard J. Mouw and Robert L. Millet (Downers Grove: IVP Academic, 2015), 203.

want to be—as great as God Himself" because "as man now is, God once was; as God now is, man may become."[21] One can finish the marathon of progression like God did, but they do so by passing the finish line with the tape already broken. God finished long before everyone else. So did the Son, whom we always follow. It is impossible to outpace God, the ultimate self-surpassing being.

Engaging the Doctrine of Eternal Progression

Presently, Latter-day Saints tend to hold this doctrine (in whatever form) close to the chest, a reserved posture to apparently prevent the casting of a theological pearl into the pigsty of criticism. To many Latter-day Saints, eternal progression is either too mysterious or too meaty a doctrine to feed spiritual juveniles and outsiders, so it's best discussed privately. Church critics who relentlessly pounce on the doctrine are partly to blame for this reserved posture, but concealing such an essential doctrine is unnecessarily reactive and evidently contrary to Smith's intentions for it. After all, he publicly revealed it to a massive crowd during a General Conference—his last, in fact—in Nauvoo with Mormons and non-Mormons in attendance. Smith thought it important enough to be publicly received, considered, and debated. And although it's rarely named from the pulpit, the sermon still today shapes how many Latter-day Saints explore core questions about God, humanity, and what it means to be exalted.[22] So, hiding it only raises suspicion about the church's theological transparency, as does minimizing its importance.[23] The King Follett Discourse is not a fringe or obscure sermon, as it is sometimes framed. But if Latter-day Saints should not shy from this doctrine publicly, then neither should traditional Christians weaponize it. Instead, let the doctrine of eternal progression be subject to biblically formed and informed dialogue, with the end goal of discovering the truth about the nature of God and his image bearers. Not talking about it at all, or talking about it in caricatured forms, is helpful to no one.

Relatedly, the traditional Christian idea of becoming like God is not the same as LDS eternal progression, nor does the LDS belief easily square with

---

21. Lorenzo Snow, "The Grand Destiny of Man," *Deseret Evening News*, July 20, 1901. This expression, known as "the Lorenzo Snow couplet," is too reductive a reflection of LDS anthropology. Mormonism does not teach a person can become literally like God is now because who God is now is beyond one's ability to meet, let alone surpass. Perhaps a more accurate version reads "as man now is, God once was; as God has been, man may be."
22. See James E. Faulconer and Susannah Morrison, "The King Follett Discourse: Pinnacle or Peripheral?" *BYU Studies* 60, no. 3 (2021): 85–104. The authors argue that while the sermon is seldom cited explicitly, it continues to serve as a theological "mirror" and catalyst, encouraging ongoing reflection on divine nature and human potential.
23. The LDS Church tacitly agrees, having published an anonymous article addressing concerns over the doctrine. For an in-depth critique of this discourse, see Richard Sherlock, "Becoming Like God: A Critique," in The *LDS Gospel Topics Series: A Scholarly Engagement*, ed. Matthew L. Harris and Newell G. Bringhurst (Salt Lake City: Signature Books, 2020), 51–68.

Orthodox doctrines of deification (Gk. *theōsis*),[24] although the latter seem very similar to Smith's teaching at first.[25] While *theōsis* is a dynamic concept in Orthodox thought, it is generally defined as humans becoming like the Son of God because his incarnation enabled a "divine-human exchange,"[26] or as a mystical transformation whereby humans are adopted as sons of the Son of God (i.e., the "Christification" of the saints),[27] or as participation in the divine energies—but never the divine *essence*—of the Trinity.[28] Deification, and its related glorification in other Christian thought, is essentially the culmination of human salvation in mysterious communion with God so complete that individuals are said to be like God, but never *as* God.[29]

Here, then, is the core difference: traditional Christianity denies God and humans are of the same species because God is absolutely inaccessible in his essence, so any divine likeness humans experience will always be ontologically disparate from God's nature.[30] The doctrine of deification has more to do with divine likeness (*imago Dei*), not divine sameness, and "the restoration of our true humanity," not the activation of our latent divinity. Christianity has long confessed the Son of God became a son of man so we might become "*partakers*

---

24. For a concise survey of Orthodoxy deification, see Nikolaos Asproulis, "Eucharistic Personhood: Deification in the Orthodox Tradition," in *With All the Fullness of God: Deification in Christian Tradition*, ed. Jared Ortiz (New York: Fortress Academic, 2021), 29–57.
25. Some Latter-day Saints see in Smith's doctrine of eternal progression the Christian doctrine of *theōsis*. See, for example, Keith E. Norman, "Divinization: The Forgotten Teaching of Early Christianity," *Dialogue* 1 (1975): 15–19; Norman, "Deification, Early Christian," in *Encyclopedia of Mormonism*, ed. Daniel H. Ludlow, 5 vols. (New York: Macmillan, 1992), 1: 369–70; Craig J. Blomberg and Stephen E. Robinson, *How Wide the Divide?: A Mormon and an Evangelical in Conversation* (Downers Grove: InterVarsity Press, 1997), 80–81; Stephen E. Robinson, "LDS Doctrine Compared with Other Christian Doctrines," in *Latter-day Saint Essentials: Readings from the Encyclopedia of Mormonism*, ed. John W. Welch and R. Devan Jensen (Provo, UT: RSC, BYU, 2002), 177–81.
26. Paul M. Collins, *Partaking in Divine Nature: Deification and Communion* (New York: T&T Clark, 2010), 50.
27. See Panayiotis Nellas, *Deification in Christ: Orthodox Perspectives on the Nature of the Human Person*, trans. Norman Russell (Crestwood, NY: St Vladimir's Seminary Press, 1987).
28. Even if one distinguishes between God's energies (or activities) and his essence (or nature), as Byzantine theologian Gregory Palamas did—whatever he meant by the distinction—*theōsis* is still restricted only to participation in the energies of the Holy Trinity and never God's nature, or *ousia*. See Tikhon Pino, *Essence and Energies: Being and Naming God in St Gregory Palamas* (New York: Routledge, 2023), 118–21.
29. For introductions to traditional Christian concepts of deification, see Norman Russell, *The Doctrine of Deification in the Greek Patristic Tradition* (New York: Oxford University Press, 2004); Michael J. Christensen and Jeffery A. Wittung, eds., *Partakers of the Divine Nature: The History and Development of Deification in the Christian Traditions* (Grand Rapids: Baker Academic, 2008); Jared Ortiz, ed., *Deification in the Latin Patristic Tradition* (Washington, DC: Catholic University of America Press, 2019); Ortiz, *With All the Fullness of God.*
30. Terryl L. Givens rightly discerned this important difference in his survey of Christian deification and Mormon exaltation (*Wrestling the Angel: The Foundations of Mormon Thought: Cosmos, God, Humanity* (New York: Oxford University Press, 2015), 256–66).

of the divine nature" (2 Pet 1:4, emphasis added), not *persons* of the divine nature. [31] The Son "became human for our sakes, not abandoning what he is—divinity—but assuming what he is not—humanity."[32] The opposite is not true. The Son was not sent to enable us to retain what we are—humanity—while assuming what we could potentially become—divinity, or gods of God's very nature, true gods from true God. The goal of deification is not some "abstract change of the nature (human) into another (the divine)" because we never cease to be our Creator's creatures.[33] Neither is deification an evolutionary process of a shared nature with God because, again, humans are ontologically other than God. There is no genetic relationship, so to speak, between God and humanity, as the ancient Gnostics maintained.

Therefore, when traditional Christians mention the "admirable exchange"—something like "the Son of God became a man to enable men to become sons of God"—they mean believers are adopted by God and hidden in Christ to enjoy a mystical transformation by the Holy Spirit but are never ontologically metamorphized into the divine essence or nature. [34] And the admirable exchange is only possible because of Christ's other exchanges: his righteousness for our sin (see 2 Cor 5:21), his heavenly wealth for our spiritual poverty (see 2 Cor 8:9), and his glory for our good (see Phil 2:5–11). The Son of God exchanged himself for us, and through faith in this exchange, believers may become sons of God, destined for immortality.

As C. S. Lewis noted, Christian scripture promises that all of God's beloved will be with Christ and will be like him, glorified in a sense beyond our comprehension,[35] so that it's "a serious thing to live in a society of possible gods and goddesses" on earth as we await heaven.[36] But "becoming like God" in Christian thought is far more concerned with the saint's adoption by God, unification with him, and conformation to the divine character than any sort of translation into his nature that blurs or demolishes the Creator-creature distinction. We are not presently like God in his nature or being. Nor is there a future in which we experience his exalted state. Instead, Christ's own are "being turned from a created thing into a begotten thing" like him, though forever a created thing, and this has nothing to do with our earning through

31. Andrew Louth, *Introducing Eastern Orthodox Theology*, 95.
32. Louth, *Introducing Eastern Orthodox Theology*, 95.
33. Jonathan M. Ciraulo, "Divinization as Christification in Erich Przywara and John Zizioulas," *Modern Theology* 32, no. 4 (2016): 479.
34. C. S. Lewis, *Mere Christianity* (New York: HarperCollins, 2001), 178. Long before Lewis, and echoed through the ages, was Irenaeus's statement (and others like it): "He who was the Son of God was made man, that man, having been taken into the Word, and receiving the adoption, might become the son of God" (*ANF* 1:448).
35. C. S. Lewis, "The Weight of Glory," in *The Weight of Glory: And Other Addresses* (New York: HarperCollins, 2001), 34.
36. Lewis, "The Weight of Glory," 45.

covenant making and covenant keeping. This work "has been done for us," said Lewis.[37] In the end, God "wants a world full of beings united to Him but still distinct."[38] The point of glory is to reflect who Christ is, not to assume the nature that Christ is, because the "goal of humanity is not to transcend that distinction of Creator and creature but to fulfill it by God becoming reproduced in them, as a portrait reproduces the person," not as parents reproduce people.[39] As Lewis summarized, "What is near Him by likeness is never, by that fact alone, going to be any nearer."[40] Deity is always something other, outside, and beyond us. We can never transform into God's substance. Doing so collapses the Creator-created distinction. As God now is, God has always been; as God always is, man will never be.

Moreover, the medals of Christ's victory are not a host of siblings enthroned in kingdoms beneath the Father and Son. Instead, the remnant scars of crucifixion on his resurrected body are an eternal reminder of his victorious work and, consequently, his glory, not ours. We will be eternally grateful to him, not for our enthronement but for his atonement. And while Latter-day Saints may—even should?—agree, there is nevertheless a mechanism in their soteriology that abets them (whether intentionally or not) to look beyond the eternal effects of Christ's atonement, if even for the briefest moment, toward one's personal kingdom rather than Christ's kingdom. And this personal kingdom is obtained not by Christ's work alone but aided with personal righteousness. "When we get in eternity, we shall be angels or Gods [and] shall advance to godhead *if* we do right," explained Brigham Young.[41] But to believe that humans may be gods is to yield, it seems, once more to the first temptation: "Ye shall be as gods" (Gen 3:5).[42]

---

37. Lewis, *Mere Christianity*, 181. For Lewis's view on becoming like God, see Douglas Beyer, "From Kenosis to Theosis: Reflections on the Views of C. S. Lewis," *Inklings Forever: Published Colloquium Proceedings 1997–2016*, vol. 5 (2006): 90–95.
38. C. S. Lewis, *The Screwtape Letters* (New York: Macmillan, 1974), 38.
39. Ben C. Blackwell, *Christosis: Engaging Paul's Soteriology with His Patristic Interpreters* (Grand Rapids: Eerdmans, 2016), 66.
40. C. S. Lewis, *The Four Loves* (New York: Harcourt, Brace & Company, 1960), 16.
41. *CDBY* 1:436 (emphasis added). Possibly *godhood*, not "godhead."
42. Paulsen and Boyd noted that this concern dates to the patristic era, especially Gregory of Nazianzen, who famously taught that in the first temptation, the serpent "cheated us with the hope of becoming gods" (*Are Christians Mormon?*, 87n64). They noted, however, that Gregory apparently also believed that Christ would "make [him] God by the power of His incarnation" (Paulsen and Boyd, *Are Christians Mormon?*, 88n64). Yet, in the same sermon, Gregory defines "gods" as "the saved." Frederick W. Norris, ed., *Faith Gives Fullness to Reasoning: The Five Theological Orations of Gregory Nazianzen,* trans. Lionel Wickham and Frederick Williams (New York: Brill, 1991), 264. Thus, becoming like God "is for him a description of the Son bringing in the saved at the time of judgement," not into a state of glorified deity sourced from a shared essence with God (Norris, *Faith Gives Fullness to Reasoning*, 163).

Summary

Joseph Smith taught that human beings have the potential to become gods through eternal progression in a way similar to that by which God himself ascended to his divine state. This doctrine of eternal progression is summarized in the oft-cited maxim: "As man now is, God once was; as God now is, man may become." Traditional Christianity rejects this doctrine largely on the basis that it violates the Creator-created distinction and lacks biblical evidence to support it otherwise. While Christianity rejects the possibility we may all become gods, it wholly affirms we may all become God's, his eternally beloved partakers *of* (not participants *in*) the divine nature.

REFLECTION QUESTIONS

1. Why do classical theism and creation *ex nihilo* prohibit eternal progression?

2. Does Mormonism teach that humans can become God or gods, and why is this distinction important to make?

3. What did early church fathers mean when they taught that the Son of God became a man so that people may become sons and daughters of God?

4. Read 2 Peter 1:4. How might a Latter-day Saint and traditional Christian interpret this passage differently?

5. Do you agree or disagree that believing humans may be as gods is an echo of the first temptation: "Ye shall be as gods" (Gen 3:5)?

QUESTION 33

Why Does Mormonism Have Temples?

"God is in His holy Temple, Sons of earth, be silent now;
Hither let the saints assemble, and before His footstool bow."[1]
~ Samuel Woodworth, American Poet

It's the most recognizable building associated with Mormonism. The massive, six-spire Gothic structure is decorated with celestial symbols—the sun, moon, and stars—representing heaven's visit to earth. The structure is adorned with a golden statue of an angel, Moroni, his lips pressed against a long trumpet in one hand, and in the other he grasps metal plates. Moroni is announcing audibly what the building communicates through symbolism: God is here, in the reconciliation of heaven and earth, the temple being a physical representation of this spiritual message. If anyone is left wondering what the building is about, then a very unassuming and mundane feature fills in the blanks. Engraved on the doorknobs is the phrase "Holiness to the Lord," the same message written on the high priest's mitre of ancient Israel (see Exod 28:36). This is the Salt Lake Temple.

For traditional Christians, the word "temple" transports their thoughts not necessarily to a place but to a time, the biblical era of priestly sacrifices and religious feasts. But that time ended long ago when the second temple of Jerusalem was destroyed by Rome in AD 70. Since then, the temple as a place has practically evaporated from the traditional Christian imagination, though its theological significance remains. Temple theology plays a significant role in understanding the nature of God and the purpose of his works. So, when early Latter-day Saints reintroduced temples as physical spaces to worship, non-Mormons scratched their heads. Some dismissed it as delusional, an extravagant

1. Samuel Woodworth, "God in His Temple," in *The Poems, Odes, Sons, and Other Metrical Effusions, of Samuel Woodworth* (New York: Abraham Asten and Matthias Lopez, 1818), 273.

exercise in religious zealotry, a place where Mormons "pretend to have remarkable revelations, work miracles, heal the sick."[2] Others were impressed but perplexed, believing that building temples outside ancient Israel was "contrary to every precept of the divine law."[3] To add to the confusion, Latter-day Saints have built not just one temple in a holy city, as the ancient Jews did. Latter-day Saints have built many temples all over the world, from Tonga to Toronto and everywhere in between. Why, then, does Mormonism have temples?

Temples in Early Mormonism

According to Mormonism, there were at least two prominent Jewish temples in antiquity. The first, of course, was Solomon's temple in Jerusalem, but the Book of Mormon described how ancient Jews built a second temple like the one in the holy city shortly after their arrival to the Americas (see 2 Nephi 5:16). Other temples were constructed, too, and served as places where people gathered to hear preaching (see Jacob 1:17; 2:11; Mosiah 1:18; Alma 16:13) and to commune with the resurrected Christ (see 3 Nephi 11:1, 7–8). Like the NT, the Book of Mormon is uninterested in temples as mechanisms for salvation after Christ's death and resurrection. The temple does, however, feature in some eschatological readings of the scriptural texts and so retains importance as a physical, but future, structure (see Ezek 37:28; Matt 24:15–16; 2 Thess 2:4; cf. 3 Nephi 24:1).[4]

Smith agreed, in part, having taught how building temples in the end times would herald Christ's imminent return, providing the Messiah with "a place to manifest himself to his people."[5] And because the Latter-day Saints were in the *latter days*, it was, perhaps, unsurprising to them when they began to receive divine commands to build temples.[6] But Smith also envisioned temples playing a critical role in the soteriological development of the Church of Jesus Christ of Latter-day Saints, spaces where the Saints would receive "knowledge of God" and retrieve "the power of Godliness."[7] Just as the Book of Mormon materialized the recovery of lost or forgotten "plain and precious truths," so too would temples be spaces in which ancient religious rituals, retrieved by revelation, could be performed. And not just any rituals. What would eventually occur in temples had the power to exalt the individual in knowledge and power and to bind them eternally to an ever-expanding networked community of the living and the dead.

---

2. "The Mormons," May 23, 1836, *Adams Sentinel* 20, no. 30.
3. "Mormonism," April 29, 1835, *New York Weekly Messenger and Young Men's Advocate* 4, no. 41.
4. Charles R. Harrell, *"This Is My Doctrine": The Development of Mormon Theology* (Salt Lake City: Greg Kofford Books, 2011), 310–11.
5. JSJ, March 27, 1836, J1:205.
6. See, for example, JS, revelation, February 9, 1831 [D&C 42:1–72], D1:252; JS, revelation, July 20, 1831 [D&C 57], D2:8.
7. JS, revelation, September 22–23,1832, D2:295 [D&C 84:20].

Smith promised the church that God would one day "endow those whom I have chosen, with power from on high," should they build him a sacred "House" according to divine design.[8] By March 1836, that day had arrived, after Latter-day Saints dedicated their first "House of the Lord" in Kirtland, Ohio. In this temple, members performed sacred ordinances such as washings and anointings, while rendering sacrifices of prayer and song.[9] Those in attendance reported intense charismatic activity, marked by prophecy and tongues in the company of angels.[10] Some even witnessed the Son of God himself "standing upon the breast work of the pulpit before them," according to Smith's journal.[11]

But the Kirtland episode would prove to be "the zenith of the Saints' ecstatic experience" after the church lost ownership of the temple and struggled to build any others during Smith's lifetime, despite being "allways [*sic*] Commanded to build" temples.[12] In the time since, however, the church has built or announced the construction of hundreds of temples on every continent (except Antarctica).

Temple Design and Activity in Mormonism

Temples are inaccessible to non-members, with very few exceptions. Unlike meetinghouses, which welcome visitors, only certain members of the church are permitted entry. Non-members will never know precisely what temples are like, but they are privy to know approximately what occurs through official church sources. As a non-member who has never been a Latter-day Saint, I have not participated in temple ritual. On several occasions I have had the privilege of touring temple spaces. What follows, then, is an amalgam of my very limited experience, official church information, and scholarly perspectives on temple design and activity.

Not all temples are designed the same, but they share the same mission: to provide sacred space for performing ordinances. Typically, the entry point of a temple is practical—an administrative foyer to greet visitors and to verify their temple recommend, which is an ecclesiastical endorsement required for entry. Because temples represent the most sacred spaces in Mormonism, only worthy members may enter. Worthiness is dependent on individual efforts to obey the

8. MRB:339 [D&C 95:8].
9. Richard Bushman, *Joseph Smith and the Beginnings of Mormonism* (Urbana, IL: University of Illinois Press, 1984), 312–13. Joseph Smith introduced temple rituals in various locations prior to the construction of any temples. The Nauvoo temple (1846) briefly served a portion of the LDS community just before their exodus westward, but it would not be until the completion of the Endowment House ten years after Smith's death that Latter-day Saints had a dedicated and long-lasting ritual space; this was before the first temples in Utah were constructed (e.g., St. George [1877], Logan [1884], Manti [1888], and Salt Lake [1893]).
10. See JSJ, March 27, 1836, J1:210–11; March 30, 1836, J1:215–16.
11. JSJ, April 3, 1836, J1:219.
12. Bushman, Joseph Smith: *Rough Stone Rolling*, 319; JS, revelation, January 19, 1841, D7:518 [D&C 124:39].

teachings of the church faithfully and is determined in interviews by officials who certify their temple recommend. Once permitted entry, members may be led to private dressing rooms where they change into special temple clothing to participate in a variety of rituals, like baptism for the dead, eternal sealings, and the endowment, all of which will be discussed in subsequent questions.

These ordinances and phased rituals are performed in different rooms. Baptism for the dead occurs in a baptistry that features a large font atop twelve outward-facing oxen, typically below ground level to simulate the grave.[13] The font design is modeled after the molten sea, a large basin used by ancient Jewish priests to ceremonially cleanse themselves (see 1 Kgs 7:23–25; 2 Chr 4:2–4). Sealings are performed in rooms specifically designated for the rituals. Sealing rooms feature kneeling altars and rows of chairs for witnesses who look on as husbands, wives, and children are sealed as families for time and eternity. The endowment takes place in phased stages. Beginning in the creation room and culminating in the celestial room, Latter-day Saints move through the narrative of LDS soteriology that represents one's ascent to celestial glory.[14] A subsequent ceremony offers participants a second anointing to complement the initiatory invitation of blessings offered in the endowment. This ritual is extremely rare; most Latter-day Saints will never experience it.[15] Having gone through these ordinances once, participants may return to stand in proxy for the deceased, ideally for their ancestors.

While each ordinance is different, a theme of covenantal vows and promises to God tie them all together. As one LDS philosopher explained, "The rites of the temple are the medium through which celebrants are made ready to receive the covenants enmeshed in those rites."[16] In other words, temple ordinances are preliminary, not necessarily conversionary; they are instructive and salvific for members, not initiates. Ordinances, in effect, open the hands of Latter-day Saints to receive exaltation, should they grasp it by keeping the related covenants, and the instruction they receive teaches them how to grasp and keep those covenants. They do so not as individuals but as a community working toward an eternal network of kinship, so that they "may be prepared to join each other hereafter in the celestial kingdom of our God," said Brigham Young.[17]

---

13. Because the ordinance of baptism simulates death and resurrection, JS explained how "the baptismal Font was instituted as a simile of the grave, and was commanded to be in a place underneath where the living are wont to assemble" (JSJ, September 11, 1842, J2:147 [D&C 128:13]).
14. James E. Faulconer, "The Mormon Temple and Mormon Ritual," in *The Oxford Handbook of Mormonism*, ed. Terryl L. Givens and Philip L. Barlow (New York: Oxford University Press, 2015), 197.
15. David John Buerger, *The Mysteries of Godliness: A History of Mormon Temple Worship* (Salt Lake City: Signature Books, 1994), 66–68.
16. Faulconer, "The Mormon Temple and Mormon Ritual," 204–5.
17. Church History Department Pitman Shorthand transcriptions, 2013–2022; Addresses and sermons, 1851–1874; Salt Lake Temple Cornerstone Laying, April 6, 1853; Church

In the end, temple ordinances are designed to channel the priesthood power of God into the lives of faithful Latter-day Saints—whether in life or death, for time and eternity—to forge a network of families that not only mirrors heaven but incorporates Latter-day Saints into it.[18]

Traditional Christianity and the Temple

If temples are so important to Mormonism, why does traditional Christianity lack them? The question is a bit misleading. Although there are no physical temples in Christianity, nevertheless, the faith depends on a robust temple theology. The temple of Jerusalem dominated the landscape of Israel's ancient capital. It was the nation's most sacred space, God's holy dwelling place, but not because he literally lived there. After all, the "heavens cannot contain him" (2 Chr 2:6), let alone a building. Instead, Israel believed the temple was an intersecting space of heaven and earth, which described God in three primary ways.

First, God *reigned* over Israel. Biblical scholars have noticed how the temple was designed in a way that parallels the Genesis creation accounts. Just as God created the cosmos in six days, so God commanded the tabernacle's construction in six phases.[19] God's creation is also a work of successive separations (e.g., light from dark, land from sea), just as the tabernacle separated people from priests and priests from the high priest as the distance between God and man narrowed. And as God rested on the seventh day of creation, so too was Israel commanded to rest on the seventh day after building the tabernacle (see Exod 31:6–17). After God saw his creation, he blessed it (see Gen 2:1–3), just like Moses saw and blessed the completed tabernacle (see Exod 39:43).[20] The implications are subtle but clear. As the God reigns over the whole cosmos, so too does he reign over all of Israel.

Second, God *resided* with Israel. Biblical scholars have long noticed the parallels of imagery and function between the tabernacle (and later the temple) and the garden of Eden.[21] Both were spaces set apart from the rest of the world for a special purpose, fitted with precious material, like gold and onyx (see Gen 2:12; Exod 28:15–20), and furnished with menorahs that evoke the tree of life. And the tabernacle was the center point of sacred presence and

---

History Library. https://catalog.churchofjesuschrist.org/assets/3f96d062-17b7-4fd0-8e7f-79eae78cc26b/0/0?lang=eng

18. See Jonathan A. Stapley, *The Power of Godliness: Mormon Liturgy and Cosmology* (New York: Oxford University Press, 2018)
19. William P. Brown, *The Seven Pillars of Creation: The Bible, Science, and the Ecology of Wonder* (New York: Oxford University Press, 2010), 33–41.
20. Carol Meyers, *Exodus* (Cambridge: Cambridge University Press, 2005), 282.
21. Donald W. Parry, "Garden of Eden: Prototype Sanctuary," in *Temples of the Ancient World: Ritual and Symbolism*, ed. Donald W. Parry (Salt Lake City: Deseret, 1994), 126–51; G. K. Beale, *The Temple and the Church's Mission: A Biblical Theology of the Dwelling Place of God*, New Studies in Biblical Theology 15 (Downers Grove: IVP Academic, 2004), 66–80.

activity. Just as God walked about (Heb. *hālak*) the garden in the cool of the day (see Gen 3:8), so too did God "walketh" (Heb. *hālak*) among his people because of the tabernacle (see Deut 23:14; see also Lev 26:11–12). It was a holy place, and to approach God's presence required holiness, a work that fell uniquely to Aaron and his descendants. God placed Adam in the garden "to dress it and to keep it" (Gen 2:15). These terms (Heb. *ʿāvad* and *shamar*) are significant, as they are later used to describe the work of priests in serving and guarding the tabernacle (see Num 3:7–8; 18:5).

Third, God *redeemed* Israel. The tabernacle was not merely symbolic. It served a practical function as well. The sins of Israel were reconciled to the holiness of God through a system of feasts, pilgrimages, and sacrifices. Israel sacrificed various offerings, like grain and animals, for forgiveness and peace with God. The holiest of these events was the annual Yom Kippur, or Day of Atonement, in which the high priest alone entered the most holy place to offer the atoning sacrifice for the sins of Israel (see Lev 16:1–27).

But Israel struggled to maintain the vision of temple life that God set out before them. Prior to the NT period, John the Baptist believed that the temple system had become irredeemably corrupt. It was then that Jesus Christ stepped forward to reveal himself as the one to whom the temple pointed. Jesus reigned not only over Israel but the whole world (see Eph 1:22–23; Phil 2:9–11; Rev 17:14). And like the temple—the space where God resided with his people—in the incarnation the Son of God "took upon him the form of a servant, and was made in the likeness of men" (Phil 2:7) as the Word of God "was made flesh, and dwelt among us" (John 1:14). Yet, unlike us, Christ was holy, completely without sin (see Heb 4:15). Most evident to the earliest Christians, then, was Christ's work of redemption, the sacrificial lamb who "was manifested to take away our sins" (1 John 3:5).

Jesus thus radically altered the Christian understanding of the temple. Jesus is the greater temple, the one to whom Israel's temple pointed (see John 2:21). And because his saints "are the body of Christ, and members in particular" (1 Cor 12:27), the church now stands as God's dwelling place on earth. The temple is no longer a building but a people. Collectively, the church is "a holy temple in the Lord" (Eph 2:21, ESV), and individually, each believer is a temple of the Holy Spirit (see 1 Cor 6:19). The shift is not from one temple to many, but from stone and shadow to Spirit and substance. That was the point all along. The temple was "symbolically designed to point to the cosmic eschatological reality that God's tabernacling presence, formerly limited to the holy of holies, was to be extended throughout the whole earth."[22] In other words, the Son of God reigns over a new kingdom, a society of "temples" (or disciples) redeemed by him and indwelled with the Holy Spirit (see 1 Cor 3:16; 6:19; Eph 2:19–22). They are the "lively stones" with whom God "built up a

22. Beale, *Temple*, 25.

spiritual house" (1 Pet 2:5), because in the end "the tabernacle of God is with men, and he will dwell with them" (Rev 21:3). As the Baptist preacher Charles Octavius Boothe exclaimed, "What a glorious work that building, that house of God, that temple, that church will be when finished!"[23]

Early Christians did not see themselves "as being merely *like* the temple of God or as supplanting the temple altogether."[24] Rather, they were convinced "that the heavenly temple had begun to break into history through the resurrection of Jesus Christ."[25] Jesus's message, the gospel, invites us to receive all that the temple represents: God's reign, residence, and redemption in the person and work of the Lord Jesus Christ by the power of the Holy Spirit.

Summary

Temples are central to Latter-day Saint worship. They provide Latter-day Saints the necessary sacred space to perform rituals that bind them together across space and time with an ever-growing familial network of heaven. These rituals include the endowment, baptisms, and sealings, for both the living and the dead. Traditional Christianity has long believed in the importance of temple theology but not the necessity of building temples. The temple was always meant to point toward Jesus Christ, the incarnation of God who reigns over all creation, resides with his people, and redeems the world.

REFLECTION QUESTIONS

1. What comes to mind when you think about temples?

2. Having briefly learned about the function of temples in Mormonism, how important do you think these spaces are for Latter-day Saints?

3. What role did the temple play in ancient Israel, and how does that inform your understanding of temples?

4. Do you agree or disagree that temples are meant to point people to Jesus Christ, specifically to recognize his reign over creation, residence with his people, and redemption of the world? Why or why not?

5. What are the similarities and dissimilarities between Latter-day Saint and traditional Christian temple theologies?

---

23. Charles Octavius Boothe, *Plain Theology for Plain People* (Bellingham, WA: Lexham Press, 2017), 81.
24. Nicholas Perrin, *Jesus the Temple* (Grand Rapids: Baker Academic, 2010), 75.
25. Perrin, *Jesus the Temple*, 75.

QUESTION 34

What Is the Temple Endowment?

"You need an endowment, brethren, in order that you may be prepared and able to overcome all things."[1]
~ Joseph Smith

The temple endowment is the central ritual of Latter-day Saint temple worship, the pinnacle ordinance in which "the power of Godliness is manifest," said Joseph Smith.[2] Without such ordinances, "no man can see the face of God."[3] As Brigham Young taught, the endowment offers participants the ability "to walk back to the presence of the Father," to return to our celestial home.[4] Due to its sacred nature, participation is restricted to worthy members of the Church of Jesus Christ of Latter-day Saints and is seldom spoken about in public. The endowment is a lesson and a gift, a mortal waypoint on the path toward immortal exaltation. For Latter-day Saints, it teaches the "purpose of Creation and our life on earth and the role of Christ in bringing us back home again."[5]

For traditional Christians, the endowment is a puzzling conundrum. Cloaked in mystery and considered a private matter for Latter-day Saints, investigating it is both difficult and feels off-limits. At the same time, the ceremony is very important to the LDS faith, so any attempt to understand Mormonism by glossing over it feels limiting. For this reason, it's natural to ask: What is the temple endowment?

Given the private nature of the ceremony, the scope of this question is restricted to public sources and scholarly reflections of its origin, purpose, and

1. JS, 1834–1836 history, H1:122.
2. JS, revelation, September 22–23, 1832, D2:295 [D&C 84:20].
3. JS, revelation, September 22–23, 1832, D2:295 [D&C 84:22].
4. *CDBY* 2:646.
5. Jennifer C. Lane, *Let's Talk About Temple and Ritual* (Salt Lake City: Deseret, 2023), 22.

practices. Some people may find public discussion of the endowment inappropriate, especially from a traditional Christian perspective, given its sacred nature and vows of secrecy. I recognize and respect this concern, so I have taken cues from the church's transparency about the endowment's purpose and practice, limiting myself to details that have been made public or alluded to in church publications.

What Is the Temple Endowment?

The temple endowment is viewed by Latter-day Saints as a divine gift to worthy initiates who enter a temple to receive instructions on growing closer to God. The ceremony is sacred and secret, a gateway to special knowledge for the initiated and safeguarded from the uninitiated. Its symbolism draws primarily from biblical narrative and practices, especially OT priestly activity as interpreted by church leaders.

Participants begin with the initiatory ceremony, or preparation to receive sacred knowledge. In this rite, participants experience ritual washing, anointing, being clothed, and receiving a new name. Latter-day Saints view their ceremonial washing and oil anointing as emulating high priestly activity (see Exod 29:5). A primary point of the endowment is to set apart people as priests and priestesses who form "a royal priesthood, an holy nation" (1 Pet 2:9), and the initiatory ceremony prepares participants for this setting apart. Initiates wear temple garments, or garments of the holy priesthood—which they are obligated to wear always, even outside the temple—as a reminder of ritual experiences inside the temple. The garments are considered sacred and are kept private, as is the initiate's new name, which they promise never to reveal nor forget.

After the initiatory ceremony, participants join an assembly to receive instructions through dramatized video and temple officiators. The group is taught the redemptive metanarrative of LDS soteriology—creation, fall, atonement, apostasy, and restoration—and arcane key words, signs, and tokens that unlock and secure spiritual knowledge and power. These signs and tokens enable a person's ability to discern spiritual truth from lies. They are so important that Smith once remarked, "No one can truly say he knows God until he has handled something [i.e., spiritual signs], & this can only be in the holiest of Holies," or the temple.[6] Thus, the endowment symbolizes one's passage from mortality to immortality and imparts the knowledge required to reach celestial glory, even God himself.

Latter-day Saints are also invited to make covenants with God in five areas of life: obedience, sacrifice, the gospel, chastity, and consecration. These covenants bind Latter-day Saints to God's commands by sacrificing their desires, repenting daily and obeying Christ's teachings, refraining from sexual

---

6. JSJ, May 1, 1842, J2:53.

immorality, and dedicating their time, talent, and treasure to the church. By keeping these covenants, Latter-day Saints demonstrate their faithfulness to God and are promised that they will become kings and queens in eternity. Thus, the endowment is instructive and salvific, a required rite for gaining exaltation, conditioned on one's worthiness by making and keeping covenants with God.

Where Did the Temple Endowment Ceremony Come From?

The temple endowment has developed over years of revelations and alterations. Interestingly, there is no trace of it in the first days of Mormonism. The Bible offers no instructions for the ritual, and the Gospels are especially silent; Christ never prompted his followers toward the endowment. His concern was chiefly the ordinances of baptism (see Matt 28:19–20; Mark 16:15–16) and the Lord's Supper (see Mark 14:22–25; Luke 22:18–20). The Book of Mormon is also relatively silent on the matter, as were Joseph Smith's earliest revelations. He hinted that temple rituals would develop over time as the church marched progressively toward "great things" and "greater blessings," which he considered necessary "to make the foundation of this church complete, and permanent."[7] This march began in 1835 after Smith introduced the earliest iteration of temple ritual at the first temple in Kirtland, Ohio.[8] It was a simple foot-washing ceremony that drew on biblical washings, like the ceremonial cleansing of Aaron, the high priest (see Exod 30:17–21), and Christ's command to "love one another" (John 13:34), which he demonstrated by humbly washing their feet (John 13:14–17).

Nothing like the temple endowment today took place until 1842, twelve years after the church was founded. In May of that year Smith gathered a small group of select men in a room above his mercantile store in Nauvoo because the temple was still under construction.[9] Smith presided over the first endowment ceremony, a more elaborate ritual than the one performed in Kirtland. He "instruct[ed] them in the principles and order of the priesthood, attending to washings, anointings, endowments and the communication of Keys," Smith recorded.[10] This ceremony was private, and its participants were sworn to secrecy, and for good reason. Smith believed it was a sign of the end times, a harbinger of Christ's imminent return, and it was apparently reserved for only a privileged few. "In this Council was instituted the ancient order of things for the first time in these last days,"[11] he elaborated, days "in which the God of heaven has begun to restore the ancient order of his Kingdom."[12]

---

7. JS, 1834–1836 history, H1:121.
8. Richard Bushman, *Joseph Smith and the Beginnings of Mormonism* (Urbana, IL: University of Illinois Press, 1984), 213–14.
9. Bushman, *Joseph Smith*, 448–49.
10. Joseph Smith, History, 1838–1856, vol. C-1, *JSP*, 1328.
11. Joseph Smith, History, 1838–1856, vol. C-1, *JSP*, 1328.
12. JSJ, January 6, 1842, J2:26 (emend.).

Brigham Young, who participated in the ritual, reportedly described the scene in greater detail:

> We were washed and anointed had our garments placed upon us and received our New Name. and after he [Joseph Smith] had performed these ceremonies. he gave the Key Words signs, togkens [*sic*] and penalties. then after we went into the large room over the store in Nauvoo. Joseph divided up the room the best that he could hung up the veil, marked it gave us our instructions as we passed along from one department to another giving us signs. tokens. penalties with the Key words pertaining to those signs.[13]

Smith thought that such sacred ordinances demanded "a proper place to communicate them," so it was imperative to finish the Nauvoo temple for the Saints to receive their endowment and sealings.[14] He was murdered before seeing it completed. But when Brigham Young took the church's reins, he directed the Saints to continue building despite plans to abandon the city and migrate westward (see question 9). The temple neared completion in the winter of 1845–46 when Latter-day Saints received their endowments by the thousands. Not only were they promised to be blessed with spiritual power and authority, but the Saints "also saw it as a promise of physical safety and health during the pending trial of the exodus."[15] The endowment was a "spiritual magnet" that drew in over five thousand men and women before trekking to Utah.[16] After resettling there, it took three decades for the Saints to build another temple, so the endowment was practiced in smaller meeting spaces. By the close of the nineteenth century, Latter-day Saints in Utah received endowments in the temples of St. George (1877), Logan (1884), Manti (1888), and Salt Lake City (1893).

The ceremony has evolved over time. Early versions included the Law of Retribution, an oath of vengeance for Joseph Smith's death. The oath fell under public scrutiny during the Reed Smoot hearings between 1904 and 1907 as many Latter-day Saints grew uncomfortable with it, too.[17] In 1924,

13. *Diary of L. John Nuttall (1834–1905): Dec. 1876—Mar. 1884* (Provo, UT: Brigham Young University Press, 1948), 18.
14. Joseph Smith, History, 1838–1856, vol. C-1, *JSP*, 1328.
15. Richard E. Bennett, "'The Upper Room': The Nature and Development of Latter-day Saint Temple Work, 1846–55," in *The Ancient Order of Things: Essays on the Mormon Temple*, ed. Christian Larsen (Salt Lake City: Signature Books, 2019), 110.
16. Bennett, "'The Upper Room,'" 110.
17. Michael Harold Paulos and Konden Smith Hansen, eds., *The Reed Smoot Hearings: The Investigation of a Mormon Senator and the Transformation of an American Religion* (Logan, UT: Utah State University Press, 2021), 143.

one church leader criticized the oath as "harsh,"[18] and three years later, LDS president Heber J. Grant jettisoned "all references to avenging the blood of the Prophets."[19] Another change came in 1990 after the removal of a disparaging portrayal of traditional Christian ministers. The ceremony implied that clergy preach under the financial influence of Satan, inferring that pastors and priests are deceived at best or, at worst, willfully deceive people for worldly gain, or "priestcraft" (see 2 Nephi 26:29). More recent changes have apparently made the ceremony more transparent and inclusive.[20]

Is the Temple Endowment Ceremony Related to Freemasonry?

When Brigham Young reported how the early endowment included "signs. tokens. [and] penalties with the Key words," he used terms commonly associated with Masonic ritual.[21] Readers may understandably wonder if a connection exists between Freemasonry and the temple endowment.

Freemasonry is a fraternal society that promotes its morality and spirituality through symbolic rituals and allegorical teachings.[22] The organization emerged from medieval European stonemason guilds and gradually formalized by the early seventeenth century. Freemasonry appealed to many men in the early American republic, and some wondered whether it complemented their Christian faith, "not simply as representing universal moral principles but as a unique order that fulfilled the purposes and proclaimed the truths of Christianity."[23] But the fraternity sailed into dire straits during the anti-Masonic Movement, which peaked around the 1830s. The Book of Mormon reflects the anti-Masonic sentiment of this period, especially with its strong rejection of "secret combinations," or secret societies (see 2 Nephi 26:22; Ether 8:15, 25; Helaman 6:22–24). By the early 1840s, however, Freemasonry was viewed with less suspicion, just about the time Joseph Smith introduced the endowment ceremony in May 1842. In fact, the first endowment took place in the same room "where the Masonic fraternity met occasionally," he said.[24]

---

18. Devery S. Anderson, ed., *The Development of LDS Temple Worship: 1846–2000* (Salt Lake City: Signature Books, 2011), 210.
19. Anderson, *The Development of LDS Temple Worship*, 218.
20. Jana Riess, "More Jesus, Less Touching: 14 Changes to the Mormon Temple Endowment Ceremony," Religion News Service, February 10, 2023, https://religionnews.com/2023/02/10/more-jesus-less-touching-14-changes-to-the-mormon-temple-endowment-ceremony/.
21. *Diary of L. John Nuttall (1834–1905): Dec. 1876—Mar. 1884* (Provo, UT: Brigham Young University Press, 1948), 18.
22. See Andreas Önnerfors, *Freemasonry: A Very Short Introduction* (New York: Oxford University Press, 2017).
23. Steven C. Bullock, *Revolutionary Brotherhood: Freemasonry and the Transformation of the American Social Order, 1730–1840* (Chapel Hill, NC: University of North Carolina Press, 1996), 163.
24. Joseph Smith, History, 1838–1856, vol. C-1, *JSP*, 1328.

Smith was a member of the Nauvoo Masonic Lodge, a Master Mason of the third degree. To gain the title, he would have donned an apron embroidered with esoteric symbols and been "given signs, due-grips, due-guards, words, pass-words, and obligations of secrecy," explained one historian.[25] Smith also learned the significance of the five points of fellowship, a bodily embrace that discreetly confirmed one's standing within the organization. The symbols were framed in an allegorical narrative that represented the transition from mortality into the spiritual world. These features were also present in the early endowment, which Smith had introduced less than two months after becoming a Master Mason.[26]

The similarities and timing are too convenient for skeptics. Smith apparently found the Masonic ceremony so captivating that he appropriated it into the endowment. And the connections were not lost on Masonic Mormons. After the endowment, one participant couldn't help but notice the "similarity of priesthood in masonry" but failed to see any conflict between the two.[27] The similarities were intentional. Smith explained how "Masonry was taken from [the] priesthood but ha[d] become degenerated."[28] In Smith's view, Masonry was a distorted remnant of ancient temple practices. He also reportedly believed that the Masonic ceremony "was the apostate endowments, as sectarian religion was the apostate religion."[29] In other words, Smith viewed Freemasonry the same way he did the Christian church, as a broken vessel in need of restoration. Smith believed he was rehabilitating Freemasonry, not appropriating it. Mormonism transformed Freemasonry, not the other way around. Thus, it is impossible to explain the endowment as "wholesale borrowing" of Masonic ritual, but "neither can it be dismissed as completely unrelated."[30]

Reflections on the Endowment Oaths and Covenants

For traditional Christians, the endowment ceremony is cryptically peculiar. There are no equivalent rites or rituals outside Mormonism. Perhaps this rift

25. Michael W. Homer, *Joseph's Temples: The Dynamic Relationship Between Freemasonry and Mormonism* (Salt Lake City: University of Utah Press, 2014), 150.
26. Smith gained the degree of Master Mason on March 16, 1842, and presided over the endowment ceremony on May 4, 1842. See Minutes, March 15–16, 1842, D9:275; JS, May 4, 1842, J2:53–54.
27. Devery S. Anderson and Gary J. Bergera, *Jospeh Smith's Quorum of the Anointed, 1842–1845: A Documentary History* (Salt Lake City: Signature Books, 2005), 9 (original spelling corrected).
28. Anderson and Bergera, *Quorum of the Anointed*, 9.
29. Benjamin F. Johnson, *My Life's Review: Autobiography of Benjamin Franklin Johnson* (Provo, UT: Grandin, 1997), 85.
30. David John Buerger, *The Mysteries of Godliness: A History of Mormon Temple Worship* (Salt Lake City: Signature Books, 1994),56. For more on the connection between Freemasonry and Mormonism, see also Jeffrey M. Bradshaw, "Freemasonry and the Origins of Modern Temple Ordinances," *Interpreter* 15 (2015): 159–237; and Cheryl L. Bruno, Joe Steve Swick III, and Nicholas S. Literski, *Method Infinite: Freemasonry and the Mormon Restoration* (Salt Lake City: Greg Kofford Books, 2022).

exposes differences in orthodox and Latter-day Saint perspectives on covenants and sanctification or the process of becoming holy. As one LDS scholar explained, covenants made in the temple enable worthy members to advance along their journey of sanctification. "By keeping our covenants," she said, "we are allowing Christ to save us. He will sanctify us as we abide in Him and His law."[31] She further elaborated how "Christ wants to be connected to us, and we choose to keep that connection alive through our covenant faithfulness."[32]

But when it comes to our redemption, where does the greater emphasis lie: in the promises we make to God, or in the promises God makes to us? The Bible is filled with broken promises to God. When God gave the law to ancient Israel, they promised him "all that the LORD hath spoken we will do" (Exod 19:8) before betraying him by worshiping a golden calf (see Exod 32:1–6). And after Peter swore to Jesus, "I will not deny you," (Matt 26:35 ESV), he denied Christ three times, just as the Savior had predicted (see Matt 26:34, 69–75).[33] Even something like the law of chastity is impossible to keep considering the Sermon on the Mount. "Ye have heard that it was said by them of old time, Thou shalt not commit adultery" (Matt 5:27), said Jesus, reinforcing the good command to remain faithful only to one's lawful spouse. But he cautioned that the mere act of lust is tantamount to adultery in the heart (see Matt 5:28). How often have commitments to the law of chastity been broken by the temptations of private lust? Each covenant promise we make with God establishes a new law for ourselves—one that God will hold us accountable to. Since we are imperfect, we will inevitably fail to obey these laws, thereby meriting nothing less than death itself (see 1 Cor 15:56). No wonder Paul cautioned against such law-based, spiritual self-improvement. Not only is it impossible to be sanctified by making and keeping covenants with God, but it nullifies the gospel's power, "for if righteousness could be gained through the law, Christ died for nothing" (Gal 2:21, NIV).

The only covenants we make with God are the ones we break. But praise God that the only covenants he makes with us are those he keeps, for it is "impossible for God to lie" (Heb 6:18), and "no matter how many promises God has made, they are 'Yes' in Christ" (2 Cor 1:20, NIV). The beginning of our redemption is not found in our promises to God but in his promises to himself for us. All people, traditional Christians and Latter-day Saints alike, must tune their ear to hear the sweet "I will" promises of Jesus. "I will in no wise cast out" those who come to me (John 6:37). "I will confess also before my Father which is in heaven" (Matt 10:32) whomever confesses Christ on earth. "I will not leave you comfortless," for those whose hearts hurt (John

---

31. Lane, *Let's Talk About Temple and Ritual*, 90–91.
32. Lane, *Let's Talk About Temple and Ritual*, 91.
33. Some Latter-day Saints have framed Peter's denial as the result of Christ's command rather than a failure of courage. This perspective is not the prevailing view, as the Gospel accounts of Peter's profound remorse and his specific restoration by Jesus (John 21:15–17) strongly support the traditional understanding of a prophesied human weakness followed by repentance.

14:18). "I will raise him up at the last day" (John 6:40) for those who place their trust not in their own faithfulness to Christ but in Christ's faithfulness to God alone (see Phil 3:9).

Summary

The temple endowment is considered a necessary step toward salvation and the Latter-day Saint's journey toward celestial glory. It is both sacred and secret, taking place exclusively in temples and kept private from outsiders. The ceremony is initiatory and instructional, guiding the participant through an allegorical journey of salvation, from mortality to immortality. Participants make covenants with God, vowing to remain faithful to their promises as they retain personal worthiness to enter his presence. Traditional Christians, however, emphasize the importance of God's covenants for us—rather than our covenants to him—all of which find their "Yes" in Christ and are made effective to the believer by faith in his righteousness.

REFLECTION QUESTIONS

1. Does your faith tradition have an equivalent to the temple endowment? Why or why not?

2. The temple endowment has evolved since it was first introduced in 1842. What factors do you suppose led to those changes, and how has it affected the ceremony itself?

3. The endowment is rich with symbolism. What role do symbols play in your faith (if any), and how can understanding Mormon symbolism help you to understand their beliefs?

4. How do the similarities between Masonic ritual and the temple endowment inform our understanding of the historical and religious context in which Mormonism emerged?

5. Do you agree or disagree that the only covenants we make with God are the ones we break? Why or why not?

QUESTION 35

Why Do Latter-day Saints Baptize for the Dead?

"There is baptism for those who are alive, and baptism for the dead, all who died without the knowledge of the gospel."[1]
~ Joseph Smith

Jane Harper Neyman pinched her nose and clutched the elder's arms as he dipped her beneath the surface of the Mississippi River in September 1840.[2] It wasn't her first baptism, but it wasn't for her anyway. She restirred the waters on behalf of her son, who had died before having the chance to receive an ordinance so important to Latter-day Saints that entry into celestial glory is prohibited without it. How, exactly, Neyman's vicarious work would reach her son in the afterlife was then a mystery, but that was of little concern to her. A month earlier, her prophet, Joseph Smith, had promised that living members could be baptized on behalf of those closest to them "who had departed this life."[3] Should the departed choose to receive baptism in the hereafter, they would be saved not only to themselves but into an eternal family. Neyman wouldn't just see her son again in heaven. They would be rejoined in familial kinship forever.

As the elder pulled Neyman up out of the water, she became the first known Latter-day Saint to be baptized on behalf of the dead. She was certainly not the last. Today, members of the Church of Jesus Christ of Latter-day Saints

---

1. JS, discourse, May 12, 1844, 14:483 (emend.).
2. See Johnny Stephenson and H. Michael Marquardt, "Origin of the Baptism for the Dead Doctrine," *John Whitmer Historical Association Journal* 37, no. 1 (2017): 132–446.
3. Andrew F. Ehat and Lyndon W. Cook, eds., *The Words of Joseph Smith* (Provo, UT: RSC, BYU, 1980), 49.

perform proxy baptisms for many deceased men, women, and children from around the globe. So why, exactly, do Latter-day Saints baptize for the dead?[4]

The Development of Proxy Baptism in LDS Thought and Practice

Neyman wasn't alone in losing a loved one who she wished to see again one day. Joseph Smith was seventeen in 1823 when his beloved older brother, Alvin, died unexpectedly. Nearly two decades later, Joseph still recalled the "pangs of sorrow that swelled my youthful bosom and almost burst my tender heart, when he died."[5] His grief was apparently compounded by a minister who opined that Alvin was suffering in hell for belonging to the wrong church.[6] But the early 1820s marked the dawn of Joseph's restoration movement, and with it, new answers to old questions. What is the fate of the dead who never had a chance to hear the gospel? This question arose among European Christians who encountered indigenous people in the New World. Clearly, the latter could not have heard the gospel in the many centuries following Christ's resurrection. How could they? There were no Christians west of Greenland prior to the Age of Discovery.

But if "faith cometh by hearing, and hearing by the word of God" (Rom 10:17), then why would a just God allow entire ethnicities to be devoid of the gospel for so many generations? The Book of Mormon answered this question, in part, at least for indigenous people. The Native Americans—Christ's "other sheep," according to the Book of Mormon (3 Nephi 15:21; cf. John 10:16)—had, in fact, heard the gospel, but had largely rejected it and, like their ancient kin across the globe, had sunk into apostasy. But what about people like Alvin who heard the gospel but died prior to its "restoration"? We might call them the *mis*evangelized, from Smith's perspective. What was the fate of those trapped in sectarianism absent of the kind of salvific ordinances that could secure celestial glory? The Book of Mormon answered the question about the fate of the unevangelized across the globe. Now, Smith would answer the question about the fate of the misevangelized across time.

---

4. This question deals solely with postmortem salvation and baptism as a rite for the dead. For the LDS theology of baptism, see question 29.
5. JS, reflections, August 16–23, 1842, D10:423.
6. William Smith, Joseph's younger brother, reported that the minister presiding over Alvin's funeral "intimated very strongly that he had gone to hell, for Alvin was not a church member" sixty years after the fact ("Another Testimony," *Deseret Evening News*, January 20, 1894; originally printed in *Zion's Ensign*). Contemporary evidence, however, is lacking. Lucy Mack Smith never mentioned such a condemnation, and historical records show Rev. Benjamin Stockton was not yet pastor in Palmyra at the time of Alvin's funeral, making William's late recollection questionable. It is more likely that the family's memory condensed later Calvinist teachings into a symbolic narrative of Alvin's exclusion, shaped by grief and theological tension rather than a single funeral sermon.

Smith's answer began to take form in 1836 after he reported a visionary experience in which he "beheld the celestial kingdom of God."[7] The imagery was striking; an overwhelming "transcendent beauty" and "blasing throne of God" arrested Joseph's attention as he saw something completely unexpected. Alvin was there, in full celestial glory. Joseph "marveled how it was that he had obtained an inheritance in that kingdom."[8] After all, his brother died six years before the LDS Church organized and before all the restored authority and rites Joseph taught were necessary for salvation. How could Alvin be in God's presence without having received the latter-day gospel? God himself answered the question in the vision: "All who have died without a knowledge of this gospel, who would have received it, if they had been permitted to tarry, shall be heirs of the celestial kingdom of God."[9]

This moment marked a doctrinal pivot in Smith's view of salvation. He now denied "that the destiny of man is irretrievably fixed at his death" but wondered how one's eternal destiny might be altered if eternal destinations depend on hearing the gospel and responding through rites and ordinances in this life.[10] Protestants in Smith's day generally rejected the possibility of a second chance or purgatorial state in the afterlife, grounding their belief in the plain reading of Hebrews 9:27, that "it is appointed unto men once to die, but after this the judgment." In the absence of an explicit teaching on postmortem conversion in the Bible, this interpretation is most popular among traditional Christians today.[11] The Book of Mormon, too, appears to leave little room for postmortem salvation, teaching that the days of our lives offer us a chance to "repent while in the flesh" (2 Nephi 2:21) since afterward we are consigned either to "paradise" (Alma 40:12) or "outer darkness," a hellish state where "there shall be weeping and wailing, and gnashing of teeth" (Alma 40:13; cf. Matt 22:13).[12] But Smith thought "there are sins which may be forgiven in the world to come," evidenced by Christ's descent into death to preach to the spirits in prison and "bring them out of the prison house" (see 1 Pet 3:18–20;

---

7. JS, revelation, January 21, 1836, D5:158 [D&C 137:1].
8. JS, revelation, January 21, 1836, D5:159 [D&C 137:6] (emend.).
9. JS, revelation, January 21, 1836, D5:159 [D&C 137:6] (emend.).
10. JS, "Baptism for the Dead," *T&S*, April 15, 1842, 3:759.
11. A notable exception is James Beilby's reading that the verse serves to "reinforce the idea that death only occurs once" rather than excluding a postmortem opportunity for salvation. "[If] this text is an argument against any particular position or belief," he clarified, "it is reincarnation" (*Postmortem Opportunity: A Biblical and Theological Assessment of Salvation After Death* [Downers Grove: IVP Academic, 2021], 109).
12. Charles R. Harrell highlights this point. He thought it odd that the Book of Mormon omits Christ's introduction of salvation for the dead "during [Christ's] visit to the Nephites—even though, according to LDS doctrine, he had just visited the spirits in prison and opened the door for their salvation." Harrell concluded that "the whole notion of vicarious work for the dead seems incongruous with Book of Mormon theology" (*"This Is My Doctrine": The Development of Mormon Theology* [Salt Lake City: Greg Kofford Books, 2011], 361).

4:6).[13] The unevangelized and misevangelized would, in fact, have the opportunity to hear the "restored gospel" in the afterlife. Salvation awaited them, should they choose to accept it. But what about baptism?

Smith taught that baptism by a proper priesthood authority was necessary for entry into celestial glory.[14] It's one thing to offer the gospel message to postmortem souls, but how can the dead be baptized to secure their positive reception of God's invitation? They can't, of course. Dead bodies cannot be baptized. By 1840, however, Smith introduced the solution.[15] He cited 1 Corinthians 15:29, in which the apostle Paul wondered rhetorically, "Else what shall they do which are baptized for the dead, if the dead rise not at all? why are they then baptized for the dead?" Smith explained how Paul "was talking to a people who understood baptism for the dead, for it was practiced among them."[16] And because the "doctrine of baptism for the dead is clearly shown in the New Testament," Smith reasoned, the practice must be good. Otherwise, if it "is not good then throw away the New Testament," he said rather bluntly.[17] No wonder Smith invited people to proxy baptisms "to save all who were willing to obey the requirements of the law of God," one of which is baptism.[18] Jane Harper Neyman was the first to take him up, and later Smith clarified this new practice in a letter to his apostles. "The saints," he explained, "have the privilege of being baptized for those of their relatives who are dead, who they feel to believe would have embraced the gospel if they had been privileged with hearing it," particularly those who receive the gospel in the afterlife.[19] In doing so, Latter-day Saints could expand their eternal kinship network and participate, in some mysterious way, as secondary "saviors" of Christ for the dead.[20] So important is this connection that Smith tied the dead's salvation to the living (see D&C 128:15).

---

13. Joseph Smith, "Baptism for the Dead," *T&S*, April 15, 1842, 3:760 (emend.). Relatedly, for an evangelical assessment of Christ's descent into Hades, see Matthew Y. Emerson, *"He Descended to the Dead": An Evangelical Theology of Holy Saturday* (Downers Grove: IVP Academic, 2019).
14. Joseph Smith cited John 3:5 as evidence for his position: "Except a man be born of water and of the Spirit, he cannot enter into the kingdom of God" (JS, "Baptism for the Dead," 3:761).
15. See JS to Quorum of the Twelve, December 15, 1840, D7:469–70.
16. Ehat and Cook, *The Words of Joseph Smith*, 49.
17. JS, discourse, June 11, 1843, D12:386 (emend.).
18. Ehat and Cook, *The Words of Joseph Smith*, 49.
19. JS to Quorum of the Twelve, December 15, 1840, D7:470 (emend.). Elsewhere, JS taught that "those who are baptized for their dead are the Saviours on mount Zion" (JS, discourse, May 12, 1844, reported by George Laub, *JSP*).
20. See Samuel M. Brown, "Early Mormon Adoption Theology and the Mechanics of Salvation," *Journal of Mormon History* 37, no. 3 (2011): 3–52; Ryan G. Tobler, "'Saviors on Mount Zion': Mormon Sacramentalism, Mortality, and the Baptism for the Dead," *Journal of Mormon History* 39, no. 4 (2013): 182–238.

Today, the rite is performed exclusively in temple baptismal fonts supported by a host of genealogists whose research identifies deceased candidates for baptism. With each vicarious baptism performed, Latter-day Saints believe another person is offered the chance to join their kin in an ever-expanding community across dispensations of redemptive history.

Postmortem and Vicarious Salvation in Christianity

While Mormonism finds vicarious baptism critical to salvation, traditional Christians reject the practice. Why? In the absence of direct biblical teaching, most traditional Christians do not believe an opportunity exists beyond the grave to alter one's eternal destiny.[21] While the Bible speaks vaguely about an intermediary state prior to judgment (see, e.g., 1 Cor 3:10–15), it never suggests that one's destiny can change after death. Instead, the Bible assumes the finality of one's destination after divine judgment (see Matt 25:31–46). Even the Roman Catholic doctrine of purgatory contends for an intermediary space reserved to purify those who "die in God's grace and friendship," not as an intermediate state capable of altering one's eternal trajectory.[22] What, then, becomes of those who never hear the gospel?

Theologians have traditionally proposed three possibilities for the fate of the unevangelized, each with its own nuanced subcategories. These three categories are particularism, inclusivism, and pluralism.[23] Particularism maintains saving faith in Jesus Christ is only available by hearing and responding to the gospel.[24] Inclusivism sees saving faith possible through revelatory means given by God through myriad ways, but is ultimately secured through Christ's atonement.[25] Pluralism believes God honors alternative religious

---

21. For notable exceptions, see Gabriel Fackre, "Divine Perseverance," in *What About Those Who Have Never Heard?*, ed. John Sanders (Downers Grove,: IVP Academic, 1995); Jerry L. Walls's "modified orthodox view" in *Hell: The Logic of Damnation* (Notre Dame, IN: University of Notre Dame Press, 1992), 54, 91–93; and Beilby, *Postmortem Opportunity*.
22. *CCC*, 1030. See Paul O'Callaghan, *Christ Our Hope: An Introduction to Eschatology* (Washington: Catholic University of America Press, 2011), 286–308.
23. For an introduction to religious exclusivism, inclusivism, and pluralism, see Robert McKim, *On Religious Diversity* (New York: Oxford University Press, 2012), 52–130. See also Gerald R. McDermott and Harold A. Netland, *A Trinitarian Theology of Religions: An Evangelical Proposal* (New York: Oxford University Press, 2014), 12–45.
24. See Alister McGrath, "A Particularist View: A Post-Enlightenment Approach," in *Four Views on Salvation in a Pluralistic World*, ed. Dennis L. Okholm and Timothy R. Phillips (Grand Rapids: Zondervan Academic, 1995), 151–80; R. Douglas Geivett and W. Gary Phillips, "A Particularist View: An Evidentialist Approach," in *Four Views*, ed. Okholm and Phillips 213–45.
25. See Clark H. Pinnock, *A Wideness in God's Mercy: The Finality of Jesus Christ in a World of Religions* (Grand Rapids: Zondervan Academic, 1992); and *Flame of Love: A Theology of the Holy Spirit* (Downers Grove: IVP Academic, 1996); Terrance L. Tiessen, *Who Can Be Saved? Reassessing Salvation in Christ and World Religions* (Downers Grove: IVP Academic, 2004). For a critique of Pinnock's position, see Daniel Strange, *The Possibility*

paths to his saving presence.[26] Christianity largely rejects universalism—the belief that eventually all are saved—given the volume and weight behind NT teachings on the eternality of life in Christ or death apart from him (see Matt 12:32; 18:6–8; 2 Thess 1:8–9; Rev 20:13–15).[27] And even though the LDS theology of heaven secures room for nearly every child of God, an eternal state of outer darkness still awaits the most obstinately wicked and unrepentant (see Alma 40:13–14; cf. 2 Nephi 10:23; Jacob 6:8–10). An absolute religious pluralism, too, is blunted in traditional Christian and LDS doctrines of salvation because, in the end, it is the particularity of Jesus Christ's atonement—his unique work alone—that crowns God's redemptive plan for the world.

Traditional Christianity is less interested in the possibility of a postmortem reception of the gospel than the necessity of belief in Christ's resurrection and confession of his lordship in *this* life, to be born again before we die (see John 3:3; Rev 20:14). It follows that if eternal destinies are fixed after death, there is no need for proxy baptism and, from a Protestant perspective, even less so considering the doctrine of *sola fide*, or justification by faith alone.[28]

But what of that enigmatic verse from 1 Corinthians? Did Paul endorse vicarious baptism for the dead, and if so, is it a lost practice from the ancient church that ought to be restored?

Vicarious Baptism in the New Testament

Admittedly, this verse is challenging to interpret. Why the Corinthian church practiced baptism for the dead is perplexing. No other biblical passages (nor the Book of Mormon) support the practice, a fact evidenced by the early church's eventual dismissal of it.[29] Biblical scholars have made numerous

---

of Salvation Among the Unevangelized: An Analysis of Inclusivism in Recent Evangelical Theology (Eugene, OR: Wipf & Stock, 2002).

26. Hans Küng, "The World Religions in God's Plan of Salvation," in *Christian Revelation and World Religions*, ed. Josef Neuner (London: Burns & Oates, 1965). For a critique of pluralism, see D. A. Carson, *The Gagging of God: Christianity Confronts Pluralism* (Grand Rapids: Zondervan Academic, 1996).
27. For a differing view, see Robin Parry (pseud. Gregory MacDonald), *The Evangelical Universalist* (Eugene, OR: Cascade, 2012). The crux of Parry's argument orbits the reconciliation of sin to God's attributes of justice and love. While God must punish sin to maintain his justice, he must also forgive sin to uphold his love, lest he fall short of being truly love. Parry finds it "odd" that Christian theologians—especially those of the Reformed tradition—who confess that "God is love" nevertheless "subordinate divine love to divine justice so that God *has* to be just but does not *have* to love" (Parry, *Evangelical Universalist*, 21–22, emphasis original).
28. As Herman Bavinck summarized: "All the benefits of grace have been completely and solely acquired by Christ; hence, they are included in his person and lie prepared for his church in him. Nothing needs to be added to them from the side of humankind, for all is finished" (*RD* 3:591).
29. Early extra-canonical Christian writings apparently offer room for the practice (e.g., Shepherd of Hermas, Apocalypse of Peter, and Apocalypse of Paul), but these date to the second century AD and later, indicating a developed tradition rather than one received. The early church

unsuccessful attempts to pull the hermeneutical sword from this exegetical stone.[30] As Gordon Fee rightly pointed out, "When there is such a wide divergence of opinion, no one knows what in fact is going on."[31] Given the array of interpretations, "we dare not be dogmatic in upholding any one of them," added Craig Blomberg.[32]

Perhaps the better question to ask is why the *Corinthian* church—not the universal church—baptized on behalf of the dead. Paul was troubled by some members of the congregation who, having accepted his full gospel, later denied a critical element of it: the resurrection (see 1 Cor 15:12). If there is no resurrection, Paul argued, then "your faith is vain" (1 Cor 15:14, 17). To prove his point, he asked rhetorically why "they" (1 Cor 15:29)—some in the congregation or in the church's proximity—baptized for the dead. If there is no resurrection, the dead have no hope anyway, so what's the point of proxy baptism? Whatever the apostle meant by this, one thing is certain: "Paul's theological shorthand here made clearer sense to the Corinthians than it does to us."[33] It's equally clear that Paul's concern isn't vicarious baptism per se but the meaninglessness of any baptism whatsoever—whether it's for the living or the dead—if the promise of resurrection is hollow. After all, the apostle elsewhere argued, "we are buried with him [Christ] by baptism into death" so that just as Christ rose from death, "even so we also should walk in newness of life" (Rom 6:4; see also Col 2:12). A crucial purpose for baptism is to rehearse today what God has promised for tomorrow—life beyond the grave.

---

fathers were far more interested in Christ's evangelistic mission into Hades (see 1 Pet 4:6) than they were with the dead's descent into a watery grave. And while the gnostic Marcion sect practiced it, by the fourth century, theologians were at a loss for why the Corinthians did. Ambrosiaster wondered whether "some people were at that time being baptized for the dead because they were afraid that someone who was not baptized would either not rise at all or else rise merely in order to be condemned" (Gerald Bray, ed., *1–2 Corinthians*, Ancient Christian Commentary on Scripture: New Testament 7 [Downers Grove: IVP Academic, 1999], 166). Chrysostom simply thought it was ridiculous (*Saint Chrysostom: Homilies on the Epistles of Paul to the Corinthians* [*NPNF* 1 40]). Vicarious baptism was rejected by the Council of Carthage (419), though technically the council forbade baptism for dead bodies.

30. Anthony Thiselton catalogued the interpretive possibilities into four categories. First, the dead Paul speaks of are the spiritually dead baptismal candidates. Second, the dead are martyrs whose baptism is associated with persecution (cf. 1 Cor 15:31–32). Third, baptism means ritual washing (i.e., the cleansing of recently deceased believers). Fourth, Paul describes the Corinthian practice of "*vicarious baptism* on behalf of people who are dead" (Anthony C. Thiselton, *The First Epistle to the Corinthians*, New International Greek Testament Commentary (Grand Rapids: Eerdmans, 2000),1240, emphasis added). Within these categories are dozens of interpretations have left contemporary scholars shrugging their shoulders as "none of them seems to fully satisfy" (*First Epistle to the Corinthians*, 763).
31. Gordon D. Fee, *The First Epistle to the Corinthians*, New International Commentary on the New Testament (Grand Rapids: Eerdmans, 1987), 763.
32. Craig L. Blomberg, *1 Corinthians*, NIV Application Commentary (Grand Rapids: Zondervan Academic, 1994), 304.
33. Keener, *1–2 Corinthians*, 128.

This explanation is as far as the verse may be taken. Paul did not seem particularly bothered by vicarious baptism, but neither did he affirm it. He was more interested in the bigger picture: not baptism for the dead but resurrection of the dead. By emphasizing resurrection over baptism, Paul reminds us that an ordinance is less important than the thing it represents. In the end, the eternally blessed are those whom God ushers into his celestial presence—who "enter the city by the gates" (Rev 22:14 ESV)—with cleansed robes, not having washed their souls by water but having "washed their robes and made them white in the blood of the Lamb" (Rev 7:14 ESV).

Summary

Baptism for the dead is among the most unique practices in Mormonism. Although there are no explicit statements or instructions for the practice in the Bible or Book of Mormon, Joseph Smith introduced proxy baptism after a visionary experience led him to revisit the possibility of salvation among deceased unevangelized and misevangelized people. Traditional Christianity largely rejects baptism for the dead due, in part, to common interpretation of Hebrews 9:27 while also recognizing the possibility of its practice in the ancient Corinthian church (see 1 Cor 15:29). In the end, Christians ought to concern themselves more with belief in the resurrection of the dead over baptism for the dead because "if the dead rise not," the apostle Paul said, "let us eat and drink; for tomorrow we die" (1 Cor 15:32).

REFLECTION QUESTIONS

1. Joseph Smith sought an answer to the question of the unevangelized and misevangelized who die before hearing the gospel, like his older brother. Have you ever asked the same question?

2. Smith's solution came in a vision, one that suggested to him the possibility of postmortem salvation. Do you agree or disagree with the potential for salvation after death? Why or why not?

3. How is Smith's vision of the afterlife similar to or different from purgatory?

4. Most traditional Christians reject the possibility of salvation after death based on Hebrews 9:27, "And as it is appointed unto men once to die, but after this the judgment." How do you interpret this verse?

5. How do you interpret 1 Corinthians 15:29? How is your interpretation informed by your belief in the eternal state of the soul?

QUESTION 36

Why Don't Latter-day Saints Drink Coffee?

"Teach them to keep the 'Word of Wisdom' . . . that they may have strong bodies, and be entitled to the promise that follows obedience to this commandment."[1]
~ Zina D. H. Young, Relief Society President

With a few hours to spare before the conference, I searched for a café in my map app and headed to the nearest one. It was a local place, one tucked away in a shopping strip and not easily seen from the busy road. I could have gone to one of the major coffee chains in town, but I like supporting local businesses.

As I walked into the café, it seemed more like a bakery than the coffee shops I'm used to. "No matter," I thought to myself. As long as they were brewing that black elixir of goodness I was looking for, I'd be happy.

"No, sir, we don't serve coffee here," the cashier said.

"Sorry?" I replied. The confused and disappointed look on my face must have asked the question for me.

"No, sir. Sorry, no coffee."

Surely, she was kidding. I leaned to the right a bit to peer over her shoulder, desperately looking for coffee makers or canisters or something. Even a single-pod coffee maker would have sufficed.

"Sir," she interrupted with a smile. "This is Provo."

1. "First General Conference of the Relief Society," *Woman's Exponent*, April 15, 1889, 17:172.

That's when it hit me—Latter-day Saints don't drink coffee, and I was trying to order some in one of the densest concentrations of Latter-day Saints in the world.

Sheepishly, I ordered a muffin to go, of course, then retreated quickly to the green mermaid, hoping she could fulfill my order.

I knew Latter-day Saints don't drink coffee, or tea or alcohol for that matter. And they don't use tobacco, either. All that had just slipped my mind. Coffee is such a common part of the American experience, its absence at that moment was jarring to me. Of course, there's coffee in Utah. Some of the best I've ever had, in fact. But my interaction that morning turned my attention to one of Mormonism's more unique practices (or abstinences).

Why Don't Latter-day Saints Drink Coffee?

The answer is straightforward: the Word of Wisdom strictly prohibits coffee. This health code also forbids the use of tobacco (see D&C 89:8) and the consumption of alcohol and "hot drinks" (D&C 89:5–7, 9). Conversely, it endorses the consumption of certain types of food (see D&C 89:10–17). It is commonly misunderstood that the Word of Wisdom prohibits caffeine, likely due to the interpretation of "hot drinks" as caffeinated beverages like tea and coffee.[2] But soda is permitted, and not all heated beverages are prohibited. Latter-day Saints enjoy herbal teas and hot chocolate, for example. The principle behind the law, however, prohibits narcotics, vaping, and substance abuse of any kind.

Good health is the Word's goal but not its ultimate purpose. Adherents who observe this "principle with promise" (D&C 89:3) can anticipate not only physical well-being but also spiritual blessings. The Word is an LDS expression of the NT's command to "glorify God in your body" (1 Cor 6:20). Thus, the Word correlates to the similar dietary laws of other religious traditions, like *kosher* or *halal*, which categorizes the Word as a spiritual discipline rather than merely a health code. The Word is not advice for physical health alone; it's tied to the soul as well. To accept its prohibitions is to receive a richer relationship with God. Traditional Christians struggle to see it the same way. While caution against tobacco and alcohol feels familiar, the prohibition of hot drinks and meat seems arbitrary, more like "the commandments and doctrines of men" (Col 2:22) than heavenly wisdom. The apostle Paul warned against submitting to the 'touch nots' and 'taste nots' of human norms (see Col 2:21). "Let no man therefore judge you in meat, or in drink," he wrote (Col 2:16).

2. As early as 1842, Joseph Smith's brother, Hyrum Smith, clarified the meaning of "hot drinks" to the church. "Many who wonder what this can mean," he said, "whether it refers to tea, or coffee, or not. I say it does refer to tea, and coffee" ("The Word of Wisdom," *T&S*, June 1, 1842, 3:799).

Perhaps this is why some early Latter-day Saints followed the Word selectively, though leadership generally warned that failure to heed its advice was detrimental for the individual and community.[3] The Word came to the Church of Jesus Christ of Latter-day Saints "not by commandment or Constraint" but by revelatory counsel.[4] This language reminds readers of the way NT apostles sometimes counseled the church "not by commandment" (2 Cor 8:8) but as a gentle prompt to incline the saints toward obedience, "not by constraint, but willingly" (1 Pet 5:2). Congregations were given the opportunity to demonstrate their willingness to serve others in their community, "not because you have to, but because you want to please God" (1 Pet 5:2 MSG). If Joseph Smith had this model in mind, then he may have issued the Word, in part, to offer the church a way to demonstrate their fidelity to the community. Whether such a prompt was warranted has less to do with its content than with one's view of Smith's authority.

Where Did the Word of Wisdom Come From?

While the exact circumstances that led Smith to dictate the Word in early 1833 are unknown, historians have noticed a few contextual clues. Broadly speaking, the Word came at a moment when the LDS Church was overshadowed by health epidemics (like cholera) that raged during the early 1830s. Scholars have noticed how much of the Word's content reflected medical treatments of the day.[5] At that time, the medicinal use of tobacco and alcohol

---

3. LDS apostle Wilford Woodruff recalled a conversation with church leaders in November 1841 concerning obedience to the Word. After a lengthy discussion, the men reached consensus "that it was wisdom to deal with all such matters according to the wisdom which God gave" but also recognized that "a forced abstinence was not making us free but we should be under bondage with a yoke upon our necks" (*WWJ* 1:482 [emend.]). Unsurprisingly, adherence was not always consistent. For example, at a wedding just three years after the Word of Wisdom was published, LDS guests, including Joseph Smith, "took some refreshment" and "were made glad with the fruit of the vine" (JSJ, January 14, 1836, J1:153). Smith's home in Nauvoo, which doubled as a hotel, featured a large bar, and as late as 1844 Smith journaled that he had "Drank a glass of beer" (JSJ, June 1, 1844, J3:269). Such an admission today would have jeopardized his temple recommend. And while Brigham Young eventually became a major advocate for keeping the Word, he permitted the private production and consumption of wine, whisky, and rum in Utah Territory. See Sherry Monahan and Jane Perkins, *The Golden Elixir of the West: Whiskey and the Shaping of America* (Guilford, CT: Twodot, 2018), 43–55. By the early nineteenth century, however, and with the rise of Prohibition, adherence to the Word grew stronger. See also Lester E. Bush, "The Word of Wisdom in Early Nineteenth-Century Perspective," *Dialogue* 14, no. 3 (1981): 47–65.
4. JS, revelation, February 27, 1833, D3:20 [D&C 89:2].
5. Clyde Ford, "The Origin of the Word of Wisdom," *Journal of Mormon History* 24, no. 2 (1998): 129–54. See also Steven C. Harper, *The Word of Wisdom: Setting the Record Straight* (Orem, UT: Millennial Press, 2007); "Word of Wisdom," *Mormonism: A Historical Encyclopedia*, ed. W. Paul Reeve and Ardis E. Parshall (Santa Barbara, CA: ABC-CLIO, 2010), 122–23.

were prescribed to reduce symptoms of some illnesses. For example, tobacco was a popular ingredient in many home remedies ranging anywhere from diuretics to healing rattlesnake bites.[6] Alcohol, too, was well-known for its antiseptic power, even though the relationship between microbes and hygiene was then unknown. The Word apparently reflected these medical practices when it explained how "strong drinks are not for the belly, but for the washing of your bodies" (for hygiene and not inebriation), and "tobacco is not for man but is for bruises" (for topical application, not smoking or chewing).[7]

But some medical professionals in Smith's day promoted complete abstinence from drinking and smoking as a preventative measure to avoid sickness altogether. They believed the body was perfectly capable of staving off illness on its own and that our immunity to fight disease was weakened by habitual and prolonged use of these substances. Alcohol, for example, was thought to be "destructive to the bloom of youth," according to a medical journal published the same year as the Word.[8] That same journal also theorized how "excessive use of hot drinks" like coffee, tea, and hot chocolate could "weaken the organs of digestion."[9] Some of these substances could be used medicinally, but it was best to stay away from them altogether and let the body heal itself. Others, however, found moderate intake of alcohol and tobacco to be healthy. "Very moderately taken," argued a pair of physicians, "[tobacco] quiets restlessness, calms mental and corporeal inquietude, and promised a general state of languor or repose."[10] The debate was far from settled.

Latter-day Saints also believed that God had blessed them with the spiritual gift of healing through prayer and blessings. One historian observed how early Mormonism contrasted itself against the cessationism that guided Protestantism away from the miraculous healing. In the early days of the church, "elders either commanded the sick to be made whole or prayed over the sick and laid their hands on them, reflecting divine instruction given through Joseph Smith exhorting the saints to ritually administer to the sick."[11] And this practice was not restricted to men. In fact, a major role of the Relief Society, a women's organization within the church, was faith ministry to the sick. So members questioned their reliance on the medical practices of their

6. George B. Wood and Franklin Bache, *The Dispensatory of the United States* (Philadelphia: Grigg and Elliot, 1833), 629; Samuel North, *The Family Physician . . . Medical Herbal* (Waterloo, NY: Wm. Child, 1830), 117.
7. JS, revelation, February 27, 1833, D3:21 [D&C 89:8]. The revelation apparently permitted "mild drinks" or light ales, but the term could also refer to low- or non-alcoholic barley drinks used for indigestion (22).
8. *The Toilette of Health . . . of Both Sexes* (Boston: Allen and Ticknor, 1833), 84.
9. *The Toilette of Health*, 85.
10. Wood and Bache, *The Dispensatory*, 629.
11. Jonathan A. Stapley, "'Pouring In Oil': The Development of the Modern Mormon Healing Ritual," in *By Our Rites of Worship: Latter-day Saint Views on Ritual in History, Scripture, and Practice*, ed. Daniel L. Belnap (Salt Lake City: Deseret, 2013), 285.

day. Early Latter-day Saints generally adopted a "faith against medicine" posture.[12] If there was any medical wisdom to be trusted, then it was in botanical medicine, healing that came through herbs created by God and a regulated diet guided by wisdom.

With converts joining from an array of backgrounds and beliefs, the early church may have found itself confused by these competing views on health. Are tobacco and alcohol good or bad, or good for medicine but bad for recreation? Should the faithful rely on God's healing power rather than worldly medicines? These questions—and the inevitable debate that accompanied them—undoubtedly fueled dissenting opinions. The Word came at an opportune time to offer the church surety amid confusion.[13]

The Word of Wisdom and 1 Corinthians 8

There is another clue that sheds light on the Word of Wisdom's origin, one that frames the revelation as a mechanism to preserve unity by alleviating tension between "strong" and "weak" Latter-day Saints. While the text is addressed to the whole church, it is especially concerned with "the weak & the weakest of all Saints."[14] Readers are reminded of the apostle Paul's teaching concerning the consciences of the weak brothers who stumbled in their faith at the indifference some church members held toward meat sacrificed to idols. "We know that an idol is nothing in the world" (1 Cor 8:4), Paul wrote, but not everyone felt the same way. Some weaker saints were aghast that fellow Christians would eat food dedicated to false gods. It shook their delicate conscience and threatened to undo their faith and lead pagan converts back to their old ways (see 1 Cor 8:10). Why would the church tolerate such a thing, Paul wondered. "Shall the weak brother perish, for whom Christ died?" (1 Cor 8:11). The answer, of course, was no. "Take heed lest by any means this liberty of yours become a stumblingblock to them that are weak" (1 Cor 8:9), warned the apostle. Personal liberty ought to be freely given up in love to preserve unity in the church.

---

12. Courtney S. Campbell, *Moral Realities: Mormonism, Medicine, and Bioethics* (New York: Oxford University Press, 2021), 34–39. This posture is far from the LDS Church's approach to medicine today, as the institution is presently led by a heart surgeon, President Russell M. Nelson.
13. Brigham Young offered a simpler, albeit more anecdotal, explanation for why the Word was needed. He recalled how students of Smith's habitually smoked pipes during instruction, clouding their small meeting place with smoke and veneering the floor with spit. "This, and the complaints of his wife at having to clean so filthy a floor, made the Prophet think upon the matter," Young said (*CDBY* 5:2532). Smith questioned whether it was appropriate for the Saints to keep such habits and apparently prayed about tobacco and other health-related concerns. Young explained that "the revelation known as the Word of Wisdom was the result of his inquiry" (*CDBY* 5:2532).
14. JS, revelation, February 27, 1833, D3:20 [D&C 89:3].

Smith's careful use of the term "weak" to discuss matters of conscience in the church helps explain why he wrote the Word. Some early Latter-day Saints thought alcohol and tobacco use was permissible, whether for consumption or medicinal purposes. But others thought consuming alcohol and tobacco was immoral and that using them for medicinal purposes was a sign of weak faith in God's ability to supernaturally heal. The Word offers the church a unifying avenue to walk amid this tension, throwing its weight behind giving up a liberty for the sake of health, both personal and ecclesiastical. Just as Paul advocated giving up a personal liberty for sake of the weak brother, Smith advocated giving up the liberty of leisure and folk remedies, all for the sake of "the weak & the weakest" in the church.[15]

The Word of Wisdom Today

Despite it coming to the LDS Church "not by commandment or Constraint," adherence to the Word of Wisdom has been generally compulsory since the beginning of the twentieth century. In part, the Word functions as a symbolic designator that distinguishes Latter-day Saints from Christian denominations. As one historian has argued, Mormonism once distinguished itself by plural marriage, but after its repeal in the late-nineteenth century, Latter-day Saints "reemphasized certain doctrines and practices that had been relatively dormant, such as the Word of Wisdom," to set themselves apart from the culture.[16]

Today, more Latter-day Saints than not choose to abstain from tobacco, alcohol, and tea. But not all Latter-day Saints strictly follow the Word, as younger members opt to consume coffee and alcohol at higher rates than earlier generations.[17] And despite the Word's explicit guidance to reserve the meat of "beasts & of fowls" for famine or winter, steakhouses in Utah find no shortage of business during the summer months.[18] Still, understanding and obeying the Word is prerequisite for baptism and one's temple recommend. It serves modern Latter-day Saints much the same way it did their theological forebearers: to demonstrate their willingness to set aside habits and tailor diets in exchange for bodily and spiritual blessing.

---

15. JS, revelation, February 27, 1833, D3:20 [D&C 89:3].
16. Thomas G. Alexander, *Mormonism in Transition: A History of the Latter-day Saints, 1890–1930,* 3rd ed. (Urbana, IL: University of Illinois Press, 2012), 11; see also 273–84.
17. Jana Riess, *The Next Mormons: How Millennials Are Changing the LDS Church* (New York: Oxford University Press, 2019),157–62.
18. The Word of Wisdom states that the "flesh also of beasts & of fowls" is permissible to eat; however, "they should not be used, only in times of winter or of famine" (JS, revelation, February 27, 1833, D3:21–22 [D&C 89:12–13]). The use of the word "only" here is prepositional to indicate exception (i.e., meat should not be consumed *except* during winter or famine).

Summary

Latter-day Saints typically refrain from drinking coffee in adherence to the Word of Wisdom, a spiritual health code given by Joseph Smith. If Smith had in mind NT apostolic models for offering counsel rather than commands, then the Word represents spiritual advice meant to alleviate the burden of "weaker" members of the Church of Jesus Christ of Latter-day Saints who then wrestled with the efficacy and benefit to substances like coffee, tea, alcohol, tobacco, and meat. While early Latter-day Saints apparently kept the Word inconsistently, the church today upholds it as a measure of fidelity to the tradition.

REFLECTION QUESTIONS

1. How is the Word of Wisdom similar and dissimilar to other religious dietary laws, like kosher or halal?

2. What health benefits come from following the Word of Wisdom? Are there disadvantages?

3. Read Colossians 2:20–23. Do you agree or disagree that this passage relates to something like the Word of Wisdom?

4. How does the historical context around the Word of Wisdom frame your understanding of it?

5. Read 1 Corinthians 8. Do you agree or disagree that the Word of Wisdom has a parallel to Paul's counsel?

PART 5

Approaching Mormonism

QUESTION 37

What Are Concerns Latter-day Saints Have About Traditional Christianity?

"They were all wrong."[1]
~ Joseph Smith

During the First Vision (see question 7), Joseph Smith prayed to know which church he should join. The answer was startling: "Join none of them," for "they were all wrong."[2] Hidden deep in this short reply are two concerns Mormonism has long harbored against traditional Christianity. The first is how churches are described as "them" and "they," emphasizing the plurality of Christianity rather than its unity. If Christians are meant to be a people of "one Lord [and] one faith" (Eph 4:5), why are they divided into denominations? The second concern is related. Smith learned from the vision that all churches "were all wrong," especially their creeds, or summaries of belief. If Christianity ought to reflect "the faith which was once delivered unto the saints" (Jude 3), why are there so many theological disagreements and deviations?

This question explores these concerns, as well as the possibility that Mormonism suffers from similar conditions.

Traditional Christianity Was Hellenized

Mormonism asserts that Greek thought (sometimes called Hellenism) altered early Christianity, which produced a religion based on the philosophies of men mingled with scripture. The view of God as the ineffable, transcendent First Cause is more at home among disciples of Plato than of Christ. Trinitarianism is a philosophical compromise, a way to reconcile Athens to Jerusalem. Greek

1. JS, H1:214 [Joseph Smith–History 19].
2. JS, H1:214 [Joseph Smith–History 19].

philosophy initially gave early Christians the necessary framework to explain and defend the faith to unbelievers, but it ceased to describe Christian doctrine and started informing it over time. As noted by LDS scholars, "What began as a Jewish religion founded on revelation and faith became an appendage of classical civilization."[3] Orthodoxy, then, is an unintended hybrid of divine and worldly ideas, and its ecumenical creeds represent the "conceptual merger of Christian doctrine with Greek philosophy."[4] In short, Christianity "became hellenized and was transformed in the process."[5] Thus, a major reason for the LDS restoration.

There should be no doubt about the intricate and extensive interaction between Christian and Greek thought in the early church. The question is not whether but *how* the two influenced one another. Adolf von Harnack, a nineteenth-century historian, popularized the Hellenization (or Greek influence) interpretation of Christian history in his *History of Dogma*. According to Harnack, the development of early Christian thought is best explained primarily as a process of assimilation with Greco-Roman thought. Bearing in mind the Great Apostasy, Mormonism instinctively adopted this interpretation because it helps explain how the post-apostolic church "apostatized from the truth and lost the priesthood," a point Smith argued but hesitated to elaborate in detail.[6] Syncretism could be a reason for apostasy—or even the outcome of apostasy—as the church gradually forfeited its doctrinal birthright for the pottage of Greek philosophy.

Harnack's interpretation of early Christianity, however, is not unchallenged among scholars. Historian Robert Louis Wilken has argued for a more convincing interpretation that inverts Harnack's narrative. Christianity was not Hellenized; instead, Hellenism was Christianized. Wilken argued that the writers of the patristic era displayed far greater interest in scripture and worship than in embracing Greco-Roman intellectual frameworks. In fact, "Christian thinking, while working within patterns of thought and conceptions rooted in Greco-Roman culture, transformed *them* so profoundly that in the end something quite new came into being."[7] Is it the case, as Harnack argued, that Christianity was Hellenized, or is Wilkin's assessment correct, that Hellenism underwent Christian baptism? The debate is unsettled, of course, but Harnack's story ought not to be received uncritically.[8]

---

3. Daniel W. Graham and James L. Siebach, "The Introduction of Philosophy into Early Christianity," in *Early Christians in Disarray: Contemporary LDS Perspectives on the Christian Apostasy*, ed. Noel B. Reynolds (Provo, UT: Maxwell Institute, BYU, 2005), 233.
4. "Are 'Mormons' Christian?," The Church of Jesus Christ of Latter-day Saints, lds.org/topics/christians.
5. Graham and Siebach, "The Introduction of Philosophy into Early Christianity," 233.
6. Joseph Smith, History, 1838–1856, vol. F-1, *JSP*, 105.
7. Robert Louis Wilken, *The Spirit of Early Christian Thought* (New Haven, CT: Yale University Press, 2003), xvi–xvii (emphasis added).
8. Relatedly, for a measured and charitable overview of early Christianity from Latter-day Saint scholars, see Jason R. Combs et al., eds., *Ancient Christians: An Introduction for Latter-day Saints* (Provo, UT: Maxwell Institute, BYU, 2022).

Additionally, Latter-day Saints are not alone in noticing how early Christians utilized Greek philosophy to communicate their doctrine. Dutch theologian Wilhelmus à Brakel, for example, noted how the concept of *autexousia*, or the notion of free will or agency, "was introduced into the church by Platonic philosophers who had been converted to Christianity," which is perhaps why the "word is not to be found in Scripture."[9] Brakel theorized that early Christianity was introduced to *autexousia* in the second century by Justin Martyr. "Of course the idea itself was not original with Justin," explained one historian. "The notion of *autexousia* as a prerogative of all men is so abundantly present in scripture, particularly in the New Testament, that it is an essential of Christian thought."[10]

Other Platonic concepts, like the premortal existence and unconditional immortality of the soul, resonate deeply with Mormon thought. Indeed, sometimes patristic writers seem to affirm Mormon doctrine. Deification, for example, captured the imagination of church fathers who argued the *telos* (i.e., purpose) of humanity was to become "gods" like God (see question 27). Latter-day Saints have been quick to see classical thought or practices as evidence that "early Christians still retained many Gospel truths and the same verities were revealed to the Prophet Joseph Smith."[11] But when the ancients disagree with Mormon doctrine—e.g., Trinitarianism or original sin—their writings are dismissed as "pagan philosophies being mingled with the doctrines of the gospel to form the apostate Christianity."[12]

In the end, humility and charity are always warranted when interpreting another religion's historical development. We should consider that whatever we find distasteful in the other story may lurk in our own. This point is especially true of the Mormon objection to traditional Christianity that stems from its many denominations.

Traditional Christianity Is Fractured

In Christ's high priestly prayer, he asked the Father that his disciples would "be one, as we are" (John 17:11). His request was profound, that the church in its ideal

9. Wilhelmus à Brakel, *God, Man, and Christ*, vol. 1 of *The Christian's Reasonable Service*, ed. Joel R. Beeke, trans. Bartel Elshout (Grand Rapids: Reformation Heritage, 1992), 407. While Plato never explicitly tackled the issue of free will, later philosophical traditions informed by his thought offered more straightforward theories. Aristotelian ethics, for example, explored voluntary actions, deliberation between choices, and the development of character that followed.
10. William Telfer, "Autexousia," *Journal of Theological Studies* 8, no. 1 (1957): 124.
11. Milton R. Hunter, *The Gospel Through the Ages* (Salt Lake City: Stevens and Wallis, 1945), 109. Joseph Smith made a similar claim when pointing to John Chrysostom's report that some early Christians practiced baptism for the dead: "The church of course at that time was degenerate," Smith clarified, "but the thing is sufficiently plain in the scriptures" (JS, "Baptism for the Dead," *T&S*, April 15, 1842, 3:761). For Chrysostom's comment, see Chrysostom, *Homilies* (NPNF 1 12:244).
12. Bruce R. McConkie, *Mormon Doctrine* (Salt Lake City: Bookcraft, 1958), 410.

state would share the same kind of oneness as the Father and Son. The fledgling church sustained this ideal state in the opening chapters of Acts as it grew "with one accord" (Acts 1:14), even when adding converts at an astounding rate (see Acts 2:41–47). But already during the later apostolic era, disunity threatened the church for a handful of reasons. Some threats were cultural, like how to integrate Gentile converts into the predominantly Jewish church (see Gal 2:12–14). Other threats were over practice. If Gentiles were allowed to become members of God's covenant community, should they become circumcised? The so-called circumcision party (Gal 2:12 ESV) thought so and opposed those who disagreed (see Acts 11:1–3; Gal 5:2–3; 1 Cor 7:19). Relatedly, issues over authority and allegiance divided a single congregation into at least four groups (see 1 Cor 1:12), like a mirror dropped on the floor and shattered. This fracturing led the apostle Paul to conclude it was "necessary that there be factions among you" to determine who was "approved" by God (1 Cor 11:19 CSB).

The Greek word for factions, *hairesis*, is the source of the English term "heresy." Unlike today, it didn't originally hold a negative connotation. The word *hairesis* simply meant "a collection of persons who have chosen for themselves a particular way of living and of thinking about things."[13] Yet, sometimes a particular group drifted from the faith, which led the apostles to warn against "divisions" in the church (Gal 5:20 ESV) caused by "destructive heresies" (2 Pet 2:1 ESV). Such heresies continued to develop over generations (e.g., Docetism, Gnosticism, Arianism, Pelagianism, Nestorianism). At significant inflection points, the church assembled councils to discern truth amid differences, striving to maintain the unity for which Jesus Christ prayed. Still, Christianity has suffered from denominationalizing throughout its history, from the East-West schism to the many Protestant traditions of the Reformation.

Mormonism has long pointed to denominations as a sign of Christianity's distress and need for restoration. After Smith made an "intimate acquaintance with those of different denominations," he concluded their non-alignment with scripture was so severe that "there was no society or denomination that built upon the gospel of Jesus Christ."[14] From Rome to Cane Ridge, every church "had apostatized from the true and living faith" and needed complete restoration.[15] In Smith's lifetime, major divisions included Roman Catholicism, Eastern Orthodoxy, Lutheranism, Anglicanism, Presbyterianism, Congregationalism, Baptists, Methodism, and Restorationism. Since then, even more churches have formed, like those of the Pentecostal and Charismatic movements.

Smith's concern about the apparent disunity of Christianity was warranted. Christians must be "eager to maintain the unity of the Spirit in the

13. Steve Nemes, *Orthodoxy and Heresy: Elements in the Problems of God* (Cambridge: Cambridge University Press, 2022), 2.
14. JS, H1:11 (emend.).
15. JS, H1:11 (emend.).

bond of peace" (Eph 4:3 ESV). The church is the bride of Christ (see Eph 5:23), and he has only one bride, not many. Unity and love are the foundation on which our common faith rests (see John 13:35; 17:11). Despite spanning time and space, all Christians ought to affirm the same, central faith, which is less a codified body of doctrines housed in an institution than it is the simple trust that sinners place in Christ alone for their salvation. Every true believer must affirm the simplicity of the faith that was "once delivered unto the saints" (Jude 3), which is this: The Lord Jesus Christ died for our sins, was buried for three days, and rose again before the apostles, all according to scripture (see 1 Cor 15:3–5). Believing this is "most important" (1 Cor 15:3 CSB) because rejecting Christ's resurrection places one outside the community of faith. In other words, despite all appearances to the contrary, Christianity has always been (and will always be) the "one faith" of the crucified and resurrected Lord Jesus. To confess Christ as Lord and to believe in his resurrection is to be part of that one faith (see Rom 10:9), to be "sealed with that holy Spirit of promise" (Eph 1:13). "Whoever has the Holy Spirit is in the church," said Augustine.[16]

The church is united not by polity or creeds but by the lordship of the resurrected Son of God, who transcends confessional and institutional boundaries. As German theologian Jürgen Moltmann explained, "Where so far as Christ rules, there, consequently, the church is to be found."[17] Christ is the unifying authority of mere Christianity, the landlord of C. S. Lewis's great hall of faith "out of which doors open into several rooms," or different Christian traditions. All rooms are connected by the great hall, a corridor of common confessions to core beliefs, but "it is in the rooms, not in the hall, that there are fires and chairs and meals. The hall is a place to wait in, a place from which to try the various doors, not a place to live in."[18] So Christians are encouraged to settle in the room of a church while also recognizing that they share a roof with the neighboring churches around them, all of whom live in—and, better, all of whom *are*—the house of the Lord (see Matt 16:18; 1 Cor 3:16; 6:19; 2 Cor 6:16). "Just as there are many rays of the sun but one light," so there are many churches but one faith, taught Cyprian, a third-century theologian.[19] In other words, institutional disunity does not reflect disunity of the faith, as Smith apparently feared.

Besides, Mormonism suffers from the same kind of division as traditional Christianity. A handful of branches sprouted during Smith's life, and his movement suffered severe fragmentation after his death. Today, the original church he founded in 1830 has split into hundreds of groups with thousands

---

16. *ACD* 5:31.
17. Jürgen Moltmann, *The Church in the Power of the Spirit: A Contribution to Messianic Ecclesiology*, trans. Margaret Kohl (Minneapolis: Fortress, 1977), 338.
18. C. S. Lewis, *Mere Christianity*, xv.
19. *ACD* 5:61.

of members.[20] Mormonism is no monolith. It is better understood as a collection of Mormonisms, with each group calling the other to return to the "true" church. Perhaps it is wisest for those who worship in glass churches not to cast stones. Instead, we ought to recognize that strife and division are often rooted in pride, which is common to all people whether they are traditional Christians or Latter-day Saints. May we all humbly retreat into Christ's high priestly prayer for unity through what is most important to our own individual faith.

Summary

Mormonism has historically objected to traditional Christianity in two ways. First, Mormonism argues that the faith was deeply influenced by Greco-Roman ideas and thus has forfeited its purity and authority. Second and consequently, Christianity has fractured into countless denominations, which is evidence of its apostasy and need for complete restoration. These concerns, however, are a double-edged sword. Mormonism resonates with Greek ideas and has splintered into myriad factions since founding of the original Church of Jesus Christ of Latter-day Saints. Perhaps it is best that these concerns be refined into more substantive and self-reflective criticism or be retired altogether.

REFLECTION QUESTIONS

1. Joseph Smith was concerned about the divisions of traditional Christianity. Do you share his concern? Why or why not?

2. A common concern Mormonism harbors against traditional Christianity is its apparent Hellenization, or influence by Greco-Roman thought. Do you believe this concern is warranted?

3. Why do you believe there are denominations of Christianity? What is the ideal state of the faith, considering high priestly prayer of the Lord Jesus?

4. Mormonism also expresses affinity for ideas that were posited by Greek philosophy. If you agree with this statement, how does it inform your view of the Great Apostasy?

5. Do you believe that Mormonism suffers the same kind of divisions as traditional Christianity? If so, what does this fractionalization say about the human heart?

---

20. See Steven L. Shields, *Divergent Paths of the Restoration: An Encyclopedia of the Smith-Rigdon Movement*, 5th ed. (Salt Lake City: Signature Books, 2021).

QUESTION 38

Should We Pray About Whether the Book of Mormon Is True?

"We request all that wish the truth on [the Book of Mormon], to enquire of the Lord, who will always answer the pure in heart."[1]
~ *Evening & Morning Star* (1832)

The conversation has occurred countless times before: A traditional Christian rejects the Book of Mormon as a forgery, while a Latter-day Saint challenges this view. The Christian dismisses its origin story as unbelievable; however, the Latter-day Saint reminds them that God often works in extraordinary ways to confound the wise. The Christian counters that the canon of scripture is set, but the Latter-day Saint asks why God would limit his ability to bring forth new revelation. Finally, the apparent lack of external proof for the Book of Mormon's historicity is countered by an appeal to consider current evidence and have patience—perhaps more evidence will emerge in time. In the end, if a person wants to know whether the Book of Mormon is true, then "there is no other way to find it out, but to receive intelligence from whence it professes to have come," wrote an early LDS apologist.[2] Since the book claims to be from God, ask him to confirm it.

The Book of Mormon makes a similar plea and "presses us for a decision."[3] As it concludes, readers are invited to pray about whether "these things are not true" (Moroni 10:4). If a person asks God "with a sincere heart, with real

1. "The Book of Mormon," *EMS*, June 1832, 1:8
2. Benjamin Winchester, "History of the Ancients of America," *The Gospel Reflector* (Philadelphia) 1, no. 6, March 15, 1841.
3. Robert L. Millet, "Book of Mormon," in *LDS Beliefs: A Doctrinal Reference*, ed. Robert L. Millet et al. (Salt Lake City: Deseret Book, 2011), 80.

intent, having faith in Christ, he will manifest the truth of it unto you, by the power of the Holy Ghost" (Moroni 10:4). This request often surprises traditional Christians. The Bible never asks the same of its readers, and religious experience is not high on their list for confirming knowledge. Still, it's not wrong to desire a more profound experience with scripture. As the psalmist wrote, "How *sweet* are thy words unto *my* taste!" (Ps 119:103, emphasis added). Objective evidence supporting scripture is helpful but unnecessary. In the end, "God alone can properly bear witness to his own words," explained John Calvin, so that the words of God "will not obtain full credit in the hearts of men, until they are sealed by the inward testimony of the Spirit."[4]

So, if the Book of Mormon claims to be the word of God, should we pray about whether it is true?

Exploring the Book of Mormon's Invitation

The answer to this question should begin by examining the invitation itself.

> Now I, Moroni . . . write unto my brethren, the Lamanites. . . . Behold, I would exhort you that when ye shall read these things, if it be wisdom in God that ye should read them, that ye would remember how merciful the Lord hath been unto the children of men, from the creation of Adam even down until the time that ye shall receive these things, and ponder it in your hearts. And when ye shall receive these things, I would exhort you that ye would ask God, the Eternal Father, in the name of Christ, if these things are not true; and if ye shall ask with a sincere heart, with real intent, having faith in Christ, he will manifest the truth of it unto you, by the power of the Holy Ghost. And by the power of the Holy Ghost ye may know the truth of all things.[5]

In this passage, the Book of Mormon urges readers to receive, ponder, and pray "if these things are not true" (10:4). "It is this very challenge to test the truthfulness of the Book of Mormon through personal prayer that remains a key feature of LDS life and missionary work in the twenty-first century," observed one scholar.[6] Indeed, this prayer functions almost like a non-salvific ordinance in LDS practice—as an instrument God uses to communicate his mercy and grace—though it is not recognized as an ordinance. According to LDS Church leaders, "an essential part of conversion is receiving

4. Calvin, *Inst.* 1.7.5.
5. Moroni 10:1–5.
6. Douglas J. Davies, *An Introduction to Mormonism* (Cambridge: Cambridge University Press, 2003), 58.

a witness from the Holy Ghost that the Book of Mormon is true."[7] Today, many Latter-day Saints report receiving this confirmation in prayer, classically describing the experience as a "burning in the bosom," though there are many kinds of experiences, and not all are solely dependent on feelings. What if a person prays about the Book of Mormon but does not receive a witness or feels negatively toward it? Those scenarios say more about the prayer than the book. Only the insincere feel nothing, like when a person renders "a sacrament [e.g., the eucharist] *in*effectual by a lack of real intention."[8] Readers are encouraged to try again, but this time, with more sincerity.

Moroni's invitation is open to all people, but a close reading of this text suggests it was initially (and primarily) for Lamanites, not necessarily Gentiles. These Book of Mormon terms describe two groups of people (see question 13). Early Latter-day Saints applied the first term, *Lamanite*, to descendants or associates of Laman, son of Lehi, a Hebrew tribal leader who emigrated from Jerusalem to the Americas. The early church believed that Native Americans were descendants of the Lamanites and focused missionary efforts on converting them.[9] The second term, *Gentile*, was given to any person who neither descended from the Jews or Lamanites nor was a member of the church (i.e., White Americans, and typically Christians).

Moroni, a descendant of Lehi, exhorted his "brethren, the Lamanites" that "*they* should know" the Christian message written by Nephite prophets (Moroni 10:1, emphasis added). This book contained shocking information for future Lamanite readers about their "true" ethnic origin. It posits that Native Americans were not created to dwell in their ancestral lands and interact with a pantheon of deities and departed ancestors. Instead, they were children of Abraham, kin to a people in a faraway land, and descendants of people miraculously brought to the Americas who worshiped only one God. Native readers of the Book of Mormon were not only asked to expand their existing spiritual beliefs, like non-native Christians who would need to accept the book in addition to the Bible. No, the Natives were asked to accept a radically different spiritual paradigm and origin story. Surely they would struggle to accept it. What would it take for them to lay aside their ancestors' spiritual beliefs, ideas, and traditions? Nothing short of the Spirit of God could convince them. Thus, Moroni invited his "brethren" to "ask God" to manifest the

---

7. Gary James Bergera, ed., *Statements of the LDS First Presidency: A Topical Compendium* (Salt Lake City: Signature Books, 2007), 49.
8. Matthew Barrett, ed., *Reformation Theology: A Systematic Summary* (Wheaton, IL: Crossway, 2017), 611 (emphasis original).
9. In 1830, the same year the Book of Mormon was published, Joseph Smith gave a revelation to LDS apostle Oliver Cowdery, to "go unto the Lamanites & Preach my Gospel unto them & cause my Church to be established among them," doubtlessly by sharing the Book of Mormon, which hints at one of its original intentions (JS, revelation, September 1830, D1:185 [D&C 28:8]).

integrity of their alternative origin story, identity, and destiny. Should they ask, "with a sincere heart, with real intent," God would confirm it "by the power of the Holy Ghost" (Moroni 10:4).

Gentiles may also do the same, though they were not the primary audience. The Lamanites were in focus because they had the taller barrier of disbelief to overcome. Gentiles may have already accepted the gospel, albeit in a pre-'restored' form. They needed to receive the 'restored' gospel too, but to do so was conditioned on the belief that God still spoke in their day. The canon wasn't set; it was missing the Book of Mormon. It's unsurprising that the remainder of Moroni's exhortation argued forcefully against cessationism, that God's ability to reveal spiritual truth "never will be done away, even as long as the world shall stand" (Moroni 10:19).

In short, the invitation of Moroni 10:1–5 was written primarily to indigenous non-Christians, and nonindigenous "Gentiles" were only secondarily in view. Thus, the central thrust behind Moroni 10:1–5 is for Moroni's "brethren," the Lamanite descendants, to ask God whether the Book of Mormon, and their 'true' origin story, is true. It is a missionary text aimed at Native Americans. Granted, others are welcome to do the same. Nothing in the text prohibits it.[10] In fact, a reasonable deduction of the invitation welcomes all seekers, but for this passage to be primarily a call for all people to discern the truthfulness of the Book of Mormon is at odds with the text's original and primary intent.

Still, Moroni 10:1–5 is a quintessential missionary text. LDS missionaries use it to urge seekers who have formed positive beliefs about the Book of Mormon, however small, to seek divine confirmation of their predetermined conclusions. And this is where traditional Christians feel off balance. They do not reject that God confirms truth in their hearts. After an encounter with the resurrected Lord Jesus, the two disciples on the road to Emmaus pondered Christ's words: "Did not our heart burn within us?" (Luke 24:32). But early Christians also confirmed truth by assessing it with what God has revealed earlier, like the ancient Bereans (see Acts 17:10–12). These early Jewish converts "received the word with all readiness of mind" and together "searched the scriptures daily, whether those things were so" (Acts 17:11). Smith himself offered the same advice: "When you have heard go & read your bible" to confirm "if the things are not verily true."[11] Truth ought to be sought in community as much as individually and in concert with Scripture as much as with prayer. Private religious experience is only one of many ways Christians

10. The Book of Mormon offers hermeneutical permission to "liken all scriptures unto" (1 Nephi 19:23) the reader, to apply the text to oneself even if it was written to a specific person or people. This permission was initially offered to "a remnant of the house of Israel" (1 Nephi 19:24), that is, Lamanites, inviting them to apply the Torah to themselves.
11. JSJ, January 29, 1843, J2:251.

discern and confirm truth. In doing so, they rely on what God's Spirit says in prayer and has said in the Bible, and they do so together in a godly community.

Religious Experience and Knowing Scripture

Indeed, traditional Christians have long upheld the relationship between scripture and the Holy Spirit. To recognize a text as inspired is to affirm its origin in God, the wellspring of truth. Supplementary evidence, like apologetics, is helpful to build confidence in scripture, but that confidence must always be built atop the foundation of the Spirit's testimony. The Lord Jesus promised that the Holy Spirit would "guide you into all truth" (John 16:13). He is "the spirit of wisdom and revelation" (Eph 1:17), the only one who can illuminate our hearts and minds to understand and comprehend the word of God. This principle is apparently in play for the Book of Mormon's invitation. If the Holy Spirit inspired scripture and the Christian's heart to recognize scripture, then why not apply it to the Book of Mormon?

As John Calvin noted, the Holy Spirit was promised to us "not to form new and unheard-of revelations, or to coin a new form of doctrine . . . but to seal on our minds the very doctrine which the gospel recommends."[12] In other words, the Spirit does not confirm *new* things; instead, he confirms the *true* things already revealed in his gospel. This is precisely why traditional Christians feel caution when the Book of Mormon asks its readers to pray to receive private revelation to confirm its message. Not only does granting the Book of Mormon the status of scripture rob the Bible's sufficiency, but it also raises questions about the nature of scripture (see question 12). Is scripture an inspired text *about* God's word, or *is it* God's word, his very voice? While Latter-day Saints typically view the Bible as a testament *to* God's voice, many Christians (especially conservative ones) view the Bible *as* God's voice. So, when Christians pray about scripture, they not only ask the Holy Spirit, "Is this *true*?" They also ask, "Is this *God*?" As Puritan reformer John Owen stated, "We do not affirm that the Spirit immediately, by himself, saith unto every individual believer, This book is, or contains, the word of God. We say not that the Spirit ever speaks to us *of* the Word, but *by* the Word."[13] Thus, traditional Christians demonstrate great sincerity and trust in God when they retreat to his well-known voice in the Bible to discern truth. As Jesus said, "My sheep hear my voice, and I know them, and they follow me" (John 10:27). When faced with a test of spiritual truth, it's only natural to turn toward the Good Shepherd. Should a Christian decide to "ask with a sincere heart, with real intent" whether the Book of Mormon is valid, they should also search with a sincere heart and real intent the words God has already revealed for the same reason.

---

12. Calvin, *Inst.* 1.9.1.
13. William H. Goold, ed., *The Works of John Owen*, 24 vols. (Edinburgh: T&T Clark, 1862), 16:325–26.

As Owen argued, God gifts Christians "an infallible assurance" of the Bible that we are not simply reading "cunningly devised fables" (see 2 Pet 1:16).[14] It is the "glory and power" of the Bible that distinguishes it from all other texts.[15] The Bible declares the gospel, which is the "power of God" (Rom 1:16; 1 Cor 2:4–5), the word of Christ's cross (see 1 Cor 1:18), God's "holy scriptures, which are able to make thee wise unto salvation" (2 Tim 3:15). God's word is "able to save your souls" (Jas 1:21) because its gospel is "the effectual working of his power" (Eph 3:6–7). No wonder it is commended to us as the "quick and powerful" saving force, "sharper than any two edged sword, piercing even to the dividing asunder of soul and spirit" (Heb 4:12). In the end, the word of God—and not us—is the "discerner of the thoughts and intents of the heart" (Heb 4:12). It is never a sign of insincerity or lack of faith when we turn our hearts toward the Bible to discern the truth of all things. Quite the opposite is true. Searching the scriptures to discern truth shows great trust in God because we submit our curiosity, knowledge, and wisdom to what he has previously and finally revealed.

Summary

The Book of Mormon tells a unique history of Native Americans and invites their descendants to consider whether their origin lies in Abraham rather than their traditional sources. For this reason, the Book of Mormon asks Native readers to pray whether its telling of their history is accurate. Nonindigenous people, like traditional Christians, are also challenged to consider whether God continued to expand his canonical revelation beyond the Bible. While traditional Christians have long relied on religious experience to inform their beliefs, they have also been wary of venturing beyond what God has already revealed in his word, the Bible. It is a sign of sincere trust in God when Christians pray *and* study the Bible to discern spiritual truth.

REFLECTION QUESTIONS

1. Joseph Smith argued that the invitation to pray about the truthfulness of the Book of Mormon (Moroni 10:1–5) was originally meant primarily for indigenous people and only secondarily to nonindigenous people. How does this form your understanding of the invitation?

2. What role do you believe religious experience plays in believing the Bible?

3. If the Book of Mormon is considered scripture, what does this say about the sufficiency of the Bible?

---

14. Goold, *Works of John Owen*, 16:325.
15. Goold, *Works of John Owen*, 16:325.

4. When discerning truth, it is helpful to pray and study scripture, not in isolation but also in godly community. What does this look like in your personal life?

5. Do you believe traditional Christians should pray about whether the Book of Mormon is true?

QUESTION 39

How Might a Traditional Christian Best Approach Mormonism?

"Probe every heart to the bottom
and you will find one want: it is rest."[1]
~ Dwight Lyman Moody, American Evangelist

On a snowy Easter Sunday, April 2, 1899, Dwight L. Moody stood from his chair to approach the pulpit. Most heads in the congregation were bowed in prayer as the famous evangelist shuffled across the stage. There were thousands of them—upwards of 6,500 people—and they were quite unlike the people to whom he was accustomed to preaching.[2] Moody, the Protestant evangelist, stood in Salt Lake City's famous Mormon Tabernacle, facing a sea of Latter-day Saints. It wasn't his first time preaching in Salt Lake City. In fact, he spent the day before preaching elsewhere in the city, and twenty-eight years earlier, in June 1871, he preached at the exact same spot in the Tabernacle. But when the prayer concluded, and all eyes drew upward to Moody, he doubtlessly felt the significance: a Protestant preaching to Latter-day Saints in their primary assembly space. What did he say, and how was it received?

It may seem strange to mention Moody's experience now. After all, doesn't this question ask how traditional Christians might approach Mormonism? Perhaps in a book like this one you expected a how-to guide for sharing the good news with Mormons for when they come calling. While plenty of others offer such advice, I have chosen a different route: a case study of how a traditional Christian, Dwight L. Moody, *approached* Mormonism. By reflecting on Moody's experience, this book aims less for a call to action and more for a call

1. "Moody to Women," *Salt Lake Herald*, April 2, 1899.
2. "Rev Moody's Sermon," *Salt Lake Herald*, April 3, 1899.

to affection, empowered by the gospel invitation for all to "come unto Christ" and find their eternal rest in him.

Character and Reputation

Let's start by asking the obvious question: Why did a Protestant evangelist preach in the Mormon Tabernacle? Moody was returning home to Chicago from California when he detoured in Salt Lake City at the invitation of ministers to preach before their congregations. Moody understood the unique context preaching to Christians beneath the shadow of the Salt Lake temple. He had been there before, and in the late-1890s, the Church of Jesus Christ of Latter-day Saints was experiencing change. 1899 marked the end of the decade when plural marriage was officially discontinued, yet many members of the church—including its new president, Lorenzo Snow—were still intertwined in the polygamous relationships that had once branded Mormonism. As years passed, traditional Christians would eventually shift their attention away from the peculiarities of Mormon practices (e.g., polygamy) to its unique doctrines (e.g., eternal progression). Snow's famous couplet acted as a lightning rod for criticism (see question 32).

But this shift was only just beginning when Moody stepped off the train and was welcomed in Salt Lake City in April 1899. He was likely only aware of the catalogue of differences between his faith and that of the Latter-day Saints. Surely he hadn't mastered them. But that apparently didn't matter to him, and neither did it seem to bother church leadership. Moody's reputation earned him an invitation to the city and Tabernacle. In the days leading up to his arrival, newspapers anticipated hearing from the "celebrated evangelist,"[3] a man they considered "noted"[4] and "great."[5] His reputation walked the streets of Salt Lake City before he did.

Moody provides a worthy example to follow. Do you want the opportunity to approach Mormonism? Then earn it. You do not need a platform as large as a nineteenth-century celebrity evangelist, but you do need the kind of reputation that exudes Christlikeness. The apostle Paul required church leaders to be "well thought of by outsiders" (1 Tim 3:7 ESV) for a reason. A good reputation is tied to quality character. It's impossible to have the former without the latter. Moody's genuine Christian character upheld his solid reputation, something he said could be lost in the blink of an eye.[6] Approaching Mormonism begins with submitting one's heart to the lordship of Jesus Christ and living in such a way that your character and reputation precede you.

---

3. "Evangelist Moody Coming," *The Salt Lake Tribune*, March 25, 1899.
4. "The Coming of Dwight L. Moody," *The Deseret Evening News*, March 28, 1899.
5. "Evangelist Moody Tonight," *The Salt Lake Herald*, March 29, 1899.
6. So Moody: "I have been forty years building up a Christian character, but I can blast it before the sun goes down tonight; it takes long to build up, but a short time to tear down" ("His Tabernacle Sermon," *The Deseret Evening News*, April 3, 1899).

Speaking Among Latter-day Saints

Moody's preaching tour in Utah began with, "I want to talk to Christians."[7] Whether he considered Latter-day Saints Christian is impossible to say with certainty, but he didn't preach to them, at least not initially or intentionally.[8] He delivered his first sermons in the First Congregational Church of Salt Lake City, on home turf at an away game. Still, he was keenly aware that he spoke among Latter-day Saints. Mormon spectators filled the stands. What's striking about his messages is not what Moody said about Mormonism. It's what he didn't say. The evangelist never addressed the theological elephant in the room. Mormonism, the LDS Church, and Latter-day Saints are completely absent from his talks. Instead, Moody preached freely about his gospel convictions—Christ's precious crucifixion,[9] the Holy Spirit's regenerative work,[10] and eternal rest in the Lord Jesus.[11] Moody didn't ignore Latter-day Saints; in fact, he honored them by treating them with the same dignity he did his fellow Protestants, as people blessed to hear his gospel message. Moody's example is worth following. The way traditional Christians speak about Latter-day Saints matters. Are they duped victims of a mind-control cult, objects of our feigned compassion who are—in reality—bizarre aberrations of the Christian faith? Or are they fellow image bearers of God and the objects of his deep, abiding love, people who may live in potential or authentic union with Jesus Christ?

Nineteen years after Moody's trip to Utah, John E. Brown published *In the Cult Kingdom*.[12] Like Moody, Brown was a popular evangelist with a lasting legacy. Both men founded evangelical institutions, Moody Bible Institute and John Brown University. Unlike Moody, however, Brown took an uncharitable aim at Latter-day Saints. He offered no unique or substantial analysis of Mormonism, opting instead to steamroll the religion with incendiary rhetoric, painting Latter-day Saints as "ignorant, unthinking masses"[13] whose religion "is the humbuggiest humbug that ever humbugged a humbuggy people."[14] If you choose to approach Mormonism by this route, you'll find a well-worn path. Many have walked this wide and easy way before. But by choosing the better

7. "Evangelist D. L. Moody Campaigns Against Evil," *The Salt Lake Herald*, April 1, 1899.
8. It is unlikely Moody considered Mormonism a part of orthodox Christianity; however, he refrained from commenting on the matter in public. In an interview a few months after his Tabernacle sermon (and just two months before his death), Moody told reporters, "I am not going to talk about Mormons. I don't know that they are any worse than we are." "The Country Changing," *Boston Daily Globe*, October 13, 1899.
9. "Evangelist D. L. Moody Campaigns Against Evil," *Salt Lake Herald*, April 1, 1899.
10. "Moody In Salt Lake," *The Salt Lake Tribune*, April 1, 1899.
11. "Crowds Hear Moody," *The Salt Lake Tribune*, April 2, 1899.
12. John Elward Brown, *In the Cult Kingdom: Mormonism, Eddyism, and Russellism* (Siloam Springs, AR: International Federation Publishing, 1918).
13. Brown, *In the Cult Kingdom*, 113.
14. Brown, *In the Cult Kingdom*, 45.

route—speaking graciously, wisely, and truthfully (see Col 4:4–6)—you might be surprised at where the path leads. In the end, the difference between Brown and Moody is profound. Brown spoke *about* Latter-day Saints to evangelicals while Moody earned an invitation to speak *to* Latter-day Saints as an evangelical.

Speaking to Latter-day Saints

Sometime after he preached to the First Congregational Church, representatives from the LDS Church invited Moody to speak on Easter Sunday at their Tabernacle. The opportunity must have thrilled him. He jumped on it right away, although he undoubtedly felt some apprehension. What would an evangelist say to a Latter-day Saint audience of thousands? Moody chose to preach from Galatians 6:7 to emphasize Paul's warning that "whatsoever a man soweth, that shall he also reap."[15] Perhaps Moody chose this verse because it represented neutral ground, an opportunity to explore common concerns shared by Christians and Latter-day Saints (e.g., lying, adultery, alcoholism). These sins frayed the social fabric of America, which was a message both churches agreed on. "What this nation needs is a revival of righteousness," he bellowed to an affirming audience.[16]

His message was well-received. One LDS reporter described Moody's sermon as "full of truth" and "told with vividness and dramatic force."[17] It was different from his earlier sermons, though. Previously, he focused on the necessity of being born again and coming to Christ to find rest. But in the Tabernacle, Moody offered his audience the kind of moralism that resonated with the ethical code of the church. Sowing sin and worldliness means reaping sadness and death. Still, something was missing from the Tabernacle sermon. "As a rule it is not fair to criticize a sermon for what is not in it," the reporter acknowledged, "but to a great many it seemed strange that the celebrated speaker, before an audience of six or seven thousand people . . . did not explain the plan of salvation." True, the evangelist "emphasized with terrible force" the consequences of sowing sin, "but of the remedy little or nothing was said."[18] They *wanted* to hear the gospel according to Moody. Speaking on behalf of his fellow Saints, the reporter added, "We recognize the fervor and sincerity of his efforts" but lamented that Moody's sermon was gospel-less, lacking what is of "paramount importance."[19]

---

15. "Moody In Tabernacle," *The Salt Lake Tribune*, April 3, 1899. The sermon was apparently based on a book he published a few years earlier (Dwight L. Moody, *Sowing and Reaping* [Chicago: Fleming H. Revell, 1896]).
16. "Rev Moody's Sermon," *Salt Lake Herald*, April 3, 1899.
17. "Moody at the Tabernacle," *Deseret Evening News*, April 3, 1899.
18. "Moody at the Tabernacle," *Deseret Evening News*, April 3, 1899.
19. "Moody at the Tabernacle," *Deseret Evening News*, April 3, 1899.

The evangelist teaches us an important lesson: finding common ground with Latter-day Saints is a good thing. As ecripture commands, "Whatever is true, whatever is honorable, whatever is just, whatever is pure, whatever is lovely, whatever is commendable, if there is any excellence, if there is anything worthy of praise, think about these things" (Phil 4:8 ESV). If we can think about these things together with Latter-day Saints, all the better. That's what Moody did. But he also had a testimony of God's faithfulness in his life, the truest and greatest praiseworthy thing—the gospel—and he didn't share it, to the disappointment of his audience. If "faith cometh by hearing, and hearing by the word of God" (Rom 10:17), then why not share it with Latter-day Saints to challenge, encourage, comfort, and invite them into his rest? In an earlier sermon, he rightly argued the human heart suffers from exhaustion, flitting to and fro looking for rest but never finding it. "If I wanted to find rest," he said, "I would go to some man or woman who had listened to the voice of Christ."[20] Be that man or woman who repeats their Lord's invitation, "Come unto me, all ye that labour and are heavy laden, and I will give you rest" (Matt 11:28). There is no sweeter invitation to an exhausted heart.

Summary

Dwight L. Moody's 1899 trip to Salt Lake City offers traditional Christians valuable lessons for approaching Mormonism. Moody's reputation preceded him, which earned him an invitation to speak to Latter-day Saints in their primary gathering place. In his preaching to fellow evangelicals, he never bashed Mormonism or Latter-day Saints, but neither did he shy away from his gospel convictions, knowing that Latter-day Saints were listening in. In his Tabernacle sermon to Latter-day Saints, he taught about the common convictions they and traditional Christians shared but fell short of explaining to Latter-day Saints his beliefs about the gospel. In light of Moody's experience, a traditional Christian ought to approach Mormonism with a virtuous reputation and gospel convictions that are not belligerent but graciously transparent and thorough.

REFLECTION QUESTIONS

1. Can you think of a person who exemplifies what it means to have a gospel reputation precede them? What kind of life do/did they live?

20. "Moody to Women," *Salt Lake Herald*, April 2, 1899.

2. Moody was aware of his context but apparently chose not to address differences between his beliefs and Mormonism in any of his sermons. Do you agree or disagree with his approach?

3. What does it mean to earn the opportunity to approach Mormonism?

4. Compare Moody's and Brown's approaches to Mormonism. Which do you find more attractive, useful, and/or biblical?

5. Moody apparently neglected to express his gospel convictions in his famous Tabernacle sermon, disappointing Latter-day Saints. How does this episode in his life inform your approach to Mormonism?

QUESTION 40

How Can a Traditional Christian Dialogue with a Latter-day Saint?

"My dear brothers and sisters, understand this:
Everyone should be quick to listen, slow to speak, and slow to anger."
~ James 1:19 CSB

Reaching the end of a book like this one invites an obvious question: Now what? Perhaps nothing at all; you've reached the journey's end. I suspect, however, that this isn't the case for most readers. You've read this book to gain new insight into Mormonism in preparation for encountering it, specifically Latter-day Saints. Maybe you've just moved to an area where many Latter-day Saints live. For the first time in your life, you are a religious minority in a spiritually strange land. Maybe you've befriended a Latter-day Saint or had a loved one join the Church of Jesus Christ of Latter-day Saints, and now, having gained some awareness of their beliefs and practices, you're wondering what steps to take next. Perhaps you're like me. When people ask why I'm so interested in Mormonism, my most honest answer is also frustratingly terse: "I just am." There's no need to explain it. Sometimes, it's best to step aside and let the Holy Spirit guide the passion of your heart where he wills. "Where is that for me?" you might wonder. There are many possibilities. Some are assertive, posted on a street corner passing out evangelistic tracts. Others are more reserved, sharing a couch with opened Bibles and closed, praying hands. I won't bother judging the usefulness of these approaches, but I am very open about my favorite way of approaching Latter-day Saints.

Dialogue aims to create positive and constructive interactions between traditional Christians and Latter-day Saints through humility, respect, and mutual understanding. Participants ask quality questions and listen well to learn about a person's story, beliefs, and practices. Dialogue has tangential benefits, such as discovering areas of cooperation, but ultimately, dialogue should point every participant to the Lord Jesus Christ. His model interaction with the Samaritan woman in the gospel of John reminds us that the goal of dialogue should always be him (see John 4:1–45). In doing so, we honor Jesus as Lord over our lives and interactions, seeking peace and holiness through truth.

Discernment

Before asking how a traditional Christian might dialogue with a Latter-day Saint, it's important to ask *why*. This question is related to one we've already answered: Why should traditional Christians learn about Mormonism (see question 1)? The common reasons listed in that question are not exhaustive, although the Greatest Commandment should be our starting point, which is especially true of dialogue. Truly knowing someone empowers us to love them as ourselves. Is that Latter-day Saint a person you want to approach, or do you want a *project*, something to refashion after your own spiritual image? Do you want a *Mormon* friend or simply a friend? Your heart must be in the right place—beneath the lordship of Jesus Christ (see 1 Pet 3:15). If your heart isn't submitted to the Lord, neither are you.

Is your mind prepared? I'm not speaking necessarily in terms of knowledge. It's helpful to know about Mormonism when dialoguing with Latter-day Saints, but there's no prerequisite level. The right mindset is a state of readiness, marked by humility, curiosity, and conviction. Are you ready and willing to listen more than you speak (see Jas 1:19)? Are your spiritual convictions secure and mature enough to handle scrutiny (see 1 Cor 16:13)? The right mindset is also being ready to speak with the person in front of you, not the person you *want* to be in front of you. Just as there are many types of traditional Christians, so there are also many types of Latter-day Saints. The LDS Church appears extremely uniform from the outside, but Mormonism is dynamic, and its people are diverse. Some Latter-day Saints are true believers whose thoughts are tightly correlated with their church. They are active, temple recommend-holding, missionary veterans whose lives orbit their faith. Others, however, parted ways with their beliefs long ago but still identify with Mormonism. They might have left the church bitter or indifferent; others mourn their loss. Many are in between, wrestling with their religion but not wanting to leave. You may even encounter Latter-day Saints with no religious convictions at all, practical atheists who remain members of the church. Are you open to approaching and even befriending people where they are and for who they are? This is especially true when it comes to dealing with disagreements.

Disagreement

Obviously, if it were not clear by now, there are many irreconcilable differences between Mormonism and traditional Christianity. Approaching Mormonism inevitably leads to disagreement. Some people see disagreement as permission to act uncharitably toward Latter-day Saints, and in righteous indignation, they command rhetorical "fire to come down from heaven, and consume them" (Luke 9:54), forgetting that Jesus Christ rebuked such behavior among his disciples. "Ye know not what manner of spirit ye are of," he warned (Luke 9:55). Other people, however, yearn to maintain civility, so they shy away from the tension differences create. They are tempted to ignore or downplay the things that make us different, to sidestep contention, and worse, to avoid our faults and failures, hiding behind dialogic fig leaves to conceal our naked souls from the Other. But these are dangerous pitfalls in dialogue.

Imagine a young couple engaged and about to be married. Suppose they have never spoken about their differences for fear of upsetting each other. They only ever talked about things on which they agreed. This couple will struggle the first time they clash over conflicting preferences after their wedding day. You might say they don't even truly know who the other person is, which is a poor foundation for friendship, let alone marriage. We *must* talk about differences, or else we don't really know the other person.

Conversely, imagine the couple discussing only their differences, things that divide them, arguing all the time about why the other should come closer to their own beliefs and opinions. They'd never have gotten married because no one wants to be with someone who constantly dissents, dismisses, and disagrees with them. Herein lies another pitfall in dialogue: focusing only on disagreement. Doing so inevitably leads to hostility and quarreling. If downplaying differences robs our ability to really know a person, then amplifying differences does just the opposite; the person won't truly want to be known.[1]

This tension between civility and conviction can derail dialogue if not managed well. While people with great convictions often "lack civility, the civil often lack conviction," observed religious scholar Martin Marty.[2] "Civility is important," wrote theologian Richard Mouw, "and so is conviction."[3] What's needed, then, is a blend of both, or what Marty and Mouw called "convicted civility," dialogue with the Other that preserves (and even honors) personal convictions without sacrificing gentleness and respect.[4] We wrongly suppose the price of civility is holding convictions lightly or setting them aside

1. As a side note, I often sense a fear of association that comes with traditional Christians engaging Mormonism, but it's unfounded. Simply because you associate with Latter-day Saints does not mean you endorse all of Mormonism. Finding areas of public cooperation does not automatically invite private capitulation. We must discuss the areas where we agree, or again, we don't really know the other person.
2. Martin E. Marty, *By Way of Response: Journeys in Faith*, ed. Robert A. Raines (Nashville: Abingdon, 1981), 81.
3. Richard J. Mouw, *Uncommon Decency: Christian Civility in an Uncivil World*, 2nd ed. (Downers Grove: InterVarsity Press, 2010), 17.
4. For an example of the fruit of such an approach, see the scholarly dialogue between Latter-day Saints and evangelicals in *Talking Doctrine: Mormons and Evangelicals in Conversation*, ed. Richard J. Mouw and Robert L. Millet (Downers Grove: IVP Academic, 2015).

altogether. But is it really *you* if your deepest, most fundamental spiritual beliefs are sidelined for the sake of pleasantry? And if you only ever quarrel and interrogate the Other, do you really want to know them, to love them? Differences matter, but they are not ammunition to be expended in the conflict of rhetoric. What we need instead is "heart-felt contestation between respectful free agents," empathetic and honorable people who interact truthfully without toeing party lines.[5] We must keep "aloof from strife" (Prov 20:3 ESV) and never "quarrel over opinions" (Rom 14:1 ESV). Listen with the intent to learn; it's the "fool" who "does not delight in understanding, but only wants to show off his opinions" (Prov 18:2 CSB). So, wisely "make a defense" (1 Pet 3:15 ESV) for your hope in the gospel by "always showing gentleness to all people" (Titus 3:2 CSB).

Devotion

Remember, it's only possible to dialogue as a traditional Christian if you are one. Dialogue is a precious opportunity for self-reflection. Before asking a Latter-day Saint, "Are you devoted to Christ?" ask yourself the same question. Are you devoted to the Savior whom you intend to discuss? Christ is devoted to you by faith, and your devotion to him is empowered by his grace. Genuine devotion involves a commitment grounded in trust and cultivated through continuous mercy and response through faith and repentance. Devotion sustains our most meaningful relationships, especially friendship, and friendship is the most natural space for conversations about faith. As traditional Christians, we first devote ourselves to Christ, who brings us peace through reconciliation.

Relatedly, the Bible implores us to "seek peace, and pursue it" (Ps 34:14), to "strive for peace with everyone" (Heb 12:14 ESV). There is a great need for peace between Latter-day Saints and traditional Christians, so we ought to seek it by earning their respect and then building trust with them. Few Christians before us have found such peace with Latter-day Saints, but for those who have, opportunities of untold joys blossomed before them. After all, we are called not only to "strive for peace with everyone," wrote the author of Hebrews, but also to strive "for the holiness without which no one will see the Lord" (Heb 12:14 ESV). It is toward that holiness—and the one who brings us to it—that we must orient our hearts (see 1 Thess 3:11–13). "So then let us pursue what makes for peace and mutual upbuilding" (Rom 14:19 ESV). Be a person of peace; seek people of peace; point all people (yourself included) to the Prince of Peace.

One Sunday morning in 1849, Henry Kroh, a German Reformed minister, rose to deliver a powerful gospel sermon. His message wasn't unique, but the setting certainly was. Like Dwight L. Moody in the decades after him

5. Charles Randall Paul, *Converting the Saints: A Study of Religious Rivalry in America* (Draper, UT: Greg Kofford Books, 2018), xvi.

(see question 39), Kroh preached before an audience of Latter-day Saints and their prophet, Brigham Young. Kroh was elated at the opportunity, and his sermon was received in kind. "[He] has preached good things to us," Young told his people, encouraging them to "do those things as far as you have been taught."[6] If such an exhortation seems out of character for a Mormon prophet, according to Mormonism it shouldn't. Joseph Smith instructed Latter-day Saints "to receive truth let it come from where it may."[7] Despite his skepticism of the ecumenical creeds, Smith drew from the Apostles' Creed when describing the "fundamental principles" of his religion: "that [Jesus Christ] died, was buried, and rose again on the third day, and ascended up into heaven."[8] If ever there was a space for approaching Mormonism, it is here in God-honoring dialogue, in our mutual pursuit of truth, our only way to eternal life, the crucified and risen Lord Jesus Christ (see John 14:6).

Dos and Don'ts of Dialogue

I empathize with skeptics of dialogue. Its abuses and misuses are many. Dialogue should never water down one's faith. Sacrificing personal convictions is too expensive for too little gain—a synthetic peace sewed together by defeatist self-censorship. Those who see the benefit to dialogue are sometimes tempted to use it incorrectly. Dialogue is not a Trojan horse for evangelism. Approaching the dialogue table with concealed motivations is unethical. Don't bait-and-switch Latter-day Saints with a veneer of friendliness that masks your disinterest in learning from them. If you want to proselytize, then do it. Never engage in stealth evangelism; always "refuse to practice cunning" (2 Cor 4:2 ESV). Be upfront and open about your intentions. Never be duplicitous, speaking one way to Latter-days Saints to their face but another way when they aren't around, especially uncharitably (or what I call "anti-Mormon locker room talk"). Remember, "people will give account for every careless word they speak" (Matt 12:36 ESV).

Think about how you'd want to be treated in dialogue, "then grab the initiative and do it for *them*" (Matt 7:12 MSG, emphasis original). No one wants to be a proselytism project. Bear the fruit of the Holy Spirit (see Gal 5:22–23) and express "genuine love; by truthful speech, and the power of God" (2 Cor 6:6–7 ESV). Put on "compassionate hearts, kindness, humility, meekness, and patience" (Col 3:12 ESV), and when it comes to disagreements, discuss them with gentleness (see 2 Tim 2:25). Never perpetuate caricatures or outright lies about Mormonism, as this is tantamount to bearing false witness against your neighbor. Such behavior "shall not be unpunished" (Prov 19:5) because, again, Jesus warned "on the day of judgment people will give account for

6. Smith, *Brigham Young*, 1:173 (emend.).
7. JSJ, July 9, 1843, J3:55 (emend.).
8. JS, *EJ*, July 1838, 1:44.

every careless word they speak" (Matt 12:36 ESV). Tame your tongue (see Jas 3:8) and, in our digital age, tame your thumbs, too. Don't post things about Latter-day Saints privately that you wouldn't say publicly. Foster dialogue that is edifying (see 1 Cor 14:26), charitable (see Col 4:6), and conveys genuine care (see Gal 5:14; Jas 2:8). Avoid unnecessary controversy (see Titus 3:9). "Refrain from anger and give up your rage" (Ps 37:8 CSB) because "an offended brother is harder to reach than a fortified city" (Prov 18:19 CSB). Latter-day Saints are especially averse to anger because the Book of Mormon warns them that "he that hath the spirit of contention is not of me [Jesus Christ], but is of the devil" (3 Nephi 11:29). Abhor pride (see Prov 27:2); it shouldn't be in your heart, let alone in the dialogue. "Follow not that which is evil, but that which is good" (3 John 11). Glorify God through Christ by acknowledging him in all things, "and he shall direct thy paths" (Prov 3:6) by the Holy Spirit. "Let all that you do be done in love" (1 Cor 16:14 ESV).

Pray

Finally, and most importantly, never consider dialogue complete without prayer. Ask Latter-day Saints to pray with you. If they decline, that's okay—pray for them privately. Bring yourself and your dialogue partner to God's throne. Pray they would be called into his grace (see Gal 1:6), be sanctified in truth (see John 17:17), and that the Lord would bless and keep them and their loved ones (see Num. 6:24). Ask God to gift them with faith that works through the love of God (see Gal 5:6), and never anything less—not merited righteousness of their own, only ever the Lord Jesus's perfect and completed faithfulness to God's holy law. Ask that they would come to Christ, those who "labour and are heavy laden" (Matt 11:28), to receive rest in his righteousness alone. And ask God to grow your sincere and deep love of neighbors for no other reason than to love them as he does. Then see where the Holy Spirit leads you.

Summary

Dialogue provides a space to know and be known by Latter-day Saints. With virtuous motivations and spiritual readiness, traditional Christians may learn who a Latter-day Saint truly is, avoiding contentious disagreement or exaggerating commonalities. With convicted civility, it's possible to seek peace and discuss devotion to Jesus Christ, to share gospel convictions in the mutual pursuit of truth. Above all, pray for Latter-day Saints as sincerely and fervently as any other person whom God brings to you.

REFLECTION QUESTIONS

1. Do you agree that dialogue is a good way to approach Mormonism? What are its benefits and drawbacks?

2. How do you discern your motivation for approaching Mormonism?
3. How ought we handle disagreements with Latter-day Saints?
4. How would you apply convicted civility in a dialogue with a Latter-day Saint?
5. How should you pray for Latter-day Saints?

Scripture Index

Acts

Romans

1 Corinthians

Moses